Political Economy of Foreign Policies in Contemporary China

A Japanese Point of View

Political Economy of Foreign Policies in Contemporary China

A Japanese Point of View

Ken Morita

Hiroshima University, Japan & Hiroshima Shudo University, Japan

World Scientific

NEW JERSEY • LONDON • SINGAPORE • BEIJING • SHANGHAI • HONG KONG • TAIPEI • CHENNAI • TOKYO

Published by

World Scientific Publishing Co. Pte. Ltd.
5 Toh Tuck Link, Singapore 596224
USA office: 27 Warren Street, Suite 401-402, Hackensack, NJ 07601
UK office: 57 Shelton Street, Covent Garden, London WC2H 9HE

Library of Congress Cataloging-in-Publication Data
Names: Morita, Ken, 1947– author.
Title: Political economy of foreign policies in contemporary China : a Japanese point of view / Ken Morita, Hiroshima University, Japan & Hiroshima Shudo University, Japan.
Description: New Jersey : World Scientific, [2025] | Includes bibliographical references and index.
Identifiers: LCCN 2024053288 | ISBN 9789819806232 (hardcover) | ISBN 9789819806249 (ebook) | ISBN 9789819806256 (ebook other)
Subjects: LCSH: China--Economic policy. | China--Foreign relations. | China--Foreign economic relations. | China--Foreign relations--Japan. | Japan--Foreign relations--China.
Classification: LCC HC427 .M67 2025 | DDC 330.951--dc23/eng/20250206
LC record available at https://lccn.loc.gov/2024053288

British Library Cataloguing-in-Publication Data
A catalogue record for this book is available from the British Library.

For any available supplementary material, please visit
https://www.worldscientific.com/worldscibooks/10.1142/14129#t=suppl

Desk Editors: Aanand Jayaraman/Sandhya Venkatesh

Typeset by Stallion Press
Email: enquiries@stallionpress.com

To My Beloved Late Wife

Preface

This book is a sequel to the previous book written by the author (Morita, 2017b). Consequently, the first chapter of this book partly overlaps with the last chapter of the author's previous book.

The first part of this book provides analyses on "Sino-American relations," with the aim of understanding "China's behavior." As described in the chapters of this book, "China's behavior" is based on the theory of "offensive realism." It means that due to China's actions to protect its own national security, it might not act like a "status-quo country" but as a country aspiring toward "hegemony (or regional hegemony)."

If this is correct, it would be reasonable to think that China's behavior could become similar to the behavior of the United States.

However, from the viewpoints of economics, the difference between the United States' "excess consumption" and China's "excess saving" ("underconsumption") is significant. Therefore, one can assume that the "excess consumption" and "underconsumption" established the foundation for a "codependency" relationship between the United States and China.

Also, at the same time, there existed the "exorbitant privilege" of the United States (which has supported the "excess consumption") and the "undervaluation of the renminbi" in China (which has supported the "underconsumption" and also produced a great disparity between the rich and the poor in China). That is to say, the relationship between the "exorbitant privilege" of the United States and the "undervaluation of the renminbi" in China epitomizes the characteristics of Sino-American relations.

According to Ito (2011), China's strategy involves biding its time, waiting for a good opportunity, maintaining the desire for revenge, and concealing its abilities. Ito mentioned that the essence of the Chinese foreign policy includes a move toward hegemony. Thus, Ito (2011) asserted in the year 2011 that China would continue its "peaceful rise" strategy with which it could avoid being seen as an enemy by the United States. However, in books and articles written by him, Mearsheimer claimed that China does not have peaceful aspirations. However, even if the main intention of China seems to be "unpeaceful" and "regional hegemony," as of now, the Chinese strategy is to avoid making an enemy of the United States. If it is called a "peaceful rise," Chinese strategy could be called a "peaceful rise."

Because the "codependency relationship" between the United States and China is connected to the "peaceful rise" strategy, if China decides to antagonize the United States, then the "codependency relationship" between the two countries will cease to exist. Therefore, the relationship between the United States' "excess consumption" and China's "underconsumption" should not be seen as "symmetric" but as "asymmetric." Chinese "underconsumption" (in the centralized system) can be more easily (relatively) amended.

We can assume that as soon as China decides to confront the United States, the "codependency relationship" between the two countries will cease to exist. Then, the "unpeaceful rise" of China (as Mearsheimer asserted) will become clearer. We should understand that the "codependency relationship" between the United States and China is a property of the political economy.

The aim of the second part of this book could be said as discovery and development of the appropriate method to catch an occurrence of "non-economic situations" by framework of economics. To be more specific, the main subject of the analysis is the "Taiwan situation."[1] That is to say, the occurrence of "non-economic situations" means the "annexation of Taiwan by China." Therefore, it could be said that the discovery and development of the method means to appropriately recognize the "Taiwan's emergency situations" by framework of economics.

The former prime minister Shinzo Abe asserted that "Taiwan's emergency is Japan's emergency." As we mention in the book, it is correct to recognize the situation in Taiwan as Mr. Shinzo Abe did. It means that the "annexation of Taiwan by China" will undoubtedly have a major impact

[1]In this book, Taiwan is recognized as a country (not as a region), for no other intention than to avoid complications.

in Japan. Does Japan have a strategy ready for a "Taiwan's emergency" which will break out sooner or later? And will the Japanese strategy work effectively?

For most Japanese people, an efficient strategy means the involvement of US Forces in Japan. To be more specific, it means the involvement of nuclear weapons owned by the United States, which is usually called the "nuclear umbrella." Therefore, for the Japanese strategy for a "Taiwan's emergency" to be effective, it is indispensable that the "nuclear umbrella" work effectively. Then, will the United States' "nuclear umbrella" work effectively for Japan? Japan must seriously consider this question.

Japanese peoples' question if the United States' "nuclear umbrella" could work effectively means what the US–Japan security alliance has been all about. Most Japanese people do not even know the United States' real intentions in establishing the US–Japan security alliance.

Kanehara directly mentioned in Ohta *et al.* (2022) that at the US–Japan Summit, the nuclear issue was never a topic of serious discussion and the Japanese side never asked to be brought under the US's "nuclear umbrella." It goes without saying, because it has never been necessity for the US side to declare the "nuclear umbrella" could work effectively, it has continued to this day that no validation of effectiveness of "nuclear umbrella" has been conducted.[2]

The "Taiwan emergency situation" could have a significant impact on the security of countries in the Asia-Pacific region. Therefore, Australia will also be forced to respond. Actually, Chinese extending to Australia was illustrated by Hamilton (2018) entitled *Silent Invasion: China's Influence in Australia*. Therefore, "AUKUS" (the international security

---

[2]The "nuclear umbrella" indicates the following. Assuming a hypothetical nuclear-armed state (called "country A" here) were to engage in nuclear intimidation against Japan, at that time, the United States would use nuclear weapons to protect Japan. Therefore, it would mean that when country A attacked Japan with nuclear weapons, the United States would counterattack with nuclear weapons in the defense of Japan. It indicates that country A would also attack the United States with nuclear weapons due to the US's defense of Japan. To clarify, according to the current capability of nuclear weapons (according to Kan Ito in his internet program entitled *Earnest Chat*), due to a nuclear attack by country A, perhaps nearly 100 million Americans will die (not in the defense of the United States but in the defense of Japan). Common sense would suggest that it is reckless for the United States to perform such an action. Thus, it means that the "nuclear umbrella" of the United States would not work for Japan.

framework established by the United States, UK, and Australia in September 2021) has enabled Australia to obtain the technology to build nuclear submarines.

However, for Australia, Japan, and especially Taiwan, economic relations with China are extremely important. Therefore, decoupling economic relations with China might be crucial for those countries.

In part two of this book, (1) we investigate the deep interdependence between China and the countries concerned and (2) we highlight the issues that might lead to decoupling and then assess the economic implications of those issues.

1. Four Chapters of Part I

Hereinafter, we provide a preview of the respective chapters.

1.1. *Chapter 1*

In Chapter 1, we focus our attention on the complicated international relations or diplomatic relations among the United States, China, and Japan in order to consider the fundamental framework of international relations. We note that Japan has never had an independent military strategy. Furthermore, with regard to the diplomatic strategy of the United States about the US–Japan alliance, Japan has had insufficient recognition. As far as the diplomatic strategy of China is concerned, it is indispensable to observe calmly.

In international society, many countries offer excessive consideration toward China. It might be an economically rational reaction by taking into account the growth of the Chinese economy. At the same time, it might be indispensable for international society to require their cool judgment about the future relationship with China

In Chapter 1, we investigate international relations from the point of view of the "selection of Japan" and the "selection of China," which fall under the framework of "realism," particularly "offensive realism."

The author thinks that both "selection of Japan" and "selection of China" are appropriate expressions. If necessary, "national selection of Japan" and "national selection of China" might be more appropriate. But they seem to be needlessly long and to be unnecessarily cumbersome.

With respect to the "selection of Japan" (especially in the "US–Soviet bipolar era"), the aim of Japan was to take actions as a "small country" under the influence of a great power (the United States) and not take action as a country wanting to acquire the position of "regional hegemon." That "selection of Japan" to be a "small country" became also convenient for another pole of the "bipolar system" (USSR).

In contrast, the "selection of China" has been completely different. The national strategy of China has undoubtedly been to acquire the position of "hegemon" (or at least the position of "regional hegemon").

Assuming that is the case, it seems like the occurrence of serious conflict between the United States and China might be inevitable. We think, therefore, that it is too optimistic to suppose that the "G2" system (between the United States and China) could proceed peacefully. Even if in the future China surpasses the United States in various positions, it might be difficult to expect such a system to proceed peacefully.

1.2. *Chapter 2*

In Chapter 2 of this book, we analyze the economic "codependency relationship" between the United States and China.

The "codependency relationship" between the United States and China involves the two countries relying on each other to balance the excess consumption of the United States and the excess savings of China. The excess consumption of the United States results in a trade deficit and the excess savings in China results in a trade surplus. These two situations are theoretically separate but, because the two countries have large-scale economic dealings with each other, the situations have led to a "codependency relationship."

Such excess consumption in the United States and excess savings in China would undoubtedly establish the basis for a "codependency relationship" between the United States and China. At the same time, we should indicate that in the United States there exists an "exorbitant privilege" which could support the excess consumption and that in China there exists an underestimation of the exchange rate of the Chinese renminbi which could lead to a bigger disparity and excess savings. In other words, the "exorbitant privilege" of the United States and the underestimation of the exchange rate of the renminbi would also help establish the contemporary "codependency relationship" between the United States and China, which is different from the relationship between any other two countries.

In Chapter 2, we concentrate our attention on China and try to analyze the Gini coefficient and labor distribution ratio in China by taking the disparity as a crucial factor, in accordance with Kaldor's (1955–1956) assertion.

That is to say, suppose the Gini coefficient in China is the same as that in the United States, the consumption–GDP ratio in China would be higher. Improvement of the disparity could cause expansion of consumption and could reduce excess savings.

Also, suppose the labor distribution ratio in China is around the same as that in the United States, the consumption–GDP ratio in China would be higher. That is to say, an increase in the labor distribution ratio could increase consumption and reduce excess savings.

If the disparity in China could be improved (expressed as the revision of the numerical value of the Gini coefficient and the labor distribution ratio), the underconsumption in China (domestic demand shortage) could also be improved. Therefore, the "codependency relationship" between the United States and China would also be revised. Therefore, one of the effective policies is the revision of the underestimation of the renminbi exchange rate.

1.3. *Chapter 3*

In Chapter 3 of this book, we focus mainly on the United States and its political economy and then investigate the "codependency relationship" between the United States and China.

The viewpoint in Chapter 3 is as follows. When we focusing on the United States, it is not realistic for the "codependency relations" between them to suppose to reach a resolution.

Roach (2014) was the first to consider the "codependency relations" in his writing. He stated, one "of the tragic ironies of codependency is that partners often subsume their sense of self into an increasingly destructive relationship." (To new economic realities) a "failure to adapt risks collision – the Bad Dream of a trade war, or worse." "Trust is key to resolving the political disconnect between the two" (pp. 267–268). Frictions "could undermine not only the two countries' relationship but the entire global economy. The imbalances of codependency will drive the economic agendas of the United States and China. Rebalancing will define their future — separately and collectively" (p. 268).

Roach's (2014) following insistence provides us with useful information:

> "Saving is the central unifying element in the codependency between the United States and China. All you have to know at this point is one thing: Savings-short nations run multilateral trade deficit. Without sustained improvement in domestic saving, America will never pull itself out of its current account and trade deficits. And that means China, with its large trade and saving surplus, will probably remain in Washington's political crosshairs for as long as this key issue is unresolved" (p. 131).

A trade deficit means a savings shortage. It is certain that Japan (which had a trade surplus and a huge amount of savings) was the target of continued attacks from Washington. However, it is not certain if China is a target of Washington's political attacks. Sure enough, at present or in the near future, one country which could be the target of political attacks is China and the country that would attack is the United States. However, (after China would endure difficult situations) it might become real that the United States would be the target of Beijing's political attack. In fact, we should recognize that US–Japan relations and Sino-American relations are basically different.

In any case, when we consider the situation at present or in the near future, emphasizing the "codependency relationship" and emphasizing rebalance without friction might not give the same benefits to the United States and China.

As described in Chapter 3, there have existed different arguments. For example, Mearsheimer asserted that the "US policy on China is misguided." Mearsheimer's analysis suggested that "the United States has a profound interest in seeing Chinese economic growth slow considerably in the years ahead. For much of the past decade, however, the United States has pursued a strategy intended to have the opposite effect." Such a US policy on China is misguided because "A wealthy China would not be a status quo power but an aggressive state determined to achieve regional hegemony."

As indicated by the assertions by Roach and Mearsheimer, different ways of thinking have coexisted. Roach presumed that "trust is key to resolving the political disconnect between the two." However, according to Mearsheimer, "If China continues its impressive economic growth over the next few decades, the US and China are likely to engage in an intense security competition with considerable potential for war." Thus, in Mearsheimer's view, we could not find any indications considering that "trust is key."

In that sense, it should be understood that "indicating the codependency relations between the United States and China" and "urging the necessity of probiosis" could easily become benefit for China (at the least from a mid-to long-term perspective), but not easily become benefit for the United States. Therefore, the codependency relationship between the two has rather strong implications, suggesting that the relationship is "by China" and "for China." Then, which side has started to resolve the codependency relationship? The side seems not for the United States but for China. On earth why is it?

The Chinese strategy has been called a "peaceful rise." As Ito (2011) indicated, however, China has a strategy of waiting for a good opportunity, maintaining the desire for revenge, and concealing its abilities. Ito mentioned that the essence of the Chinese foreign policy includes a move toward hegemony. Therefore, Ito carefully asserted in 2011 that, until around 2020, China would continue its "peaceful rise" strategy and avoid turning the United States into an enemy.

However, in books and articles written by him, Mearsheimer claimed that China does not have peaceful aspirations. However, even if the main intention of China seems to be "unpeaceful" and "regional hegemony," as of now, the Chinese strategy is to avoid making an enemy of the United States. If it is called a "peaceful rise," Chinese strategy would become a "peaceful rise."

Therefore, because the "codependency relationship" between the United States and China is connected to the "peaceful rise" strategy, if China decides to antagonize the United States, then the "codependency relationship" between the two countries will cease to exist. Therefore, the relationship between the United States' "excess consumption" and China's "underconsumption" should not be seen as "symmetric" but as "asymmetric." Chinese "underconsumption" (in the centralized system) can be more easily (relatively) amended.

Thus, we can assume that as soon as China decides to confront the United States, the "codependency relationship" between the two countries will cease to exist. Then, the "unpeaceful rise" of China (as Mearsheimer asserted) will become clearer. We should understand that the "codependency relationship" between the United States and China is a property of the political economy.

1.4. *Chapter 4*

In Chapter 4, we focus our attention (in the first 3 sections) on the topics of "trade," "military expenditure," and "technology" *vis-à-vis* the United States and China. "China's rise" has been tremendous, especially in terms of the Chinese technology policy and its exponential growth.

In the Section 4 of Chapter 4, concerning the "Sino-American friction," we (1) describe the issue, (2) consider the speech of US Vice President Michael Pence, (3) investigate whether or not "China's rise" could be termed peaceful, and (4) examine its rise under the framework of "offensive realism."

The conclusion of Chapter 4 is presented as follows (because situations are still evolving, it is difficult to judge decidedly): (1) The economic interdependence between the United States and China is based on the "economic structure" and "institutional mechanism." Therefore it cannot be easily revised. (2) Confrontation between the United States and China seems to have intensified because of the "US's decrease" and "China's increase" in military expenditure. (3) We consider the occurrence of abnormal value by the Grubbs-Smirnov Test on the Chinese number of patent applications. And the result indicated that an abnormal value occurred in the year 2011. (4) It is extremely difficult to accept that China's rise can be peaceful. (5) Judging from the circumstances, China's national strategy falls under the framework of "offensive realism." (6) China's behavior under the framework of "offensive realism" might be similar to the US's behavior (as a regional hegemon). (7) Assuming that the previous point is true, "Sino-American friction" could be a confrontation not relating to a trade balance but relating to hegemony. (8) Therefore, we should recognize that "Sino-American friction" could move toward an extremely serious confrontation (although it might be a long-term prospect).

2. Four Chapters in Part II

2.1. *Chapter 5*

In Chapter 5 of this book, we analyze the following assertions: (1) The Sino-Japanese war was devised by Germany. Although it does not matter here whether or not the above-mentioned assertion is correct, the facts were; (1) the "German–Japanese Anti-Comintern Pact" was concluded (2) Germany provided conveniences for China (a belligerent country with Japan) which should undoubtedly be the acts of disloyalty. From such a situation, we can understand the characteristics of German relations with China. (2) The existence of China in German trade and the existence of Germany in Chinese trade has been completely different. To put it briefly, the important countries for German trade are China and the United States (and France and Netherlands); in contrast, the important countries for Chinese trade are the United States and Japan (and Hong Kong and South Korea) but not Germany. Thus, from the viewpoint of trade relations, if Germany and China establish an alliance, it will be initiated by the German side, not the Chinese side. (3) German FDI in China has seemed to be rather large in light of the economic relations between them. In contrast, however, Chinese FDI in Germany has never been large. Therefore, similar circumstances in trade relations could be recognized also in FDI relations. From the viewpoint of FDI relations, if Germany and China establish an alliance, it will be initiated by the German side, not the Chinese side. (4) VW's relationship with China is very interesting when we consider Sino-German relations. One of the main reasons why VW achieved the same automobile sales as Toyota was its permeation into the Chinese market. The rapid sale of 10 million VW cars was mainly due to the sales in China. However, it did not have any substance. On the other hand, due to its focus on China, VW was late in establishing luxury car brands in the United States compared with BMW and Mercedes-Benz. In such circumstances, VW installed illegal software to bypass US emission testing for its diesel cars in order to reach the top position in terms of car sales. (5) VW was also denounced as an accomplice of the Chinese Communist Party in oppressing the Uyghurs because VW constructed a factory in Urumqi (Xinjiang Uyghur Autonomous Region) and utilized Uyghur "forced labor." (6) With considering such situations, it is appropriate to estimate that the possibility of change of German attitude to China could become small. Even if VW would be denounced as profit oriented with no conscience and as the accomplice in Uyghur oppression with Chinese Communist Party, it seems to be reasonable to suppose that Germany would make an effort to continue the international relations with China. (7) However, in the present situation, there are many uncertainties. Supposing that situations which were occurred by Chinese Communist Party administration could be revealed and to which even both Chancellor Merkel and VW (which have conciliatory attitudes towards China) are hard to accept, it could become possible that German attitude to China might change.

2.2. *Chapter 6*

In Chapter 6 of this book, we consider Sino-Australian relations, focusing on the economic aspects, we also investigate Sino-Australian relations by comparing the economic aspects of Sino-Japanese relations and Sino-German relations. Our main focus is on Sino-Australian relations in 2018 and 2019 (based on the decisive deterioration in relations in 2017).

As the result of our considerations in Chapter 6, we could say that it is difficult to verify the recognition asserting that "the decisive deterioration in Sino-Australian relations occurred in 2017."

Outline of considerations in Chapter 6 is as follows: (1) In 2019, the military expenditure of Australia equaled 25.912 billion US dollars, Japan 47.690 billion US dollars, and Germany 49.277 billion US dollars. In contrast, the military expenditure of China reached 261.082 billion US dollars (China's military expenditure in 2019 was 10 times more than Australia's military expenditure). The military expenditure of Australia in 2018 was smaller than in 2017 and the expenditure in 2019 was smaller than in 2018. (2) Concerning the ranking and ratio of import partner countries and export partner countries of Australia, Chinese position of the ranking occupied the first in both import and export, and Chinese position of the ratio indicated that the ratio of 2018 was larger than of 2017 and the ratio of 2019 was larger than of 2018. With regard to the trade balance of Australia (keeping in mind the decisive deterioration in Sino-Australian relations in 2017), the Australian trade surplus (both with China and the whole world) in 2018 was larger than in 2017 and that (both with China and the whole world) in 2019 was larger than in 2018. (3) With respect to the degree of dependence on foreign trade in Australia, Japan, China, and Germany, the average value in 2018 and 2019 for each country was Germany 67.90 percent, Australia 32.80 percent, Japan 26.74 percent, and China 38.57 percent. Compared with Germany, the average value of Australia was substantially smaller. The degree of dependence on foreign trade in Australia was larger in 2018 than in 2017 and larger in 2019 than in 2018. (4) With regard to the directional trade ratio with China, the numerical value for Germany was small. The numerical value of the ratio for Australia and Japan was undoubtedly larger than that of Germany.

However, after 2013, the ratios of Australia were larger than those of Japan. The directional trade ratio of Australia with China in 2018 was larger than the ratio in 2017 and the ratio of 2019 was larger than that in 2018. (5) In the same way, the trade linkage index of Germany with China was small; in contrast, the trade linkage indices of Australia and of Japan with China were rather large. After 2009, the numerical values of Australia indicated an upward tendency but the numerical values of Japan had a downward tendency. The trade linkage index of Australia with China in 2018 was slightly smaller than the index in 2017 but the index in 2019 was substantially larger than the index in 2018. (6) The degree of export dependence of Australia on China was undoubtedly larger than the degree of dependence of Germany and Japan. The degree of export dependence of Australia on China had peaked in 2013 and after that the value had a downward trend, in which the numerical values in 2018 and 2019 were slightly smaller than before. Therefore, as a general trend, since the year 2014, the "degree of deviation from comparative advantage" in the sense of this chapter in Australian export to China has become smaller. (7) The FDI–trade index of Germany with China has become larger than that of Japan and Australia. Compared with the Japanese FDI–trade index with China, the Australian FDI–trade index with China has become smaller. The FDI–trade index of Australia with China from 2014 to 2017 was negative; in contrast, in both 2018 and 2019, the FDI–trade index was positive. Thus, in 2018 and 2019 the FDI–trade index of Australia with China was smaller compared with the index before 2017.

Therefore, in short, based upon the consideration in Chapter 6, although it could be recognized "the decisive deterioration in Sino-Australian relations" in the aspect of international politics and national security, at this moment we could confirm no influence coming from "the decisive deterioration" in the economic aspect.

2.3. *Chapter 7*

In Chapter 7, we consider the following: (1) If we consider Chinese behavior within the framework of "offensive realism," we would reach a rational conclusion that China's rise could never be peaceful. Thus, within the framework of "offensive realism," it might also be rational to conclude that a conflict involving Taiwan will break out sooner or later. (2) If we call the Chinese way with "the actual use of force" as "Taiwan's emergency situations," and when China becomes a regional hegemon, "Taiwan's emergency situations" would absolutely be occurred. The only country which has the incentive to instigate a "Taiwan emergency situation" is China, and not Taiwan, Australia, the US, Japan, or European countries. (3) Taiwan recorded a positive growth rate (3.12 percent) in 2020 due to the following reasons: (a) The negative influence on economic activities of the novel coronavirus was rather slight, (b) new business opportunities were created due to the application of new technology and remote working, and (c) the increase in export of electronic components and information and communication equipment boosted external demand. (4) The trade balance of Taiwan recorded a robust surplus trend, which was different from the trends of Australia and Japan, which fluctuated repeatedly. (5) We also examine the ratio of military expenditure in 2020 to 2002. The expansion of China's military expenditure was predominantly the largest. In contrast, the expansion of Taiwan's and Japan's military expenditure was smaller, which is interesting as both countries have been exposed to Chinese military attacks. (6) The Chinese ratio of Taiwanese exports equaled 27 percent – 29 percent and the Chinese ratio of Australian exports reached 32 percent–38 percent. The Chinese ratio of Taiwanese import equaled 19 percent–20 percent, and the Chinese ratio of Australian import reached 22 percent–25 percent. Obviously, the Chinese ratios occupied in Australian export and import were larger than in Taiwanese export and import. However, both situations in which the ratios were predominantly large and the rankings were the first were in common. (7) The ratios of China and of ASEAN in Taiwanese export and import were increased in China and, in contrast rather decreasing (export) and remained unchanged (import) in ASEAN. If the "New Southbound Policy" of the Tsai Ing-wen administration in Taiwan aimed to reduce dependence on China, it has not shown results. (8) Since 2013, the directional trade ratio between China and Australia has been larger. The ratios between China and Taiwan and between China and Japan have been smaller than the ratio between China and Australia. The directional trade ratio between China and Taiwan has shown a gradual upward trend since 2016. (9) When we observe the degree of export dependency II of Taiwan, we recognize that there has never been reduced dependence since 2016. Rather, it was the bottom in 2015 and after then "dependence on China" might be said to be tending to rise. If the "New Southbound Policy" of the Tsai Ing-wen administration in Taiwan aimed to reduce dependence on China, it has not shown results. When we describe the degree of export dependency III, we recognize that the numerical values of export dependency III of Taiwan increased in 2016 and 2017 and after that gradually decreased. However, it seems that the decrease was not obvious. (10) The Taiwanese FDI to China rapidly decreased. Although the Taiwanese FDI to Vietnam and Singapore was never large compared to the FDI to China, it was generally steady (in particular, the Taiwanese FDI to Vietnam seems to be flat or moderately increasing). Therefore, with respect to the Taiwanese FDI to China, it has shown a "reducing dependence on China." This becomes clearer when we observe the corresponding values of Taiwanese FDI to other countries. (11) However, with respect to the "FDI concentration index," (with keeping in mind the "New Southbound Policy" of Tsai Ing-wen administration in Taiwan) we could not recognize the declining trend since 2016 in Taiwanese FDI concentration index in China. (12) The Taiwanese FDI–trade index with China has fluctuated greatly (since 2016 keeping in mind the "New Southbound Policy" of the Tsai Ing-wen administration in Taiwan), making it difficult to judge accurately.

2.4. *Chapter 8*

In Chapter 8, we mentioned that, with referring Akita (2022), the three conditions for the future of Sino-Japanese relations as "cold peace" (meaning to successfully-without armed conflict-maintain the relations) are submitted. The three conditions are as follows. First, a channel for multilayered talks for government leaders, cadremen, and government authorities can be constructed. Second, economic cooperation for mutual benefit can be promoted. Third, a stable military balance can be secured between "China" and "the USA and Japan."

As investigated in Chapter 8, because the Japanese economy deeply depends upon the Chinese economy, if Japan proceeds the decoupling with China, the economic cost from which Japan suffers has to be surely big. Also, with regard to the "military balance," Japanese national security completely depends on the "nuclear umbrella" of the United States. In order to secure a military balance with China (which has spent a huge amount of money in the military sector with the possibility of further enlarging the expenditure and also has nuclear power), it is indispensable for Japan to have an independent nuclear deterrent force. As Akita (2022) indicated, when the military balance largely collapses, a dispute easily occurs.

Judging from the present situation of US–Japan security arrangement, it might not be easy for Japan to reach the status of an independent nuclear deterrent force. However, it is quite necessary for Japan that unless Japan proceeds the decoupling with China and unless Japan changes their deep economic dependence upon China, and in order to successfully (without armed conflict) maintain the Sino-Japanese relations under the "cold peace," the first thing for Japan to do is a verification whether or not the "nuclear umbrella" of the United States could effectively work. That is the first thing to do and developing an independent nuclear deterrent force is the next thing.

The chapters of this book are based on the author's analysis, some of which were presented at international academic conferences and some of which were further elaborated in other books and papers published by (no particular order) Ashgate Publishing (UK), World Scientific Publishing (Singapore), and *The Hiroshima Economic Review* (Hiroshima University). Nevertheless, each chapter was originally published in *The Hiroshima Economic Review* (in Japanese). The month and year when each chapter was published are as follows: Chapter 1 (March 2017), Chapter 2 (November 2017), Chapter 3 (March 2018), Chapter 4 (March 2019), Chapter 5 (November 2020), Chapter 6 (November 2021), Chapter 7 (March 2022), and Chapter 8 (March 2023). The designations of persons mentioned in each chapter were accurate as of the date of original publication. Also, the ways of thinking of persons referred in each chapter reflected the thinking at the time of original publication (which might differ from the current way of thinking). Needless to say, each chapter has been revised from the original articles based on helpful comments given to the author.

As circumstances have constantly changed, each chapter entailed many corrections and previous analyses have been reconsidered. As a result, some chapters have overlapping portions. However, taking into consideration the convenience of the reader, we did not make significant revisions.

Because through the publication of this book, the author came to recognize new unresolved problems, the author intends to address these problems on a future occasion.

About the Author

Ken Morita, Ph.D., is Emeritus Professor at both Hiroshima University and Hiroshima Shudo University. He is a well-known author of numerous articles and books, including *Economic Reforms and Capital Markets in Central Europe*, Farnham, Ashgate Publishing, 2004, and *Emerging Capital Markets and Transition in Contemporary China*, Singapore, World Scientific Publishing, 2017.

Contents

List of Figures

Chapter 5

Chapter 6

Chapter 7

Chapter 8

List of Tables

Chapter 3

Chapter 4

Chapter 6

Chapter 7

Chapter 8

Part I

Chinese Foreign Relations: With the United States

Chapter 1

A Political Economy of International Relations: Selections of Japan and China

1. Introduction

The aim of this chapter is to investigate the fundamental framework of international relations and diplomatic strategies among Japan, China, and the United States, which have become more complicated recently.

As a matter of fact, one cannot say that Japan has never had an independent military strategy; moreover, regarding the "US–Japan Alliance" led by the United States, Japan has never had enough information about the diplomatic strategy of the United States.[1] It is also quite necessary for Japan to make dispassionate observations about the diplomatic strategy of China. In international society, there seems to be "excess consideration for China" as it were. However, it could be said that such consideration is a retroaction of international society (which also includes the future perspective of Chinese economy). At the same time, it is indispensable for Japan to make dispassionate judgments about other countries.

The purpose of this chapter is to carefully consider the judgments.

The structure of this chapter is as follows: In the first section, we review the selection of Japan, which was disputed in the 1980s, and try to reconsider the issue from contemporary viewpoints. In the second section,

[1] With regard to that point, see Ito (2011, 2012).

we focus on the selection of China and the "G2 system of US and China," which we investigate from the perspective of "Sino-American relations." In the last section, we submit the conclusion of this chapter.

2. The Selection of Japan

In the 1980s, there were controversial issues in Japan which were frequently called the "selection of Japan." The following factors provide some background for the issues: (1) the positions Japan occupied in some international indicators of development, (2) the gradual deterioration of US hegemony, and (3) the withdrawal of Soviet-type planned economy, which was easily recognized as a sign of change in international economic relations with the USSR. The above-mentioned points depict the uncertain state of affairs for the superpowers that had established the bipolar system of the US and USSR.

Moreover, there existed the widely recognized and chronic "friction phenomenon" between the US and Japan that continued from the beginning of the 1980s, which was rather serious in the sense that the closed nature of the Japanese market as a whole was seen as the cause of this phenomenon. Concerning the USSR, after the Gorbachev administration was established, the Soviet advances towards the Asia-Pacific region were clearly noticeable. In particular, the USSR's advances toward Japan in order to intensify the economic and technological exchanges were easily perceived.

With respect to the fundamental strategy of diplomatic policy in Japan, How should we properly recognize? We try to analyze such problems.

Needless to say, as it is impossible to discuss each aspect of such major problems in this chapter, we proceed with the analysis by keeping in mind the fundamental framework of the Japanese foreign policy and the international economy.

2.1. *Fundamental strategy: Preparation of international trade*

After the Second World War, in particular after the reconstruction of the economic disorder caused by the Second World War, it could be said that the fundamental strategy of Japanese diplomatic policy was the maintenance and intensification of a system in which economic interests could be converted to order and peace. This expression was originally stated by Polanyi (1957). As Polanyi stated, it seems obvious that people doing economic activities to gain economic benefit do not particularly love peace and are not exceptionally virtuous, but order and peace are still necessary for them to gain economic benefit.

There exists an apparatus in the international system to convert economic benefits to order and peace, and in order for the system to fully work, it is necessary for goods, services, and capital to move freely.[2] As a result, a system that has such an apparatus can work efficiently.

Because such an apparatus has a property of public goods, it is usually called international public goods. Public goods do not exclude consumption by other persons, other companies, other organizations, and other countries; thus, if any country (which has comparatively larger benefit from international public goods than other countries) bears an appropriate share of the burden, as a result, excess burden phenomena (which means that they pay more than own appropriate share) could occur. It is called the "free rider phenomenon."[3] After the Second World War, the United States undoubtedly shouldered excess burden. We can state that Japan received the benefits of a "free rider" and contributed to the stabilization of international order by acquiring economic benefits.

This fundamental strategy of Japanese foreign policy can be considered a cooperative policy toward the United States. Needless to say, "cooperative policy to the United States" was, at first, the measures associated with defeat in the Second World War. Later (although it is difficult to specify when), it became recognized as Japanese autonomous selection.[4]

---

[2]It is quite doubtful that, until at least the end of the 1960s, Japanese policymakers of international trade and industrial policies performed policy operations based upon the above-mentioned concept (see Komiya, 1984). However, since the impact on the Japanese economy on international society has been recognized, such a concept seemed to have become pervasive.

[3]See, for example, Hamada (1982) and Olson and Zeckhauser (1966). If as long as any country bears the expenses corresponding to own benefits, it would not for that country to pay excess burden. However, if every country bears the appropriate burdens corresponding to its benefits, each country would bear only smaller burdens (although that country could gain the same benefit). In that sense, the situation (in which any country bears more burden on a comparative scale) can be called as excess burden.

[4]It could have another assertion whether or not it was "autonomous selection," particularly in the aspect of military power. With regard to such an issue, see Chapter 8 of this book.

Therefore, it seems appropriate that the fundamental strategy of Japanese foreign policy was to maintain and strengthen the apparatus in the international system to convert economic benefits to order and peace.

Since the end of the 1960s and the beginning of the 1970s, judging from various economic indicators and the international situation, the hegemony (or regional hegemony[5]) of the United States began to deteriorate. It is indicated that the time when shortage of international public goods and possibility to lead to functional incompetence of abovementioned apparatus has come. What were the main reasons for the shortage? What could Japan do to deal with them?

It goes without saying, if supply of international public goods could become profitable for the United States (although it might be excess burden), it would not be inconvenient for the United States. Nevertheless, there are two reasons why shortage of international public goods was closely related with the deterioration of US hegemony.

The first reason is a phenomenon called "the hegemon's dilemma."[6] When international public goods are provided mainly by a hegemonic country and when the active transfer of goods, services, and capital occurs, then the active transfer of economic and managerial resources from the hegemonic country to non-hegemonic countries can take place. Then, countries which have comparatively less burden of supplying international public goods can comparatively increase their economic scale, thereby comparatively reducing the economic scale of the hegemonic country. Needless to say, both Japan and Germany are typical examples.

The second reason is the existence of an opposing camp. If the behavior of the opposing camp becomes more aggressive or if the ability of the opposing camp increases, the corresponding benefit for international public goods (particularly national security) becomes greater. However, the cost to do so might also dramatically increase. Because of such cost and benefit considerations, it becomes possible that US (marginal) cost exceeds US (marginal) benefit related with international public goods

---

[5] It is difficult to strictly define the term "hegemony." Its definition varies from one author to another. See, for example, Inoguchi (1987), Keohane (1984), Murakami (1985), Sakamoto (1986), and Olson (1982). It is also difficult to strictly define "hegemon" or "regional hegemon." In this chapter, we would use the term "worldwide hegemon" or "regional hegemon" without definition. With regard to this definition, see, for example, Waltz (1979) and Mearsheimer (2014).

[6] See, for example, Gilpin (1975) and Olson (1982).

provision. Military expansion of opposed camp (mainly of USSR) seemed to be an important reason.

Alongside the above-mentioned two reasons, it might be important to indicate the following two.

First, in the case of the hegemon's dilemma, if the comparative economic scale of the United States becomes smaller, it would not be possible for it to provide international public goods in a profitable manner. However, in the case of the opposing camp reason, the situation is different. When cost (curve) rises (shifts), it is adjusted for optimum benefit to be deteriorated (for example, the range of security areas becomes reduced). Thus, the possibility of decreasing the provision of international public goods increases more in the first case. Another one is that the reasons of deterioration of the US hegemony vary from one period to another. If it is taken the long period, it could be said that, from the second half of 1960s (and at the beginning of 1970s) until the second half of 1970s, relatively above-mentioned first reason was dominant. However, after the second half of 1970s, in association with military expansion of USSR, above-mentioned second reason became relatively dominant.

Therefore, after the second half of the 1980s, a rapid deterioration of US hegemony and a reduction in international public goods supply occurred, mostly due to the military power of the USSR.

When we suppose the selection of Japan to deal with the above-mentioned situation, it seems to be desirable that Japan would bear the burden to supply international public goods. The reasons are as follows:

First, as far as the "dilemma of hegemony" is concerned, it cannot be applied to Japan. It might be possible to categorize Japan as a country that acquires net benefit associated with the burden of international public goods supply.

Second, because the movement of goods, services, and capital would undoubtedly increases, even if the cost of international public goods supply increases, the net benefit could become positive.

Third, if the collapse of the international order is realized, it would be closely connected with Japanese behavior (which means Japan would bear a relatively smaller the burden for international public goods supply). The burden of international public goods supply (from which Japan could have net benefit) might be undoubtedly more desirable selection compared with the occasion of collapse of international order and compared with the policy in cooperation with USSR.

Fourth, if the following two conditions are satisfied, it could be possible that, as far as net benefit is concerned, the case of Japan as a free rider would have less benefit than the case of Japan as an international public goods supplier: (A) if the opposing camp becomes stronger and US's cost to countervail it becomes greater, the cost increase for Japan might become relatively smaller[7]; (B) if the benefit for Japan is largely increased, the increase of benefit for the United States would be reduced. Such a situation could occur if the benefit associated with international public goods supply increases greatly and if the comparative position of Japan in the world also increases, thereby making it difficult for another country (or other countries) to take the place of Japan.[8]

Thus, the fundamental strategy of Japanese foreign policy was to maintain and strengthen the apparatus in which economic benefit could be converted into peace and order; even if US hegemony gradually declined, it was desirable for Japan to bear the cost of international public goods supply.

2.2. *Confirmation of fundamental strategy: Foreign economic relations of the USSR*

As stated in the previous section, the fundamental strategy of Japanese foreign policy was to maintain and strengthen the apparatus in which economic benefit could be converted into peace and order and the movement of goods, services, and capital could increase. This could be called a cooperative relationship with the United States.

Are there any other feasible alternatives for the foreign policy of Japan? One feasible alternative in those days might have been a cooperative relationship with the USSR.[9]

---

[7]Thus, at this stage, an assumption which is different from that of Olson and Zeckhauser (1966) is introduced.

[8]For more detailed assertions, see Olson and Zeckhauser (1966) and Snidal (1985).

[9]Okazaki (1983, 1984a, 1984b) persuasively asserted that, because the substance of power in Far East could be always USSR and Anglo-Saxon (1984b, p. 175), in practice, alternative of Japanese strategy about the foreign policy could be limited to "cooperative relationship with USSR" or "cooperative relationship with Anglo-Saxon." Therefore, the alternatives in this chapter would fundamentally be based upon such a way of thinking. During the 1980s, international relations were as mentioned in this chapter. Furthermore, the alternatives in those days did not include a "cooperative relationship with China."

However, Japan selected a cooperative relationship with the United States. Why would Japan prefer a cooperative relationship with the United States? There are many reasons for this, one of which relates to a difference in adjustment systems. Economic relations among capitalist countries, although varying depending on the countries involved and the periods, are fundamentally adjusted by the market. However, in socialist countries, including the USSR, economic relations among countries were dependent on intergovernmental negotiations. Japan deemed a world whose adjustment was done by markets to be better than a world whose adjustment was done by intergovernmental negotiations. It was rational selection because Japan was comparatively superior to the USSR in economic activities.

If Japan had changed its strategy into a cooperative relationship with the USSR, it would not have been easy to precisely predict the situation after the change. Our estimation indicates that the share of international trade at the time was 45–50 percent for socialist countries, 35–40 percent for Western advanced industrialized countries, and around 15 percent for developing countries.[10] Such a framework of international trade was determined by bilateral intergovernmental negotiations, the economic efficiency of which was remarkably inferior. As a result, the ability to acquire convertible currencies significantly decreased and gain from trade became undoubtedly smaller. With regard to the life of the Japanese people, there would have been an excessive demand for food and consumer goods. In compensation for inadequate economic activities in the comparative advantageous field of Japan, it could occur considerable net loss compared with the case in cooperative relationship with the United States.

Suppose that the military power between the Eastern bloc and Western bloc was balanced and suppose the Japanese economy had reached a certain level in the 1980s, the fundamental strategy of the Japanese foreign policy of a cooperative relationship with the United States would not have been inconvenient for the USSR due to the following reasons.

As the domestic and international relations of socialist countries are not clear, with regard to economic relations between East European

[10] Such numerical values include East Germany and Czechoslovakia; moreover, it should be noted that the Asia-Pacific region is distant from the central region of the USSR and East European countries.

countries and the USSR, the following two cases should be considered separately.[11]

First, the USSR made East European countries into a buffer zone in order to safeguard its own national security. In return for their political, social, and cultural support, the USSR would supply cheaper raw materials and mineral fuel (lower than market price) to East European countries (as substantial aid).[12] If Japan had formed a "cooperative relationship with the USSR," Japan would have also become a buffer zone for the USSR and would have received substantial aid as compensation. How much would Japan have required as compensation in order to do this? Needless to say, if Japan had become a socialist country, a large amount of money for economic and military purposes might have been necessary. Thus, in order for Japan to comply with the USSR and not deviate from its cooperative relationship, more economic compensation would have been required (due to a relatively high level of economic standard) than the amount provided to the GDR, Czechoslovakia, Hungary, and (geopolitically important) Poland. The Soviet economy would have been unable to bear such a compensation.[13]

Second, the USSR exploited East European countries economically.[14] Even in this case, it is doubtful that the USSR would have made Japan a socialist country. If we make a comparison between (A) socialist Japan and (B) capitalist Japan, socialist Japan would have been inefficient and would have had poor technology from which the USSR could have exploited only marginal benefit. On the contrary, the USSR could have implemented economic exchange with capitalist Japan, from which it could have benefited much more economically and technologically. If we take into consideration the costs required to control and manage socialist Japan, the net benefit gained by economic exchange with capitalist Japan would have been larger than that exploited from socialist Japan.[15]

---

[11] In this chapter, we exclude the case in which Japanese people evaluate the socialism ideology and join socialist countries of their own free will.

[12] Such a supposition seemed to be quite ordinary. See, for example, Dietz (1986), Holzman (1974), and Marrese and Vanous (1983).

[13] With regard to a "united Germany," the same assertions were made by Rosecrance (1986).

[14] See, for example, Mendershausen (1959, 1960).

[15] On such a way of thinking, see Kimura (1987).

Therefore, the Japanese fundamental strategy of a cooperative relationship with the United States was not inconvenient for the USSR.

However, the real possibility of a remarkable expansion of economic exchange between the USSR and Japan was insignificant. The main reason was the USSR's Soviet-type planned economy. In this chapter, we provide an example, which involves the Soviet advance into the Asia-Pacific region.

We suppose that the Soviet advance into the Asia-Pacific region was caused by the tremendous development of the economy in that region and also because of the prosperous economic activities in the eastern region of the USSR. However, judging from the ratio of the USSR's trade, the Soviet advance into the Asia-Pacific region was limited to China, North Korea, and Vietnam. Soviet trade with non-socialist countries like Japan decreased in the second half of the 1970s and the beginning of the 1980s. The reasons for the poor economic relations between the USSR and non-socialist countries in the Asia-Pacific region are as follows. First, the quality of industrial products made in the USSR was poorer than those made in Western countries. Second, there was a shortage of convertible currency. Although the poor ability to acquire convertible currency was closely related to the first reason, there is more to the issue. The shortage of convertible currency was incorporated into the mechanism of the planned economy (as currency inconvertibility and commodity inconvertibility[16]). Therefore, although the quality of industrial products was relatively poorer and convertible currency was in short supply, large-scale international trade among socialist countries was possible due to the implementation of barter trade. Third, the international trade of the USSR with Asia-Pacific countries, particularly Japan, was on a smaller scale compared to that of West European countries, particularly West Germany and Finland. The USSR selected import markets according to the products imported because of limited solvency. With regard to Western developed countries at the beginning of the 1980s, the main export products to the USSR from the United States and West European countries were based on the comparative advantages of the respective countries. However, Japan's main export products to the USSR were not based on its

[16]With regard to currency and commodity inconvertibility, see, for example, Holzman (1976) and Spero (1985). Also, there existed the USSR's side assertion which said that above-mentioned situation should not be overestimated. See Ершов и Станковский (1988).

comparative advantage.[17] It should be recognized as results of USSR trade authority's selection about the import market.

The above-mentioned third reason gradually changed as economic activities in the eastern region of the USSR increased vigorously, and, as a result, international trade between Asia-Pacific countries and the USSR expanded. However, the first and second reasons, which were the poor quality of industrial products and the shortage of convertible currency, respectively, could not be nullified unless drastic economic reforms were successfully implemented. Thus, it would be appropriate to judge that the possibility to remarkably expand the USSR's economic exchange with Asia-Pacific region countries particularly Japan might not become so large.[18]

It can be concluded that the USSR's international economic relations (including Asia-Pacific countries) did not have any influence on the fundamental strategy of Japan's foreign policy.[19]

2.3. *US–Japan relations: An interpretation*

The 1980s saw the enactment of the "two-pole system of the United States and USSR." Under such a system, Japan did never employ an alternative to become a "large country" (which means that Japan has selected an alternative to be a "small country").[20] It seemed as if Japan entrusted its own national security to the United States and endeavored to maintain and

[17]Concerning such situations, see Morita (1988b).

[18]Therefore, with regard to the assertion insisting (in the years 1987 and 1988) that it might be probable for Japan to lose (USSR) export market because Japan would lag behind other capitalist countries in economic exchange with USSR, it would not be misunderstanding and it might be economically appropriate not to lag behind other countries. However, it seemed that the effects were incorrectly judged. Regarding the above-mentioned issue, see Станковский (1988).

[19]Even if Japan had attempted to further cooperation with the USSR, due to the circumstances of the USSR, no change would have occurred.

[20]Opting to become a "small country" is not a selection unique to Japan. For example, Iceland has been a member of NATO and its per capita GDP was 51,262 US dollars (value estimated by the IMF in 2014). However, Iceland has no armaments if its own. (Although Iceland has a large per capita GDP, the nation's size is a little bigger than Hokkaido, Japan. Iceland's population was only 330,610 as of June, 2015.) (Based upon the homepage of Japanese Ministry of Foreign Affairs.)

strengthen an apparatus in which economic benefit could be converted into peace and order. Such a Japanese strategy could become possible because of (1) the circumstances in which Japan could dedicate own time to that strategy (for maintaining and for strengthening the apparatus in which economic benefit could be converted into peace and order) were completed and (2) the strong US position as a "hegemon" (or a "regional hegemon"), which enabled it to create the above-mentioned apparatus.

This Japanese strategy of "offensive realism" did not establish the survival of one's own nation as the most important strategy. However, the strategy, in which one's own country is regarded as a "small country" and one's own survival is entrusted to a "big country" can be called a rational strategy.

Nevertheless, there were several possible problems for a country regarded as a "big country" economically but a "small country" militarily. In this section, we will focus our attention on such problems.

The above-mentioned framework was observed from the viewpoint of economics. Moreover, there was an important occurrence in US–Japan relations in those days, i.e., "US–Japan friction." In this section, we discuss the "US–Japan" friction and then interpret that friction from the viewpoint of the framework of international relations and international politics.

The relations between two specific countries can deteriorate to a "serious situation." One of the principal reasons seems to be a connection with a "hegemonic country" or "regional hegemonic country." US–Japan relations reached a point of serious "friction" in the 1980s due to the presence of a "hegemonic country" or "regional hegemonic country." We now outline the cause of the US–Japan friction.

2.3.1. *The US–Japan friction*

The trade friction between the United States and Japan can be divided into different "waves." For example, according to Komiya (1983), the period from the 1950s to the middle of the 1960s was a time when Japanese export of sundries and fibers to the United States rapidly increased; however, the trade problems of those days involved an accumulation of respective concrete matters. There was a history to "the US–Japan friction."

The first wave of "trade friction" occurred from 1968 to 1972 and involved a confrontation between the two countries because of tough negotiations between the US and Japan on textiles. The second wave occurred between 1976 and 1978 and was caused by the "export drive effect," meaning that, because of slumping domestic demand at the time of a recession, Japanese export drastically expanded. Neither the first wave nor the second wave led to serious friction," which calmed down after the Japanese trade deficit. Instead, serious friction accompanied the "oil crisis."

The third wave started after the beginning of the 1980s and led to the extremely serious "US–Japan friction." This wave of friction was triggered by the relatively minor recession (associated with the oil crisis) in Japan compared to other developed countries because of which Japanese export of industrial products rapidly increased from the second half of the 1980s.

The main products involved in the third wave of the "US–Japan friction" were automobiles and semiconductors. The characteristics of the third wave were developed to exclusive criticism in Japan not only in economic aspect but also in military, social and cultural aspects, because Japan was criticized as its unfair behaviors to protect own domestic market from US import and was criticized as its catch up behaviors (with the United States) not only in such individual industries as automobile and semiconductor, but also in advanced technology industry.

The economic background for the US's criticism of Japan included the following two points: (1) the increased ratio of Japanese GNP to that of the whole world (Table 1)[21] and (2) the increased ratio of Japanese trade surplus to the overall trade deficit of the United States (Table 2).

As shown in Table 1, the ratio of Japanese GNP to the whole world reached 10.0 percent in 1978. It seemed to suppose that there existed a concept in the US saying that a country which had 10 percent GNP ratio to the whole world could not be intolerable with its unfair behaviors. Also, at the same time, the ratio of the US GNP to the whole world declined from 30 percent to 20 percent. In 1980, the ratio of the GNP of the former EC countries to the whole world exceeded the ratio of the USA and also the relative difference between the ratio of USA and the ratio of USSR (which was a leader of confrontationally camp) made frustration of USA stronger.[22]

---

[21] We use the term GNP, and not GDP, as used in the original article and in that period.

[22] The aggregate ratio of GNP (to the whole world) of USA and USSR occupied 48.9 percent, 46.1 percent and 33.1 percent in 1960, 1970 and 1980 respectively. They were the ratio of GNP to the whole world in the period called as "USA and USSR two poles system."

Table 1. The ratio of countries' GNP to the whole world (1955–1980) (in percent).

	1955	1960	1970	1978	1980
Japan	2.2	2.9	6.0	10.0	9.0
USA	36.3	33.7	30.2	21.8	21.5
China	4.4	4.7	4.9	4.6	4.7
EC	17.5	17.5	19.3	20.2	22.4
USSR	13.9	15.2	15.9	13.0	11.6
USA + USSR	50.2	48.9	46.1	34.8	33.1

Source: Komiya (1983, p. 9).

Table 2. The amount and ratio of the Japanese trade surplus to the total trade deficit of the USA (1972–1981) (100 million US dollars).

	1972	1974	1976	1978	1980	1981
Amount of trade deficit of USA to Japan	40	19	10	106	98	163
Ratio	62.5	42.2	10.7	31.3	38.7	41.1

Source: Komiya (1983, p. 10).

As indicated in Table 2, the ratio of the trade surplus of Japan to the total trade deficit of the USA occupied larger numerical values. In 1978, when the US trade deficit against Japan rapidly increased, the ratio of the US trade deficit against Japan exceeded 30 percent.

It goes without saying, above-mentioned (1) was the US anxiety against Japan which seemed for US to approach them towards a "hegemon." With respect to (2), the US recognized that the huge amount of its trade deficit was caused by Japan's huge amount of trade surplus with the US.

The phenomenon of US trade deficit has existed since the 1970s. In the 1970s and 1980s, Japan was recognized as having a huge amount of trade surplus with the US. Therefore, it is safe to assume that the US–Japan friction was caused by the huge amount of US trade deficit.

However, on the whole, if the "trade friction" had remained at the level of "trade negotiations," the friction would not have been so serious. As Komiya (1994) asserted, the "trade friction" changed to "economic friction" (p. 43). As Hanai (1988) called the friction to be "3*B* friction" which means "trade friction" (*b*oueki masatsu), "defense friction" (*b*ouei masatsu) and "cultural friction" (*b*unka masatsu), when the friction came up not only trade and overall economy but also came up the culture, institution and society, it is never easy to settle.

2.3.2. *What was the US–Japan friction about?*

As far as the US–Japan friction is concerned, the "Komiya–Koo dispute," i.e., arguments between academics Komiya (1995) and Koo (1994, 1996), became well known. The dispute concerned various topics aside from economics. In the following, we consider such interesting topics.

In this section, we start with a discussion by Bergsten and Cline (1985). According to them, Japan definitely had the largest trade amount (the first rank); however, the ratio of trade surplus to the whole trade amount (export plus import amount) was not the largest (the fifth rank). The four countries and regions of Romania, Taiwan, Brazil, and Hong Kong had ratios greater than that of Japan (Table 3). That is to say, Japan had a large amount of trade surplus with the US because the total trade amount with the US was large and not because only Japanese export to the US was large.

The conclusion reached by Bergsten and Cline based on statistics and data on the reasons for the US–Japan friction was as follows: (1) the large amount of trade surplus of Japan with the US and (2) the wide circulation of a negative image of Japan which proclaimed that Japan had unfair trade practices (Bergsten and Cline, 1985, Japanese version p. 34).

Table 3. Each country's trade balance with the USA (1984) (million US dollars, in percent).

	Amount of trade balance	**Rank**	**The ratio of the trade balance to the total trade amount with the USA (in percent)**	**Rank**
Brazil	5,633	7	51.6	3
Canada	20,387	2	18.0	14
West Germany	8,726	4	32.4	10
Hong Kong	5,837	6	48.8	4
Japan	36,795	1	43.8	5
South Korea	4,044	9	25.3	12
China	337	19	5.9	19
Romania	720	15	59.1	1
Taiwan	11,065	3	52.2	2

Source: Bergsten and Cline (1985, p. 33), Japanese version.

However, the large trade surplus that Japan had with the US was not solely due to Japanese domestic factors. Basically, it was the result of US consumers' preferences. At the same time, the amount of Japanese imports from the US was large, and Japanese trade surplus ratios to total trade amount (export plus import amount) were smaller than those of Romania and Taiwan. Thus, it was wrong to say that the US–Japan friction was caused by Japanese export-biased trade with a large amount of trade surplus. Instead, it was because of Japan's supposed unfair trade practices and the large amount of trade surplus. This made the US–Japan friction a more serious political issue.

Unfair trade practice issue started with criticism from the US government and congress. They claimed Japan as a target of unfair trade practice by which US accumulated the trade deficit. However, the assertion of unfair trade practices was highly obscure. As a matter of fact, it was indispensable that there existed such a player to perform to build up negative unfair image and to raise a fever of friction.

The key player who was thought to have contributed to the expansion and establishment of such an image, thereby increasing frictional fever was the "Maekawa report" (and the member of the committee). Actually, in "Section II. Proposal of the Maekawa report," such statements in Point 3 as further improvement of market access, promotion of manufactured imports could be recognized for Japan (and Japanese enterprises) to be reformed as internationally cooperative. Needless to say, unless reform could be successfully implemented, the circumstances that caused the friction could not be changed.

Why was such a report prepared in 1986? Komiya (2008) claimed that the "Maekawa report" was prepared in time for the then prime minister Nakasone's visit to the US as it was assumed that the then US President Reagan would accept this report as a show of deference (thus, it was written to please the US). Komiya (2008) also mentioned that the then USTR (US Trade Representative) Yeutter criticized the report because it seemed to pander to the US and Yeutter considered it a dangerous precedent.

Such an usual way which was criticized by the trade representative (responsible for the trade negotiations) was nothing but a behavior to raise a fever of friction.

However, the Japanese government's attitude of showing deference seemed to have a reason. For example, if Japan had strong defense capability against the US, the Japanese government would have had no necessity to show deference. This asymmetry in defense capability possibly caused the Japanese government to defer to the will of the US.

It is quite doubtful actually that the "Komiya–Koo dispute" can be recognized as a dispute, because it is extremely difficult to find economists who agree with Koo's assertion. The aim of this section is not to criticize Koo's assertion but to confirm the US misrecognition saying that appreciating the exchange rate of Yen could improve US trade deficit situation, and that Japan could accumulate trade surplus because of Japanese closed nature of the markets to foreign countries' export.

Actually, the discussions between the two countries during the days of the US–Japan friction influenced discussions between the US and China on Sino-US relations. The US requested the appreciation of the Chinese Renminbi when the US had a huge amount of trade deficit with China in order to decrease the US trade deficit, which is what it had done with Japan. In that sense, both the US–Japan trade friction and Sino-American relations basically had the same characteristics from an economic point of view.

Another point of contention in the "Komiya–Koo dispute" concerns the US–Japan trade imbalance, for which Japan did not take responsibility (in terms of the exchange rate and the closed nature of the market).

If that was the case, why did Koo, who actively worked in Japan, dispute Komiya's "absorption approach," which almost all economists in both countries agreed with?

What was the chief reason behind Koo's argument? We could approach the question with chapter 12 of Koo (1996). The title of Chapter 12 of the book is "select US or select China." To briefly summarize it, Koo said that Japan should strengthen its relations with the US. If Japan did not, it would become a vassal state of China. Under such circumstances, it was not good for Japan to have friction with the US; moreover, as an industrialized country, Japan should have recognized that it needed to follow the accepted principles of democracy and liberalism.

Needless to say, the argument on selecting the US or selecting China is completely unrelated to the "US–Japan trade imbalance." The argument on "select US or select China" is an issue related with the selection of Japan, and it is quite reasonable for Japan to argue against unjustified assertions concerning trade imbalance.

The problem is, however, why such an issue as selecting the US or selecting China was established in the first place. Such issues after all lead us to military conflicts.

2.3.3. *Background of US–Japan defense friction*

In the previous section, it was pointed out that the overall friction started due to trade issues in the 1980s.

Since the second half of the 1970s, particularly in the 1980s, the US economy was in the worst shape since the post-war period. The economic performance of the US in the 1980s was extremely bad. It was sometimes termed the decline of a hegemon, which we describe in the following.

Table 4 shows the main economic indices of the US. Undoubtedly, in the 1980s, the US economy was worse than in other periods. Compared with other periods, the economic growth rate was lower, the unemployment rate was higher, the budget deficit was larger, and corporate profit was smaller. As a matter of fact, the real GDP growth rate was 2.7 percent on average annually, which was the lowest it had been. The growth rate of labor productivity in the 1980s was 1.4 percent on average annually, which was almost half of what it was in the 1960s. Also, the accumulated deficit of current account balance became larger which led the US to become a debtor country in the 1980s.

Table 5 indicates the scenarios and actual results of Reaganomics (the economic policies of Ronald Reagan). In 1986, five years after the Reagan administration was inaugurated, the only positive result was consumer price; the fiscal balance whose scenario in 1986 was 28.2 billion US dollars surplus, but whose actual result was significant deficit to be 221.2 billion US dollars.

Table 4. Main economic indices of USA (1960s–1990s).

	1960s	**1970s**	**1980s**	**1990s**
Real GDP growth rate (in percent)	4.6	3.2	2.7	3.3
Consumer price (in percent)	2.4	7.1	5.5	2.8
Unemployment rate (in percent)	4.8	6.3	7.1	5.6
Current account balance (100 million US dollars)	333	▲31	▲8,513	▲15,991
Current account balance (ratio to GDP) (in percent)	0.5	0.0	▲1.8	▲2.0
Fiscal balance (100 million US dollars)	▲565	▲3,654	▲17,862	▲14,825
Fiscal balance (ratio to GDP) (in percent)	▲0.8	▲2.2	▲3.8	▲2.1
Corporate profit (ratio to GDP) (in percent)	10.7	8.7	7.2	8.6

Source: Marumo (2002, p. 12).

Table 5. Scenarios and actual results of Reaganomics (1986).

	Scenarios	Actual results
Real GDP growth rate (in percent)	4.2	3.4
Consumer price (in percent)	4.2	1.9
Unemployment rate (in percent)	5.6	7.0
Fiscal expenditure (100 million US dollars)	282	▲2,212

Source: Marumo (2002, p. 15).

The main reason for the fiscal deficit was undoubtedly military expenditure.

As a matter of fact, the period when the Reagan administration started was the same period of aggravation of defense friction, which was the beginning of 1980s.

At that time, the United States and Japan had signed the Treaty of Mutual Cooperation and Security. Article 10 of the treaty provided that each signatory nation could notify its intention to terminate the treaty to the other signatory nation; thus, this treaty could have been terminated one year after the notice was given. If the treaty is terminated, which signatory nation would have been more seriously impacted in terms of its security?

Needless to say, even though the US might have faced some sort of impact, for Japan, it might have become a matter of life and death. Those impacts are perfectly asymmetrical. For example, if Japan could not defend its sea lanes, the Japanese economy would be shaken thoroughly. It means that, even Japan has had a rather crucial vulnerability as a state, Japan had more than 10 percent ratio of GDP to the whole world. The US military umbrella contributed substantially to Japan's economic expansion after the Second World War. Japan's circumstances as a free rider in a military sense made the friction with the US much more serious.

Another circumstance behind the US–Japan defense friction was the existence of the USSR, which was called an "evil empire" by the then US President Reagan. When the US–Japan defense friction became serious, the USSR invaded Afghanistan, which was closely connected with discussions on Japan's security.

In terms of the defense asymmetry between the US and Japan, Japan was called the "free rider." The Japanese position meant that its defense cost was kept lower and the security of its own country depended completely upon the US (moreover, Japan enjoyed a higher rate of economic growth). At this time, the US recognized that it had taken on an excess burden for international public goods, providing order and peace to the international society.

2.3.4. *Komiya–Koo dispute: Different viewpoints*

As considered in a previous section, the "Komiya–Koo dispute" focused on the US trade deficit with Japan based on the "absorption approach." However, the argument made by Koo also covered different topics, particularly Japan's security issues.

The "absorption approach" is a theory according to which current account surplus (and deficit) equals the difference between total savings and total investments. The "absorption approach" is a standard theory of international macroeconomics. Thus, it is undoubtedly a basic error to say that one's own country's trade deficit depends on another country's excess savings.

Apart from discussions on "absorption approach," we should make note of the Japanese circumstances, which were asserted by Koo (1996, Chapter 12). As referred to earlier, the title of Chapter 12 of Koo's book was "select US or select China." As of the year 1996, circumstances might have still been vague, but possible selection could have been obvious. Needless to say, selecting the US or selecting China would not have fostered independence as one selection would have made Japan a protectorate of the US and the other a protectorate of China.

Koo's assertion was clear, which was to strengthen the US–Japan alliance. He then introduced the words of Lee Teng-hui (former Chinese premier). When Koo visited Lee Teng-hui in Taipei in September 1995, Lee said to him that Japan should have strong relations with the US. Koo indicated that one Japanese government official said that Japan did not need the US as it could foster a relationship with China. To make sure, foreign relations as of the days were that, from the Japanese perspective, we did neither care about relations with the US nor care about relations with the West, China would follow us (Koo, 1996, p. 314). Koo further stated that if such Japanese perspective would continue, what would the results become 5 years later and 10 years later. From the present point of view, Koo's comment should be considered very insightful.

As Koo asserted, Japan could not become the leader of Asia, and if there is a country that can be a leader of Asia, it has to be China (Koo, 1996, p. 314).

In short, as of 1996, for 15 consecutive years, China had recorded a nearly 10 percent economic growth rate and (keeping step with the high rate of economic growth) expanded its military expenditure, which would lead to its rise.

Koo's assertion as clearly mentioned earlier was to strengthen the US–Japan alliance, which would restrain China and release the tension between China and Taiwan (for relaxation of China–Taiwan relations), leading to Asian security. Koo criticized the Japanese government; he claimed that the US tried to deal with its problems with China by approaching Japan, but instead the Japanese government started a quarrel with the US about trade issues (p. 330).

Moreover, what Koo mentioned in Chapter 12 of his book seemed to be quite suggestive:

"When we think about the future of Japan, what is the most crucial thing for Japan to consider is that, after 10–15 years later when China becomes more powerful country in the sense of economy and military, what should Japan do against so powerful China? Then, would Japan be obedient to China? Would Japan rearm in a fluster? If not rearm, what should US–Japan relations become? Such kind of topics are indispensable for present Japan to discuss" (p. 331). "It should be argued now much more about Japanese correspondence to (the future) such powerful China" (p. 331).

The fundamental concept behind Koo's assertion was that both the US and Japan had some common principles such as liberalism and democracy. According to Koo, Japan had the following choices: (1) side with the US (strengthen its relations with the US), (2) side with China (become a vassal state of China), and (3) rearm itself. Koo's choice was undoubtedly (1). Although the meaning of "rearmament" is not necessarily obvious, if Japan is neither obedient to the US nor a vassal state of China, the only way for it to have independent defense is to rearm itself.

2.3.5. *US–Soviet bipolar era*

In this section, we look at the "selection of Japan" and US–Japan relations from the viewpoints of international relations and international political economy.

According to the framework of international relations and international politics, the international system is classified into "realism" or "idealism," in which "realism" is also classified into "offensive realism" and "defensive realism."

In light of such a framework, the Japanese strategy (as mentioned in previous sections) seems to be based on a situation that has the USA as a "hegemon" (at least a "regional hegemon" in the East Asian region). If such an assumption can be established, it might be meaningful for a country to make efforts to maintain and intensify the system in which economic interests are converted into order and peace. However, the main player for the national security of Japan is the United States. Then, could such a Japanese strategy be based on a framework of "idealism"? As a matter of fact, under a unipolar system in which the US is a "hegemon," Japan could entrust its national security to the US and acquire economic benefits as a "free rider."

However, that is not necessarily the case. In order to correctly recognize the international relations, we refer to Mearsheimer (2014). According to Mearsheimer (2014), power in the international system is usually arranged in three different ways: bipolarity, balanced multipolarity, and unbalanced multipolarity. The core of his argument is that bipolar systems tend to be the most peaceful and unbalanced multipolar systems are most prone to deadly conflict. A balanced multipolar system will fall somewhere in between (p. 335).

During the Cold War, the "US–Soviet bipolar era" (persisted until by and large 1990) was a highly stable system. Mearsheimer's framework (2014) describes the situation precisely.

From the viewpoints of Japanese strategy, under the bipolar system of the USA and USSR, Japan performed like a "small country."[23]

In the 1980s, Japan opted to perform as a "small country," which meant that Japan could entrust its national security to the US and have the US deal with the burden of international public goods. Then, what about contemporary China? In the following section, we focus on the "G2" system in which the main players are China and the US.

3. The Selection of China: The "G2" System

In this section, we consider the "G2" system with a focus on China and the US.

---

[23]The meaning of a "small country" as described in this book is as follows. The most important aim for each nation is to survive; in order to accomplish the aim, the country concerned could not act like a hegemon (and a regional hegemon) but act to maintain the status quo which is called here as a "small country." We would not refer here the relations with the concept of "defensive realism."

An article in the *People's Daily* (the Japanese version of the state media of Beijing, 8 January 2009) reported that the then FRB Chairman Ben Bernanke asserted that the reason for the US's trade deficit was not only the excess consumption of Americans but also the excess savings of foreigners.

It is reasonable to assume that the foreigners referred to by him are Chinese.

Most Japanese people had a sense of "déjà vu" upon reading the article. When the US faced a huge trade deficit with Japan in (the second half of) the 1970s and the 1980s, the US government stated that it was due to excess savings by the Japanese people (the US made the Japanese government reform its policy so as to decrease its citizens' propensity to save).

Such a misdirected argument is unusual. People who have studied international economics would refute such an argument. It can be understood that a country's trade deficit is due to its own excess consumption.

Article 10 of the Treaty of Mutual Cooperation and Security between the US and Japan states the following: "After this treaty has been valid for 10 years, each signatory nation could notify an intention to another signatory nation of terminate the treaty. Under these circumstances, this treaty terminates one year after the notice is given." In other words, the US could terminate the treaty simply by notifying Japan of its intention to do so. Japan could do the same. However, in order to be symmetric between the US and Japan, it is indispensable that the security situation between the two countries could be symmetric.

As is well known, the security circumstances between the US and Japan are undoubtedly asymmetric. The US can ensure its own security; however, Japan cannot do so. Unless Japan safeguards the treaty with the US, its security as a nation-state might be in jeopardy.[24]

The characteristic features of Sino-American relations are very different from US–Japan relations. Bernanke's statement seemed to trigger "déjà vu" for the Japanese; however, it was not so crucial for Sino-American relations. "G2" relations are much more important than

[24] Ito (2012) described that, according to the calculation by international political scientists, the countries (which were merged or disappeared by attack or invasion by other countries) reached 51 in the past 200 years. Thus, when we recognize the death rate of countries over the past 200 years, it was 24 percent (p. 152). This death rate statistics of the countries might be beyond imagination in size for the majority of Japanese people.

US–Japan relations. As regards Bernanke's statement, the period around 2009 requires careful attention.

Around the year 2009, discussions on the "G2" system changed — they became more gloomy and less hopeful. In that period, both the US and Japan started to reconsider their foreign policies toward China. For both the US and Japan, concerning the foreign policy to China, it could be said that it has become necessary for them to approach based on the framework of "realism" not on the framework of "idealism." Undoubtedly, China has managed its foreign policy with realism and its own interest.

The US and Japan have to reconsider their foreign policy toward China because of the rapid expansion of the Chinese economy and Chinese military expenditure.

3.1. *Basic statistics and data: Current situations of USA, China, and Japan*

In this section, we take a look at several statistics and data from three countries: USA, China, and Japan.

Table 6 shows the GDP of the three countries and Figure 1 shows the GDP in the form of graphs.[25] As regards the GDP, the main points are (1) whether or not China can surpass the US and (2) if it can surpass the US, when that would happen, for which there are several estimates. However, concerning estimates, there are many uncertain factors due to which it is quite difficult to have convincing results. In the year 2014, the GDP of the US was 17 trillion US dollars, China was 10 trillion US dollars, and Japan was 4.6 trillion US dollars. As shown in Figure 1, the Chinese GDP has expanded rapidly; in contrast, the US GDP has increased gradually. The Japanese GDP has been generally level.

Table 7 compares the GDP of each country (USA, China, and Japan) to that of the whole world. Figure 2 indicates the same graphically. As of the year 2014, the US's share was 22.5 percent, China's 13.4 percent, and Japan's 6.0 percent. China's ratio has increased sharply; in contrast, Japan's ratio has decreased remarkably and the US's ratio has remained around 22–23 percent (but with a declining tendency). In 2011, the Chinese GDP increased more than 10 percent and has since increased steadily.

---

[25] According to the GDP data concerned, the year when the Chinese GDP overtook that of Japan was 2009. Undoubtedly, such statistics and data vary.

Table 6. Nominal GDP of USA, China, and Japan (1990–2014) (100 million US dollars).

	USA		China		Japan	
	Rank	**GDP**	**Rank**	**GDP**	**Rank**	**GDP**
1990	1	59,796	11	3,925	2	31,037
1995	1	76,641	8	7,319	2	53,339
2000	1	102,848	6	12,053	2	47,310
2005	1	130,937	5	22,686	2	45,724
2006	1	138,559	4	27,298	2	43,568
2007	1	144,776	3	35,233	2	43,563
2008	1	147,186	3	45,589	2	48,492
2009	1	144,187	2	50,597	3	50,351
2010	1	149,644	2	60,395	3	54,987
2011	1	155,179	2	74,925	3	59,089
2012	1	161,553	2	84,615	3	59,572
2013	1	166,632	2	94,908	3	49,196
2014	1	173,481	2	103,565	3	46,024

Source: IMF (Data: Global Note).

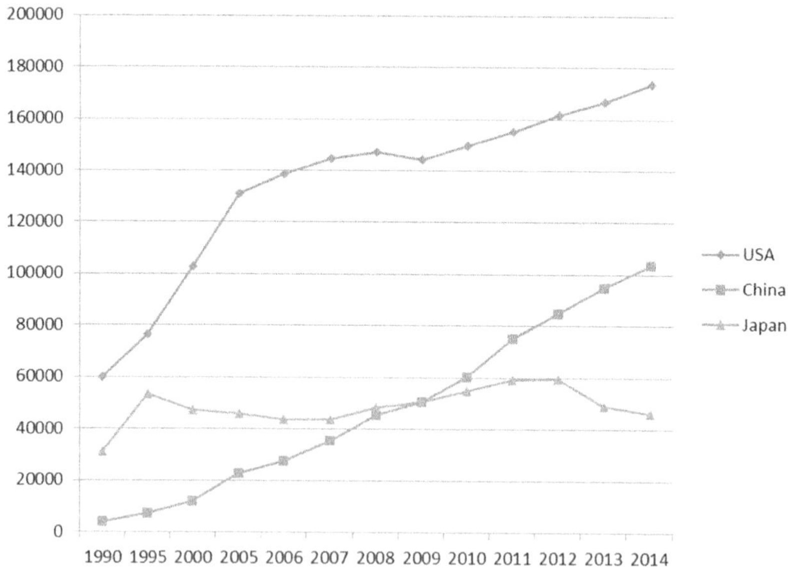

Figure 1. Nominal GDP of USA, China, and Japan (1990–2014).

Source: IMF (Data: Global Note).

Table 7. Each country's GDP ratio to the whole world's GDP (1990–2014) (in percent).

	USA	China	Japan
1990	25.8	1.7	13.4
1995	25.0	2.4	17.4
2000	30.7	3.6	14.1
2005	27.8	4.8	9.7
2006	27.2	5.4	8.6
2007	25.2	6.1	7.6
2008	23.4	7.2	7.7
2009	24.4	8.5	8.4
2010	22.9	9.2	8.4
2011	21.4	10.3	8.2
2012	21.9	11.5	8.1
2013	22.1	12.6	6.5
2014	22.5	13.4	6.0

Source: IMF (Data: Global Note).

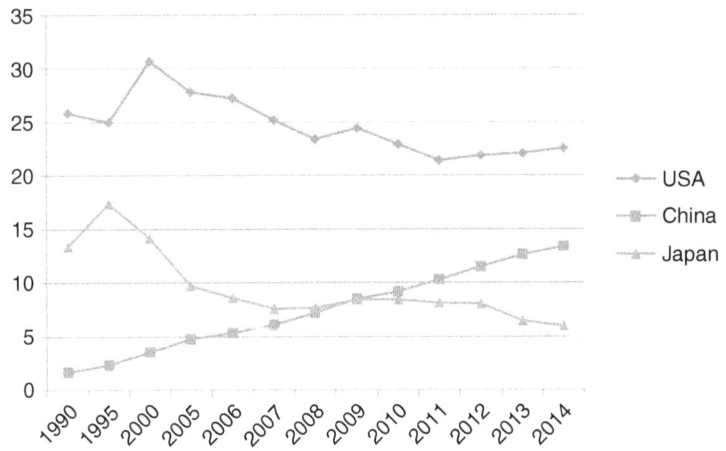

Figure 2. Each country's GDP ratio to the whole world's GDP (1990–2014) (in percent).
Source: IMF (Data: Global Note).

Table 8 lists military expenditure and the corresponding illustration is shown in Figure 3. The tendency of them has become more obvious than GDP. That is to say, as of the year 2014, the US's military expenditure was 600 billion US dollars, China's was 380 billion US dollars, and Japan's

Table 8. Military expenditure of USA, China, and Japan (1990–2014) (100 million US dollars).

	USA		China		Japan	
	Rank	**Military expenditure**	**Rank**	**Military expenditure**	**Rank**	**Military expenditure**
1990	1	3,061.7	7	290.3	10	191.1
1995	1	2,788.6	3	383.4	9	263.5
2000	1	3,016.9	2	677.7	8	319.7
2005	1	5,033.5	2	1,344.2	8	380.2
2006	1	5,276.6	2	1,588.4	8	393.5
2007	1	5,569.6	2	1,826.9	8	405.9
2008	1	6,211.3	2	2,016.2	8	413.6
2009	1	6,685.7	2	2,438.2	9	416.9
2010	1	6,981.8	2	2,523.7	10	423.0
2011	1	7,113.4	2	2,714.3	8	448.9
2012	1	6,847.8	2	3,036.2	9	457.6
2013	1	6,397.0	2	3,335.6	8	456.9
2014	1	6,099.1	2	3,766.7	8	460.9

Source: World Bank (Data: Global Note).

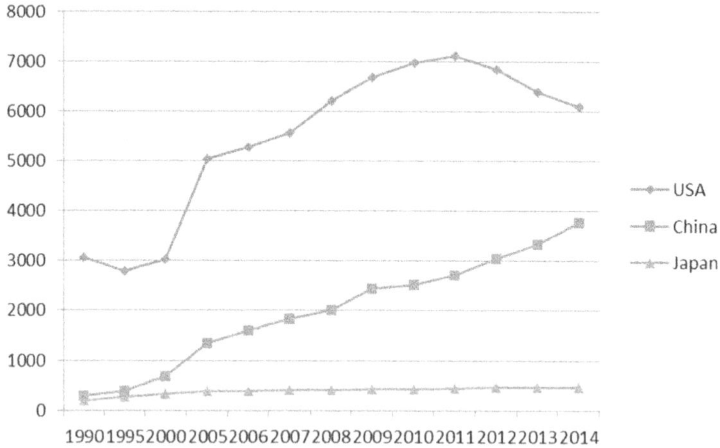

Figure 3. Military expenditure of US, China, and Japan (1990–2014).

Source: IMF (Data: Global Note).

Table 9. Each country's ratio of military expenditure to GDP (1990–2014) (in percent).

	USA	China	Japan
1990	5.1	7.4	0.6
1995	3.6	5.2	0.5
2000	2.9	5.6	0.7
2005	3.8	5.9	0.8
2006	3.8	5.8	0.9
2007	3.8	5.2	0.9
2008	4.2	4.4	0.9
2009	4.6	4.8	0.8
2010	4.7	4.2	0.8
2011	4.6	3.6	0.8
2012	4.2	3.6	0.8
2013	3.8	3.5	0.9
2014	3.5	3.6	1.0

Source: IMF, World Bank (Data: Global Note).

was 46 billion US dollars. Figure 3 shows that the US's military expenditure had a declining tendency, with that of Japan generally leveling, in contrast to China's rapidly increasing military expenditure.

Table 9 shows the ratio of military expenditure to GDP, which is indicated graphically in Figure 4. China's ratio decreased, and in 2010, it was below the ratio of the US. Although the military expenditure of China has increased sharply, as GDP has also expanded, the ratio of military expenditure to GDP has been declining. The Japanese ratio of military expenditure to GDP was undoubtedly smaller and remained roughly around 1 percent.

As of the year 2014, the Chinese circumstances were as follows: The GDP was around 60 percent that of the US and the military expenditure was around 62 percent that of the US. As of the year 2000, those ratios were 12 percent (GDP) and 22 percent (military expenditure). For 15 years, China has been closing its gap with the US. As of the year 2014, Japan's circumstances were as follows: The GDP was roughly 27 percent that of the US and military expenditure was around 8 percent that of the US. In the year 2000, those ratios were 46 percent (GDP) and 11 percent

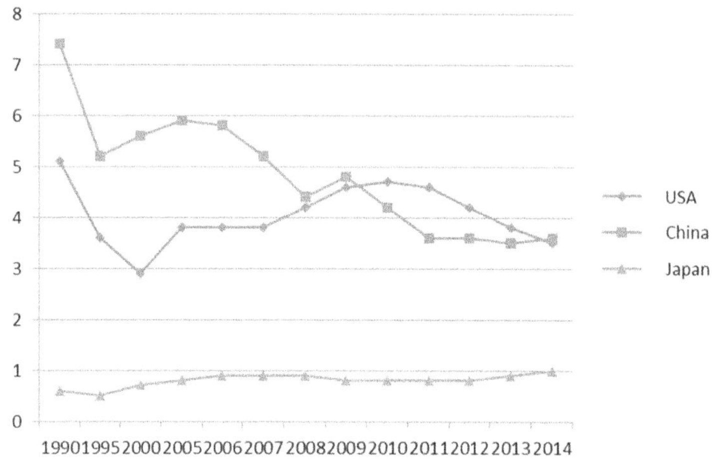

Figure 4. Each country's ratio of military expenditure to GDP (1990–2014) (in percent).
Source: IMF, World Bank (Data: Global Note).

(military expenditure). Thus, Japanese circumstances worsened to a great extent in terms of GDP and military expenditure over 15 years. At any rate, China is quickly catching up with the US.

Next, we consider trade relations and foreign currency reserves.

Table 10 indicates the trade balance, a graphical illustration of which is shown in Figure 5. In 2014, the US had a deficit of 735.8 billion UD dollars and Japan had a deficit of 99.2 billion US dollars. Only China had a surplus of 435.0 billion US dollars. In general, one can note a huge deficit in the trade balance of the United States, a huge surplus in the trade balance of China, and a large trade surplus in the trade balance of Japan (although it becomes a trade deficit after the year 2011).

Table 11 lists the ratio of the trade balance to GDP in the three countries (US, China, and Japan). The ratio in the year 2014 is −4.2 percent for the United States, −2.2 percent for Japan, and +4.2 percent for China. Figure 6 clearly indicates a situation in which China was undoubtedly better placed than the US and Japan.

Table 12 shows the amount of foreign currency reserves and Figure 7 illustrates the same in a graphic format. As of 2014, the United States had 434.4 billion US dollars, China had 3900.0 billion US dollars, and Japan 1260.7 billion US dollars in foreign currency reserves. The amount of foreign currency reserves in China has been significant and has reached 10 times the amount in the United States.

Table 10. Trade balance of each country (1990–2014) (100 million US dollars).

	USA	China	Japan
1990	▲1,110	92	693
1995	▲1,742	181	1,318
2000	▲4,469	345	1,148
2005	▲7,828	1,197	1,067
2006	▲8,373	1,961	951
2007	▲8,212	2,908	1,206
2008	▲8,325	3,419	553
2009	▲5,097	2,352	581
2010	▲6,487	2,455	1,085
2011	▲7,406	2,361	▲45
2012	▲7,421	2,978	▲535
2013	▲7,017	3,518	▲896
2014	▲7,358	4,350	▲992

Source: UNCTAD (Data: Global Note).

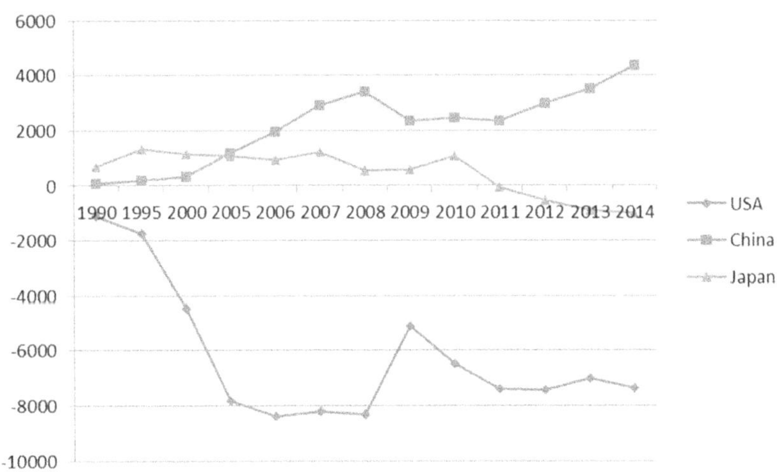

Figure 5. Trade balance of each country (1990–2014).

Source: UNCTAD (Data: Global Note).

Table 11. Each country's ratio of trade balance to GDP (in percent) (1990–2014).

	USA	China	Japan
1990	▲1.9	2.3	2.2
1995	▲2.3	2.5	2.5
2000	▲4.3	2.9	2.4
2005	▲6.0	5.3	2.3
2006	▲6.0	7.2	2.2
2007	▲5.7	8.3	2.8
2008	▲5.7	7.5	1.1
2009	▲3.5	4.6	1.2
2010	▲4.3	4.1	2.0
2011	▲4.8	3.2	▲0.1
2012	▲4.6	3.5	▲1.0
2013	▲4.2	3.7	▲1.8
2014	▲4.2	4.2	▲2.2

Source: UNCTAD (Data: Global Note).

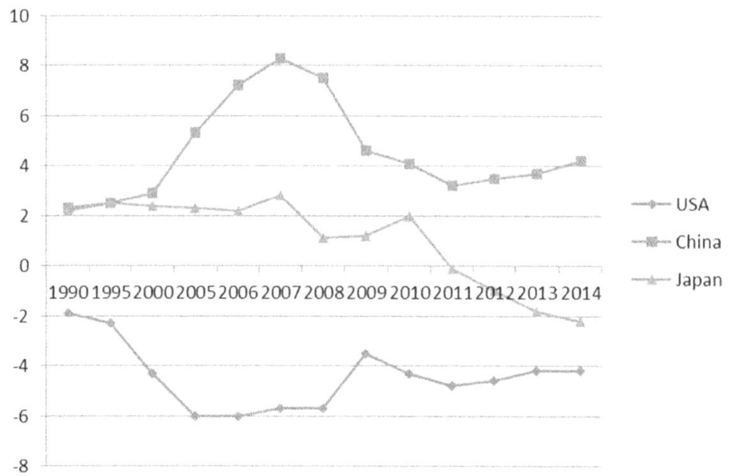

Figure 6. Each country's ratio of trade balance to GDP (1990–2014) (in percent).
Source: UNCTAD (Data: Global Note).

Table 12. Foreign currency reserves of each country (1990–2014) (100 million US dollars).

	USA	China	Japan
1990	1,731	345	878
1995	1,760	803	1,926
2000	1,284	1,718	3,616
2005	1,883	8,314	8,469
2006	2,211	10,808	8,953
2007	2,775	15,464	9,733
2008	2,940	19,660	10,308
2009	4,041	24,529	10,490
2010	4,889	29,137	10,961
2011	5,373	32,547	12,958
2012	5,743	33,875	12,681
2013	4,485	38,804	12,669
2014	4,344	39,000	12,607

Source: World Bank (Data: Global Note).

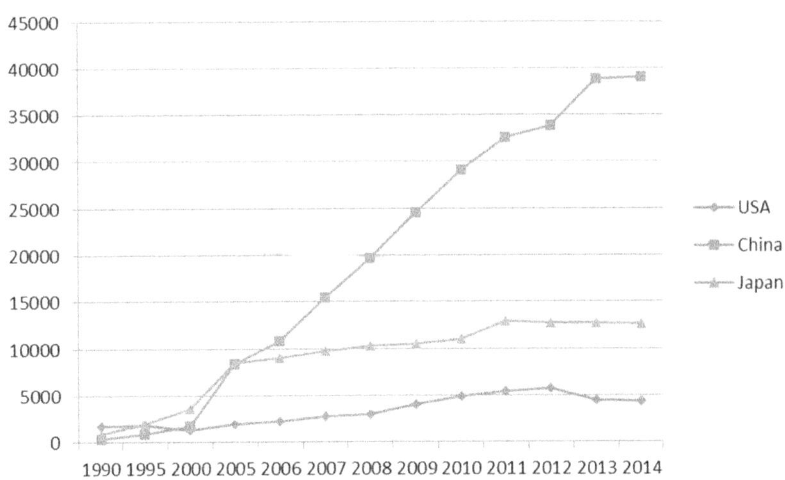

Figure 7. Foreign currency reserves of each country (1990–2014).

Source: World Bank (Data: Global Note).

Therefore, the numbers relating to trade and foreign currency reserves in China were remarkably large. In contrast, the corresponding numbers for the United States were significantly small with no signs of improvement in the trade deficit.

Next, we consider the ratio of exports and imports for the three countries after the year 2009.

Table 13 shows the ratios of China and Japan of the total export to and import from the United States. The Chinese export and import ratios in relation to the United States are particularly large. In the years 2013 and 2014, the import ratios were 19.4 percent and 19.9 percent, respectively. Japan's import ratios were 6.1 percent in 2013 and 5.7 percent in 2014. The difference in the ratios between China and Japan is undoubtedly significant.

Table 14 indicates the ratios of the United States and Japan of total exports to and imports from China. Needless to say, those values correspond to the values in Table 13, thereby clarifying the significant Chinese ratios of import to the United States. In 2013 and 2014, the export ratios of the US in relation to China were 16.7 percent and 16.9 percent, respectively. Correspond to the numbers in Table13, Chinese import from Japan

Table 13. Chinese Japanese ratios of total exports to and imports from the United States (2009–2014) (in percent).

	2009		2010		2011		2012		2013		2014	
	Export	Import	Export	Import	Export	Import	Export	Import	Export	Import	Export	Import
China	6.6	19.0	7.2	19.1	7.0	18.1	7.1	18.7	7.7	19.4	7.6	19.9
Japan	4.8	6.2	4.7	6.3	4.4	5.8	4.5	6.4	4.1	6.1	4.1	5.7

Source: JETRO Global Trade and Investment Report (Annual Edition) and author's calculation.

Table 14. The ratios of the United States and Japan of total exports to and imports from China (2009–2014) (in percent).

	2009		2010		2011		2012		2013		2014	
	Export	Import	Export	Import	Export	Import	Export	Import	Export	Import	Export	Import
USA	18.4	7.7	18.0	7.3	17.1	7.0	17.2	7.3	16.7	7.8	16.9	8.1
Japan	8.1	13.0	7.7	12.7	7.8	9.4	7.4	9.8	6.8	8.3	6.4	8.3

Source: JETRO Global Trade and Investment Report (Annual Edition) and author's calculation.

occupied large ratio which was replaced by import from the United States. In contrast, Chinese import from Japan has been stagnant. For example, in 2009, Chinese imports from Japan amounted to 13.0 percent but in 2014, the ratio decreased to 8.3 percent. Chinese imports from the United States amounted to 7.7 percent and 8.1 percent in 2009 and 2014, respectively.

Table 15 lists the ratios of the United States and Chinese of total exports to and import from Japan. By and large, the ratios relating to Japan are larger than of the United States and China. For example, the Japanese import ratio from China was more than 20 percent (corresponding to the Chinese export ratio to Japan in the same year, indicated in the vicinity of 8 percent). Also, Japanese export ratios to the United States in 2009 and 2014 were 16.1 percent and 18.6 percent, respectively (in contrast, the United States' import ratios from Japan in 2009 and 2014 were 6.2 percent and 5.7 percent, respectively).

That is to say, the ratios of exports and imports clearly displayed larger value for Japan compared with the values for the United States and China (whose values were asymmetrically smaller).

Table 16 indicates the Chinese ratio and Japanese ratio of trade surplus to the total trade deficit of the United States. As of the year 2014,

Table 15. The ratios of the United States and China of total exports to and imports from Japan (2009–2014) (in percent).

	2009		2010		2011		2012		2013		2014	
	Export	**Import**	**Export**	**Import**	**Export**	**Import**	**Export**	**Import**	**Export**	**Import**	**Export**	**Import**
USA	16.1	10.7	15.4	9.7	15.3	8.7	17.5	8.6	18.5	8.4	18.6	8.8
China	18.9	22.2	19.4	22.1	19.7	21.5	18.1	21.3	18.1	21.7	18.3	22.3

Source: JETRO Global Trade and Investment Report (Annual Edition) and author's calculation.

Table 16. Chinese ratio and Japanese ratio of trade surplus to the total trade deficit of the United States (2007–2014) (in percent).

	2007	**2008**	**2009**	**2010**	**2011**	**2012**	**2013**	**2014**
China	32.2	33.3	45.1	43.0	40.6	43.1	46.2	47.2
Japan	10.4	9.1	8.9	9.5	8.7	10.5	10.6	9.2

Source: JETRO Global Trade and Investment Report (Annual Edition) and author's calculation.

the Chinese ratio was 47.2 percent and the Japanese ratio stayed at 9.2 percent, which undoubtedly showed the China's large ratio to the US overall trade.

These data prove China's rapid expansion, the US's gradual reduction, and Japan's stagnation.

Such statistics and data (as pointed out in Tables 13–16) simply denote that, although the three countries have dominated the world economy, the numbers for Japan were obviously small (and have become smaller) compared with the numbers for the USA and China.

What we can recognize from the above-described data is the Chinese behavior, which has been defined as "offensive realism" (including its aim to become a "regional hegemon" in order to survive) and also the US's behavior (about which Mearsheimer was worried). That is to say, although it was beneficial for the US to slow down the growth of the Chinese economic, the US implemented a strategy for decades that had completely opposite effects. Such a US policy toward China was wrong because an affluent China will not become a status-quo country but an aggressive country aiming to become a "regional hegemon."[26]

3.2. *Foreign policies of USA*

3.2.1. *On the intention of US foreign policy: Ito's assertion*

Koo's assertion was made in the medium of 1990s, when his book was published. The reason we look back it is the suggestive involvement of his assertion.

Actually, the above-mentioned three choices are appropriate at present. Of the three choices, the US's intention for a US–Japan alliance is not obvious and (when Japan becomes a vassal state) China reaction toward Japan is not clear. In particular, one cannot make a pronouncement on the US–Japan alliance without understanding the actual intention of the US foreign policy. Depending on the US's actual intention, it might be necessary for Japan to have an independent defense policy.[27]

With regard to the three choices mentioned earlier, a very interesting argument was put forth by Ito (2011, 2012) and Kusaka and Ito (2011). As the intention of the US concerning the US–Japan alliance was not

---

[26]Mearsheimer (2001, p. 517), Japanese version.

[27]It is unclear whether or not the "independent defense" means "nuclear armament."

straightforward, the assertions of Ito (2011, 2012) have been extraordinary for most Japanese people.

It is accepted in some quarters that the true intention of the US foreign policy (of an asymmetric alliance) is not to secure other countries from attack but to regard the protectorates (e.g., Japan) as potential enemies. Thus, the US has opposed a Japanese independent defense. If this interpretation of the US's foreign policy toward Japan is accurate, then Japan has almost no space to maneuver. Furthermore, if Japan refuses to become a vassal state of China, then its only choice is "rearmament" or "independent defense."

What does "rearmament" or "independent defense" mean? It usually indicates the security system in which a country secures its own independence (not dependent upon another country's military power). According to Ito (2011, 2012) and Kusaka and Ito (2011), "independent defense" means "nuclear armament." However, most Japanese people undoubtedly would refuse nuclear armament. It automatically means Japan will not have an independent defense system. Thus, if Ito's way of thinking is correct, Japan cannot dependent on the US's military power and also cannot have an independent defense system. In such a case, Japan can only reach one conclusion. If China gains more economic power and military power than the US in the near future, it might be necessary for Japan to become a vassal state of China.

Therefore, Ito's assertion is that Japan cannot avoid nuclear armament in the future. Ito's assertion has been accepted by Huntington, Mearsheimer, and Waltz. If we follow Ito's logic, we reach the following conclusions: (A) Japan cannot depend on the US for its security, (B) Japan would not accept becoming a vassal state of China, and (C) it might be necessary for Japan to have nuclear weapons as it is surrounded by nuclear powers like the USA, China, North Korea, and Russia.

Thus, in this section, we study the important presupposition of Ito's discussion, called "balance of power," in which international society must insist on a multipolar system, not a unipolar system.

3.2.2. *International political system and realism*

There is a crucial difference between a "unipolar system" and a "multipolar system" in terms of the international political system. In addition, there is also a difference between "realism" and "idealism."

A system in which there is only one powerful state and international public goods (meaning the order and stability in international society) are provided with numerous countries possibly receiving benefits is called a "unipolar system." In contrast, if there are several powerful states, they could form a "multipolar system" where there is an international society with a "balance of power." When we look at international politics over the past few centuries, we could recognize by and large there could existed power balance situation. That might be regarded as the mainstream perspective. As far as the "Cold War" period is concerned, which started around 1947 and ended in 1990, it is usually understood to have been a "two-polar system with the US and the USSR" or is also recognized frequently as "Pax Americana" in which the US had overwhelming economic and military power. The potential enemy for the US was the former Soviet Union and there was keen competition between the two in terms of military power. Therefore, the "free rider" behavior of Japan seemed to irritate the US, leading to criticism.

The annoyance of the US could have been caused by the rapid expansion of the Japanese economy. In other words, US intention which was actualized at the period of US–Japan friction was to equalize the powers among USSR, EC and China, and also US–Japan friction was an expression of tendency towards the collapse of power balance (if the balance had not been disturbed, the hegemony of the United States would not have been unstable). In other words, the US intended to maintain a balance among the USSR, EC countries, China, and Japan. As a matter of fact, as regards power distribution in those days, USSR existed (opposed to US, as shown in Table 1, USSR occupied the ratio of GNP to the whole world in 1970 and 1978 which was 15.9 percent and 13.0 percent respectively), EC existed (as obvious also in Table 1 upon the ratio of GNP to the whole world, EC accounted for 19.3 percent in 1970 and 20.2 percent in 1978). Figure 8 shows the increase in Japan's GNP ratio, in contrast with the US's decrease in GNP ratio. It can be assumed therefore that the US headed the warning signs of Japan's rise.

When we pose the question of whether a unipolar or multipolar system is preferable, we could not find any undoubted grounds to object the "realist view," which has been said as the mainstream perspective in the field of international politics. However, as regards the classification of "offensive realism" or "defensive realism," we can accept Waltz's assertion that the theory of realism is neither "offensive" nor "defensive" and that realism is the best strategy.

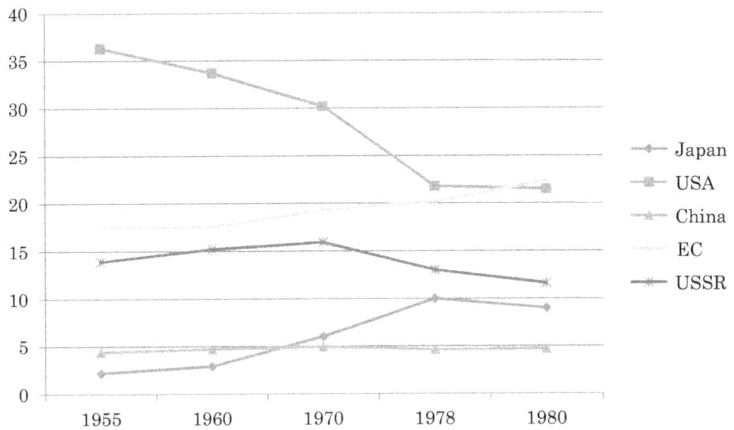

Figure 8. Each country's and region's ratio of GNP to the whole world (1955–1980) (in percent).

Source: Komiya (1983, p. 9).

The necessary condition, whether "good" or "bad," for any state to create a pole system is to have an independent defense capability, especially nuclear capability. In accordance with Mearsheimer's assertion, both Germany and Japan have potential abilities to become great powers based only on population and wealth. However, these two countries lack independent security and depend upon the US for the same. Thus, Germany and Japan can be called "semi-sovereign states," not great powers. Neither Germany nor Japan has nuclear weapons; instead, both depend on the protection provided by the US, which has nuclear weapons.

Concerning nuclear weapons, Germany and Japan are decisively different. Germany participates in nuclear sharing, while Japan does not. In other words, Germany can be called a "semi-nuclear power state," but not Japan.

Actually, Japan maintains its security via an asymmetric alliance called the Treaty of Mutual Cooperation and Security with the United States. Japan is under the nuclear umbrella of the United States. And also Japan has the "Three Non-Nuclear Principles."

That has been the nature of the relationship between the United States and Japan, under which US–Japan friction occurred.

In recent years, most Japanese people have not wanted to remain under the nuclear umbrella of the US. In an imaginary scenario, if China or North Korea attacks Japan with nuclear weapons, Japan does not believe that the US would fight back against China or North Korea with nuclear weapons as the US accepts that the two countries could counterattack the US.

In this section, we investigated the US foreign policy toward Japan in relation to the US–Japan friction. However, the US's intention toward Japan is unclear The Japanese public does not believe that the US nuclear umbrella would work effectively for Japan. Moreover, according to Ito (2012), US has regarded Japan as a "potential enemy" and therefore has made Japan a protectorate.

If Ito's assertion is correct, we can assume that the US has attempted to balance the power among neighboring countries by weakening the strength of "potential great powers" like Germany and Japan.

Then, how does the US relate to China, which is one Japan's neighbors and undoubtedly a potential great power?

In the following section, we focus our attention on the "G2" (Sino-American relations).

3.3. *Sino-American relations*

In this section, we analyze the US's strategy on foreign policy and the international political system in relation to China.

As discussed in previous sections, it is difficult to find a reasonable economic interpretation of the US–Japan friction. The decline in the hegemony of the US and the reduction in its share of international public goods in the 1980s were caused not by Germany or Japan but by the USSR. The friction between the US and Japan started around the same period.

Sino-American relations have a similar theoretical framework. As stated in the beginning of this chapter, the then FRB Chairman Ben Bernanke's assertion reported by the *Peoples' Daily* (the Japanese version of the state media of Beijing, 8 January 2009). It would likely appear as the "déjà vu" ("already seen") to many Japanese people.

However, the main features of the US–Japan friction and conflict in Sino-American relations are completely different.

US–Japan friction was caused by the asymmetric balance of power between the stronger allied power (US) and the weaker allied power (Japan). After all, the asymmetrically weak ally had no choice but to follow the intentions of the asymmetrically strong ally. Thus, Japan had no other choice but was inevitably plunged into the economic stagnation with no end in sight.

Although there were several factors that caused the friction, Japan has been forced to become a weaker power as shown in Tables 6, 7, and Tables 10 to 12 compared to the US and China.

Once again, US–Japan relations and Sino-American relations are essentially different. "The rise of Japan" irritated the US when the Japanese ratio of GNP to that of the whole world reached more than 10 percent and the Japanese ratio of trade surplus with the US to the total trade deficit of the US was more than 30 percent. However, as of the year 2014, China's economy has advanced much further than Japan's. The Chinese ratio of GDP was than 13 percent and the Chinese ratio of trade surplus with the US to the total trade deficit of the US reached 47 percent.

From the viewpoints of GDP and military expenditure, both US and China are more advanced than other countries and can be labelled "G2."

In the next section, we consider the "G2" and compare the benefits and drawbacks of promoting the G2 or taking precautions against it.

3.3.1. *Assertions to promote G2*

Niall Ferguson and Moritz Schularick coined the term Chimerica in a chapter published in *International Finance* in 2007. The word "Chimerica" is composed of "China" and "America." According to the authors, this term expresses the coexistence and coprosperity of the two countries.

In the abstract of their chapter, they stated the following:

> "Over the past five years the world has witnessed a spectacular boom in asset prices. This chapter reviews different explanations for this phenomenon, and argues that future financial historians will point to the divergence between high returns on capital and the low cost of capital, not to excess liquidity or asset shortage, as the driving force in global asset markets. The integration of the massive Asian labor force into the world economy has significantly increased global returns on capital while the cost of capital as measured by long-term real interest rates has not increased, but has actually fallen. We label this two-sided phenomenon "Chimerica" because it is in large measure consequence of the symbiotic economic relationship that has developed between the

> People's Republic of China and the United States of America. Not only has plentiful Chinese and Asian labor increased global returns to capital; Chinese excess savings have also depressed US and global interest rates. We show that the Chinese "savings glut" was not primarily a function of precautionary household behavior, but of surging corporate profits in China due to increasing exchange rate undervaluation" (originally from abstract of Ferguson and Schularick, 2007).

In short, Ferguson and Schularick focus on two phenomena, namely, (1) the high returns on capital and (2) the low cost of capital, which exist behind the dramatic increase in asset prices. They consider the phenomena to be the result of the mutual economic coexistence between US and China. The keywords in such economic relations are the Chinese labor force, Chinese excess savings, Chinese corporate profits, and the Chinese exchange rate. What should be careful about China is that many of the mechanisms at work there are those of China's socialist market economy and various phenomena have arisen as a result of the mutually beneficial relationship between the United States and China. The underestimation of the renminbi exchange rate has made corporate profits larger, which has led to excess savings in China. This, in turn, reduced the interest rate. The underestimation of the renminbi exchange rate is not the result of the market mechanism but the result of the exchange rate policy of the Chinese government.

If Ferguson and Schularick recognize economic relations of mutual coexistence between US and China, even apart from the year of 2007, it should be said as nothing less than a rather peculiar optimism. If there is "mutual coexistence" between the US and China, it only existed when the economic power and military power of China were poorer compared to those of the US. However, we easily suppose it could not be possible that China would take actions which would abandon independent defense, like Japan did.

As indicated earlier, it was in 2007 or 2008 that terms like "Chimerica" and "G2" were used to describe Sino-American relations. In addition, active controversy has begun about the two countries' relations.

Bergsten (2008) positively supported the "G2" concept. According to the abstract of the assertion expressed on *Foreign Affairs* (Japanese version), it is as follows.

The present US approach to China involves encouraging China to take part in the existing global economic order; on the other hand, China has felt uncomfortable being integrated into a system where it had no room to play a role in institutional building, and in some cases, it showed moves to challenge the system. Washington should not concentrate shortsightedly on the issues relating to just the two countries but should construct a proper partnership in order to jointly lead the global economic system with Beijing. The only way to create an environment conductive to China's new role as a global economic superpower, legitimate system designer, and defender of the international economic order is through the G2 plan between the United States and China. This seems to be an extremely efficient way of attempting to provide a solution by replacing the dispute between the US and China with an issue relating to institution management.

In short, the US must construct a proper partnership with China by designing a legitimate framework for Sino-American relations and enabling China to play the role of protector of the international economic order.

However, for a partnership led by the US, it is not certain whether or not China concurs. It is not clear at all whether or not China wishes to protect the international economic order (which is the order led by the US). It is not clear whether or not the international economic order led by the US is consistent with the national interests of China. Furthermore, when it is said as the national interests of China, it is also unclear what and whom "China thinks of itself as China" refers to.

A more serious problem is that the world "order" created and led by the US has been made more favorable for the US unilaterally. When the US–Japan friction occurred, the US demanded that Japan abolish a tax relief system for small-sum savings, which was then actually abolished. What was the reasoning for this demand? It was due to the assertion that the US trade deficit was not only due to excess consumption by the US but also because of excess savings by foreigners. That is to say, if the logic of the United States itself is inconvenient, it would be almost impossible. What exists is an inextricable confrontation with the Chinese government.

3.3.2. *Assertions to take precautions against G2*

Experts who have cautioned against China's "realist approach" have not only been pessimistic about the "G2" system but are also critical of opinions suggesting the successful functioning of the "G2" system. One of the experts strongly cautioning against the G2 is Mearsheimer (2001). From the perspective of Mearsheimer's so-called "offensive realism," this is rather a natural claim. In Chapter 10 of Mearsheimer's book (2001), he expresses his views as explained in the following.

China is viewed as a possible thread in the future as it is likely to become much stronger and a "potential hegemon," which is a situation that the US has not confronted in the 20th century. Even such empires as the Weimar Republic, the Japanese Empire, Nazi Germany, and the Soviet Union did not have the military power in their heydays to compete against present-day US. However, if China becomes a "giant Hong Kong," it would have four times greater military potential than the US. China would be able to achieve a decisively advantageous position over the United States in Northeast Asia militarily. If such circumstances are realized, China would undoubtedly become a competitor of the US. Moreover, it is possible that China could become a superpower like the US, as a result of competition with the US (originally from Mearsheimer, 2001, Japanese version, pp. 516–517 — the same hereinafter).

Such opinions by Mearsheimer (2001) lead us to the view that the US would benefit if China's economic growth was slower (p. 517). However, the US has implemented a strategy whose effects have been completely to the contrary (p. 517). Therefore, Mearsheimer's assertion is that US policies toward China have been misguided (p. 517).

Actually, if China were richer than it is now, it could become a predatory country aiming for regional hegemony, which seems to be a natural outcome. This is because it is best for every country to be a regional hegemon in order to ensure its survival (p. 517). Furthermore, it takes many years to obtain enough military power to establish oneself as a regional hegemon. It is not too late to work toward slowing down Chinese development to deter the rise of China (p. 518).

Mearsheimer (2001) closes his book by mentioning that America's political culture is rather liberal and is keeping to be oppositional against realist's idea, and turning away from the principles of realism would lead America to make fatal mistakes (p. 518).

Mearsheimer's book was published in the year 2001, which is more than 20 years ago. As a matter of fact, his "Balance of power in Asia (2000)" table, as shown in Table 17, is very different from the present circumstances.

The GNP levels cited in Mearsheimer (2001) were 1180 billion US dollars for China and 4090 billion US dollars from Japan, which showed

Table 17. Balance of power in Asia (2000).

	Potential power		Actual power	
	CNP (1000 billion US dollars)	**Population (million)**	**Size of armed forces**	**Number of nuclear ballistic**
China	1.18	1,240	2,200,000	400
Japan	4.09	126	151,800	0
Russia	0.33	147	348,000	10,000

Source: Mearsheimer (2001, p. 43), Japanese version.

that the Chinese GNP was only 28.9 percent of that of Japan. As indicated in Table 3, the GDP levels of China and Japan in 2014 were 10,000 US dollars and 4,600 billion US dollars, respectively, which undoubtedly pointed out that the Chinese GDP is 2.2 times greater than that of Japan.

However, if the United States has employed the wrong policy toward China and has turned its back on a realist principle, thereby inadvertently supporting China in establishing a regional hegemonic system, it is not reasonable for other countries to blame the US. Actually, Mearsheimer's argument saying that, just after the demise of Cold War, Japan was confident that economic interdependence developed in Asia could make the relations with China perpetually peaceful. However, after the mid-1990s, the Japanese view on China considerably changed and Japan started to worry about Chinese strategic objectives from a realistic point of view (p. 484). Japan was also wrong against China. Undoubtedly, Japan supported the growth of the Chinese economy.

From the viewpoints of offensive realism by Mearsheimer, the United States aims to encourage China to play a role as a defender of the international economic order by building a true partnership, referred to as G2, which would accelerate fatal mistakes.

Economy and Segal (2009) kept a wary eye on Bergsten's G2 propulsion discussions which was insisted on *Foreign Affairs*.

Similar to Bergsten (2008), Economy and Segal's state the following arguments in the abstract of *Foreign Affairs* (Japanese version).

For the United States to respond to global challenges, Chinese cooperation is necessary. However, even if the United States tries to strengthen its relationship with China from the viewpoint of global tasks, it might be extremely difficult to construct a successful partnership. This is mainly because there could exist very real differences in political values, enforcement capacities, and what the two countries want and when they want it. The time has come to acknowledge that although working with China sounds easy, it is not. After all, both countries repel each other when they confront real disorder. To escape this downward spiral, Washington must solicit the help of the rest of the world. The United States is not alone in recognizing that China affects all the critical issues of the day or in seeking more from China as an emerging global power. Throughout the world, countries are realizing that the issues that currently define their relationships with Beijing cannot simply be negotiated bilaterally. Therefore, if the United States wants to move its relationship with China forward in the next 30 years, it needs the rest of the world, not just China, on board.

In short, they assert that it is necessary for the United States to recognize the difficulty of constructing a proper partnership with China and understand the necessity of cooperation with the rest of the world, not with just China.

In other words, Bergsten thinks that Sino-American relations could become a proper partnership; in contrast, Economy and Segal recognize that constructing a partnership between the United States and China is extremely difficult.

In both papers, many pages are occupied in expressing how China's behavior has caused problems with the United States, Europe, Japan, etc. Based on the indicated problems, Bergsten insists that constructing a proper partnership between the United States and China is important and of the first priority. As opposed to Bergsten's assertion, Economy and Segal advocate that it is extremely important to create a framework that included other countries such as Canada, Europe, and Japan.

In other words, the difference is whether the United States promotes to construct proper partnership with China or to progress multilateral relations including other countries. It is clear that the United States can negotiate more easily with Canada, Europe, and Japan than with China. The reason for this, as Economy and Segal (2009) mention, is that the United States has more in common with such countries as Canada, Europe, and Japan than with China.

3.3.3. *Some considerations: Offensive realism*

The views on "G2" seemed to gradually change in 2009 and 2010 (though, concerning Japan, as Mearsheimer appropriately referred, until the middle of 1990s Japanese view of China considerably stiffened and Japan started to be worried about Chinese strategic objectives). Actually, as Hosoya (2012) pointed out, Sino-US cooperation gradually increased and the foreign policy of the Obama administration depended excessively upon cooperation with China. The main reason for the resumption of Sino-US cooperation was China's stronger attitude toward the "core interests" of foreign policy (Hosoya, 2012, p. 324). The reason for China's change in attitude was its growth in economic and military power in contrast with the (comparative) reduction of the powers of the United States and Japan.

As mentioned earlier, it is unclear who or what the word "China" refers to. At present, it could refer to the administration of the Chinese Communist Party. We should consider whether or not it could serve the best interests of the nation. Thus, if China intends to serve its own best interests, it would promote a partnership with the United States. However, to the contrary, China would not pursue the partnership with the United States if it does not align with its own interests. The Chinese strategy is reasonable in a realist view.

If judged in such a way, the difference of opinions between the "promotion" of and the "precaution" against the "G2" concept is solvable. Undoubtedly, the Chinese strategy could be interpreted as a realist's view. In order to construct a proper partnership with China, the United States has to demonstrate that the partnership could serve the best interests of China. In addition, in order for China to play the role of a defender in the international economic order, the US has to clearly show that being the defender could serve the best interests of China.

It is not so difficult to understand the Chinese foreign policy toward the United States from past Chinese experiences. Even when the economic and military power of the United States overwhelmed China, it has not been submissive but has avoided serious conflict with the United States. However, when China's economic and military power become stronger than that of the United States, the attitude changed. Depending on the situation, it would undoubtedly be possible for the Chinese to engage in a conflict (possibly a war) against the United States.

It is not a peaceful story, however, if (repeatedly saying we call the administration of the Chinese Communist Party as "China") maximizing China's national interests would mean that China possesses overwhelmingly large economic and military power in the world, enabling it to enjoy a hegemonic position. It would be unavoidable to occur serious conflicts with the United States. It might be thus excessively optimistic to think that the "G2" system between the United States and China would advance peacefully.

4. Conclusion

As investigated in this chapter, such strategy on international relations as the "selection of Japan" and the "selection of China" seems to be by and large recognized with "realism" particularly "offensive realism."

That is to say, with respect to the "selection of Japan," the aim of Japan was to take actions as a "small country" under the great power, not to take actions as a "regional hegemon." The "selection of Japan" became also the convenient position for another pole of the "bipolar system" (USSR).

In contrast, the "selection of China" has been completely different. The national strategy of China has undoubtedly been to acquire the position of "hegemon" (or at least the position of "regional hegemon").

Assuming that is the case, it seems that the occurrence of serious conflict between the United States and China might be inevitable. We think, therefore, that it is too optimistic to suppose the "G2" system (between the United States and China) could proceed peacefully. Even if in the future China were to supersede the United States in various spheres, it might be difficult for such a system to proceed peacefully.

Chapter 2

An Economic Analysis of the Codependency Relationship between the USA and China: The United States' Excess Consumption and China's Underconsumption

1. Introduction

On 15 August 2017, the United States Department of the Treasury announced the US national bond holding value of each country at the end of June 2017. According to the announcement, the Chinese holding value reached 1,146.5 billion US dollars and the Japanese holding value was 1,090,8 billion US dollars. This meant that the Japanese holding value (which had retained the top place from October 2016) had been overtaken by the Chinese.[1]

What are the reasons for such a high holding of the United States national bond by China? The Vice-Chief Spokesperson of the Foreign Ministry of China, Hua Chun Ying, mentioned that it was a sign of integrating the mutual benefits of China and the United States and also that the Chinese people hoped the two countries would make efforts to maintain satisfactory relations in terms of the economy and international trade. There is no doubt about the "mutual benefit" of cooperation between China and the USA. However, what are the specific benefits for China?

[1]For example, see the article in *Nihon Keizai Shimbun* (16 and 17 August 2017).

It goes without saying that China's holding of US national bonds increases through the use of foreign exchange reserves obtained by export and through China's intervention by selling renminbi and buying US dollars. What is the main purpose of the increase of China's holding value of the United States' national bond? There are two reasons: (1) an increase in foreign exchange operations and (2) protecting the currency (by selling renminbi and buying US dollars). Additionally, this gives China a strong bargaining position during negotiations with the USA. A newspaper article stated that when the United States increased the national bond issue in large quantities to deal with the Lehman crisis in 2008, China accepted a large percentage of that national bond. When a rating company downgraded the credit rating of the United States in August 2011, the New China News Agency published a review article mentioning that China was the largest creditor nation for the US and that China had every right to request the United States to guarantee the safety of US dollar-denominated assets. The New China News Agency then demanded that the United States cut down its military budget.

In short, China stands to gain from being in the position of the largest creditor nation to the USA.

At the political context of that increase of China's US national bond holding, there was the fact that the Trump administration in the US expressed dissatisfaction with China's foreign policies and trade practices (particularly on the issues related with North Korea).[2]

However, as regards Sino-American relations, we recognize the fundamental structure beyond the economic conditions and policy tasks of each era. Roach (2014) termed such relations between the United States and China as "codependency." According to him, "codependency becomes problematic when one participant in the relationship starts to grow away from the other"[3] (p. 81). For a country in the position of "hegemon" like

[2]It was reported on 14 August 2017 that President Donald Trump had initiated an investigation into unfair trade practices by China based on Section 301 of the Trade Act which relates to intrusion of intellectual property rights (*Nihon Keizai Shimbun*, 15 August 2017).

[3]According to Roach (2014), psychologists will warn that "codependency becomes problematic when one participant in the relationship starts to grow away from the other" (p. 81). However, based on the usage in Roach, it could be considered to have the same meaning as the interdependence that we usually use (although there might be some differences). Needless to say, the participant that started to grow away from the other is China (not the USA).

the United States, it is inevitable that another country will develop faster that it.

As far as Sino-American relations are concerned, the critical phrases related to the "codependency" were the "excess consumption" of the United States and the "underconsumption" of the Chinese. When there is a savings shortage and excess consumption, the trade balance swings toward a deficit. In fact, the trade deficit in the United States can be traced back to the 1970s when the United States' trade balance was consistently in a deficit. As the absorption approach asserts, the trade deficit of a country indicates the excess consumption or savings shortage of that country. On the contrary, China which has excess savings acquired a trade surplus. Although there is no logical necessity, China has increased its holding of United States national bonds.

However, it is the economic mechanism that a country's excess consumption results in a trade deficit while another country's underconsumption results in a trade surplus, and that a country with a trade deficit becomes a capital account surplus country while a country with a trade surplus becomes a capital account deficit country. The critical phrases related to the "codependency" were the "excess consumption" (or "savings shortage") of the United States and the "underconsumption" (or "domestic demand shortage") of China. As mentioned above, the phenomena that excess consumption of a country results in a trade deficit (and a capital surplus) and underconsumption of a country results in a trade surplus (and a capital deficit) are naturally occurring, not only for US–China relations. Then, what are the characteristic features of the US–China relationship?

In this chapter, we consider the current situation and the prospect of Sino-American relations from the viewpoints of the "codependency" concept. In the first section, we discuss a general view of the Sino-US codependency and in the second section, we analyze Sino-US trade relations. In the third section, we investigate the role of the contemporary Chinese economy. In the fourth section, we consider the current situation of Sino-American relations focusing on the "consumption–GDP ratio." In the fifth section, we try to analyze the symmetric phenomenon, meaning the relationship between the "trade linkage index" and the "consumption–GDP ratio." In the sixth section, we investigate the savings ratios, disparity, and exchange rate intervention. Finally, in the seventh section, a summary of this chapter is provided.

2. Sino-American Relations: What Are the Problems?

As submitted earlier, the crucial words related to the "codependency" were the "excess consumption" (or "savings shortage") of the United States and the "underconsumption" (or "domestic demand shortage") of China.

In that sense, it is not the first time that the US has established a "codependency" relationship with another country. As a matter of fact, from the 1970s to the beginning of the 1990s, there was a similar relationship with Japan in which the US had "excess consumption" and Japan had "excess savings." Such US–Japan relations caused rather serious frictions, after which Japan accepted the US claims and employed policies to reduce savings.[4]

Moreover, the US has an "exorbitant privilege," which is a concept presented by Giscard d'Estaing (French finance minister). According to Eichengreen (2011), it "costs only a few cents for the Bureau of Engraving and Printing to produce a 100 dollars bill, but other countries have to pony up 100 dollars of actual goods and services in order to obtain one" (p. 3). Furthermore, the United States can be "importing more than it exports and consuming more than it produces year after year without becoming more indebted to the rest of the world" (p. 4). Other countries "question whether the United States should have been permitted to run current account deficits approaching 6 percent of GDP in the run-up to the crisis" (p. 5). However, as long as other countries utilized US dollars as the currency of settlement, the "exorbitant privilege" would persist. Also when the central banks of such other countries hold as their foreign exchange reserves in US dollars, it means that those other countries are offering low-interest financing to the United States, which also reduced the interest rate of the US. Therefore, "poor households in the developing world ended up subsidizing rich ones in the United States" (p. 5).

Long years of trade deficit of the United States had been supported by this "exorbitant privilege."[5] If the paper currency printed by the US Bureau of Engraving and Printing could be used to exchange

[4] One serious effect of such policies in Japan was the financial bubble.

[5] Both "excess consumption" and "exorbitant privilege" of the United States not only affect Sino-American relations but are characteristics of the United States. However, in this chapter, we do not focus on the United States, but on China in terms of the Sino-American relations.

foreign-made goods and services (also if it had not been necessary to convert the paper currency to gold), it would have been quite easy for the US to have "excess consumption" and trade deficit.

However, at the same time, lots of countries (other than the United States) voluntarily use US dollars as the currency of settlement and hold US dollars as their foreign exchange reserves. Regardless of Giscard d'Estaing sentiment, as long as other countries voluntarily use US dollars as the currency of settlement and foreign exchange reserve, the "exorbitant privilege" position of the United States would continue.

A serious problem of the "exorbitant privilege" of the United States was the friction between the USA and Japan.

The friction between the USA and Japan transformed, as Komiya (1994) described, from "US–Japan trade friction" to "US–Japan economic friction." Hanai (1983) called it "3B friction," which meant that it incorporated "trade friction," "defense friction," and "cultural friction,"[6] thereby extending beyond trade and economy into culture and society. When friction extends to culture and society, it is extremely difficult for the countries concerned to reach a solution.

The economic backgrounds of US–Japan friction were as follows: (1) increasing the ratio of Japanese GNP to the world total (Table 1) and (2) increasing the ratio of Japanese trade surplus to the United States' total trade deficit (Table 2)

As Table 1 indicates, the ratio of Japanese GNP to the world total was 10 percent in 1978. The United States could not tolerate another country having such a ratio and considered it to have engaged in unfair trade practices. At the same time, the US ratio to the world total GNP decreased from 30 percent to 20 percent. In 1980, the ratio of former EC countries exceeded the ratio of the United States, which angered the US.

As Table 2 shows, the ratio of the Japanese trade surplus to the total US trade deficit was more than 30 percent in 1978. Such a big ratio could not be overlooked by the US.

However, the US's criticism against Japan was caused by an obvious misrepresentation as an elementary level of international economics knowledge would clearly disprove US assertions against Japan. Such a

---

[6] In Japanese language, "*b*oueki" means trade, "*b*ouei" means defense, and "*b*unka" means culture. Thus, Hanai (1983) took up the first letter of three words and named coined the term "3B friction."

Table 1. The ratio of each country's GNP to the world total (1955–1980) (in percent).

Country \ Year	1955	1960	1970	1978	1980
Japan	2.2	2.9	6.0	10.0	9.0
USA	36.3	33.7	30.2	21.8	21.5
China	4.4	4.7	4.9	4.6	4.7
FormerEC	17.5	17.5	19.3	20.2	22.4
USSR	13.9	15.2	15.9	13.2	11.6

Source: Komiya (1983, p. 9).

Table 2. The ratio of the Japanese trade surplus to the United States' total trade deficit (1972–1981) (billion US dollars, in percent).

Item \ Year	1972	1974	1976	1978	1980	1981
Japanese trade surplus	4.0	1.9	1.0	10.6	9.8	16.3
Ratio (in percent)	62.5	42.2	10.7	31.3	38.7	41.1

Source: Komiya (1983, p. 10).

misunderstanding can be clarified by the following well-known equation:

$$X - M = S - I$$

X indicates export, M import, S saving, and I investment. Therefore, the equation means that disequilibrium of trade balance equals the amount of difference between whole savings and whole investment. We can say, thus, that a trade-surplus country has a big amount of savings and a trade-deficit country has a small amount of savings. It means therefore that the reason for the trade deficit equals is excess consumption and small savings of the country concerned. It is simply a misrepresentation to claim that the excess savings of other countries are to blame.

Nevertheless, the United States criticized Japan which had a large amount of trade surplus with the US; it blamed Japan's excess savings, unfair trade practices, and free rider behavior (meaning that Japan had very little military expenditure because of its dependence on the military capability of the United States).

The above-mentioned well-known equation indicates the "codependency" relationship of the United States with other countries. The left side of the above equation shows the trade balance, trade surplus country like Japan expands the foreign exchange reserves and increases money supply. If other things remain unchanged, with such a mechanism, the price of the money market, that is to say, the interest rate, decreases. On the contrary, a trade-deficit country like the United States reduces foreign exchange reserves[7] and decreases the money supply. If other things remain unchanged, with the same mechanism, the interest rate of the United States would increase. Because of the difference in interest rates between the countries concerned, capital movement occurs between them (from other countries to the United States). Thus, a trade-surplus country becomes a capital-account-deficit country, and to the contrary, a trade-deficit country becomes a capital-account-surplus country, which is the rational adjustment in the economic sense.

If the above-mentioned adjustment smoothly works, one country has trade surplus and capital account deficit and the other has trade deficit and capital account surplus. It could be said that such an adjustment is a reasonable consequence of economic mechanisms. Therefore, if a crucial part of the adjustment mechanism leads to the "codependency" relationship, such a "codependency" relationship would occur between "excess-consumption" countries and "excess-savings" countries.

However, as regards Sino-American relations, there could exist unpredictable characteristics because the market mechanism are not clear and there is plenty of space for political intervention. Those unpredictable characteristics are closely connected with (1) the US's problem of sustainability of its "exorbitant privilege" and (2) China's problem of sustainability of the "exchange rate intervention." It is quite unpredictable if these problems could be adjusted by market mechanisms. That unpredictability indicates lots of space for political intervention.

As mentioned earlier, "codependency" relationships are caused by the "excess consumption" of the United States and the "excess savings" of China. According to Roach (2014), "the two pieces of the Sino-American saving story together gets right to the heart of the powerful codependency between these two economies. America, the deficit saver,

---

[7]However, actually, because the United States has "exorbitant privilege," the Bureau of Engraving and Printing could print the United States dollars to compensate for the reduction of foreign exchange reserves.

needs imported capital in order to grow. China, the surplus saver, needs to make certain that its export demand is well supported by the deficit economy. Two unbalanced economies, each needing support from the other. The ultimate symbiosis of codependency" (p. 135).

That is not all. Roach (2014) further stated the following: "Saving is the central unifying element in the codependency between the United States and China. All you have to know at this point is one thing: Saving short nation run multilateral trade deficit. Without sustained improvement in domestic saving, America will never pull itself out of its current account and trade deficit. And that means China, with its large trade and saving surpluses, will probably remain in Washington's political crosshairs for as long as this key issue is unresolved" (p. 131). Roach worried that China would remain in Washington's political crosshairs, creating a situation similar to the pressure the US put on Japan during the period of friction between the United States and Japan.

Ferguson and Schularick (2007) studied the asset market and international financial market. In their article (2007), they use the word "Chimerica," which is a compound word including China and America. According to them, it expresses "prosperous coexistence relations" between the United States and China. In their article (2007), they analyzed a drastic upturn of asset prices over five years. They noticed two phenomena behind the drastic upturn: high profit of capital and low cost of capital. They thought that the two phenomena were a consequence of the "prosperous coexistence relations" between the United States and China.

The following were of great consequence in the relations between the US and China: the labor force in China, the excess savings in China, corporation profit in China, and exchange rate in China. Much of the working mechanism in China is due to its "socialist market economy." Undervaluation of the exchange rate made the corporation profit higher, which produced excess savings in China[8] and also produced a lower rate of interest. Undervaluation of the renminbi was not due to market mechanisms but due to the exchange rate policy of the Chinese government.[9]

---

[8]The correlation between the exchange rate of the renminbi against the US dollar and the Gini coefficient in China is significant (at a 1 percent significance level). That is to say, it shows that the correlation between the appreciation of exchange rate of the renminbi against the US dollar and lowering of the Gini coefficient in China would become significant.

[9]Although it was claimed that "there is no evidence to protest that the exchange rate of renminbi is significantly undervalued" (Shirai, 2004, p. 162), here we suppose that

Ferguson and Schularick changed their viewpoint on "Chimerica" in 2009. They presented an article entitled "The End of Chimerica."[10]

A summary of their article was also published in the Harvard Business School Working Paper (2009).

The financial crisis that happened from 2007 to 2009 was the start of the end of "Chimerica." The economic model of China from1998 to 2007 was similar to the model employed by West Germany and Japan after the Second World War. Trade surplus with the United States contributed to their economic growth. However, there are two critical differences between West Germany and Japan and China. The first difference was the exchange rate intervention by the Chinese government, which was unprecedented caused a "distortion" in the world economy. The second difference was the fact that the Chinese government resisted the appreciation of the renminbi; in contrast, both West Germany and Japan had agreed on the appreciation of their currency. Thus, "Chimerica" relations could not persist like the relationships the US had with West Germany and Japan. Just like in the 1970s, it is indispensable for the adjustment of world economy to significantly change the exchange rates. When the US dollar depreciated, maintaining "Chimerica" relations would have brought about a new and risky distortion into the world economy.

In other words, artificial intervention in the exchange rate and strong preferences regarding the undervaluation of the renminbi by the Chinese government caused a new and risky distortion in the world economy.

As mentioned earlier, critical factors to establish the contemporary Sino-American relations are, (1) consumption and saving (US excess consumption and Chinese excess saving), (2) exchange rate intervention by

---

exchange rate intervention was implemented by the Chinese socialist government. Concerning the problem of undervaluation of the renminbi, we concur with Ferguson and Schularick because of their sharp insights into policies of the Chinese socialist government. As considered later, we think that the principal factor of distortion shown by the symmetry in the "trade linkage index" (which means that the distortion from potential comparative advantage structure) would exist the undervaluation of renminbi. In other words, we understand that the distortion in the "trade linkage index" could be proposed as "indirect" evidence of the undervaluation of the renminbi.

[10]The article was published in *International Finance* in 2011; however, the article was presented in the Harvard Business School Working Paper (10-037) in 2009.

Chinese government and,[11] and (3) the "exorbitant privilege" of the United States. In this chapter, we analyze these factors using statistical verification.[12]

3. Trade Relations between the United States and China

3.1. *Current situation*

In this section, we provide an overview of the current situation of international trade between the United States and China. We also explain the two tools used hereafter in this book.

The first tool is the "directional trade ratio." This ratio is used to measure the closeness of trade relations as follows:

$$F_{mn} = \frac{1}{2}\left(\frac{t_{mn}}{T_m} + \frac{t_{mn}}{T_n}\right)$$

In this equation, t_{mn} indicates the amount of trade between country m and country n, T_m indicates the total amount of trade of country m, and T_n indicates the total amount of trade of country n. Table 3 displays the directional trade ratio between the United States and China.

As Table 3 indicates, the ratio between the United States and China has a numerical value of 0.14–0.15. Thus, the closeness of trade relations between the two countries was high. The ratio of the total trade amount between the United States and China to the total trade amount of the US is shown in Table 4.

Table 4 shows that the ratio would become gradually higher and reached around 0.15-0.16.

Just for reference, the directional trade ratio between the United States and Japan and the ratio of the total trade amount between the United States and Japan to the total trade amount of the United States have been provided in Tables 5 and 6, respectively.

---

[11] We do not matter in this book whether or not the modification of exchange rate intervention implies the change to the floating exchange rate system.

[12] In this book, as regards the "exorbitant privilege" of the United States, we only offer the necessity minimum explanation and do not provide a detailed investigation on it.

Table 3. Directional trade ratio between the United States and China (2006–2015).

Year	Ratio
2006	0.157
2007	0.151
2008	0.140
2009	0.153
2010	0.148
2011	0.137
2012	0.140
2013	0.141
2014	0.143
2015	0.156

Source: JETRO, *International Trade and Investment Report* (Annual Edition) and author's calculation.

Table 4. The ratio of the total trade amount between the United States and China to the total trade amount of the United States (2006–2015).

Year	Ratio
2006	0.119
2007	0.124
2008	0.120
2009	0.140
2010	0.143
2011	0.136
2012	0.140
2013	0.146
2014	0.149
2015	0.160

Source: JETRO, *International Trade and Investment Report* (Annual Edition) and author's calculation.

Table 5. Directional trade ratio between the United States and Japan (2006–2015).

Year	Ratio
2006	0.124
2007	0.115
2008	0.099
2009	0.097
2010	0.093
2011	0.087
2012	0.093
2013	0.092
2014	0.092
2015	0.101

Source: JETRO, *International Trade and Investment Report* (Annual Edition) and author's calculation.

Table 6. The ratio of the total trade amount between the United States and Japan to the total trade amount of the United States (2006–2015).

Year	Ratio
2006	0.074
2007	0.069
2008	0.059
2009	0.058
2010	0.058
2011	0.054
2012	0.057
2013	0.053
2014	0.051
2015	0.051

Source: JETRO, *International Trade and Investment Report* (Annual Edition) and author's calculation.

As Table 5 indicates, the directional trade ratio between the United States and Japan is nearly 0.1, which demonstrates a smaller ratio than that between the United States and China. Table 6 shows the ratio of the total trade amount between the United States and Japan to the total trade amount of the United States. It presents a tendency toward gradually getting smaller (in contrast to the ratio between the United States and China). In other words, the directional trade ratio between the United States and Japan, nearly 0.1, was mostly contributed by the Japanese side.

The second tool is the "trade linkage index." This index focuses on whether or not there exists a trade distortion between the United States and China. The trade linkage index is used as a measure of the distortion of trade.[13] The distortion in the trade between the United States and China (to be explained not by comparative advantage but by specific factors in China and/or the United States) is analyzed.

The numerical value of the distorted portion of the trade is defined as follows:

$$B_{ij} = \frac{X_{ij}}{X_{ij}(-)}$$

$$\left(\text{Here, } X_{ij}(-) = X_j \bullet \frac{X_i}{X}\right)$$

In this equation, *Xij* indicates the export amount from China to the United States, *Xi* indicates the total import amount of the United States, *Xj* indicates the total export amount of China, and *X* indicates the total export amount of the whole world. That is to say, it is a ratio of the "actual import amount" of the United States from China and the "hypothetical import amount" of the United States from China. The "hypothetical import amount" is the Chinese potential export amount to the United States, which includes all the goods that are exported based on the potential comparative advantage of China against the United States. If the Chinese actual export amount to the United States equals the hypothetical export amount to the United States, the numerical value of *Bij* could become 1.0. If the numerical value of *Bij* becomes higher (or lower) than 1.0, it is recognized that the "distorted portion of the trade" becomes bigger.

[13] Concerning the trade linkage index, see, for example, Yamazawa (1971).

Table 7. Trade linkage index of China with the United States (2006–2015).

Year	Index
2006	1.355
2007	1.343
2008	1.386
2009	1.501
2010	1.407
2011	1.377
2012	1.349
2013	1.352
2014	1.325
2015	1.317

Source: JETRO, *International Trade and Investment Report* (Annual Edition) and author's calculation.

Table 7 shows the trade linkage index of China with the United States.

As Table 7 indicates, the trade linkage index of China with the United States has a value of more than 1.0; in other words, the Chinese actual export amount to the United States is more than the Chinese potential export amount to the United States (which means the export amount is based on the potential comparative advantage). This is a result of an inference on the basis of the "trade linkage index."

To the contrary, we have the same calculation on the trade linkage index of the United States with China. The results of the calculation are shown in Table 8.

The numerical values indicated in Table 8 are undoubtedly less than 1.0. There exists a "distortion" in which the actual export amount of the United States to China is less than the potential export amount of the United States to China.

Tables 7 and 8 represent the characteristics of trade between the United States and China. The Chinese actual export amount to the United States is more than the Chinese potential export amount to the United States. To the contrary, the United States' actual export amount to China is less than the United States' potential export amount to China.

It is not realistic to assume that the economic policies of China are based on market mechanisms. Supposing that market mechanisms in

Table 8. Trade linkage index of the United States with China (2006–2015).

Year	Index
2006	0.805
2007	0.807
2008	0.780
2009	0.833
2010	0.773
2011	0.724
2012	0.707
2013	0.721
2014	0.715
2015	0.795

Source: JETRO, *International Trade and Investment Report* (Annual Edition) and author's calculation.

China work smoothly, it is reasonable to think that such "distortions" can be eliminated by adjusting the market mechanisms. However, in reality, market mechanisms do not work.

Such "distortions" in international trade result in a trade surplus in China and a trade deficit in the United States (because adjusting market mechanisms does not work). The inclination of the trade balance from 1985 to 2015 is indicated in the following figures: Figure 1 shows the trade balance of China and Figure 2 the trade balance of the United States. The figures undoubtedly present both the trade surplus of China and the trade deficit of the United States, which have high values.

Table 9 provides statistics such as Chinese exports to the United States, Chinese imports from the United States, the Chinese trade surplus with the United States, the total trade deficit amount of the United States, and the ratio of the Chinese trade surplus to the total trade deficit of the United States from 2006 to 2015.

As is shown in Table 4, the ratio of the trade amount between China and the United States to the total trade amount of the United States has the tendency of gradually increasing, with numerical values in the range of 0.12 to 0.16. As presented in Table 9, the ratio of the Chinese trade surplus to the total trade deficit of the United States is 0.2–0.3. Compared to the

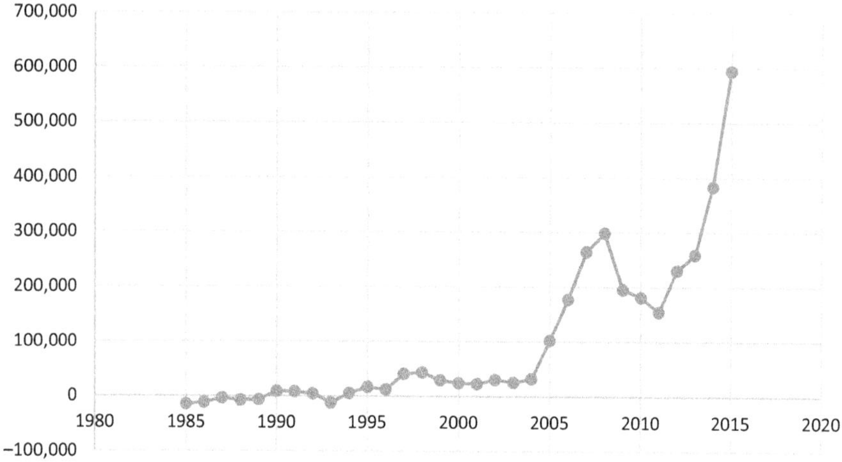

Figure 1. Trade balance of China (1985–2015).
Source: UNCTAD (Data: Global Note).

Figure 2. Trade balance of the United States (1985–2015).
Source: UNCTAD (Data: Global Note).

above-mentioned ratio of 0.12 to 0.16, the ratio of 0.2–0.3 is undoubtedly bigger.

The main reasons for such differences are (keeping in mind that the Chinese economy is a socialist economy and not a market economy)

Table 9. Several statistics on the trade between China and the United States (2006–2015) (million US dollars, in percent).

Year	Chinese export to USA	Chinese import from USA	Chinese trade surplus with USA (A)	Total trade deficit of USA (B)	A / B (in percent)
2006	203,472	59,209	144,263	817,303	17.65
2007	232,704	69,379	163,325	794,483	20.56
2008	252,297	81,440	170,857	1,049,937	16.27
2009	220,816	77,443	143,373	503,582	28.47
2010	283,304	102,038	181,266	634,897	28.55
2011	324,493	122,154	202,339	727,392	27.82
2012	351,796	132,886	218,910	729,611	30.00
2013	368,427	152,575	215,851	688,728	31.34
2014	396,082	159,036	237,046	727,153	32.59
2015	409,538	148,737	260,801	745,660	19.35

Source: JETRO, *International Trade and Investment Report* (Annual Edition) and author's calculation.

(1) the United States' excess consumption and China's underconsumption and (2) the artificial rigorousness of the exchange rate of the renminbi (in other words, an artificially higher US dollar rate and an artificially lower Chinese renminbi rate).

Table 10 indicates the savings rate of the United States and China from 2000 to 2015 and Figure 3 depicts the same in image format.

It is quite clear from one glance that the savings rate of the United States is extremely low and, on the contrary, the savings rate of China is considerably high. This indicates the "excess consumption of the United States" and "excess savings of China" (in other words, "under saving of the United States" and "underconsumption of China").

If we assume that market mechanisms work smoothly, as the absorption approach presents, the trade balance of each country will equal the savings and investment balance. Therefore, the trade balance of an excess-consumption country becomes a deficit and the trade balance of an under-consumption country becomes a surplus. This disequilibrium of trade balance can be adjusted by capital account balance, which is the standard mechanism of the market economy.

This mechanism produces the "codependency" relationship between the United States and China.

Table 10. Savings ratio of the United States and China (2000–2015) (in percent).

Year	USA	China
2000	5.9	35.8
2001	4.4	37.4
2002	3.0	39.0
2003	2.3	42.6
2004	2.6	45.9
2005	2.7	46.2
2006	3.7	48.5
2007	1.6	50.9
2008	▲0.6	52.3
2009	▲2.1	51.0
2010	▲0.8	52.1
2011	▲0.1	50.1
2012	2.0	49.6
2013	2.5	48.6
2014	3.4	49.2
2015	3.4	47.1

Source: OECD.

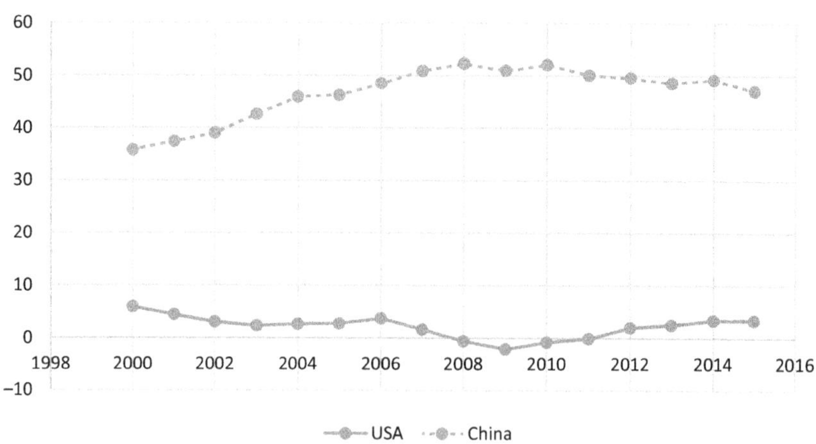

Figure 3. Savings ratio of the United States and China (2000–2015) (in percent).
Source: OECD.

However, as just confirmed above, it must be a mechanism predicted by a well working market mechanism. Under the socialist market economy of China, we could not mention that market mechanism well works. It would be rather obvious that the distortion moves into the mechanism which is functioned between the socialist market economy China and the market economy the United States. Moreover, in the market economy of the United States, there exists "exorbitant privilege."

One of the important mechanisms which would not work well under the socialist market economy of China is the exchange rate system. As regards the movement of the exchange rate of the renminbi to the US dollar, please check Table 11. As it is usually suggested, the exchange rate of

Table 11. Exchange rate of the renminbi to the US dollar (1997–2016).

Year	Exchange rate of renminbi
1997	8.28981
1998	8.27895
1999	8.27825
2000	8.27850
2001	8.27706
2002	8.27695
2003	8.27703
2004	8.27680
2005	8.19431
2006	7.97343
2007	7.60753
2008	6.94865
2009	6.83141
2010	6.77026
2011	6.46146
2012	6.31233
2013	6.19575
2014	6.14343
2015	6.22748
2016	6.64447

Source: IMF (Data: Global Note).

the renminbi to the US dollar was underestimated. As often indicated, there might have been a similar mechanism with the Japanese yen after the Second World War, which means that the Japanese yen was underestimated under the fixed exchange rate system (when the Japanese yen was fixed at 360 yen to 1 US dollar).[14]

As it was difficult to find the equilibrium rate of the Japanese yen under the fixed exchange rate system in the theoretical sense, it is also difficult to find the equilibrium rate of the Chinese renminbi in the socialist market economy in the theoretical sense.[15] The measurement used by Ferguson and Schularick (2007) indicates that (after adjusting the productivity difference) the undervaluation of the renminbi is estimated within the range of 30 percent to 48 percent.[16]

Regardless of the exact extent of the undervaluation of the renminbi, it is commonly recognized that the renminbi has been undervalued.

In conducting trade with China, because the exchange rate in China is not recognized to be on left-hand side of the market mechanism, it might be correct to suppose that the "distortion" occurs there.

As Tables 7 and 8 indicate, one of major factors for the distortion (meaning that China's actual export amount would be greater than the potential export amount; on the contrary, the actual export amount of the United States would be less than its potential export amount) that is shown in the trade linkage index is assumed to be the "undervaluation" of the exchange rate of the renminbi to the US dollar.

Therefore, a reasonable solution (at least one of them) to the trade balance disequilibrium between the United States and China is the modification of the "undervaluation of the renminbi exchange rate to the US dollar."

Furthermore, a crucial factor that could establish the "codependency" relationship is the provision of financing by China to the United States (through Chinese excess savings). Here, we confirm that matter.

---

[14] However, the exchange rate in which 1 US dollar equaled 360 Japanese yen was not usually recognized as an underestimation of the yen. Also, we could not find any standard view about the equilibrium rate of the Japanese yen to the US dollar.

[15] It means that it is also difficult to measure the "deviation" from the equilibrium rate. However, it might not be difficult to suppose a tendency toward "overestimation" or "underestimation."

[16] See Ferguson and Schularick (2007, p. 18).

Table 12 presents the Chinese holdings amount of the US Government Bonds and foreign exchange reserves and the ratio of the two values (the US Government Bond is defined as the total amount of short-term and long-term Treasury Debt). It is shown that the ratio of the US Government Bond holding to foreign exchange reserves in China is roughly 30 percent to 40 percent. Just for a comparison, the same ratio in Japan is in the range of 70 percent to 99 percent, which is a much larger value than the Chinese ratio. Table 13 lists the ratio of the amount of the US Government Bond holding in China and Japan to the world total amount of the US Government Bond holding. We recognize that both countries have a ratio

Table 12. The amount of the US Government Bond holdings and foreign exchange reserves, and their ratios (China and Japan) (2002–2016) (million US dollar, in percent).

Year	Amount of US Government Bond holding (China)(A)	Amount of Foreign exchange reserves (China)(B)	Ratio (A/B) × 100	Amount of US Government Bond holding (Japan)(C)	Amount of Foreign exchange reserves (Japan)(D)	Ratio (C/D) × 100
2002	96,457	291,128	33.1	349,440	461,186	75.8
2003	147,128	408,151	36.0	460,452	663,289	69.4
2004	194,210	614,500	31.6	667,613	833,891	71.5
2005	297,811	821,514	36.3	666,440	834,275	79.9
2006	372,235	1,068,493	34.8	542,915	879,682	61.7
2007	477,227	1,530,282	31.2	622,337	952,784	65.3
2008	535,042	1,949,260	27.4	627,772	1,009,365	62.2
2009	915,654	2,416,044	37.9	708,087	1,022,236	69.3
2010	1,112,125	2,866,079	38.8	799,858	1,061,490	75.4
2011	1,306,976	3,202,789	40.8	881,730	1,258,172	70.1
2012	1,146,876	3,331,120	34.4	1,108,872	1,227,147	90.4
2013	1,276,650	3,839,548	33.3	1,083,271	1,237,218	87.7
2014	1,268,656	3,859,168	32.9	1,219,598	1,231,010	99.1
2015	1,270,538	3,345,194	38.0	1,196,247	1,207,019	99.1
2016	1,239,794	3,029,775	40.9	1,146,478	1,188,327	96.5

Note: The holdings of US national bond are as of each June-end, and the foreign exchange reserves are as of each year-end.

Source: The US Department of the Treasury, IMF (Data: Global Note) and author's calculation.

Table 13. The ratio of the amount of US Government Bond holdings in China and Japan to the world total amount (2000–2016) (in percent).

Year	China	Japan
2002	8.5	30.7
2003	10.6	33.2
2004	11.1	38.3
2005	15.8	35.4
2006	18.8	27.4
2007	21.8	28.4
2008	20.7	24.2
2009	26.4	20.4
2010	27.2	19.6
2011	27.8	18.7
2012	21.6	20.9
2013	22.8	19.4
2014	21.1	20.3
2015	20.7	19.5
2016	19.8	18.3

Note: The holdings of US national bond are as of each June-end, and the foreign exchange reserves are as of each year-end.
Source: The US Department of the Treasury.

of about 20 percent. For reference, regarding China, by examining the ratio of US government bond holdings as of the end of June each year (numerator) to the trade surplus with the United States for each fiscal year (denominator), we can easily recognize that the ratio has increased from the year of 2009 (Table 14).

3.2. *Analysis*

Concerning China's foreign relations with the United States, it might be evident that abnormal values in some statistics were recorded in 2008 or 2009. For example, the ratio of the US Government Bond holdings to foreign exchange reserves in China (Table 12 and Figure 4) was boosted in 2009. The amount of the US Government Bond holdings in China increased greatly in the year 2009. In Figure 5, a comparison of the trends

Table 14. The ratio of US government bond holdings to US trade surplus (2002–2016).

Year	Multiplier
2002	2.01
2003	2.29
2004	2.15
2005	2.45
2006	2.50
2007	2.77
2008	2.65
2009	5.03
2010	5.80
2011	5.91
2012	4.74
2013	5.17
2014	4.65
2015	4.31
2016	4.53

Source: The US Department of the Treasury, JETRO International Trade and Investment Report (Annual Edition).

of US Government Bond holdings by China and Japan is shown. The rapid increase in the amount held by China is clear (it is an abnormal value at the 10 percent significance level). And in Figure 6, US government bond holdings' ratio of the world is indicated.

Moreover, as shown in Table 11, the exchange rate of the renminbi to the US dollar drastically increased in the year 2008 to an undoubtedly abnormal value (at the 1 percent significance level).

In short, the values of US Government Bond holdings in China, the ratio of the amount of US Government Bond holdings to the amount of trade surplus of the United States in China, and the exchange rate of the renminbi to the US dollar were abnormally high in 2008 and 2009.

Moreover, the correlation between the exchange rate of the renminbi to the US dollar and the Gini coefficient in China was significant (at the 1 percent significance level).

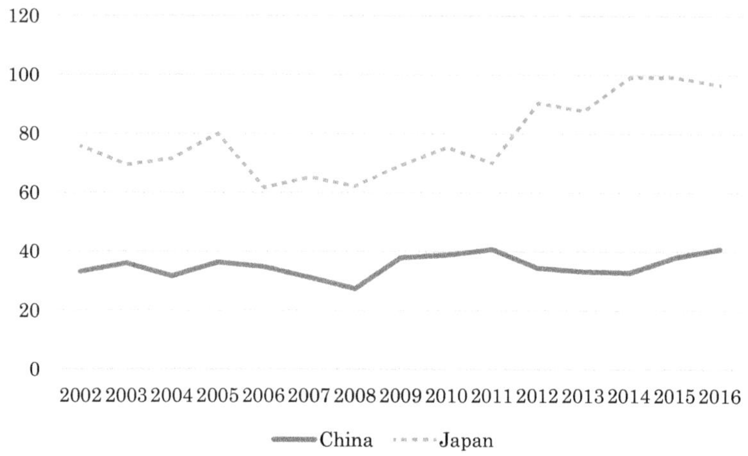

Figure 4. The ratio of US Government Bond holdings to foreign exchange reserves in China and Japan (2002–2016).

Note: The holdings of US national bond are as of each June-end, and the foreign exchange reserves are as of each year-end.
Source: The US Department of the Treasury, IMF (Data: Global Note) and author's calculation.

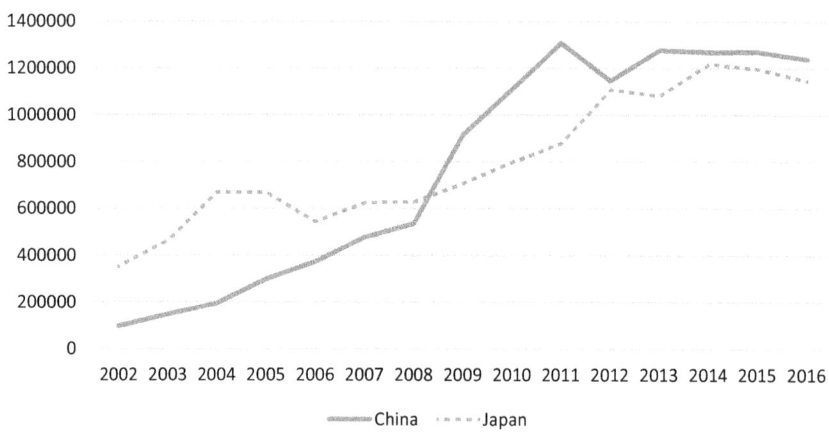

Figure 5. The trends of the amount of US Government Bond holdings in China and Japan (2002–2016).

Note: The holdings of US national bond are as of each June-end.
Source: The US Department of the Treasury.

Table 15 indicates the ratio of gold holdings to foreign exchange reserves (because of the different sources, it is possible for the sum of the ratio of US government bond holdings and the ratio of gold holdings to exceed 100 percent). Also, for comparison, the ratios of the United States and Japan have been presented.

Needless to say, the ratios of the United States, China, and Japan are obviously different from each other. Gold holdings in both China and Japan are extremely small. Particularly in Japan, as Table 15 clearly indicates, foreign exchange reserves are largely held in US government bonds (the ratio of gold holdings is extremely small, similar to that of China).

Table 15. The ratio of gold holdings to foreign exchange reserves (2000–2016) (in percent).

Year	China	Japan	US
2000	2.029	1.863	55.919
2001	2.023	1.692	55.693
2002	2.249	1.818	57.237
2003	1.929	1.520	59.244
2004	1.349	1.269	60.024
2005	1.190	1.490	71.272
2006	1.128	1.737	75.080
2007	1.040	2.108	78.554
2008	0.853	2.076	77.348
2009	1.503	2.551	70.374
2010	1.635	3.155	75.172
2011	1.594	2.907	74.517
2012	1.658	3.216	75.700
2013	1.052	2.339	70.227
2014	1.048	2.354	72.596
2015	1.764	2.115	72.236
2016	2.191	2.317	73.816

Note: The numerical value of the amount of US Government Bond holding is at the end of June, each year, and the amount of foreign exchange reserve is at the end of each year.
Source: The US Department of the Treasury, IMF and World Gold Council (Data: Global Note).

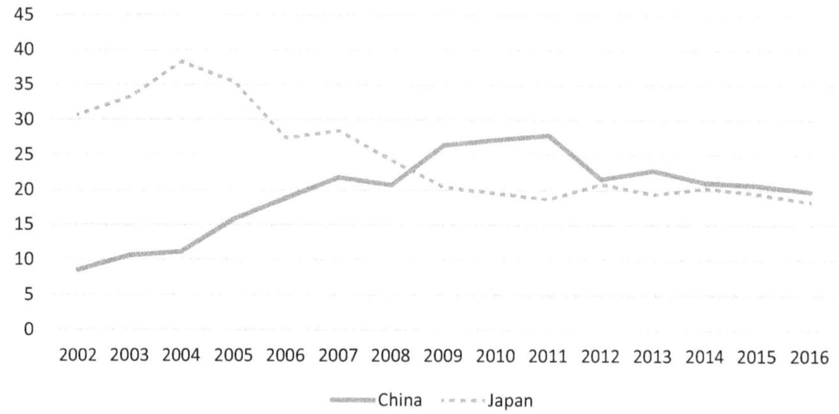

Figure 6. The ratio of the amount of US Government Bond holdings to the world total (2002–2016) (in percent).

Note: The holdings of US national bond are as of each June-end.
Source: The US Department of the Treasury.

4. The Current Situation and Problems in the Chinese Economy[17]

As is well known, the main problem in the Chinese economy is a shortage of domestic demand, namely, "underconsumption." In this section, we examine the current situation and the problems in the Chinese economy.

Since the reform and opening-up policy was implemented by Deng Xiaoping, the Chinese economy had maintained a high growth rate of around 10 percent annually (Table 16). Generally speaking, the economy of such a big country like China is led by domestic demand. However, China's degree of dependence on foreign trade (=total amount of export and import/GDP) increased from around 15 percent in the first half of the 1980s to about 65 percent in 2006. This degree recently decreased to 36.3 percent in 2015 (Table 17).

[17]This section is based on Chen and Morita (2015), chapter one. Thus, the author is indebted to Professor Yun Chen. Additional statistics have been contributed by Morita (the author of this book).

Table 16. Growth rate and per capita growth rate in China (2000–2015) (in percent).

Year	GDP growth rate	Per capita GDP growth rate
2000	8.5	7.6
2001	8.3	7.5
2002	9.1	8.4
2003	10.0	9.3
2004	10.1	9.4
2005	11.4	10.7
2006	12.7	12.1
2007	14.2	13.6
2008	9.7	9.1
2009	9.4	8.7
2010	10.6	10.1
2011	9.5	9.0
2012	7.9	7.2
2013	7.8	7.2
2014	7.3	6.7
2015	6.9	6.3

Note: Real pricing.
Source: China Statistical Yearbook (2016) and JETRO China Data File (2016).

It goes without saying, that behind the high-speed economic growth in China that is dependent on foreign demand , there exists a specific risk. The comparative advantage of Chinese export products depends on low production costs. It is possible in China to eliminate the two big costs of "rights and interests of laborers" and "environment." In the short run, producers contribute to the Chinese economy by the huge amounts of exports, earning lots of foreign exchange reserves, thereby promoting economic growth. However, in the long run, such malicious transmission mechanisms in Chinese policies are recognized to hinder the sustainable development of Chinese economic society.

Hereafter, we look at such situations concretely.

The first situation is investment-led economic growth and excessive production capacity. Table 18 shows the component ratio of GDP. After the reform and opening-up policy, the ratio of investment in the component of GDP in China decreased; however, after the year of 1982, it started

Table 17. Degree of dependence on export, import, and foreign trade in China (2000–2015) (in percent).

Year	Export	Import	Foreign trade
2000	20.7	18.7	39.4
2001	20.0	18.3	38.3
2002	22.3	20.2	42.5
2003	26.6	25.0	51.6
2004	30.6	28.9	59.4
2005	33.7	29.2	62.9
2006	35.7	29.1	64.8
2007	34.9	27.3	62.3
2008	31.7	25.1	56.8
2009	23.7	19.9	43.6
2010	26.2	23.2	49.3
2011	25.5	23.4	48.8
2012	24.2	21.5	45.7
2013	23.3	20.6	43.9
2014	22.6	18.9	41.6
2015	20.9	15.4	36.3

Source: JETRO China Data File (2016) and author's calculation.

to increase, and fluctuated between 1987 and 1992, reached 42.6 percent in 1991. Thereafter, in the year of 2003, when the new period of economic expansion started in China, that ratio moved upward to 70 percent. After 2005, that ratio indicated a declining trend, reaching 42.6 percent in 2015. Investment-led economic growth has many problems. Because of excess investment, the macroeconomic situation can become overheated. However, as domestic demand is quite limited, excess production capacity must be released through exports. On the other hand, the ratio of consumption to GDP decreased from 67.1 percent in 1981 to 58.1 percent in 1995 and 35.4 percent in the year 2003. Thereafter, the trend by and large rose and reached 59.9 percent in 2015.

Generally speaking, the stagnation of consumption is connected with domestic demand shortage and lowering of the growth rate of import, and the export market becomes the target of domestic production capacity.

Table 18. The component ratio of GDP in China (2000–2015) (in percent).

Year	Consumption	Investment	Net export
2000	78.1	22.4	▲0.5
2001	49.0	64.0	▲13.0
2002	55.6	39.8	4.6
2003	35.4	70.0	▲5.4
2004	42.6	61.6	▲4.2
2005	54.4	33.1	12.5
2006	42.0	42.9	15.1
2007	45.3	44.1	10.6
2008	44.2	53.2	2.6
2009	56.1	86.5	▲42.6
2010	44.9	66.3	▲11.2
2011	61.9	46.2	▲8.2
2012	54.9	43.4	1.7
2013	47.0	55.3	▲2.3
2014	48.8	46.9	4.3
2015	59.9	42.6	▲2.5

Note: Real pricing.
Source: China Statistical Yearbook (2016).

The second situation is the lower rate of labor distribution and a domestic demand shortage in China. After the reform and opening-up policy, the ratio of labor income to GDP in China continued to lower. As shown in Table 19, the ratio of labor income to GDP in the year 2000 was 53.3 percent; however, it decreased to 48.9 percent in 2008. Although it increased to around 51 percent in 2013, the ratio was still low. For a comparison, the ratios of labor income to GDP of the United States and Japan were 71.1 percent (USA) and 72.1 percent (Japan) in 2000 and 66.3 percent (USA) and 69.4 percent (Japan) in 2013. The ratio of labor income to GDP in China is undoubtedly lower. A low ratio of labor income to GDP results in domestic demand shortage.

Because of the low wage rate for laborers and the poor social security system, the consumer sentiment of the Chinese people (particularly people in rural areas) is conservative, leading to a domestic demand shortage.

Table 19. The ratio of labor income to GDP in each country (2000–2014) (in percent).

Year	USA	China	Japan
2000	71.1	53.3	72.1
2005	68.5	50.6	67.9
2008	70.7	48.9	69.6
2009	69.9	49.9	71.5
2010	67.9	49.4	68.9
2011	67.2	50.1	70.5
2012	66.4	51.0	69.7
2013	66.3	50.9	69.4
2014	66.5		69.4

Note: In the United States and Japan, the labor distribution ratio = Compensation of employees/National income (in factor cost indication) × 100, and in China, the labor distribution ratio = Compensation of employees/Total national income × 100.

Source: Japan Institute for Labor Policy and Training Data Book International Comparison of Labor (2016).

The third situation is trade friction. Due to the domestic demand shortage, the Chinese economy more depends on the international market, leading to trade friction with foreign countries and increased lawsuits. Specifically, cheap consumer goods made in China invade the markets of countries that are targeted for export. This invasion would cause a stagnation of production in the country concerned. Needless to say, that stagnation of production decreases the employment opportunities for laborers in the country targeted for export. Those laborers react against the Chinese system, which leads to a trade friction.

The fourth situation is the negative externality problem due to the elimination of environmental costs. The exclusion of environmental costs by producers helps to lower production costs at the expense of workers' rights and benefits, and is an important factor in the comparative advantage structure of Chinese products. However, the occurrence of negative externality cannot be ignored because (1) serious problems are caused due to environmental pollution in China, affecting peoples' health. At the same time, (2) due to weak environmental legislation, enterprises do not have any incentives to introduce and develop environmentally friendly technology and improve the process of production and management. Therefore, a bottleneck of resources and energy has developed in the Chinese economy, which has influenced (increased) the international prices of oil and resources. In other words, if the incentive problem of enterprises cannot be eliminated, it would become impossible for Chinese products to transform from price competitiveness to technology competitiveness.

The fifth situation is the economic influence of producers' sovereignty. Under the whole nation's system, the era of personal homes and cars is rapidly sweeping across Chinese society. The consumption boom for personal homes and cars has directly driven the ratio of heavy industry in China.

The heavy industry ratio (which means the ratio of heavy industry within the total industry) in China was 56.9 percent in the year 1978, which gradually decreased to 50.6 percent in 1990. Thereafter, that ratio increased to 71.9 percent in 2012. There has been considerable development of heavy industries. The increase in heavy industries ratio can be positively evaluated by way of "Hoffman's Law." However, with regard to China, it is necessary to pay attention to the following two points.

The first point is that the foreign dependency on resources is increasing. Because China's economic development model is one of consuming energy and resources, the import dependence on strategic resources like oil, iron ore, manganese, copper, lead, and zinc increases each year. The second point is the excessive investment and the overproduction that have occurred several times in China's macroeconomy since the 1980s. According to the Chinese Ministry of Industry and Information (2012), of the problem of excess production capacity has occurred in 19 different industries including raw materials, such as iron and steel, and chemicals.

At present, after joining the WTO, as some domestic and foreign factors are compounded, it is possible that price increases in raw materials and energy led to a cost-push-type inflation. Also, the asset bubble occurred because of the consumption boom, involving the purchase of cars and homes, and an unhealthy financial system. If China cannot solve these problems, then the Chinese economy will be seriously impaired.

The Chinese leadership, concerned about these issues, designated the expansion of citizens' consumption capacity as a key task for 2006 at the 2005 central economic working conference of 2005. Thereby, in addition to the correction of income disparity, they demanded for a policy conversion from an emphasis on the one-sided importance of the real estate industry's contribution to economic development to prioritizing the consumption restricting effects of rapidly rising real estate prices on consumers.

In short, the characteristics of the Chinese economic model involve a stagnation of consumption, a low rate of labor distribution, delayed countermeasures against environmental pollution, producer sovereignty, etc. These characteristics contributed to the expansion of foreign exchange reserves (of US dollars) in China, which led to "codependency" between the United States and China.

5. Current Situation of Sino-American Relations: Consumption–GDP Ratio

As mentioned earlier, both "excess consumption" in the United States and "underconsumption" in China are important factors that led to "codependency" between the United States and China.

Usually, the "excess consumption" means a savings shortage, giving rise to a trade deficit from the viewpoint of savings and investment balance. In this book, we focus on the "excess consumption" involving the ratio of private consumption to GDP.

That is to say, the percentage of a country's private consumption in the world is used as the numerator, and the percentage of the country's GDP in the world is used as the denominator, from which we have the ratio. In this book, we will call it the "consumption–GDP" ratio. Therefore, if the ratio of the GDP of a certain country to the GDP of the whole world is 5 percent and if the ratio of the private consumption of a certain country to the private consumption of the whole world is 5 percent, then the "consumption–GDP" ratio of that country is 1.0. In that case, the consumption of that country is neither in excess nor deficient.

However, in almost all cases, the "consumption–GDP ratio" is either more than 1.0 or less than 1.0. In this book, "more than 1.0" is termed "excess consumption" and "less than 1.0" is termed "underconsumption."

Table 20 shows the "consumption–GDP ratio" of some major countries[18] (the word "major" means that both the consumption and GDP are large).

---

[18]As indicated in Table 20 and Figure 7, major countries are the United States, China, Japan, Germany, France, the United Kingdom, Brazil, Italy, India, Canada, and Russia (the scale of GDP and consumption fluctuate year by year).

Table 20. Consumption–GDP ratio of major countries (2010–2015).

Countries \ Year	2010	2011	2012	2013	2014	2015
USA	1.186	1.209	1.200	1.194	1.195	1.183
China	0.618	0.637	0.644	0.646	0.657	0.661
Japan	1.005	1.023	1.029	1.034	1.023	0.981
Germany	0.977	0.971	0.977	0.973	0.955	0.938
France	0.975	0.977	0.975	0.975	0.969	0.957
UK	1.133	1.140	1.147	1.147	1.139	1.130
Brazil	1.048	1.056	1.076	1.081	1.094	1.100
Italy	1.062	1.077	1.079	1.072	1.070	1.057
India	0.960	0.988	1.000	1.016	1.012	1.035
Canada	0.988	0.980	0.984	0.979	0.982	1.000
Russia	0.896	0.888	0.907	0.948	0.942	0.939

Source: United Nations (Data: Global Note) and author's calculation.

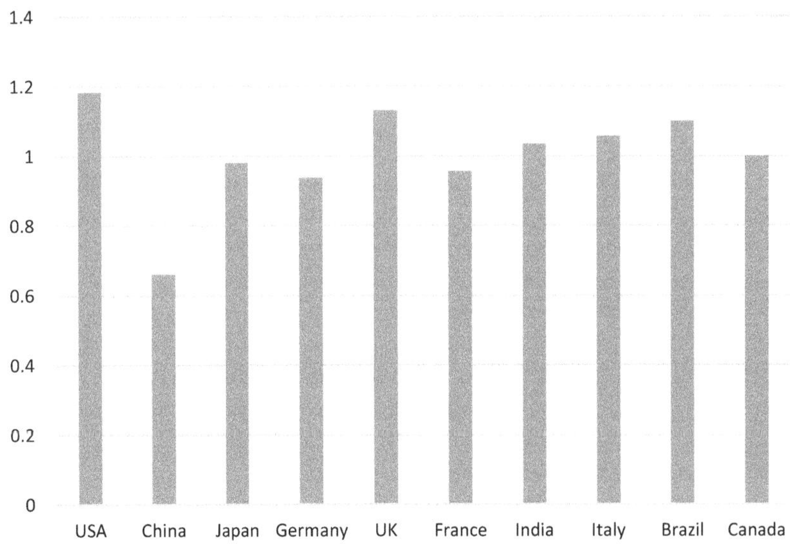

Figure 7. Consumption–GDP ratio of major countries in 2015.

Source: United Nations (Data: Global Note) and author's calculation.

Figure 7 shows the consumption–GDP ratio of the countries concerned in the year 2015. As regards the year 2015, the "excess-consumption" countries are the United States, the United Kingdom, Brazil, Italy, and India and "underconsumption" countries are China, Japan, Germany,

France, and Russia. Canada is neither in excess nor deficient. In Figure 7, we clearly recognize that the United States is an "excess-consumption" country and China is an "underconsumption" country. Table 20 also shows the values of "excess consumption" of the United States and "underconsumption" of China.

The ratios of private consumption to GDP of the US and China are extremely different. In 2015, if the consumption–GDP ratios of the United States and China were both 1.0, the consumption of the United States would be 1,899.9 billion US dollars less than the true value and consumption of China would be 2,172.8 billion US dollars more than the true value.[19]

6. Symmetry in Sino-American Relations: "Trade Linkage Index" and "Consumption–GDP Ratio"

The symmetry between the "trade linkage index" and the "consumption–GDP ratio" is shown in Tables 7, 8, and 20. In this section we create Table 21 from Tables 7 and 8, and extract part of Table 19 to present as Table 22.

---

[19]That calculation is as follows. The estimation in this chapter is done under the condition of "other things being equal" and also no "spillover effect" is assumed. In 2015, the GDP of the United States was 18,036.6 billion US dollars and the GDP of China was 11,158.5 billion US dollars. Also in the year 2015, the private consumption of the United States was 12,283.7 billion US dollars and the private consumption of China was 4,251.4 billion US dollars.

In 2015, the ratio of the GDP of the United States to the GDP of the whole world was estimated to be 24.31 percent and the ratio of private consumption of the United States to the world total was 28.76 percent. In the case of China, in 2015, the ratio of the GDP of China to the GDP of the whole world was estimated to be 15.04 percent and the ratio of the private consumption of China to the world total was 9.95 percent. Then, if the ratio of the private consumption of the United States would become, the same as the ratio of GDP, 24.31 percent, and if the ratio of China would become, the same as the ratio of GDP, 15.04 percent, (because private consumption of the whole world in 2015 was 42,714.3 billion US dollars) private consumption in the United States equals to 10,383.8 billion US dollars and in China it becomes 6,424.2 billion US dollars. Therefore, if the ratios of consumption–GDP of the United States and China were 1.0, then the private consumption of the United States would be 1,899.9 billion US dollars less and the private consumption of China would be 2,172.8 billion US dollars more.

Table 21. Trade linkage index between the United States and China (2010–2015).

Item \ Year	2010	2011	2012	2013	2014	2015
Chinese trade linkage index with USA	1.407	1.377	1.349	1.352	1.325	1.317
USA trade linkage index with China	0.773	0.724	0.707	0.721	0.715	0.795

Source: Jetro International Trade and Investment Report (Annual Edition) and author's calculation.

Table 22. Consumption–GDP ratio of the United States and China (2010–2015).

Countries \ Year	2010	2011	2012	2013	2014	2015
USA	1.186	1.209	1.200	1.194	1.195	1.183
China	0.618	0.637	0.644	0.646	0.657	0.661

Source: United Nations (Data: Global Note) and author's calculation.

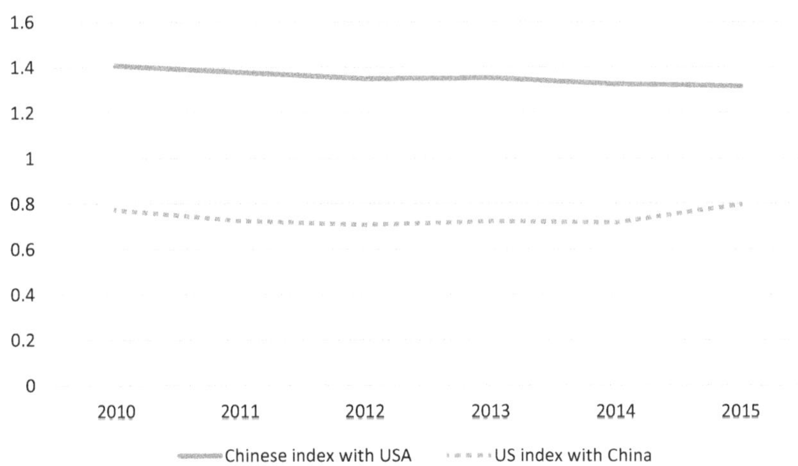

Figure 8. Trade linkage index between the United States and China (2010–2015).
Source: Jetro International Trade and Investment Report (Annual Edition) and author's calculation.

In order to clarify the situation, we provide Figure 8 (trade linkage index) and Figure 9 (consumption–GDP ratio). It could undoubtedly be understood that both Figures 8 and 9 show values ranging from 0.8 to 1.4 (Figure 8) and from 0.6 to 1.2 (Figure 9) around the boundary of 1.0. In Figure 8, the upper line indicates China and the lower line the

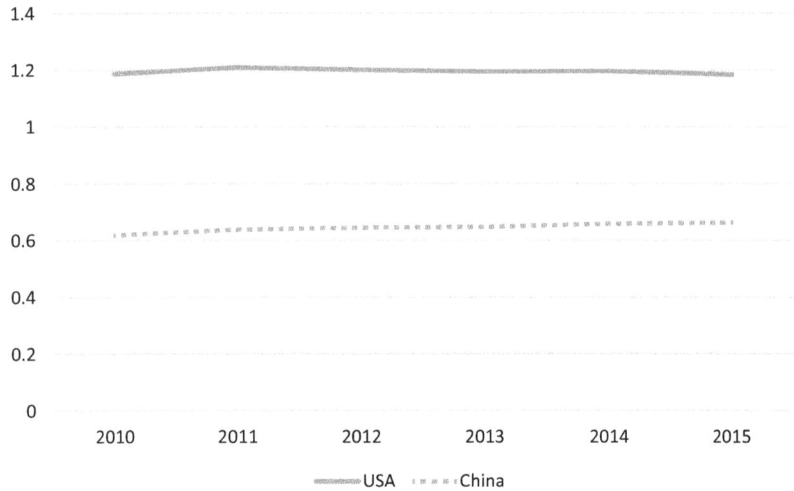

Figure 9. Consumption–GDP ratio of the United States and China (2010–2015).
Source: United Nations (Data: Global Note) and author's calculation.

United States. In Figure 9, to the contrary, the upper line indicates the United States and the lower line China. It could be said that they present clear symmetry.

In Figures 8 and 9, what do the numerical values of the United States and China (which exist symmetrically with the border of 1.0) demonstrate?

Here, we confirm the following. The "trade linkage index" measures the distortion from the potential comparative advantage and the "consumption–GDP ratio" shows excess or deficient consumption in the country concerned (based on the ratio as a proportion of the world's total consumption). Also, as mentioned earlier, the main factor which produces "symmetry" as indicated in Table 22 and Figure 9 could be the "distortion" of the exchange rate between the US dollar and the Chinese renminbi. We speculate that the main factor producing "symmetry" as shown in Table 22 and Figure 9 is the "distortion" of the Chinese economic structure, indicated in the savings rate and labor distribution rate, and the "exorbitant privilege" of the United States.[20]

[20]As suggested before, in this book, we have no explanation for the "exorbitant privilege" of the United States.

The "artificial manipulation of exchange rate" by the Chinese government is often indicated. If either the US dollar or the Chinese renminbi is artificially manipulated, it will certainly have an effect on exports and imports. It is surely indicated as a "distortion" from a "potential comparative advantage." As mentioned earlier, "The values of China and the United States, which symmetrically exist around 1.0 as indicated by trade linkage index, are likely a reflection of the above explained assertion. If Chinese renminbi would be underestimated to US dollar, the United States export to China is distorted to a lower place because of high US dollar rate, on the contrary, Chinese export to the United States is distorted to a higher place because of low Chinese renminbi rate. Such distortion could be indicated by the "symmetry" as shown in Table 21 and Figure 8.

The "distortion" in the economic structure, as indicated by savings rate and labor distribution rate, is often pointed out. The savings rate is indicated in Table 10 and Figure 3 and the labor distribution rate is shown in Table 19. Focusing on China, undoubtedly the savings rate is high and the labor distribution rate is low. In addition to a low labor distribution rate, savings rate from labor income becomes high, which leads to a low rate of consumption. Therefore, the Chinese economy as a whole could have a low rate of labor distribution, a low cost of environmental measures, and cheap export goods production, and it would be easy for the Chinese economy to capture the export markets. Furthermore, the underestimated renminbi could support the capture of the export markets.

The United States supplies a big export market to China, which means that China's economy has become more active due to support from the United States.

At the same time, the United States also depends upon China. Because the "excess consumption" of the United States means "under saving," the United States has an investment shortage. Necessary investment (which could not be acquired in a domestic economy because of "excess consumption") has to be provided by the "excess-saving" country. As clearly shown in Table 10 and Figure 3, the savings rate in China is extremely high; as Tables 20 and 22 and Figure 9 indicate, the consumption rate in China is considerably low. Therefore, we recognize that excess savings in China provide investment for the United States. The reason is not the "altruism" of China, but the "exorbitant privilege" of the United States. In other words, China can depend on the strength of the United States economy.[21]

[21] As mentioned earlier, it is not only due to the strength of the United States economy but also the practical use of the "position" of the largest creditor nation.

The "codependency relations" between the United States and China have formed based on the United States' excess consumption and China's under consumption. The "symmetry of Sino-American relations" mentioned in this chapter is be vividly represented.

In summary, the "symmetry" as shown in Figures 8 and 9 means that, because the "consumption–GDP ratio" represented as around 0.6 implies "under consumption" in China (domestic demand shortage), it is compensated by foreign demand (export). Thus, in order to encourage foreign demand, China has a policy of distorting market mechanisms, which is nothing other than trade linkage index of China to the United States indicating by a value of 1.3 and 1.4. The contrary is true for the United States. The trade linkage index of the US to China indicating values of approximately 0.7 and 0.8, suggests the presence of policies distorting the potential comparative advantage structure of the US, and the "consumption-GDP ratio" of the US indicated as approximately 1.2 could be contributed by "exorbitant privilege," which could make trade linkage index of China to the US possible. Such a structure explains the symmetry of Sino-American relations.

Therefore, as the values represented by 1.2 and 1.4 approach 1.0, and the values represented by 0.6 and 0.8 approach 1.0, the symmetry would dissolve. It thus means that the "codependency relationship" between the United States and China would be eliminated.

Then, what is necessary to eliminate the "codependency relationship?"

The symmetry in the trade linkage index can be easily recognized. If the economic mechanism of a comparative advantage structure (by adjusting the exchange rate of the Chinese renminbi to the US dollar) could function well, the numerical values of China at 1.4 and of the United States at 0.8 could be well adjusted toward 1.0.

The case of symmetry in consumption–GDP ratio is not so easy. What is an efficient measure to move the "consumption–GDP ratio" of the United States (1.2) and the "consumption–GDP ratio" of China (0.6 and 0.7) toward 1.0? One needs to eliminate the United States' "excess consumption" and China's "underconsumption" (the expression of "not be so easy" mentioned above means that resolving China's "under consumption" does not immediately lead to resolving the US's "excess consumption"). Whether or not Chinese "underconsumption" can be eliminated, the United States' "excess consumption" (or "under saving") might still exist.

The reverse is also true.

If underconsumption (domestic demand shortage) in China can be eliminated, the Chinese growth strategy led by foreign demand could be revised. If so, the "trade distortion" indicated by the "trade linkage index" could be revised, and the United States' exports and imports with China could be revised. (However, this change cannot be related to the elimination of the "exorbitant privilege" of the United States). It just means that trade with China can be revised.

We now focus on Chinese "underconsumption."[22] Regarding 2015, it is none other than how to increase China's domestic demand by 2,172.8 billion US dollars. What variables are appropriate to interpret under consumption or excess saving, in other words, the high savings rate?

7. Disparity, Savings Rate, and Exchange Rate Intervention

With regard to variables concerning a high savings rate in China, according to Kaldor (1955–1956), a big disparity means big savings, and big savings lead to capital accumulation because rich people have a lower rate of consumption.[23]

In other words, the significant disparity in China is directly linked to the high savings rate (domestic demand shortage). Because of eliminating the disparity, the consumption–GDP ratio in China which equals 0.6 or 0.7 could move toward 1.0 (at least, such a move toward 1.0 would exist).

Suppose we measure the disparity using the Gini coefficient, we could obtain Table 23 and Figure 10, which are table and figure of the United States, China and Japan. The Gini coefficient of China is shown as 0.47 and 0.49, that coefficient of the United States as 0.35 and 0.39, and of Japan as 0.31and 0.33.

Certainly, there is not a definitive way to interpret the Gini coefficient. However, a value exceeding 0.4, as seen in China, clearly indicates

---

[22] Concerning the "excess consumption" of the United States, more analysis is necessary.

[23] See Cingano (2014). However, it is necessary to pay attention to the definition of "disparity." At any rate, in this chapter, we attribute to "disparity" the general meaning. Moreover, the correlation between the Gini coefficient and the consumption–GDP ratio in China is significant (5 percent significance level). Kaldor's assertion should be recognized as related to growth theory. See, for example, Fukuoka (1986).

Table 23. The Gini coefficient in each country (2003–2014).

	China	USA	Japan
2003	0.479	0.365	0.314
2004	0.473	0.352	0.314
2005	0.485	0.373	0.314
2006	0.487	0.376	0.323
2007	0.484	0.367	0.323
2008	0.491	0.370	0.323
2009	0.490	0.374	0.332
2010	0.481	0.375	0.332
2011	0.477	0.387	0.332
2012	0.474	0.385	0.320
2013	0.473	0.392	0.320
2014	NA	0.389	0.320

Source: OECD (Data: Global Note), China Statistical Yearbook.

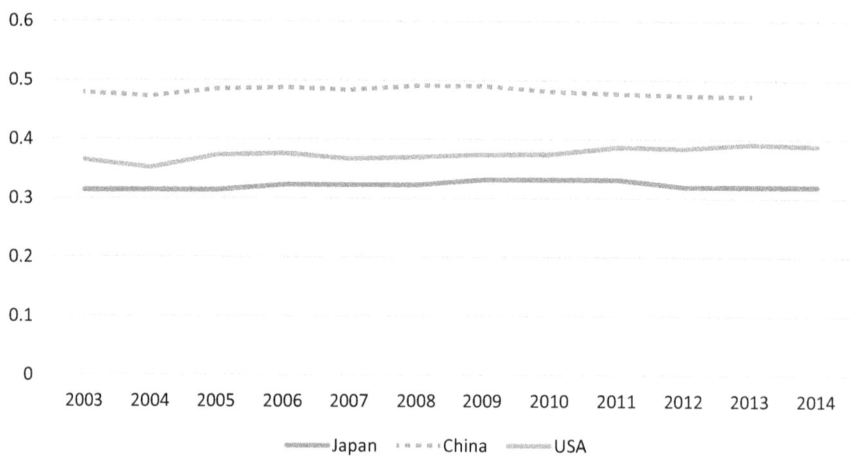

Figure 10. The Gini coefficient in each country (2003–2014).

Source: OECD (Data: Global Note), China Statistical Yearbook.

significant disparity. This big disparity leads to a lower consumption ratio and a higher savings ratio.

If China can improve its Gini coefficient to values similar to those of the United States, ranging 0.35 and 0.39, or Japan, ranging 0.31 and 0.33, it would be possible to reduce the saving ratio and increase the consumption ratio.

We confirm the situation statistically based on Table 23 (China's Gini coefficient) and Table 22 (China's consumption–GDP ratio). Suppose the numerical value of China's Gini coefficient is the same as the numerical value of the United States' Gini coefficient in the year 2013, then what is supposed to be the numerical value of the consumption–GDP ratio for China? It would be 0.9408.[24] Although it would be smaller than the actual numerical value of the consumption–GDP ratio of the United States in the year 2013 (1.194), it would be a much bigger numerical value than the actual consumption–GDP ratio of China (0.646). This implies that consumption in China could increase. Once again, suppose Gini coefficient of China is similar to that of the United States, the consumption–GDP ratio would be 0.9408, which would mean that the private consumption of China is 11.8 percent that of the world total. Thus, the private consumption of China could be 5,167.5 billion US dollars. Because the actual private consumption of China is 3,546.9 billion US dollars, the additional private consumption of China would be 1,620.5 billion US dollars, which corresponds to around 16.8 percent of the Chinese GDP. We could recognize the impact of reducing disparity on private consumption.

We also confirm the situation statistically based on Table 19 (Chinese labor distribution ratio) and 22 (Chinese consumption–GDP ratio). Suppose the numerical value of the labor distribution ratio in China is the same as the numerical value of the labor distribution ratio in the United States in the year 2014 (which is 66.5), then the consumption–GDP ratio

---

[24]The reason why we use the consumption–GDP ratio is to reach directly consumption expenditure. Above values in the text are the results by single regression analysis of "FORECAST" function of EXCEL. Although the number of data is small, correlation coefficients between the Gini coefficient in China and consumption–GDP ratio in China is minus 0.9828 which could become significant (5 percent significance level). Also if we use the same function of EXCEL for single regression analysis, the consumption-GDP ratio in China reaches 1.0 when the Gini coefficient is 0.3756.

in China would be 0.8995.[25] That ratio is less than the actual ratio of consumption–GDP in the United States (1.194); however, compared with the actual ratio in China (0.646), that ratio is undoubtedly bigger. This means that private consumption in China would increase. Once again, suppose that the labor distribution ratio of China is the same as that of the United States, then the consumption–GDP ratio of China would be 0.8995. This means that the ratio of Chinese private consumption is 11.3 percent that of the world total, and the private consumption in China equals 4,948.5 billion US dollars, which is 1,401.59 billion US dollars more than actual private consumption of 3,546.98 billion US dollars. That additional private consumption in China corresponds to a ratio of 14.5 percent to the Chinese GDP. We could recognize the improvement of labor distribution ratio on private consumption.

As shown in Table 22 and Figure 9, the consumption–GAP ratio in China is 0.6 to 0.7; how can the numerical value of that ratio move toward 1.0? Suppose the Gini coefficient of China is around the same numerical value as that of the United States, the consumption–GDP ratio of China could increase to 0.9408. Also, suppose the labor distribution ratio of China is the same as that of the United States, the consumption–GDP ratio of China could increase to 0.8995. In short, the numerical value of the consumption–GDP ratio in China could move toward 1.0.[26]

It is obvious that, if the disparity in China could be mitigated, Chinese consumption could increase after which the consumption–GDP ratio could move toward 1.0. Because of the increase of domestic demand, the dependability on foreign demand (export) would reduce. However, it would not be directly related with the consumption–GDP ratio of the United States (which is 1.2). The movement of the United States' ratio (1.2) toward

[25]As the same as in footnote 24, the reason why we use the consumption–GDP ratio is to reach directly consumption expenditure. Also the values in the text are the results by single regression analysis of "FORECAST" function of EXCEL. Moreover, as the same as in footnote 24, though number of data is small, correlation coefficients between labor distribution ratio in China and consumption–GDP ratio in China is 0.9586, which could become significant (5 percent significance level).

[26]Both a decrease in the Gini coefficient and an increase in the labor distribution ratio are closely correlated and cannot be independent. In this chapter, as mentioned in the text, it is enough to confirm the increase of the consumption–GDP ratio and the expansion of private consumption (according to the estimation in the text, a part of the increase of consumption could amount to between 14.5 percent and 16.8 percent).

1.0 is another matter altogether because the excess consumption of the United States depends on the behavior of the US's citizens themselves. As long as the "exorbitant privilege" of the United States persists, it would be difficult for the people of the United States to reduce their consumption. As mentioned before, suppose the value of the consumption–GDP ratio is 1.0, then the US consumption decreases to become 1,899.9 billion US dollars less). The "exorbitant privilege" of the United States cannot persist forever, and before long, it would cease to exist.

In this chapter, in order for China to increase private consumption and eliminate domestic demand shortage, it is important to mitigate the disparity. Thus, we have examined the importance of reducing disparity as a means to increase China's consumption and address the shortfall in domestic demand, and considered the extent to which such a reduction might have an impact. This could be one of the moves to eliminate the "codependency relations" between the United States and China.[27]

In order to eliminate the disparity and expand domestic demand, we need to recognize that they are related to the exchange rate of the renminbi. There exist significant correlations between the exchange rate of the renminbi and the Gini coefficient. The correlation between the appreciation of the renminbi by the Chinese government and the decline of the Gini coefficient in China is significant. We recognize that the correlation between the Gini coefficient in China and the savings ratio in China is also significant. It goes without saying that the correlation between the reduction of disparity in China and the expansion of private consumption in China (elimination of domestic demand shortage) is significant.

In other words, the correlation between the appreciation of the renminbi (which could be reviewed the policy of artificially undervaluing the Chinese renminbi) and the elimination of the domestic demand shortage could be significant. Therefore, we recognize that the correlation between underconsumption in China and the artificial underestimation policy of the exchange rate in China (both of which are crucial factors of the "codependency relations" of the United States and China) is significant.

An important problem ("codependency relations" between the United States and China) could be resolved by eliminating underconsumption in China. This is because, as mentioned repeatedly, "codependency

[27]Regarding a question about whether there might be any relationship between the "codependency relations" (between the United States and China) and the "exorbitant privilege" of the United States, it needs to be investigated further.

relations" are due to excess consumption in the United States and under-consumption in China. Revising the undervaluation of the renminbi against the US dollar is considered an effective measure towards its resolution.[28]

8. Summary of This Chapter

The purpose of this chapter was to analyze the "codependency relations" between the United States and China, focusing on their economic aspects.

The "codependency relations" between the United States and China were caused by the excess consumption in the United States and the excess savings in China. The excess consumption in the United States resulted in a trade deficit and the excess savings in China resulted in a trade surplus. These two situations are theoretically separate ones but, because they involve two major countries, the situations led to "codependency."

At the same time, we should indicate that in the United States there exists an "exorbitant privilege" which could support the excess consumption and that in China there exists an underestimation of the exchange rate of the renminbi which could lead to excess savings. In other words, these situations established the contemporary "codependency relationship" between the United States and China, which is different from the relationship of any two other countries.

In this chapter, we concentrated our attention on China and try to analyze the Gini coefficient and labor distribution ratio in China by taking the disparity as a crucial factor as suggested by Kaldor (1055–1956).

That is to say, suppose the Gini coefficient in China is the same as that in the United States, the consumption–GDP ratio in China would be higher. Improving disparity leads to an increase in consumption and works to reduce excess savings.

Also, suppose the labor distribution ratio in China is the same as that in the United States, the consumption–GDP ratio in China would be

[28]As stated by Ferguson and Schularick (2009), an underestimation of the exchange rate could increase corporate profit, which could generate excess savings. However, it is difficult to statistically verify this because in order to protect a deflationary effect that occurs by gradually revising the underestimation of the exchange rate, money supply could be increased and the total amount of profit could expand, due to which the savings ratio would become rather higher.

higher. That is to say, an increase in the labor distribution ratio could increase the consumption and reduce the excess savings.

If the disparity in China could be improved (expressed as a revision of the numerical value in the Gini coefficient and labor distribution ratio), underconsumption in China (domestic demand shortage) could improve. Therefore, we recognize that the "codependency relationship" between the United States and China could be revised. Reiterating from the perspective of this chapter, one of the policies with a significant correlation to this is likely the revision of the undervaluation of the renminbi exchange rate.[29]

[29]We would add a note just to be sure that such adjustments through renminbi exchange rate are not based upon the logic of "elasticity approach," which is a kind of partial equilibrium analysis. (With regard to the assertion insisting that "elasticity approach" is a kind of partial equilibrium analysis, see for example Komiya (1994)). If such policies were effective, would the "codependency relations" between the United States and China change? And if it did change, what impact would it have on the world economy? We would investigate such crucial issues in another opportunity.

Chapter 3

A Political Economy of the Codependency Relationship between the USA and China: Current Situation and Prospects

1. Introduction

In the previous chapter, we investigated the relationship between the United States and China, which is called a "codependency relationship."[1]

In this chapter, we consider the relationship between the United States and China focusing on the "exorbitant privilege" of the United States and the "tendency toward market economy" of China.

Nevertheless, when we consider such an extensive topic as Sino-American relations, it is necessary to focus on specific sub-topics. In this chapter, we focus on the "symmetry of the relations between the United States and China" (as mentioned in Section 6 in the previous chapter). A simple summary of Section 6 of Chapter 2 is provided in the following.

The "symmetry" of the relations between the United States and China indicates that the consumption–GDP ratio of 0.6 means underconsumption (domestic demand shortage) in China, which should be compensated by foreign demand (export). In order to increase foreign demand (export), a distorted policy of market mechanism is necessary in China (the Chinese trade linkage index with the United States has the numerical value of

[1] See Roach (2014).

1.3 to 1.4). The opposite position is occupied by the United States. The United States' trade linkage index with China has the numerical value of 0.7 to 0.8, which shows that there exists a distorted policy in the United States due to potential comparative advantage. Also, the consumption–GDP ratio of the United States (which is indicated as the numerical value 1.2) largely depends on the exorbitant privilege of the United States, which would make the structure that enables the high level of Chinese trade linkage index with the US (significant value of 1.3 to 1.4).

The above-mentioned assertion has been noted in the previous chapter.

In a reverse calculation, therefore, if the numerical value indicated as 1.4 to 1.2 could approach 1.0 and if the numerical value of 0.6 to 0.8 could also approach 1.0, then that tendency means that the above-mentioned symmetry could be eliminated. It would also indicate that the codependency relationship between the United States and China could be resolved.

Symmetry expressed both in the "trade linkage index" and the "consumption–GDP ratio" indicates the following: First phenomenon is caused by distortion in trade policy and international monetary policy, as represented by the distortion of exchange rate of Chinese renminbi to US dollar. Second phenomenon is caused by distortion in the economic structure, as shown by the excess consumption in the US and underconsumption in China.

Based on the above-mentioned problem, this chapter will be conducted as follows: In the second section, we present the "symmetry" and the "transposition of symmetry." In the third section, we consider the "exorbitant privilege" of the United States. In the fourth section, we investigate the issue with a focus on a "multipolar" world. In the fifth section, we consider the relations between the United States and China. In the sixth section, the "twin deficits" in the United States are investigated. In the seventh section, we examine the excess savings and disparity in China. And in the last section, we conclude this chapter. Thus, the sixth section focuses on China, while the others focus on the United States.

2. The Transposition of Symmetry

Symmetry means a phenomenon in which "if A and B exchange places with each other, nothing changes."

The symmetry in the trade linkage index and the consumption–GDP ratio are indicated in Tables 21 and 22 and shown in Figures 8 and 9, respectively, in Chapter 2. In both Figures 8 and 9, there is a boundary at 1.0, around which the numerical values of 1.4–0.8 (Figure 8) and 1.2–0.6 (Figure 9) are presented. In Figure 8, the upper part is occupied by China and the lower part by the United States. In Figure 9, the upper part is occupied by the United States and the lower part by China. They two figures show clear symmetry.

To observe the phenomenon of the "transposition of symmetry" as presented in Tables 21 and 22 and Figures 8 and 9, if the position of the United States and China are exchanges, the values indicated in the tables and figures would remain unchanged.

That is to say, it is a phenomenon where Tables 1 and 2 could become Tables 3 and 4, or Figures 1 and 2 could become Figures 3 and 4. What kind of phenomenon could be occurred?

How does the phenomenon of "transposition of symmetry" occur? And what does it mean to say something is "possible" or "impossible"? In this section, we perform an analysis.

First, we consider the "trade linkage index." We investigate whether or not the exchange rate, which is separate from the comparative advantage (needless to say, through government intervention in the middle to

Table 1. Trade linkage index between China and the United States (2010–2015).

Item \ Year	2010	2011	2012	2013	2014	2015
US trade linkage index with China	1.407	1.377	1.349	1.352	1.325	1.317
Chinese trade linkage index with US	0.773	0.724	0.707	0.721	0.715	0.795

Source: JETRO International Trade and Investment Report (Annual Edition) and author's calculation.

Table 2. Consumption–GDP ratio in China and the United States (2010–2015).

Countries \ Year	2010	2011	2012	2013	2014	2015
China	1.186	1.209	1.200	1.194	1.195	1.183
USA	0.618	0.637	0.644	0.646	0.657	0.661

Source: United Nations (Data: Global Note) and author's calculation.

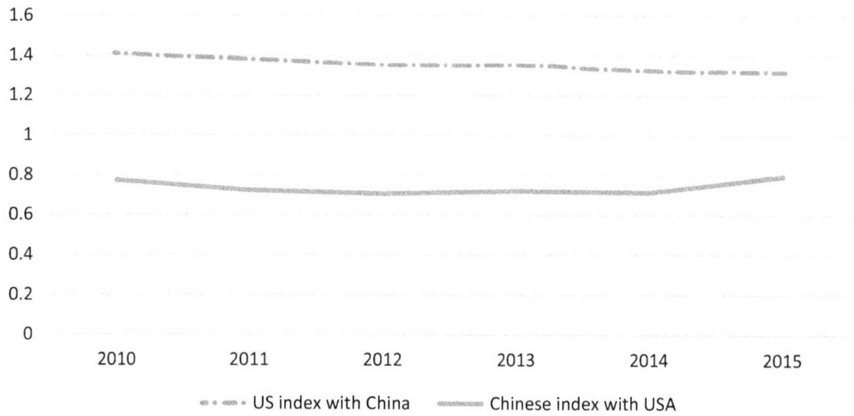

Figure 1. Trade linkage index between the United States and China (2010–2015).
Source: JETRO International Trade and Investment Report (Annual Edition) and author's calculation.

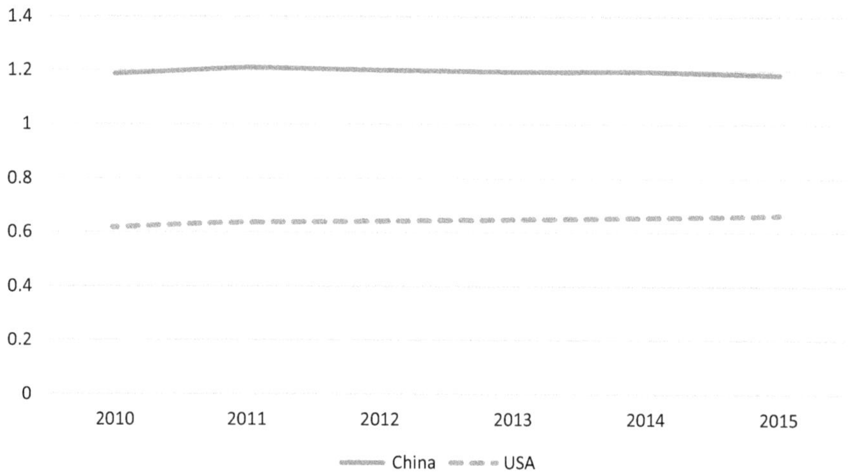

Figure 2. Consumption–GDP ratio of the United States and China (2010–2015).
Source: United Nations (Data: Global Note) and author's calculation.

long term) can be employed. The occurrence of a "transposition of symmetry" signifies that the exchange rate of US dollar to renminbi is undervalued while the exchange rate of renminbi to US dollar is overvalued, resulting in a situation of US dollar depreciation and renminbi appreciation. Such a phenomenon would not occur via market mechanisms.

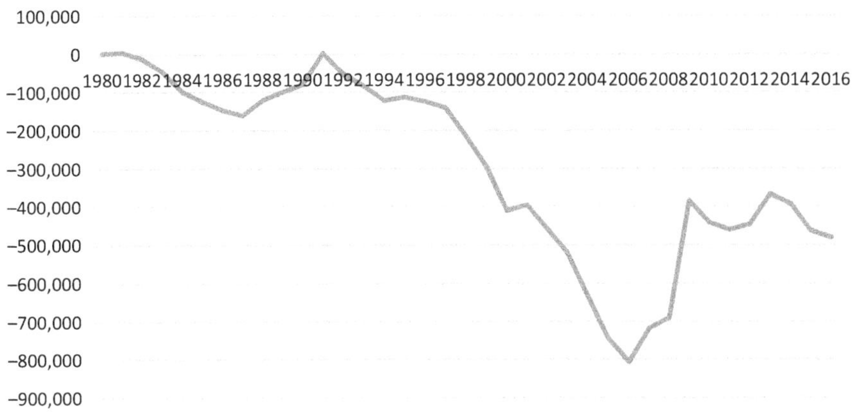

Figure 3. Current balance of the United States (1980–2016) (million US dollar).
Source: World Bank (Data: CEIC).

However, it is not entirely impossible for a situation to politically trigger a depreciation of the US dollar. The Plaza Accord situation is one example.[2] The Plaza Accord was a joint agreement signed by the G5 Finance Ministers and Central Bank Governors on 22 September 1985 to stabilize the exchange rates (in other words, to correct the US strong dollar). With regard to the Japanese yen, within 24 hours, on 23 September 1985, the rate one US dollar appreciated from 235 yen to 215 yen at an appreciation ratio of around 8 percent to 9 percent. Such a rapid (and politically artificial) adjustment of exchange rates increased the financial "bubble," which caused a lot of long-term pain in Japan.[3] Such adjustments to exchange rates, which are detached from market mechanisms, can be attributed to political factors. This was a case of "transposition of symmetry." Also, such political actions can be realized with the strong economic and military power of the United States.

However, we did not find any evidence that the "Plaza Accord" had contributed to the surplus of the current account of the United States (Figure 3).[4] The theoretical basis is, of course, the "absorption approach." In short, it is nothing but the argument asserting that disequilibrium of

[2]For the details of the Plaza Accord, see, for example, Morita (2017b).

[3]As regards the bubble in Japan, see Morita (2017b).

[4]In the following, we use the terms "trade balance" and "current balance" by and large without distinction.

trade balance equals to a difference between the amount of saving and the amount of investment in the economy concerned as a whole.[5]

Therefore, as regards the relationship between the exchange rate and trade balance, we would not insist upon the "elasticity approach." The logic of our assertion is as follows. The underestimation of the renminbi rate causes "excess savings," which leads to a trade surplus. The correction of underestimation of the renminbi rate leads to a revision of "excess savings," leading to a trade deficit in China. Furthermore, it should be added that the mechanism by which a trade surplus causes a capital deficit is not observed in the Chinese economy. As a matter of fact, there exists in China a situation where both trade balance and capital balance have been in surplus for many years (Table 3).

In that sense, it goes without saying that a model analyzing the market within the general equilibrium framework, taking into account both the trade balance and capital balance, does not fit well with the Chinese economy.

As regards the exchange rate of the renminbi, as Shibata and Hasegawa (2012) appropriately state, The so-called "internationalization of the renminbi" actually began quite recently and the "first stage" was the use of trade settlement currency. The use of the renminbi was in 2008 and 2010 (p. 202).[6] However, it should be noted that the Chinese renminbi still does not meet the conditions of an international currency. The exchange rate regime is a managed floating rate system with significant involvement from the monetary authority (People's Bank of China), and there are daily fluctuation limits in place (pp. 187–188).

The situation that Shibata and Hasegawa (2012) describe can be statistically confirmed.

Concerning the variation coefficient of the exchange rate of the currencies (in the countries concerned) to US dollar, involving China, Japan, South Korea, Australia, Canada, Germany, Denmark, Finland, Sweden, Poland, Hungary, and Czech,[7] we divide the stages into two periods:

---

[5]With regard to the "absorption approach," see Morita (2017b).

[6]According to Shibata and Hasegawa (2012), the "second stage" was 2010 to 2011, which was the stage of development of Hong Kong's offshore renminbi market, and the "third stage" was in 2012, which was the stage of the "beginning of full-scale cooperation with major industrial nations" (Chapter 5).

[7]The aforementioned eleven countries (except China) mainly consists of countries in the Euroarea and non-Euroarea in Europe, as well as Australia and Canada, and Japan and

Table 3. Balance of payment in China (2005–2015) (million US dollars).

Year	Current balance	Capital balance
2005	160,818	62,964
2006	249,866	10,037
2007	371,833	73,509
2008	426,107	189,649
2009	29,714	144,828
2010	305,374	226,045
2011	201,714	221,056
2012	193,139	▲16,816
2013	182,807	326,203
2014	277,434	▲169,174
2015	330,602	▲142,359

Source: Jetro, *China Data File*, each year.

(1) from 1995 to 2005 (Table 4 and Figure 5) and (2) from 1995 to 2015 (Table 5 and Figure 6). Period (1) involves the statistics of the period before the internationalization of the renminbi and period (2) indicates the statistics of the period after the internationalization of the renminbi.

As clearly recognized in the tables and figures, in period (1), the variation coefficient of the exchange rate of the renminbi was obviously much smaller than other currencies. On the other hand, in period (2), although the variation coefficient of the renminbi was rather small, the coefficient was not that much smaller than other currencies. We verified whether or not the variation coefficient of the renminbi was "abnormally smaller" compared with the coefficient of other currencies using the Grubbs–Smirnov test. In the period from 1995 to 2005, the result of that test was 2.3189, and in the period from 1995 to 2015, the result was 1.1589. In other words, in the period from 1995 to 2005, the variation coefficient of the renminbi was significantly "abnormal" (5 percent significance level); however, in the period from 1995 to 2015, the variation coefficient of the renminbi was not significantly "abnormal." It could be indicated that

South Korea from Asia, and are generally considered countries where the market mechanism is functioning in the foreign exchange market.

Table 4. The variation coefficient of the exchange rate of national currencies (1995–2005).

Country	Variation coefficient
China	0.004475
Japan	0.089000
South Korea	0.179346
Australia	0.147467
Canada	0.075900
Germany	0.144629
Denmark	0.140112
Finland	0.144473
Sweden	0.138717
Poland	0.170531
Hungary	0.232489
Czech	0.160433

Source: United Nations, IMF (Data: Global Note) and author's calculation.

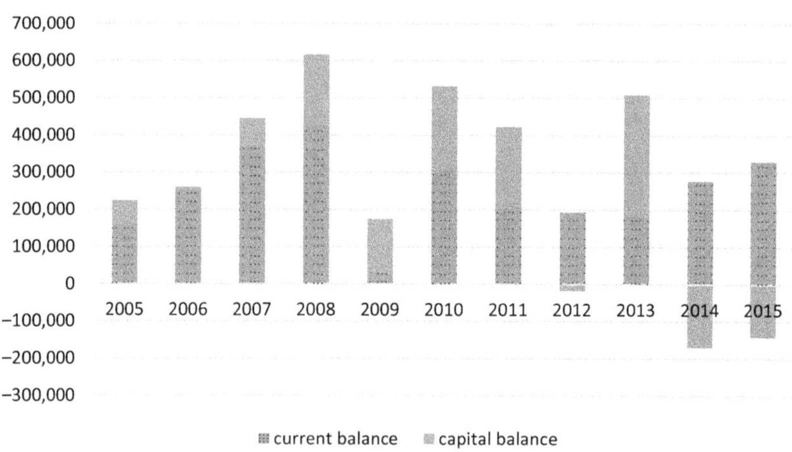

Figure 4. Balance of payment in China (2005–2015).

Source: Jetro, *China Data File*, each year.

Table 5. The variation coefficient of the exchange rate of national currencies (1995–2015).

Country	Variation coefficient
China	0.117869
Japan	0.133809
South Korea	0.141138
Australia	0.198566
Canada	0.155295
Germany	0.147577
Denmark	0.149179
Finland	0.150822
Sweden	0.139011
Poland	0.164754
Hungary	0.189117
Czech	0.261533

Source: United Nations, IMF (Data: Global Note) and author's calculation.

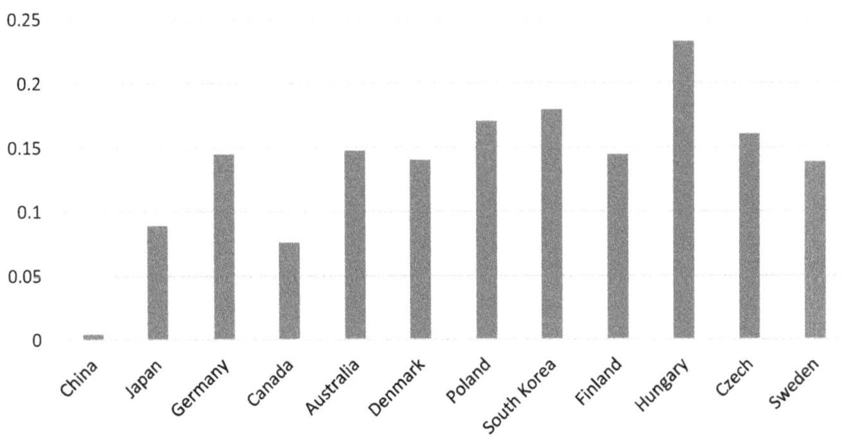

Figure 5. The variation coefficient of the exchange rate of national currencies (1995–2005).

Source: United Nations, IMF (Data: Global Note) and author's calculation.

in the period before internationalization, the renminbi rate could not fluctuate normally; however, in the period after internationalization, the renminbi rate could fluctuate without significant abnormality.

Therefore, with the gradual development in the internationalization of the renminbi, in other words, in accordance with the weakening intervention of the currency authority in China, the Chinese renminbi exchange rate to the US dollar could fluctuate as a reflection of the market mechanism. Needless to say, that change would appear as a tendency toward revising the "distorted" structure of exports and imports as judged from a "comparative advantage."

Another tendency relates to the capital balance in China.[8] As is clearly indicated in Table 3 and Figure 4, the international balance of payment in China has changed from "twin surplus" presented with the current balance and capital balance.

Still, it might be difficult to mention about the situation in which current account surplus and capital account deficit could be coexisted, however, in 2014 and 2015, the tendency toward such a normal condition could be observed. In other words, the tendency was toward more internationalization of the renminbi in China.[9]

In other words, such tendency might be judged as the revised movement from the "distorted" structure in export and import (which means that the distortion is estimated from the comparative advantage structure).

The characteristics of the "codependency relationship" between the United States and China are as follows: (1) the "distortion" in divergence from the comparative advantage structure shown as "non-marketability" of the renminbi exchange rate and (2) the "distortion" in the economic structure shown as "excess consumption" of the United States and as "underconsumption" of China. Thus, because of the movement toward "internationalization of the renminbi," the distortion mentioned in characteristic (1) might be gradually eliminated.

Needless to say, in order for the "transposition of symmetry" to be realized, the above-mentioned assertion might not be sufficient. For the

[8]In terms of the balance of payment in China, the "capital balance" consists of "capital account," "financial account" and "other investments." Concerning the balance of payment in China, see, for example, Jingu (2015).

[9]In Jingu (2015), it is mentioned that the direction of establishing "renminbi economic area" where trade and capital transactions are conducted in Chinese renminbi has become clearer (p. 15).

"transposition of symmetry," it might be necessary not only to eliminate the distortion of "underestimation" of the renminbi exchange rate but also to eliminate the distortion of the US dollar exchange rate. Moreover, it would not be a temporary phenomenon but an "underestimation" resulting from long-term government intervention.

However, it is undoubtedly unrealistic. It might be impossible for the United States, which is a democratic and market economy country, to continue to implement the same policy elsewhere as it implements for China, which is a one-party regime country.

Our judgment concerning characteristic (1) can be recognized. We observe the tendency in which the "distorted" export and import structure could be revised. Because of this tendency, the numerical value of the trade linkage index can be judged to move toward 1.0.

However, as mentioned earlier, it would be unlikely that the situation (referred to as the transposition of symmetry) envisaged in Table 1 and Figure 1, and Table 2 and Figure 2, could occur.

How do we consider the distortion mentioned in characteristic (2)?

The "excess consumption" in the United States is closely related to its "exorbitant privilege," and the "underconsumption" in China is closely related to the significant disparity in China.

As investigated earlier, it is quite obvious that the big "disparity" in China is closely related to the "non-marketability" of the renminbi exchange rate. Thus, if the "non-marketability" of the renminbi exchange rate is revised, the big disparity would also be revised, and at the same time, we would observe a tendency toward eliminating the "underconsumption" in China. However, with regard to the "excess consumption" in the United States, the situation is completely different. How does the "exorbitant privilege" of the United States continue to exist? If the "exorbitant privilege" of the United States could continue to exist,[10] the "transposition of symmetry" would never have appeared.

We will consider it in the next section.

---

[10]Although it is impossible for the "exorbitant privilege" of the United States to continue to exist in eternity, it is also difficult to estimate when the "exorbitant privilege" would cease to exist. Therefore, in this chapter, we try to investigate the issues with a time horizon of around 10 years as indicated later.

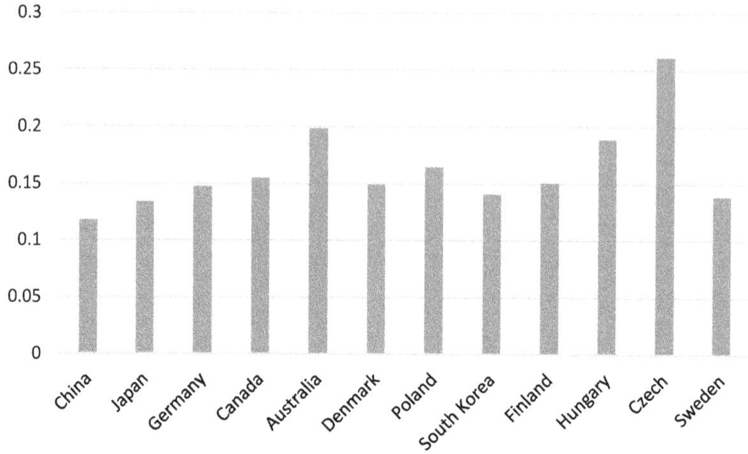

Figure 6. The variation coefficient of the exchange rate of national currencies (1995–2015).

Source: United Nations, IMF (Data: Global Note) and author's calculation.

3. The "Exorbitant Privilege" of the United States

In this section, we look back at the history of the economy of the United States after the Second World War, usually called "Pax Americana" and the history of the key currency of the US dollar.[11]

Needless to say, in the world economy after the Second World War, the United States occupied the highest ratio. For example, in the year 1950, the United States' GDP to the world total was 34.2 percent, while Japan's ratio was 2.8 percent and West Germany's ratio was 5.2 percent.[12] In 1950, the per capita GDP was 2,210 US dollars in the United States, 200 US dollars in Japan, and 640 US dollars in West Germany. Therefore, the United States' economy was 11 times larger than Japan's and 3.5 times larger than West Germany's. The United States' ratio of the export amount to the world total in 1950 was 20.5 percent, which was much more than

[11] With regard to information on the history of the United States' economy after World War II, usually called "Pax Americana," and the history of the key currency of the US dollar, the author is indebted to Spero (1985) and Marumo (2002).

[12] We take up the cases of Japan and West Germany because of the rapid growth of their countries after the Second World War.

Table 6. The ratio to the world economy to each country (1950–1999).

Item	Country	1950	1970	1980	1989	1995	1999
The ratio of GDP to the world total (in percent)	USA	34.2	26.5	25.0	24.8	25.6	30.3
	Japan	2.8	7.3	9.8	13.5	17.9	14.4
	Germany*	5.2	6.9	5.9	5.7	8.6	7.0
Per capita GDP (US dollars)	USA	2,210	4,840	11,540	20,850	26,750	33,840
	Japan	200	1,960	9,400	23,030	41,080	35,660
	Germany*	640	3,070	11,420	19,480	30,170	25,740
The ratio of export amount to the world total (in percent)	USA	20.5	15.2	11.8	12.5	11.5	12.2
	Japan	1.7	6.8	7.0	9.4	8.8	7.4
	Germany*	5.4	12.1	10.3	11.7	9.9	9.6
Exchange rate (to one US dollar)	Japanese yen	361	358	227	138	94	114
	German mark	4.20	3.65	1.82	1.88	1.43	1.84

Note: *Until 1989, West Germany.
Source: Marumo (2002, p. 5) (Data: IMF).

that of Japan (1.7 percent) and West Germany (5.4 percent). In 1970, the United States' GDP to the world total GDP was 26.5 percent, Japan's was 7.3 percent, and West Germany's was 6.9 percent. The United States' per capita GDP in 1970 was 4,480 US dollars, Japan's was 1,960 US dollars, and West Germany's was 3,070 US dollars. Thus, the United States' economy was more than 2.3 times larger than Japan's and more than 1.5 times larger than West Germany's. The United States's export amount to the world total was 15.2 percent, which was more than Japan's (6.8 percent) and West Germany's (12.1 percent) (see Table 6).

The rapid increase in GDP and the export amount for Japan and West Germany was not because of a stagnation of the economy of the United States but because of the rapid restoration of Japan and West Germany. The decade of the 1960s was called the "Golden 1960s" in the United States as the real economic growth rate reached 4.6 percent on average annually and labor productivity also continued to move upward.[13]

However, from the viewpoints of the key currency system, that period was not so smooth for the United States. The United States lost its

[13] Marumo (2002, p. 5).

overwhelming superiority as the reconstruction of European countries and Japan progressed.

The function of the key currency of the US dollar exists based on the overwhelming superiority of the United States (as shown in the 1950s). This started with the "Bretton Woods agreement."

After the Second World War, many European countries and Japan were seriously damaged; in contrast, the United States suffered no direct war damage.[14] Therefore, the undamaged superpower could support the reconstruction of advanced countries damaged by the war. This also seemed meaningful for the economic expansion of the United States itself as well as the whole world. In "1946 the total European balance-of-payments deficit with the rest of the world amounted to 5.8 billion US dollars; by 1947 it had risen to 7.6 billion US dollars."[15] In contrast, by "1948 Western Europe had only 6.7 billion US dollars of reserves to pay for these huge deficits, whereas the United States was running huge balance-of-trade surplus: 6.7 billion US dollars in 1946 and 10.1 billion US dollars in 1947."[16] At this time, dollars "flowed out through various American aid programs."[17] Through such programs as the Marshall Plan, from "1948 to 1952 the United States gave 16 Western European countries 17 billion US dollars in outright grants."[18]

As Spero (1985) indicated, such recovery aids provided by the United States to Europe and Japan came from the "American commitment to meet Soviet threats with Western political and military force."[19] Therefore, "with the vast international payments imbalances, the monetary consequences were viewed as beneficial. Thus the dollar became the world's currency, and the United States became the world's central banker, issuing dollars for the international monetary system."[20]

---

[14] *Ibid.*, p. 3.

[15] Spero (1985, p. 40).

[16] *Ibid.*

[17] *Ibid.*, p. 42.

[18] *Ibid.* The "receiver" countries of the Marshall Plan which were members of the OEEC (Organization for European Economic Cooperation): Austria, Belgium, Denmark, France, Greece, Iceland, Ireland, Italy, Luxemburg, Netherlands, Norway, Portugal, Sweden, Switzerland, United Kingdom, UK, and French-occupied Germany and US-occupied Germany.

[19] Spero (1985, p. 42).

[20] *Ibid.*, p. 43.

However, although Europe and Japan recovered and expanded, by 1960, the American-managed system was in trouble.[21] American gold holdings had been reduced in value "from 24.4 billion US dollars at the end of 1948 to 19.5 billion US dollars at the end of 1959." Also, "dollars held abroad had risen from 7.3 billion US dollars in 1948 to 19.4 billion US dollars at the end of 1959." "In 1960, for the first time, foreign dollar holdings exceeded US gold holdings."[22] It was slowly realized from November 1960 onward that the system of American management was inadequate.

After several experiences, as the system of American management was considered inadequate, "increased pluralism" was sought out.[23] According to Spero (1985), with "total reserves exceeding those of the United States, with higher levels of growth and trade, and with per-capita income approaching that of the United States, Europe and Japan were narrowing the gap between themselves and the United States"[24] (see Table 6).

The problem of imbalance between dollars held abroad and American gold holdings ended with the announcement of President Nixon on 15 August 1971 that the dollar would no longer be convertible into gold.

The dollar (inconvertible into gold) went into a trade deficit in 1971. As shown in Figure 7, since 1977, the US trade deficit has reached an enormous amount.

On the contrary, Japan recorded a huge amount of trade surplus with the United States. As indicated in Table 7, the United States' trade deficit reached 30.8 billion US dollars in 1977, and the Japanese ratio of the large US trade deficit was roughly 30 percent to 40 percent.

The key phrase for understanding these trends would be "increased pluralism." When confronting the situation in the mid-1960s and 1970s, according to Spero (1985), the United States "was no longer the dominant economic power it had been for almost two decades."[25] Needless to say, European countries and Japan caught up with the United States. A similar sentiment was echoed by Eichengreen (2011), who insisted that it "is also a reminder that the fundamental factor that has rendered the United States less dominant geopolitically is the same thing that has rendered the dollar less dominant financially, namely that the world is growing more

[21] *Ibid.*

[22] *Ibid.*, p. 44.

[23] *Ibid.*, p. 52.

[24] *Ibid.*

[25] *Ibid.*

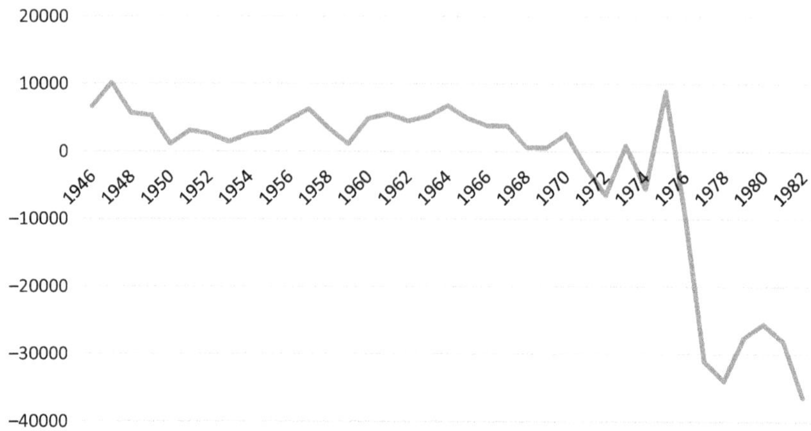

Figure 7. Trade deficit of the United States (1946–1982).

Source: Spero (1985, p. 38).

Table 7. Trade balance of the United States and Japan (1965–1981) (100 million US dollars).

Year	Trade balance of Japan	Trade balance of USA	Trade surplus of Japan with USA
1965	19	50	6
1966	23	39	8
1967	12	39	4
1968	25	0.6	12
1969	37	0.6	16
1970	40	22	15
1971	78	▲27	34
1972	90	▲64	40
1973	37	0.4	13
1974	14	▲45	19
1975	50	90	10
1976	99	▲93	55
1977	173	▲308	87
1979	18	▲273	76
1980	21	▲253	98
1981	200	▲397	163

Source: Komiya (1983, p. 10).

multipolar."[26] Eichengreen might have been referring to "the rise of China."

From the viewpoints of historical context, there was no fact that the United States, facing the "increased pluralism," ceded its position as the key currency country to other countries. In a military sense, the Soviet Union was dissolved, and in an economic sense, Japan (because of the Plaza Accord) plunged into the "lost decade" and "lost twenty years" (through the process of US–Japan friction and the occurrence and collapse of the bubble), which contributed to halt the "increased pluralism." Thus, the "Unipolar System" of the United States was complete. Afterward, the US dollar, which did not need to be converted to gold and had been created by running a rotary press in the United States Treasury, could be exchanged for actual objects such as automobiles and consumer electronics produced by other countries. The result of these economic activities made the United States a net debt country with huge amount of trade deficit for many years.

Therefore, the problem of to what extent the United States could maintain its "exorbitant privilege" could be seen as a problem of to what extent the "increased pluralism" could advance. In other words, it was a question of how high China would rise. Thus, it was also a question of the United States' "excess consumption" and China's "underconsumption."

The situation that Spero (1985) mentioned as "increased pluralism" occurred upon the restoration of Japan and West Germany after the destruction of the Second World War. In other words, the post-war period first "increased pluralism." This "pluralism" came to an end with the Japanese friction with the United States, the collapse of the Japanese bubble, and the disbanding of the Soviet Union.

The second "pluralism" of the post-war period took place with the "rise of China." What are the differences between the "rise of Japan" which occurred during the first "pluralism" and the "rise of China" which occurred during the second "pluralism?" (The answer to this question lies in the terms "balancing" and "bandwagoning."

What is the relationship between the "key currency country" and "pluralism?" After the first increase in pluralism, more than 40 years passed. How did the US dollar continue as a key currency for so long?

It is necessary for the key currency to be used as the currency of settlement and as the standard of value in international transactions. It is also

---

[26] Eichengreen (2011, p. 177).

necessary for the key currency to be held as foreign exchange reserves by governments of various countries. Therefore, generally, in order to become the key currency, the country concerned has to have (1) superior economic and military power,[27] (2) economic and political stability, (3) a developed financial market and no regulation on trade and capital transaction, and (4) a currency with stable monetary value. If a currency satisfies such requirements, other countries will put their confidence in it. Thus, the currency will be held as a reserve currency.

In short, the crucial reason why the US dollar will continue to exist as a key currency for many years is because other countries put their confidence in the superior economic and military power of the United States, the US financial market, the monetary and fiscal policies of the United States government, etc.

In a contemporary world in which "increased pluralism" has developed, what can we predict about the future of the key currency? as According to Rickards (2012), since "Bretton Woods in 1944, US dollar has been by far the leading reserve currency; however, it has never been the sole reserve currency" (p. 227). We should recognize the situation shown in Table 8, which illustrates the ratio of currency constitution of the world's foreign exchange reserves. Moreover, according to Rickards (2012), "in 2000 the dollar comprised 71 percent of total identified reserves. This decline in reserve status has been orderly, not precipitous, and is consistent with the expansion of trade between Europe and Asia and within Asia itself" (p. 227). However, according to Eichengreen (2011), data from the IMF "show the ratio of dollars in total identified official foreign exchange holdings as of the first quarter of 2010 as 61 percent, down only marginally from 66 percent in 2002–2003. If one goes back further, to the first half of 1990s, the dollar's ratio in total identified official holdings of foreign exchange was actually lower than recently" (p. 123). In any case, although the US dollar has never been the only reserve currency, it has become the currency with the most components. Then, what kind of future view can we have?

As Eichengreen described, "The dollar, the currency of the single largest economy with the most liquid markets, will remain first among equals."

[27] The growth of Japan and West Germany led to the first "increased pluralism" of the postwar period, but neither had "superior military power." The pluralism occurred due to the "balance-of-power" strategy utilized by the United States and European countries.

Table 8. The ratio of currency constitution of foreign exchange reserves in the whole world (2013 and 2014) (in percent).

Currency \ Year	2013	2014
US dollar	61.3	63.7
Euro	23.7	21.0
UK pound	4.2	4.1
Japanese yen	3.3	3.4
Australia dollar	2.2	2.1
Canada dollar	2.0	2.0
Chinese renminbi	0.7	1.1
New Zealand dollar	0.2	0.2
Swiss franc	0.2	0.2
Other currencies	2.1	2.1

Source: Mizuho Bank/Mizuho Market Topic "Current Situation of Currency Constitution of Foreign Exchange Reserves" (4 April 2017).

"The euro, the currency of a monetary zone whose economic size approaches that of the United States, will become more attractive, particularly on the periphery of Europe, if not now then once Europe has sorted out its problems." "China, for its part, is already encouraging select nonresidents to use its currency to invoice and settle merchandise transactions. In the not-too-distant future, perhaps in as few as 10 years, the renminbi will be an attractive unit, especially in Asia, for use by international investors and central banks" (p. 151). That is to say, multiple reserve currencies mainly imply the US dollar, euro, and renminbi. With regard to the "next runner," it could be the rupee (India) or real (Brazil). The conditions of economic size, population, and the scale of trade and investment are indispensable.

Rickards (2014) supposed that, after the collapse of the US dollar, the currency system would move toward (1) world money, the SDR (Special Drawing Rights), (2) a gold standard, and (3) social disorder (p. 292).

Nevertheless, as Eichengreen (2011) indicated, the US dollar could occupy the largest ratio (although the ratio might be declining) of world official foreign exchange reserves, which would be followed by the euro and renminbi (and then the rupee and real).[28]

As of now, it seems unrealistic to think that the "exorbitant privilege" of the United States might lead to disorder.[29]

What is the current situation of the Chinese renminbi? In *Nihon Keizai Shimbun* (17 December 2017), an article titled "internationalization of Chinese renminbi has been in deadlock" mentioned that "At its peak in 2015, around 30 percent of China's trade was settled in renminbi. However, by January to September 2017, this percentage had sharply declined to 14 percent. This decline is attributed to the Chinese authorities' intensified capital controls due to concerns over the rapid depreciation of the renminbi and capital outflows. These pressures on renminbi depreciation and capital outflows are a result of the massive issuance of money to support economic growth. As a matter of fact, there used to be a widespread belief that the value of the Chinese renminbi would continue to rise, and "market demand was an important driving force for its internationalization" (Gao Haihong, Chinese Academy of Social Sciences).

However, "that force has been lost, and the Chinese authorities are desperately trying to prevent money from fleeing the country through strengthened regulations." Moreover, "the stagnation of the renminbi's internationalization, which corresponds to China's growing national power, signifies a stumbling block in China's dream of becoming a "socialist modernized strong nation" by the mid-century." In short, as a title of that article, "the stalling of the internationalization of the Chinese renminbi." Although it is crucial to remove regulations for internationalization, the Chinese authority needs to tighten regulations. This indicates that the process of internationalization of the Chinese renminbi (as a candidate for multiple reserve currencies) will not be smooth.

4. Unipolar System and Multipolar System

The question of whether "increased pluralism" could be developed is closely related to the question in international politics of a "unipolar system" or a "multipolar system."

---

[28] See Eichengreen (2011, pp. 124–126).

[29] When we try to speculate, the transition of situation would be changeable depends upon the time horizon. Judged from the analysis subject of this chapter, that time horizon seems to be ten years at the longest.

What is a "unipolar system" and what is a "multipolar system?" According to Huntington, a "unipolar system" is a situation in which there exists one superstate and there are many other small countries. As a result, the superstate can behave unilaterally with almost no cooperation from other small countries, and the superstate can thus solve international problems efficiently. This situation existed during the Roman Empire and also in China (when China dominated the East Asian region).[30]

On the contrary, in a multipolar system, there exist several large countries with equivalent power and they cooperate or compete in various patterns. In this system, in order to settle important international problems, it is necessary for large countries to cooperate mutually. There existed such a situation in Europe for several centuries.[31]

An international currency system could exist in a "unipolar system," where only one currency is used for international settlements; however, under the "multipolar system," multiple currencies are used for international settlements. Judging from the current situation, under a "unipolar system," the US dollar could become the key currency and under a "multipolar system," the US dollar, euro, and renminbi can be used for international settlements. Therefore, the question arises as to whether the renminbi can become the sole key currency. In other words, this would indicate a situation in international relations where China is the only superstate and there can exist no other superpowers.

There are plenty of predictions insisting that, in the near future, the total GDP amount (not per capita GDP amount) of the United States and China might be reversed. Although it is possible, that is solely in the context of GDP. The situation would be different when considering a long-term outlook. However, even if the United States' and China's total GDP amounts are reversed, it indicates not a tendency toward a "unipolar system" dominated by China but a tendency toward a "multipolar system."

There have been many strategies such as "balancing" and "bandwagoning." According to Huntington (1998), "balancing" means that the balance of power and security can be maintained "only in an own country" or by "cooperating with other countries," and if necessary the country concerned can defeat its opponent by waging a war. "Bandwagoning" indicates that the country concerned would comply with a certain strong

---

[30]See Huntington (1996).

[31]*Ibid.*

power and would become dependent on the strong power in exchange for protection by the stronger country.

According to Huntington (1998), international relations in Western Europe fall under the "balancing" strategy. as According to Walt, when a nation considers its own well-being, it selects a "balancing" strategy. The "bandwagoning" strategy requires the weaker nation to have confidence in the stronger nation, which could be a dangerous strategy.

The strategies of "balancing" and "bandwagoning" are insightful because they are useful in understanding the clear differences between "rise of Japan" (which led to the advancement of the first wave of "increased pluralism") and "rise of China" (which is driving the second wave of "increased pluralism").

Japan seems to have employed the "bandwagoning" strategy. As a matter of fact, at the beginning of the 20th century, Japan allied with the UK because Japan recognized the UK as a leading nation. Then, in the 1950s, Japan allied with the United States, which was the strongest nation at that time and was able to protect Japan.[32] Therefore, it would not be surprising at all if the advancement of "increased pluralism" led by Japan, which has essentially adopted a "bandwagoning" strategy, has halted due to US–Japan friction and the ensuing bubble collapse of Japan.

However, the "increased pluralism" led by China is obviously different. China employs a "balancing" strategy. It is not necessary for China to rely on the United States, and , if necessary, China can wage a war to defend itself without depending on another country.

We consider this situation a bit more.[33] According to Mearsheimer (2006), China intends to become a "regional hegemon" in Asia, and with increased power, China will try to remove the United States from Asia. In fact, Mearsheimer suggested that the United States was never a "global hegemon" but a "regional hegemon" in the Western Hemisphere. In that sense, China would like to have a similar position in Asia by becoming a "regional hegemon." However, the United States will try to prevent China from becoming a "regional hegemon" in Asia. China's neighboring countries of India, Japan, Singapore, South Korea, and Vietnam would likely establish a "balancing" alliance led by the United States in retaliation for China's actions. With respect to Taiwan, the United States and Japan are unlikely to allow Chinese rule because Taiwan is a critical player in the

[32] See Huntington (1998).

[33] See Mearsheimer (2006).

"anti-China balancing coalition" and is an extremely important player in their strategy to secure a sea lane in the East Asian region. In short, according to Mearsheimer, because international politics is unpleasant and dangerous, no matter how benevolent, when a nation with the ambition to become a hegemon appears in the Eurasian region, there will be a bitter confrontation due to national security. It is the "tragedy of great power politics" as Mearsheimer indicated.

Therefore, if China wants to be a hegemon in the Asian region and if the United States (and the neighboring countries of China) wants to prevent China from being a hegemon, a bitter confrontation on national security will be unavoidable.

Moreover, according to Mearsheimer (2001), the US strategy toward China has been wrong.[34] Slowing China's economic growth is in America's interest, but America implemented strategies over the past decades that aimed for the opposite effect. This US policy toward China was wrong because a prosperous China would become an "aggressive country" seeking regional hegemony (p. 517).

What does Mearsheimer's outlook mean for the "codependency relationship" between the United States (excess-consumption country) and China (underconsumption country)?

If, hypothetically, a prosperous China were to become an aggressively expansionist country aiming for regional hegemony – something that is likely to become a reality – the "codependency relations" between the United States and China would ultimately appear to be a part of the very process of China's increasing prosperity. China would unavoidably become the regional hegemon. It can only be said that this is the result of the United States' (according to Mearsheimer, "mistaken") policy toward China.

As Morita (2017b) referred, Roach (2014) used the term that (psychologists warn that) "codependency becomes problematic when one participant in the relationship starts to grow away from the other." Needless to say, in this example, the participant growing away from the other is China, not the United States.

---

[34]Regarding the time when Mearsheimer judged that the US policy toward China was wrong, it can be recognized through an interview article (with Mearsheimer) in *NIKKEI ASIA* (21 February 2022). In that article, Mearsheimer mentioned that "the Nixon-Kissinger policy, from the early 1970s to the late 1980s, was wonderfully prudent. However, the subsequent "engagement policy" was a colossal strategic blunder.

In that sense, the second wave of "increased pluralism" is likely to be led by a country (China) that would further promote "increased pluralism," unlike the first wave of "increased pluralism." Hence, we suppose that a "multipolar system" based on the "balancing" strategy could occur.

Although the "codependency relationship" between the United States and China has become weaker gradually, at present, it will not be cancelled.

5. The United States and China

In the previous section, we referred to Mearsheimer mentioning that the United States has been executing a strategy over the past few decades that aims for the opposite effect and that such US policy towards China is wrong.

In this section, we consider the situation a bit more.

There is a question called the "Needham Puzzle." Until the middle of the 16th century, Chinese civilization led the world in terms of technology; so why is it that, since then, it is Western Europe, and not China, that has succeeded in modernization?[35]

According to Maddison (2007), Table 9 and Figure 8 indicate the source of the "Needham Puzzle." Both Table 9 and Figure 8 indicate the ratio of each country's GDP to the world's total GDP. China (and India) had significant economic power compared with other countries in 1820. However, as clearly shown in the table and figure, in 1913, China (and India) gave up its top position in terms of GDP to the United States.

If we separate the three countries of the United States, China, and India from Figure 8 and plot them into Figure 9, we can see that from the year 1900, "China and India" and "the United States" exchanged their positions.

At any rate, from viewpoints of the ratio of each country's GDP to the world's total GDP, China and India had a much larger ratio compared to other countries until around 1900. Why did the GDP ratio of China and India drastically decline?

---

[35] See Chen and Morita (2015, p. 49). As clearly shown in Table 9 and Figure 8, apart from the indicators of "civilization and technology," as long as we rely on GDP, both China and India had overwhelming economic power even in 1820; even though the ratio of GDP was slightly smaller in 1870, compared with other countries, both China and India still had a higher GDP. Thereafter, the GDP became lower in China and in India.

Table 9. The ratio of each country's GDP to the world's total GDP (1–2003) (in percent).

Country \ Year	1	1000	1500	1600	1700	1820	1870	1913	1950	1973	2003
France	2.2	2.3	4.4	4.7	5.3	5.1	6.5	5.3	4.1	4.3	3.2
Germany	1.2	1.2	3.3	3.8	3.7	3.9	6.5	8.7	5.0	5.9	3.9
UK	0.3	0.7	1.1	1.8	2.9	5.2	9.0	8.2	6.5	4.2	3.1
USA	0.3	0.4	0.3	0.2	0.1	1.8	8.9	18.9	27.3	22.1	20.6
Japan	1.1	2.7	3.1	2.9	4.1	3.0	2.3	2.6	3.0	7.8	6.6
China	25.4	22.1	24.9	29.0	22.3	32.9	17.1	8.8	4.6	4.6	15.1
India	32.0	28.1	24.4	22.4	24.4	16.0	12.1	7.5	4.2	3.1	5.5

Source: Maddison (2007, p. 381).

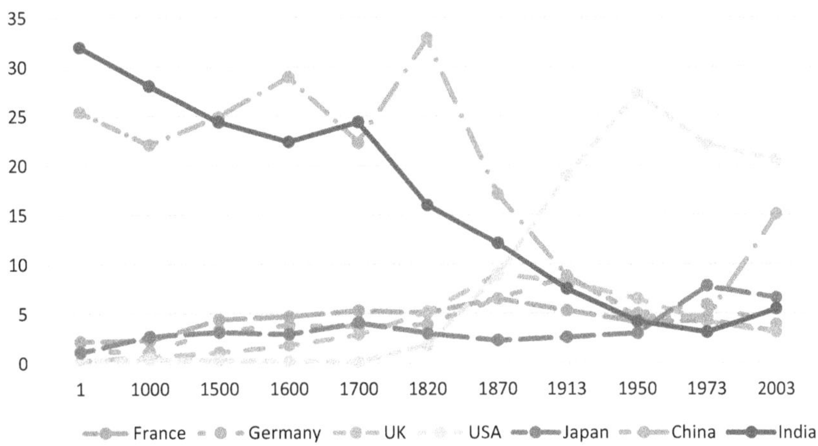

Figure 8. The ratio of each country's GDP to the world total (1–2003) (in percent).
Source: Maddison (2007, p. 381).

According to Chen and Morita (2015), the "Needham Puzzle" is a long-lasting centralization system whose driving force for institutional and technological innovation gradually declined.[36]

[36] See Chen and Morita (2015). If the single-party regime of contemporary China means the centralized system, China might not be able to get away from the "Needham Puzzle."

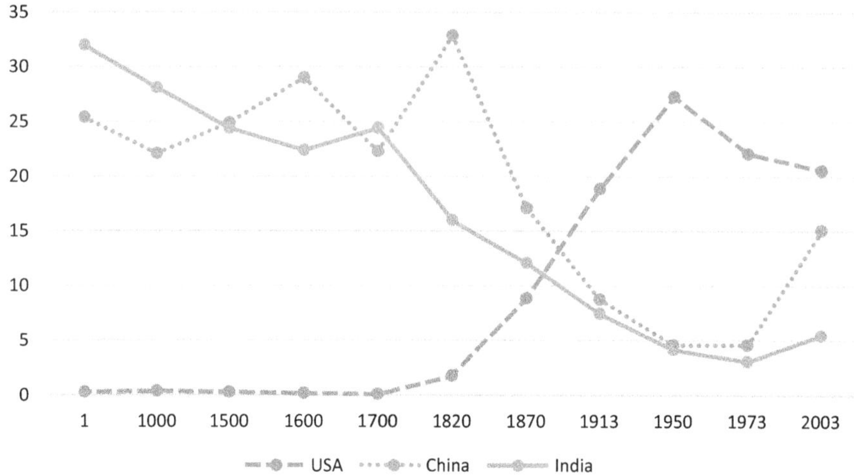

Figure 9. The ratio of each country's GDP to the world total (1–2003) (in percent).
Source: Maddison (2007, p. 381).

Chen and Morita (2015) also interpreted the "temperate zone effect" by citing Ellsworth Huntington (1915).[37] The "temperate zone effect" refers to the phenomenon where the tension between human being and environment fosters a spirit of self-supporting, leading to technological progress and advancement of civilization. On the contrary, the (para) "tropical trap" describes a situation where an overly favorable environment suppresses the manifestation of human potential.

In any case, under a centralized system and with a moderate development environment, the motivation for progress would be lost and other nations and regions that put in the effort could catch up.

as According to the ratio of GDP to the world total, until 1900, China and India were superior to Europe and the United States.

With regard to China,[38] this superiority was not limited to GDP but extended to the influence of culture and thought.

[37]Originally in Chen and Morita (2015), as the interpretation of the "model differentiation" between Zhejiang Province and Jiangsu Province, it is employed the concepts of the "temperate zone effect" and the (para) "tropical trap." Naturally, in an environment of abundance, competitiveness tends to wane, eventually leading to being outpaced by countries or regions that have honed their competitiveness through diligent effort. In that sense, similar situations would be occurred.

[38]We do not analyze the case of India in this book.

For example, the influence of Confucius has been significant. According to Matsuo (2017), Quesnay's inclination toward China was so prominent that he was given the nickname of "French Confucius" (p. 37). Quesnay praised the tyrannical system enforced by the Chinese emperors as the best political system in the world in his book *Autocratic Government Theory in China*, published in 1767 (pp. 37–38). Voltaire envied China (p. 41) and was a fervent admirer of China, inviting monarchs all over Europe to praise China, feel ashamed of themselves, and imitate China; Voltaire's even placed a portrait of Confucius in a chapel in his home, which he worshiped every day (p. 43).

Social theorists as Montesquieu and Adam Smith observed China critically because they enjoyed the freedom of thought and opinion.[39]

The influence of Chinese Confucianism on Leibnitz, the German enlightenment thinker, can be recognized. According to Matsuo (2017), Mikinosuke Ishida had claimed that Leibnitz's research on China was not only important for his own ideological thinking but also important for European ideological thought; Leibnitz's research on China triggered the "chino field (pro-Chinese)" (p. 47).

The arrival of Chinese thought in the United States was brought about by Benjamin Franklin, which created a connection between the United States and China. However, as noted by Matsuo (2017), Benjamin Franklin had the fact that he came out of the village of Ferney and met in Paris on 12 February 1778 (about three months before Voltaire's death) (p. 44), and Franklin was "a confirmed Sinophile, that is, an enthusiast for China" (p. 63). Franklin disseminated a portion of the Four Books on Confucianism through the tabloid weekly magazine "Pennsylvania Gazette," which he owned and managed, through which Confucian through spread in the US (p. 61).

The Confucian influence is still apparent in the present day. Former German Prime Minister Helmut Schmidt stated in a speech that China had a highly civilized system completely different from that of Europe and the United States and insisted that the Western world should not enforce its idea of human rights on China.[40] According to Matsuo (2017), it suggests

---

[39] In that regard, see Matsuo (2017).

[40] As Matsuo (2017) described, we could learn about the content of the speech from the following. Helmut Schmidt (2013), *Ein letzter besuch: Begegnungen mit der Weltmacht China*, Siedler Verlag, München. While its content is surprising, it provides a good example of understanding China in Europe and the United States.

a relationship between China and Germany that Japan cannot have, similar to the relationship between China and the United States (p. 37).

Matsuo describes the Germany–China relationship as what "Japan could not have." Matsuo (2017) also claimed that it was necessary for China to have a symbiotic relationship with the United States. Aside from the 3 years during the Korean War and the 22 years during China's "containment" policy, China has never been involved in a direct war against the United States. Matsuo finally concluded that the Japanese people are deeply impressed with China as it has a characteristic relationship with the United States. That relationship is very different from that of Japan and the US (p. 324).

Kase and Stokes (2012) indicated the following example. In 1936, the Franklin Delano Roosevelt administration announced a policy that was against Japan, which preceded the Japanese attack on Pearl Harbor by 5 years. President Roosevelt wanted to destroy Japan throughout the Chinese Chiang Kai-shek administration (pp. 19–20).

Why did President Roosevelt back China? In the late 1930s, the US Congress enacted the Neutrality Acts which prohibited the export of arms and munitions to nations that were in a state of war. Nevertheless, in August 1937, when the Second Shanghai Incident broke out, Roosevelt declared that the United States would not apply the Neutrality Acts to China (p. 22).

It is now well known that President Roosevelt harbored malice toward Japan. However, it is not known why he adopted such policies that supported China. According to Kase and Stokes (2012), in the United States, in those days, many people, including Roosevelt, regarded China as being within the US's sphere of influence, China accepted a large number of Christian preachers from the United States, and US citizens also had an affection for China, hoping to profit from the huge market in China.[41]

Moreover, Roosevelt had friendly sentiments toward China because of the influence of his maternal grandfather and was pleased that many Christian preachers from the United States were active all over China (p. 23). His maternal grandfather was a member of the Delano family, which was prosperous in the French–Dutch region, having amassed a colossal fortune through the opium trade with China at the end of the

[41] Because it is difficult to suppose that citizens have an affection for a country that has the power to compete with their own country, it is safe to assume that US citizens in those days did not think of China as a rival nation.

Qing Dynasty. The family had a palatial residence in Hong Kong. A lady who was President Roosevelt's mother stayed in Hong Kong during her girlhood and came to feel an attachment to China (p. 18).

The "goodwill towards China" is certainly an important factor, but even if it was one of the factors that led to the war with Japan, it is difficult to see it as a main factor. Therefore, as indicated by Kase and Stokes (2012), the standard interpretation would be as follows: Roosevelt firmly believed that Adolf Hitler was driven by an insatiable desire for conquest. He also believed that, if the UK was destroyed, the United States would also perish. Thus, Roosevelt felt that, in order to save the UK, the United States had to take part in the war in Europe. However, American isolationism blocked its participation. Isolationism stood as a formidable barrier. Therefore, Japan was forced into the war with the United States, which was a scheme to enter the European war through the back door (p. 36).

However, why was Japan used as the reason why the United States participated in the war in Europe? One answer is "the Tripartite Pact between Japan, Germany, and Italy" and the other answer is that the US opposed the Japanese invasion into China (p. 43).

According to this logic, the US national strategy can be categorized as "realism." The United States chose to support China by attacking Japan in an effort to realize the "balance of power." We could suppose, therefore, that the United States planned to contribute to the "balance of power" by strengthening China and weakening Japan.

Such an understanding seems to be in accordance with Mearsheimer's assertions. From the time of President Franklin Roosevelt, the US policy toward China has been wrong,[42] leading to the "unpeaceful rise" of contemporary China. Undoubtedly, it is difficult to condemn the balance of power policy as wrong because, by checking the strong Japan and assisting the weak China, it is possible to maintain the balance of power. However, from the viewpoints of international relations, by comparatively investigating Japan (based on the "bandwagoning" strategy) and China (based on the "balancing" strategy), it is difficult to conclude that the policy to "strengthen China" and to "weaken Japan" was correct.

In any case, if there is a bias towards China's advanced civilization behind such misguided policies, as quoted from former Chancellor

---

[42] However, we need another investigation to consider when the US policy toward China started to go wrong.

Helmut Schmidt's statement in 2013, then the roots of the "codependency relations" between the United States and China would be quite deep.[43]

In approaching the issue of the United States and China in this section, there is an indispensable name. Needless to say, it is Henry Kissinger.

According to Kissinger (2011), the United States and China are both "too big to be dominated by the other" (p. 527), and if China and the United States collide, "this is the road to disaster for both sides" (p. 528). However, Kissinger assumed that China in "facing such large domestic tasks is not going to throw itself easily, much less automatically, into strategic confrontation or a quest for world domination" (p. 525). Kissinger indicated that the "appropriate label for the Sino-American relationship is less partnership than 'co-evolution'." The concept of co-evolution "means that both countries pursue their domestic imperatives, cooperating where possible, and adjust their relations to minimize conflict" (p. 526). The concept derived from Kissinger's way of thinking could be called a "Pacific Community." The concept of the Pacific Community involves the peaceful development of the community with the participation of the United States, China, and other countries. This would enable other major countries such as Japan, Indonesia, Vietnam, India, and Australia to participate in the construction of a system perceived as a joint coalition rather than a polarized coalition between "Chinese" and "American" blocs (p. 528).

It is well known that Kissinger is an excellent scholar of international politics, and this book does not intend to deny that in any way. Moreover, it goes without saying that his major works on China (2011) (2012) are also of excellent quality.

However, like Helmut Schmidt, Henry Kissinger also backed China. As regards the "rise of China," Mearsheimer's analysis was different from Kissinger's. Kissinger as a statesman took the initiative toward restoration of diplomatic relations between the United States and China in 1971.

Unquestionably, Mearsheimer's view also suggests that both the United States and China are "regional hegemon" or are striving to become "regional hegemon." In this sense, the existence of two "regional hegemons" from the west and east of the Pacific Ocean suggests a similarity with the concept of a "Pacific Community." However, the Pacific area in

---

[43]From the Japanese point of view, the other matters to seriously consider are (1) the confidential conversation between Nixon and Mao Zedong and (2) the confidential conversation between Kissinger and Zhou Enlai. These are not discussed in this book.

which the United States and China exist as "regional hegemons" would be very different from the "Pacific Community" supposed by Kissinger (in which the United States, China, and any other nation could participate for peaceful development of the community).

For example, for Japan, it was never clear what was involved in establishing constructive relations with the United States, China, and other nations for a "Pacific Community." Japan seemed to employ the "bandwagoning" strategy and Japanese policies were adaptable in accordance with a "weakening of the United States" and a "strengthening of China" in the Asian region.[44] If China were to become the mightiest nation in that region, Japan would adopt a strategy to cooperate with China ("bandwagoning" strategy). If such a "bandwagoning" strategy with China were not accepted by a majority of the Japanese people, Japan would try to employ an independent military strategy ("balancing" strategy) as Ito (2011, 2012) and Kusaka and Ito (2011) have asserted.

In short, Kissinger's way of thinking was undoubtedly different from the "balancing" strategy suggested by Mearsheimer and Huntington.

In order to realize the "Pacific Community" urged by Kissinger, it is necessary for the participating nations, including the United States and China, to be involved in a united mechanism.

When Kissinger asserted the "co-evolution" of the United States and China, it was under the assumption that China would not pursue world domination and that both the United States and China would have confidence in each other.

Kissinger (2011, 2012) also mentioned that throughout "its history, the United States has often been motivated by visions of the universal relevance of its ideals and of a proclaimed duty to spread them" (p. 529). However, many experts might question the statement mentioning that the United States has acted according to the duty of spreading ideals. In fact, as Ito (2011, 2012) asserted, it is generally recognized that the United States talks alike an idealist but acts like a realist. If this view of the United States is correct, it would be impossible for the United States to be motivated by visions of the universal relevance of its ideals and of a proclaimed duty to spread them.

Nevertheless, we are surprised that a brilliant expert like Kissinger showed easy confidence in China and stated that China "is not going to throw itself easily, much less automatically, into strategic confrontation or

[44] Regarding such arguments, see, for example, Huntington (1998).

a quest for world domination." Such emotional assertions of confidence and favor toward China decry the scientific significance of the analyses.

In any case, in terms of Sino-American relations, it is necessary to recognize the outlook of the global system and also recognize both nations' national strategies. As we have stated in this section, if both the United States and China take a standpoint of realism and select a "balancing" strategy, regardless of the confidence between both nations, until and unless China obtains a greater military and economic power than the United States, the current situation, namely a "codependency relationship," will continue (even if it will gradually slow down). If the United States employs the wrong policies toward China, China's military and economic power could overtake that of the United States sooner, and accordingly, the "codependency relationship" could be terminated earlier.

6. Twin Deficits

We have mentioned the United States' "excess consumption" and China's "underconsumption," both of which have caused domestic problems (particularly financial issues).

A serious problem for the United States is its "twin deficits" of a current account deficit and a budget deficit.

The ratio of the government sector to the foreign sector is as follows:

$$Y = C + I + (G - T) + (X - M) \tag{1}$$

In it, Y indicates total production, C consumption, I investment, G government expenditure, T government revenue, X export, and M import. Thus, the government sector $(G - T)$ shows net government expenditure and the foreign sector $(X - M)$ shows net export.

When equation (1) is transformed, we have the following (2):

$$(S - I) + (T - G) = (X - M) \tag{2}$$

In it, S indicates saving. Therefore, if $(T - G)$ is negative, it means a budget deficit, and if $(X - M)$ is negative, it indicates a current account deficit.

As equation (2) suggests, although there exists a government deficit, if the saving–investment balance offsets the deficit, the current account balance would not become a deficit. However, if there is a savings shortage and budget balance is in a deficit, it naturally means that the current account balance is in a deficit. The situation into which the United States falls is expressed as a "savings shortage," "government deficit," and "current account deficit." That is to say, it is the situation of "twin deficits." It is possible for government expenditure to increase consumption, which would lead to an expansion of total production. It could also increase savings, which would expand government revenue. Therefore, the existence of the "twin deficits" indicates that there is neither an increase in savings nor in government revenue sufficient to trigger such mechanisms.

The ratios of primary balance to GDP of the United States, China, and Germany are presented in Table 10 and in Figure 10.

Table 10. The ratio of the primary balance to GDP in each country (2001–2016) (in percent).

Year \ Country	USA	Germany	China
2001	1.728	▲0.502	▲1.858
2002	▲1.682	▲1.327	▲2.306
2003	▲2.791	▲1.541	▲1.677
2004	▲2.399	▲1.209	▲1.033
2005	▲1.156	▲0.955	▲0.959
2006	▲0.095	0.679	▲0.694
2007	▲0.795	2.589	0.446
2008	▲4.640	2.173	0.383
2009	▲11.237	▲0.846	▲1.313
2010	▲8.891	▲2.063	0.089
2011	▲7.285	1.077	0.393
2012	▲5.673	1.829	0.187
2013	▲2.432	1.455	▲0.320
2014	▲2.034	1.705	▲0.354
2015	▲1.646	1.837	▲2.214
2016	▲2.309	1.867	▲2.944

Source: IMF (Data: Global Note).

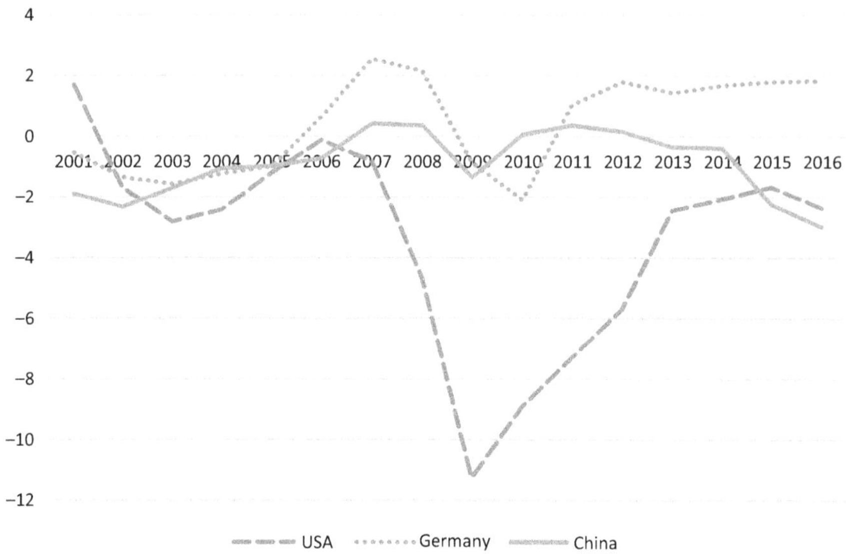

Figure 10. The ratio of the primary balance to GDP in each country (2001–2016) (in percent).

Source: IMF (Data: Global Note) and author's calculation.

As clearly shown in Table 10 and Figure 10, there were more surplus years in Germany, but a mix of surplus and deficit years in China. In the United States, there were more deficit years.

Then, what is the ratio of government revenue to GDP? It is indicated in Table 11 and Figure 11.

As clearly recognized in Table 11 and Figure 11, the ratio of government revenue to GDP in Germany was more than 40 percent and reached around 43–44 percent. On the other hand, both the United States and China had a ratio of around 30 percent, although the ratio of China increased and that of the United States remained unchanged.

It goes without saying that the "exorbitant privilege" of the United States cannot continue forever it would be desirable for such a privilege to be suspended as smoothly as possible).

It depends upon whether the economic growth of the United States could be recognized as sustainable as long as possible. In a market economy country like the United States, it could not be denied that artificial factors operate in the market, but even so, there might also be areas where the government gets involved.

Table 11. The ratio of the government revenue to GDP in each country (2001–2016) (in percent).

Year \ Country	USA	Germany	China
2001	32.133	43.796	14.729
2002	29.790	43.320	15.458
2003	29.154	43.640	15.700
2004	29.300	42.571	16.220
2005	30.652	42.783	16.729
2006	31.552	42.975	17.070
2007	31.672	43.005	18.130
2008	30.645	43.396	22.369
2009	28.430	44.341	23.751
2010	29.077	43.034	24.600
2011	29.361	43.753	26.914
2012	29.393	44.262	27.757
2013	31.617	44.548	27.703
2014	31.477	44.615	28.057
2015	31.638	44.495	28.535
2016	31.224	44.981	28.202

Source: IMF (Data: Global Note).

Therefore, in order to avoid a crisis due to its "exorbitant privilege," the US government could raise taxes and reduce expenditure. It means that the primary balance has to be in equilibrium and the ratio of government revenue to GDP has to increase.[45]

In other words, it means preventing fiscal deficits and reducing current account deficits, which ultimately boils down to an increase in the saving rate in the United States.

If a situation of an "increase in the savings rate in the United States" is realized,[46] the "codependency relationship" between the United States and China would be nullified. However, the "correction of excess con-

[45] With regard to those issues, see Eichengreen (2011).

[46] Needless to say, it would be difficult to see this as easily achievable in a democratic and market-based country like the United States. In fact, if it were possible, the problem of the US trade deficit would have been resolved long ago.

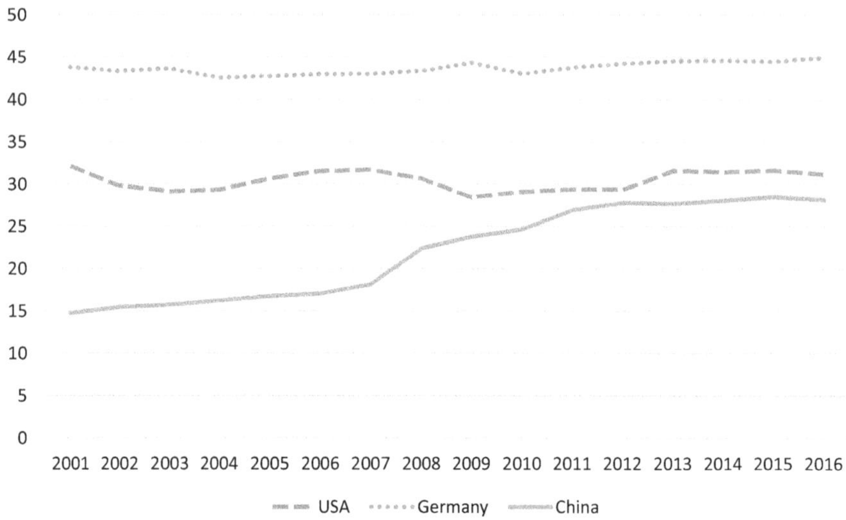

Figure 11. The ratio of the government revenue to GDP in each country (2001–2016) (in percent).

Source: IMF (Data: Global Note) and author's calculation.

sumption in the United States" cannot be separated from its "exorbitant privilege." The United States' "exorbitant privilege" could lead to its destruction and the "codependency relationship" between the United States and China could be nullified.

7. Excess Savings and Disparity[47]

In the previous section, we considered the policy of the rise of the saving rates of the United States. In this section, we analyze the "disparity of China" as there is a close connection between disparity and excess savings (or underconsumption).

The starting point in this section is the savings rate as used in the economic growth theory:

$$s = sp\frac{P}{Y} + sw\frac{W}{Y}$$

[47]As indicated in the text, we focus on China.

Here, s indicates the savings rate of the total nation concerned, sp means the savings rate from profit, and sw means the savings rate from wages. P is income from capital, W is income from labor, and Y is national income.

Moreover,

$$O < sp < 1, O < sw < 1, sw < sp$$

In other words,

$$Sp = sp\ P$$

presents the savings amount from profit; on the contrary,

$$Sw = sw\ W$$

shows the savings amount from wages.

Here, both sp and sw are constant, but s can vary according to the size of P/Y and W/Y (distribution ratio). How can it vary? If the profit of a capitalist country is large, the savings rate of the country could be large. On the contrary, if the wages of laborers are high, the savings rate of the country could be small.

The circumstances of the United States and China are shown in Tables 12 and 13. The Table 12 presents the labor distribution rate and the Table 13 indicates the savings rate of the two countries.

As the tables clearly indicate, in a country with a relatively smaller labor distribution rate like China, the savings rate as a whole is relatively larger. On the contrary, in a country with a relatively larger labor distribution rate than the United States, the savings rate as a whole is relatively smaller.

At the same time, then, in a country with a relatively smaller labor distribution rate like China, the disparity is relatively larger. On the contrary, in a country with a relatively larger labor distribution rate like the United States, the disparity is relatively smaller. The disparity is measured by the Gini coefficient as indicated in Table 13. Undoubtedly, the Gini coefficient of China is larger than that of the United States.

Concerning the policies related to distribution, it is easier for centralized China to take measures due to government intervention and more difficult for democratic United States to take measures related to government intervention. Needless to say, it would still be challenging in the case

Table 12. Labor distribution ratio of the United States and China (2000–2014) (in percent).

Year	China	USA
2000	53.3	71.1
2005	50.6	68.5
2008	48.9	70.7
2009	49.9	69.9
2010	49.4	67.9
2011	50.1	67.2
2012	51.0	66.4
2013	50.9	66.3
2014	—	66.5

Note: In the United States, labor distribution rate = compensation of employees/national income indicated by factor price ×100, and in China, labor distribution rate = compensation of employees/total national income ×100.
Source: The Japan Institute for Labour Policy and Training, *Data Book International Labour Comparison*, 2016.

Table 13. The Gini coefficient of the United States and China (2003–2014).

Year	China	USA
2003	0.479	0.365
2004	0.473	0.352
2005	0.485	0.373
2006	0.487	0.376
2007	0.484	0.367
2008	0.491	0.370
2009	0.490	0.374
2010	0.481	0.375
2011	0.477	0.387
2012	0.474	0.385
2013	0.473	0.392
2014	—	0.389

Source: OECD (Data: Global Note), Chen and Morita (2015, p. 54).

of the United States, and the mechanism should work in the same way. Thus, if the labor distribution rate in the United States becomes relatively larger, the savings rate could become relatively smaller. In the United States the disparity compared to China is smaller.

In China, the smaller labor distribution rate (meaning a larger capital distribution rate) would have a large portion contributed by exports because China has experienced economic growth due to foreign capital. We need to recognize the role of the "underestimation" of the renminbi exchange rate against the US dollar (as previously mentioned, in the sense of manifesting through excess saving) in contributing to such trade surplus.

If we say in that sense, as mentioned earlier in this chapter, the move toward the "marketization" and "internationalization" of the Chinese renminbi exchange rate to the US dollar can be seen as a step towards reducing disparity within China. At the same time, a reduction in disparity might be possible with the cancellation of the "codependency relationship" between the United States and China.

The consideration in this section focuses primarily on China. The conclusion of this section, as stated above, could be understood as a trend towards the dissolution of "codependency relations" between the United States and China.

8. Conclusion

As we indicated in the previous chapter, if the disparity in China could be improved (in terms of a numerical value of the Gini coefficient and labor distribution ratio), the underconsumption in China (domestic demand shortage) could be improved. Then we could revise the "codependency relationship" between the United States and China. One of the correlated policies is the revision of the underestimation of the renminbi exchange rate.

In this chapter, we focused mainly on the United States and its "political economy" and investigated the "codependency relationship" between the United States and China.

The viewpoint in this chapter is as follows. It is not realistic for the "codependency relationship" between the United States and China to reach a resolution (although it might gradually weaken).

According to Roach (2014), who was the first to mention "codependency relations" in his own writing, one "of the tragic ironies of codependency is that partners often subsume their sense of self into an increasingly destructive relationship." (If they fail to adapt to the new economic realities) there is a risk of conflict. This could lead to the nightmare of a trade war or something even worse. "Trust is key to resolving the political disconnect between the two" (pp. 267–268). Frictions "could undermine not only the two countries' relationship but the entire global economy. The imbalances of codependency will drive the economic agendas of the United States and China. Rebalancing will define their future — separately and collectively" (p. 268).

Roach (2014) also stated the following:

> "Saving is the central unifying element in the codependency between the United States and China. All you have to know at this point is one thing: Savings-short nations run multilateral trade deficit. Without sustained improvement in domestic saving, America will never pull itself out of its current account and trade deficits. And that means China, with its large trade and saving surplus, will probably remain in Washington's political crosshairs for as long as this key issue is unresolved" (p. 131).

A trade deficit means a savings shortage. Japan, which had a trade surplus and a large amount of savings, was once a target of Washington's political attacks. However, at present or in the near future, China could be the target of political attacks by the United States. However, is this situation unfolds, the United States would be politically targeted by Beijing. We should recognize that US–Japan relations and Sino-American relations are very different.

In any case, when we consider the situation at present or in the near future,[48] emphasizing the "codependency relationship" and emphasizing rebalance without friction might not provide similar benefits to both the United States and China.

As discussed in this chapter, there have existed different arguments. For example, Mearsheimer asserted that the US policy on China is misguided. Mearsheimer's analysis "suggests that the United States has a profound interest in seeing Chinese economic growth slow considerably in the years ahead. For much of the past decade, however, the United States has pursued a strategy intended to have the opposite effect." Such a US policy on China is misguided because "A wealthy China would not

---

[48]As mentioned earlier, this "future" is 10 years later.

be a status quo power but an aggressive state determined to achieve regional hegemony."[49]

According to Roach and Mearsheimer, different ways of thinking have coexisted. Roach presumed that "trust is key to resolving the political disconnect between the two."[50] However, Mearsheimer states that "If China continues its impressive economic growth over the next few decades, the United States and China are likely to engage in an intense security competition with considerable potential for war."[51] Thus, it does not appear that the idea of "trust is key" exists within Mearsheimer's thinking.

In that sense, pointing out the "codependency relations" between the United States and China and advocating for "coexistence" would likely be beneficial for China (at least in the medium and long term), but not necessarily for the United States. Therefore, the codependency relationship between the two seem to be "for China" and "by China." Then, which side has started to resolve the codependency relationship? The country that is beginning to move towards dissolving such "codependency relations" is not the United States, but rather China. How on earth does that occur?

China's strategy has been called a "peaceful rise." As Ito (2011) indicated, however, China bides its time, plans its revenge in advance, and then acts. Ito also mentioned that the essence of China's foreign policy was hegemony. Therefore, Ito (2011) asserted in 2011 that, until 2020, China would continue its "peaceful rise" to avoid turning the United States into its enemy.[52]

In Mearsheimer's books and articles, he claimed that China rise has been "unpeaceful." However, even if China's main intention was to be "unpeaceful" and attain "regional hegemony," as of now, the Chinese strategy is to avoid turning the United States into its enemy. If this can be called a "peaceful rise," then the Chinese strategy is indeed "peaceful."

Therefore, the "codependency relations" between the United States and China aligns with China's strategy of "peaceful rise." At the point when China becomes confident that it could afford to make the US its adversary, this relations would move towards a (swift rather than gradual) dissolution. The relationship between the United States' "excess

[49] Mearsheimer (2001, p. 402).

[50] Roach (2014, p. 268).

[51] Mearsheimer (2005, p. 1).

[52] Ito (2011, p. 224).

consumption" and China's "underconsumption" is not "symmetric" but "asymmetric." Chinese "underconsumption" (in the centralized system) can be more easily amended.

Thus, as soon China amends its "peaceful rise" strategy, its "codependency relationship" will the United States will stop. Then China's "unpeaceful rise" (as Mearsheimer asserted) would be clear. We should understand that the "codependency relationship" between the United States and China is a property of the political economy.

Chapter 4

A Political Economy of Sino-American Conflict

1. Introduction

An article in *Nihon Keizai Shimbun* (14 July 2018) reported that, on 13 July, the US Department of Commerce announced that it removed sanctions prohibiting transactions with US corporations that had been imposed on ZTE Corporation (Zhongxing Telecommunication Equipment Corporation, hereafter ZTE). According to that article, it is reported that ZTE has completed the payment of fines and the overhaul of its management, which were conditions for lifting the sanctions. However, the situation of competition, as the title of that article stated, "rivalry with high technology is still seriously," remained unchanged.

The sanction imposed on ZTE (in April 2018) stated that transactions with US corporations were prohibited for 7 years because ZTE was involved in transactions with North Korea and Iran. Due to the sanction, ZTE faced a major managerial crisis as it depended on US corporations for many components such as semiconductors, without which ZTE could not produce smartphones, communication equipment, etc. The sanction was much more effective than the US predicted and had a deep impact on China.[1] Further, the fine imposed was reported to be a maximum of 1,400 million US dollars.[2]

[1] *Nihon Keizai Shimbun* (9 June 2018).

[2] *Ibid* (8 June 2018). The amount of the fine varied from one report to another.

Moreover, the article in *Nihon Keizai Shimbun* (4 December 2018) reported that, on the previous day, the WIPO (World Intellectual Property Organization) had announced that the number of patent applications had reached 3.17 million, which was the highest on record, and that the number of patent applications from China amounted to 1.38 million, or 40 percent of all such applications, ranking China first in the number of patent applications for the seventh consecutive year.[3] Furthermore, the article also reported that applications from China were in the fields of electronic equipment, computer technology, and digital information and communication and that high-tech companies such as Huawei and ZTE has significantly increased the number of patent applications they filed. Besides, the article reported that the second place in the number of patent applications filed was occupied by the United States, with 610,000 applications, which was less than half those of China, and the third place was occupied by Japan (320,000). As the article reported, this was due to Project "Chinese Production 2025" with China devoting a large amount of money in terms of subsidy to the high-tech industry along with a positive attitude for protection of intellectual property.

However, the same article also reported that the Trump administration of the United States had criticized China due to the Chinese forcing technology transfers and violating intellectual property (As a matter of fact, the violation of intellectual property was undoubtedly the starting point of the "Sino-American friction" between the two countries).

The above-mentioned situations seem to be, by and large, similar to Mearsheimer's supposition.

Mearsheimer, through his works in 2001, 2006, and 2014, has pointed out that the US policy toward China has been wrong and has clearly accelerated China's economic growth.

The idea based on such a strategy by the United States is, needless to say, "engagement." That is to say, according to that idea, when China develops economically and democratically, China will become the "status quo" country seeking stability and will become a country that does not engage in a military expansion race with the United States.

[3]The number of patent applications will be described later. According to a report from Global Note (*Source*: WIPO), China has held the top position in this regard since 2012, and as of 2017, it has maintained this position for six consecutive years. Furthermore, the same report indicates that in 2011, Japan was in first place (475,000 applications), followed by the United States in second place (440,000 applications), and China in third place (436,000 applications).

As expressed earlier, Mearsheimer asserts that the US policy on China is misguided, and "suggests that the United States has a profound interest in seeing Chinese economic growth slow considerably in the years ahead. For much of the past decade, however, the United States has pursued a strategy intended to have the opposite effect." He stated that because a "wealthy China would not be a status quo power but an aggressive state determined to achieve regional hegemony,"[4] such a US policy toward China is misguided.

In short, both "engagement" and "containment" have been opposed. As Mearsheimer asserts, "the US policy on China is misguided" as it is based on a policy of "engagement."

However, it was only recently recognized that China would be an aggressive state determined to achieve regional hegemony and that the US policy on China is misguided.

What should be asked is, "is it still possible for the United States to change its course and take actions to slow down the rise of China ?" In other words, it essentially comes down to how we could foresee the "Sino-American relations."

The structure of this chapter is as follows: In the second section, we review the international trade between the United States and China and consider the "codependency" structure. In the third section, we review the military expenditure and in the fourth section, we investigate the technology policy of the United States and China, particularly focusing on the number of patent applications. In the fifth section, we investigate the situation often called "trade war." In the sixth and final section, we conclude the chapter.

2. International Trade

2.1. *Equilibrium and disequilibrium*

The import and export trading data of trade between the United States and China are expressed by symmetrical numbers as shown in Tables 1 and 2 and Figures 1 and 2, respectively.

As indicated in Figures 1 and 2, both the ratio of the import amount from China to the total import amount of the United States and the ratio of the export amount to the United States to the total export amount of China are demonstrated to be comparatively larger numbers.

---

[4] As referred earlier, Mearsheimer (2001, p. 402).

Table 1. The ratio of the import amount from the United States and China to the total import amount of China and the United States (2007–2017) (in percent).

Year	The ratio of the import amount from China to the total import amount of the USA	The ratio of the import amount from the USA to the total import amount of China
2007	16.4	7.3
2008	16.1	7.2
2009	19.0	7.7
2010	19.1	7.3
2011	18.1	7.0
2012	18.7	7.3
2013	19.4	7.8
2014	19.9	8.1
2015	21.5	8.8
2016	21.1	8.5
2017	21.6	8.4

Source: JETRO, *International Trade and Investment Report* (Annual Edition).

Table 2. The ratio of the export amount to the United States and China to the total export amount of China and the United States (2007–2017) (in percent).

Year	The ratio of the export amount to China to the total export amount of the USA	The ratio of the export amount to the USA to the total export amount of China
2007	5.6	19.1
2008	5.4	17.6
2009	6.6	18.4
2010	7.2	18.0
2011	7.0	17.1
2012	7.1	17.2
2013	7.7	16.7
2014	7.6	16.9
2015	7.7	19.3
2016	8.0	18.4
2017	8.4	19.0

Source: JETRO, *International Trade and Investment Report* (Annual Edition).

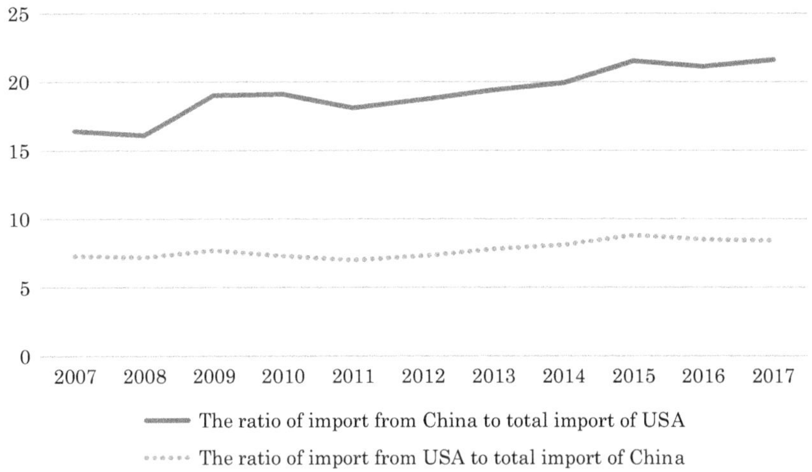

Figure 1. The ratio of the import amount from the United States and China to the total import amount of China and the United States (2007–2017) (in percent).

Source: JETRO, *International Trade and Investment Report* (Annual Edition).

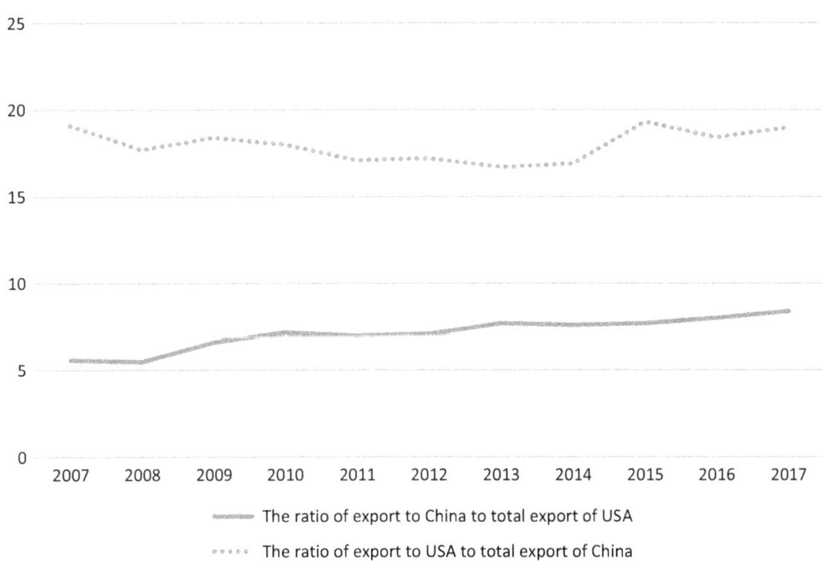

Figure 2. The ratio of the export amount to the United States and China to the total export amount of China and the United States (2007–2017) (in percent).

Source: JETRO, *International Trade and Investment Report* (Annual Edition).

When we have a look at the average value, the former value accounts for 19.17 percent and the latter value 17.97 percent. On the contrary, both the ratio of the import amount from the United States to the total import amount of China and the ratio of the export amount to China to the total export amount of the United States are demonstrated as comparatively smaller numbers correspondingly. When we take a look at the average value, the former value amounts to 7.10 percent and the latter 7.12 percent. In other words, the United States imports 19.17 percent from China and China exports 17.97 percent to the United States. And China imports 7.10 percent from the United States and the United States export 7.12 percent to China. In that sense, it seems to be generally equilibrated. Naturally, the additional levy on import duties, which will be discussed later, apply to imports from China, which account for 19.17 percent of the United States' total imports, and to imports from the United States, which account for 7.10 percent of China's total imports.

As described earlier, regarding the ratio, it is by and large balanced. However, the amount is not even.

Table 3 shows the current situation of international trade between the United States and China. With regards to the amount, China has a large amount of trade surplus with the United States, which reached 30 percent of the total trade deficit amount of the United States. As shown in Figure 3, after the ratio reached 30 percent in the year 2012, it then reached 35 percent, which is the current situation.

Table 4 shows the ratio of China's trade surplus with the United States to China's total trade surplus, and for reference, it also shows the ratio of China's trade surplus with the United States to the total US trade deficit. Clearly, the ratio to China's total trade surplus is significantly higher than the ratio to total US trade deficit.

It goes without saying that the total amount of China's (the United States') trade balance is determined by China's (the United States') saving-investment balance, not by the amount of the trade balance with the United States (China). Table 5 presents the savings rates of the United States and China. The trade deficit of the United States and the trade surplus of China could become a reflection of the saving behavior of each country, unrelated to the behaviors of other countries. Needless to say, as indicated by Morita (2017b), it is a situation that becomes clear based on the well-known formula

$$X - M = S - I. \tag{1}$$

Table 3. The current situation of international trade between the United States and China (2007–2017) (million US dollars, in percent).

Year	Chinese export to USA	Chinese import from USA	Chinese trade surplus with USA (A)	USA total trade deficit (B)	(A/B) × 100
2007	232,704	69,379	163,325	794,483	20.56
2008	252,297	81,440	170,857	1,049,937	16.27
2009	220,816	77,443	143,373	503,582	28.47
2010	283,304	102,038	181,266	634,897	28.55
2011	324,493	122,154	202,339	727,392	27.82
2012	351,796	132,886	218,910	729,611	30.00
2013	368,427	152,575	215,851	688,728	31.34
2014	396,082	159,036	237,046	727,153	32.60
2015	409,538	148,737	260,801	745,660	34.98
2016	385,085	134,402	250,682	736,794	34.02
2017	429,755	153,943	275,812	795,690	34.66

Source: JETRO, *International Trade and Investment Report* (Annual Edition) and the author's calculation.

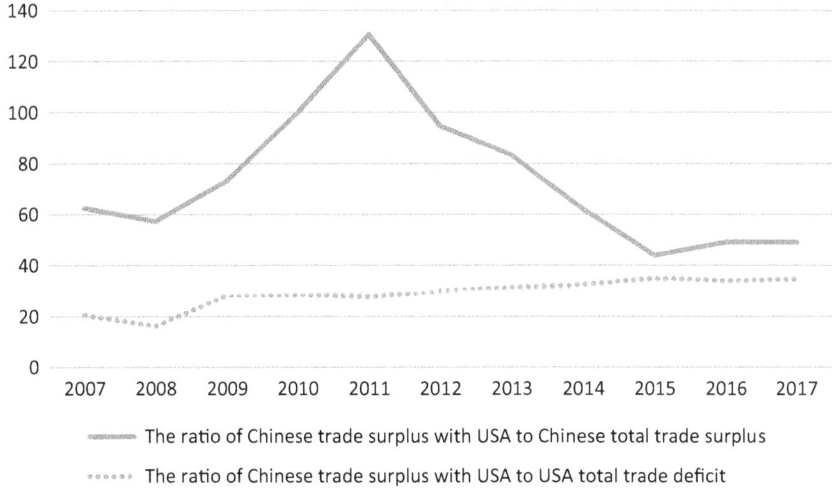

Figure 3. The ratio of Chinese trade surplus with the United States (2007–2017) (in percent).

Source: JETRO, *International Trade and Investment Report* (Annual Edition) and the author's calculation.

Table 4. The ratio of Chinese trade surplus with the United States (in percent).

Year	The ratio of Chinese trade surplus with the USA to the Chinese total trade surplus	The ratio of Chinese trade surplus with the USA to the USA total trade deficit
2007	62.38	20.56
2008	57.31	16.27
2009	73.27	28.47
2010	99.87	28.55
2011	130.63	27.82
2012	94.72	30.00
2013	83.34	31.34
2014	61.98	32.60
2015	43.98	34.98
2016	49.08	34.02
2017	49.08	34.66

Source: JETRO, *International Trade and Investment Report* (Annual Edition) and the author's calculation.

Here, X means export, M import, S saving, and I investment. Therefore, the referenced formula represents that the disequilibrium of trade balance to the difference between overall savings and overall investment.[5] A country with a trade surplus has a large amount of savings; on the contrary, a country with a trade deficit has a small amount of savings. The reason for the trade deficit is a large amount of consumption (small amount of savings) by the country concerned. In other words, it is undoubtedly wrong to assert that the reason for a trade deficit is the excess savings of another country.[6]

The above-mentioned formula applies to both Sino-American friction and US–Japan friction. In short, it is undoubtedly wrong to insist that the reason for the trade deficit of the United States is the excess savings of such countries as Japan and China.

[5] With regard to the arguments on US–Japan friction, see, for example, Komiya (1983, 1994).

[6] See, for example, Morita (2017a, 2017b).

Table 5. Savings rates of the United States and China (1995–2016) (in percent).

Year	USA	China
1995	7.24	29.60
1996	6.79	30.85
1997	6.58	31.50
1998	7.06	31.66
1999	5.19	28.80
2000	4.94	27.64
2001	5.13	27.59
2002	5.92	27.13
2003	5.57	29.30
2004	5.13	30.48
2005	2.97	30.84
2006	3.72	33.79
2007	3.49	35.49
2008	4.77	37.37
2009	6.07	37.66
2010	6.47	38.48
2011	7.01	38.02
2012	8.85	38.19
2013	6.32	37.83
2014	7.28	36.77
2015	7.78	35.74
2016	7.22	34.57

Source: OECD (Data: Global Note).

In any case, in order to investigate international trade between the United States and China more exactly, one should consider the situation in term of both quality and quantity.

First of all, we take a general view of the degree of dependence on foreign trade. The degree of dependence on foreign trade is a ratio in which the total amount of export and import is a numerator and GDP is a denominator. As shown in Table 6 (except 2009), until the year 2010, Germany and China had higher numerical values in terms of foreign trade than the whole world. However, only Germany had higher numerical values and China, Japan, and the United States had lower numerical values than the whole world. In terms of the degree of dependence on foreign trade, the order is China, Japan, and the United States. As far as the numerical values of 2017 are concerned, the foreign trade of the whole world amounted to 42.80 percent, China 32.9 percent, Japan 27.5 percent, and the United States 20.1 percent (further, Germany's foreign trade was 69.7 percent, much higher than the other three countries).

In short, as far as we can judge from the degree of dependence on foreign trade, (using the numerical values of the whole world as evaluation criteria), the values of China, Japan, and the United States are low; in particular, the amount of foreign trade of the United States was rather small.

Table 6. Degree of dependence on foreign trade of different countries and the world (2000–2017) (in percent).

Year	China	Germany	Japan	USA	World
2000	38.88	54.80	17.00	19.47	39.09
2001	37.82	55.45	16.77	17.62	37.75
2002	41.71	54.44	17.51	16.92	37.52
2003	50.42	55.54	18.42	17.27	38.96
2004	57.99	59.63	20.39	18.69	42.17
2005	54.31	57.50	21.81	19.80	42.49
2006	56.62	63.58	25.23	20.94	45.28
2007	54.39	65.71	27.43	21.63	46.50
2008	50.49	66.87	28.69	23.29	49.03
2009	39.10	56.89	19.79	18.26	40.06
2010	44.81	64.94	23.84	21.44	44.65
2011	45.03	70.17	25.73	23.94	48.40
2012	42.42	70.42	25.89	23.78	47.99
2013	40.87	68.92	28.70	23.14	47.57
2014	38.47	68.29	30.91	22.93	46.64
2015	33.04	68.90	28.57	20.76	42.97
2016	31.11	67.31	24.70	19.56	41.10
2017	32.93	69.72	27.45	20.06	42.80

Source: UNCTAD (Data: Global Note) and the author's calculation.

Next, we take a general view of the degree of dependence on export as shown in Table 7. Naturally, the degree of dependence on export is quite similar to the degree of dependence on foreign trade it goes without saying that the numerical value of the numerator is smaller, hence it is smaller than the numerical value of the degree of dependence on foreign trade.

Next, we look at the ratio of the import value. The denominator is the total world import value, and the numerator is the import value of respective country. The ratio is shown in Table 8 and Figure 4.

Similarly, we look at the ratio of export amounts. The denominator is the total export amount of the world, and the numerator is the export amount of respective country. The ratio is shown in Table 9 and Figure 5.

Table 7. Degree of dependence on the export of different countries and the world (2000–2017) (in percent).

Year	China	Germany	Japan	USA	World
2000	20.89	28.88	9.71	7.58	19.53
2001	20.20	30.07	9.21	6.84	18.84
2002	22.37	30.37	9.91	6.31	18.78
2003	26.55	30.78	10.41	6.30	19.54
2004	30.51	33.26	11.57	6.65	21.10
2005	29.84	32.16	12.03	6.93	21.37
2006	32.04	35.16	13.66	7.47	22.84
2007	31.44	36.88	15.05	8.00	23.51
2008	28.99	37.03	14.90	8.84	24.71
2009	21.85	31.31	10.44	7.37	20.26
2010	24.37	35.59	12.87	8.57	22.59
2011	24.03	38.11	12.83	9.60	24.49
2012	23.03	38.84	12.51	9.61	24.31
2013	22.30	38.22	13.48	9.48	24.16
2014	21.30	38.03	14.43	9.32	23.64
2015	19.09	38.74	14.20	8.29	21.72
2016	17.73	37.91	12.86	7.77	20.79
2017	18.47	38.93	14.18	7.95	21.64

Source: UNCTAD (Data: Global Note) and the author's calculation.

Table 8. The ratio of the import amount to the world total (2000–2017) (in percent).

Year	USA	China	Japan
2000	19.15	3.34	5.36
2001	18.66	3.75	5.08
2002	18.42	4.42	4.75
2003	17.16	5.31	4.65
2004	16.45	5.91	4.53
2005	16.86	5.62	4.63
2006	16.23	5.89	4.53
2007	14.87	6.14	4.19
2008	13.84	6.40	4.49
2009	13.22	7.40	4.09
2010	13.32	8.52	4.29
2011	12.76	8.99	4.53
2012	12.98	9.36	4.67
2013	12.72	9.92	4.35
2014	13.14	9.96	4.39
2015	14.32	9.87	3.96
2016	14.73	9.76	3.80
2017	13.88	10.23	3.79

Source: UNCTAD (Data: Global Note) and the author's calculation.

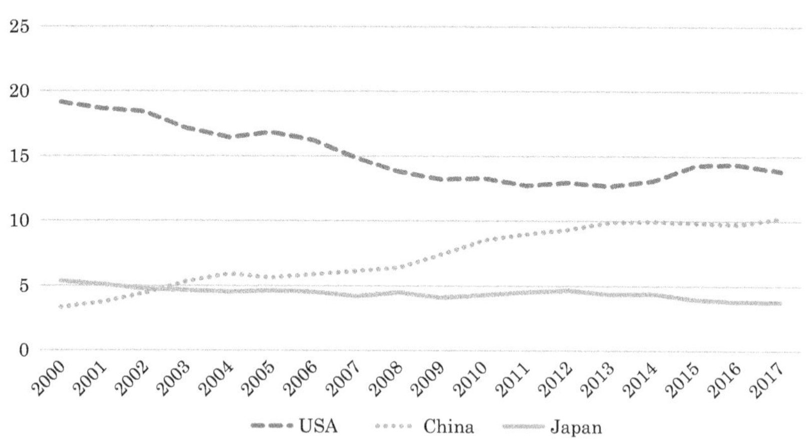

Figure 4. The ratio of the import amount to the world total in each country (2000–2017) (in percent).

Source: UNCTAD (Data: Global Note) (Annual Edition) and the author's calculation.

There is a noticeable tendency of a rapid increase in the ratio of the export amount of China to that of the whole world.

The duty battle between the United States and China has been implemented through import duty. Thus, it could become an object of judgment in which the import amount of the United States from China and that of China from the United States is predicted. Table 10 and Figure 6 show the import amount of the United States and China (from China and the United States, accordingly).

What is undoubtedly clear is that the United States' import amount from China was much greater than the Chinese import amount from the United States. Thus, if China levies the same amount of retaliative duties

Table 9. The ratio of the export amount to the world total (2000–2017) (in percent).

Year	USA	China	Japan
2000	12.23	3.88	7.16
2001	11.88	4.32	6.23
2002	10.92	5.10	6.18
2003	9.79	5.88	6.01
2004	9.07	6.55	5.94
2005	8.97	6.77	5.62
2006	8.84	7.55	5.26
2007	8.54	8.22	4.98
2008	8.32	8.48	4.77
2009	8.76	9.16	4.47
2010	8.65	9.91	4.92
2011	8.34	10.06	4.40
2012	8.57	10.83	4.26
2013	8.55	11.54	3.73
2014	8.76	12.03	3.75
2015	9.31	13.2	3.83
2016	9.26	12.65	4.04
2017	8.91	12.73	3.96

Source: UNCTAD (Data: Global Note) (Annual Edition) and the author's calculation.

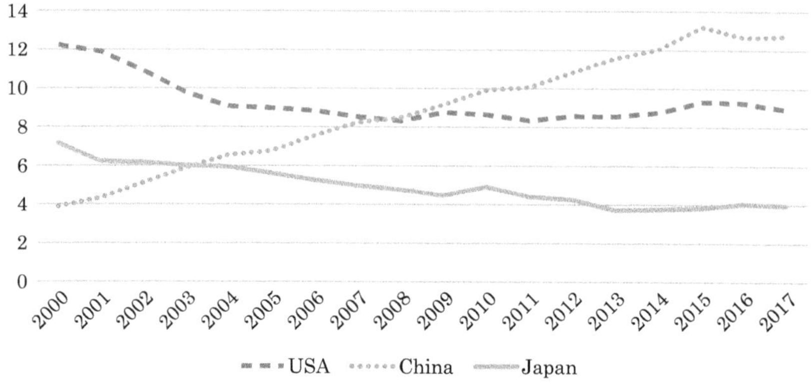

Figure 5. The ratio of the export amount to the world total in each country (2000–2017) (in percent).

Source: UNCTAD (Data: Global Note).

Table 10. The import amount of the United States and China (2007–2017) (million US dollars).

Year	USA import amount from China (A)	Chinese import amount from USA (B)	(A)/(B)
2007	321,443	69,391	4.63
2008	337,773	81,360	4.15
2009	296,374	77,460	3.83
2010	364,944	102,038	3.58
2011	399,362	122,154	3.27
2012	425,579	132,886	3.20
2013	440,448	152,575	2.89
2014	466,754	159,036	2.93
2015	483,245	148,737	3.25
2016	462,618	134,402	3.44
2017	505,470	153,943	3.28

Source: JETRO, *International Trade and Investment Report* (Annual Edition) and the author's calculation.

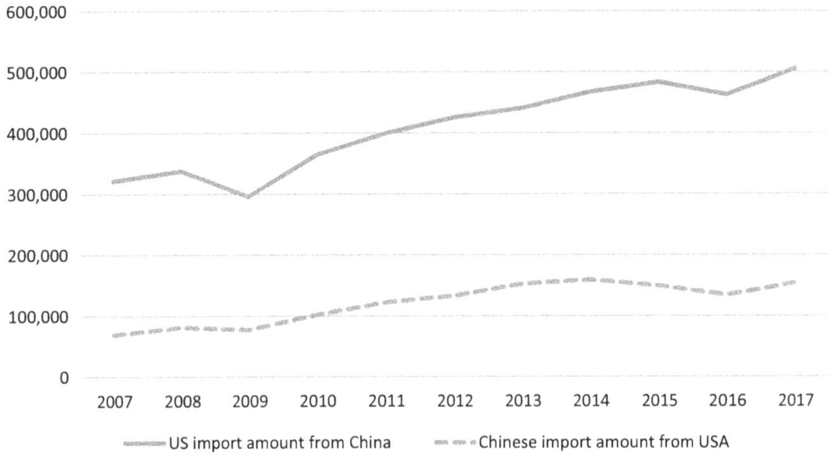

Figure 6. The import amount of the United States (from China) and China (from the United States) (2007–2017).

Source: JETRO, *International Trade and Investment Report* (Annual Edition).

(as levied by the United States as sanctions duties) on the import from the United States, it would sooner or later be exhausted.[7]

However, needless to say, there exist contrary numerical values in terms of the amount of export.

As clearly shown in Table 11 and Figure 7, China's exports to the United States are expanding significantly. We would examine the correlation with GDP scale for reference.

The correlation coefficient between the Chinese export amount to the United States (Table 11) and the GDP in China (Table 12) is 0.979212, which is significant (at a one percent significance level). In other words, if policies such as sanction tariffs negatively impact China's export to the United States, it is likely that China's GDP would also be negatively affected. Furthermore, the correlation coefficient between the United

[7]According to a report in *Nihon Keizai Shimbun* (20 November 2018), the IMF indicates that when both the United States and China charge import duties of 25 percent to the total import from the other country, there is a decrease in GDP amounting to 1.2 percent for China but only 0.2 percent for the United States. Unquestionably, economic impact of a full-scale US–China trade war would overwhelmingly disadvantage China.

Table 11. The export amount of the United States and China (2007–2017) (million US dollars).

Year	USA export amount to China (A)	Chinese export amount to USA (B)	(B)/(A)
2007	65,236	232,677	3.57
2008	71,457	252,297	3.53
2009	69,576	220,816	3.17
2010	91,881	283,304	3.08
2011	103,939	324,493	3.12
2012	110,484	351,796	3.18
2013	121,736	368,427	3.03
2014	123,676	396,082	3.20
2015	116,072	409,538	3.53
2016	115,602	385,085	3.33
2017	129,894	429,755	3.31

Source: JETRO, *International Trade and Investment Report* (Annual Edition) and the author's calculation.

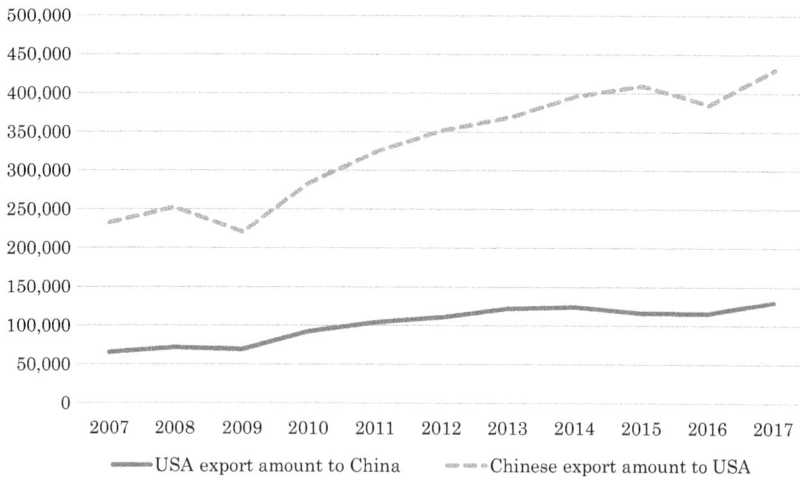

Figure 7. The export amount of the United States (to China) and China (to the United States) (2007–2017).

Source: JETRO, *International Trade and Investment Report* (Annual Edition).

Table 12. GDP in China (2007–2017) (million US dollars).

Year	GDP
2007	3,571,451
2008	4,604,285
2009	5,121,681
2010	6,066,351
2011	7,522,103
2012	8,570,348
2013	9,635,025
2014	10,534,526
2015	11,226,186
2016	11,221,836
2017	12,014,610

Source: IMF (Data: Global Note).

States' import amount from China (Table 10) and the GDP in China (Table 12) is 0.972203, which is also significant (at a one percent significance level).

In short, we undoubtedly recognize that there exists a significant correlation between the Chinese economic scale and the Chinese export amount to the United States (or the United States' import amount from China).

Now, on the contrary, let us discuss the United States.

Table 13 indicates the GDP in the United States. The correlation coefficient between the GDP in the United States (Table 13) and the United States' export amount to China (Table 11) is 0.875041546, which is significant (at a one percent significance level). Also, in other words, if there is a negative impact on the US exports to China due to policies such as sanction tariffs, it is believed that there would also be a negative impact on the US GDP. Furthermore, the correlation coefficient between the Chinese import amount from the United States (Table 10) and the GDP in the United States (Table 13) is 0.851326, which is also significant (at a one percent significance level).

Therefore, we note that the charging duty on international trade has a significant influence on the GDP of both countries.

Table 13. GDP in the United States (2007–2017) (million US dollars).

Year	GDP
2007	14,451,875
2008	14,712,825
2009	14,448,925
2010	14,992,050
2011	15,542,600
2012	16,197,050
2013	16,784,825
2014	17,521,750
2015	18,219,300
2016	18,707,150
2017	19,485,400

Source: IMF (Data: Global Note).

2.2. *Symmetric property*

Both Figure 1 (the ratio of the import amount from the United States and China to the total import amount of China and the United States) and Figure 2 (the ratio of the export amount to the United States and China to the total export amount of China and the United States) show the same symmetric property between trade linkage index and consumption–GDP ratio as mentioned in Chapter 2.

Although it might be redundant, we would add the following explanation for clarity.

The trade linkage index measures a distortion from a potential comparative advantage structure. And, the consumption–GDP ratio (based on the share in the world total) indicates the excess or deficiency of consumption expenditure of the each country. The principal reason for the occurrence of symmetry in the trade linkage index seems to be a distortion of the exchange rate (exchange rate of renminbi to US dollar). Also, the principal reason for the occurrence of symmetry in the consumption–GDP ratio seems to be the distortion of the economic structure represented by the savings rate, labor distribution ratio, etc., in China and the exorbitant privilege in the United States.

In order to clearly show the situation, the figures of symmetry of the trade linkage index and consumption–GDP ratio are indicated in Figure 8 of Chapter 2 (trade linkage index) and Figure 9 of Chapter 2 (consumption-GDP ratio). In these two figures, it can be observed that the graph exists both above and below around the threshold of 1.0. As indicated in Figure 1 (the ratio of the import amount from the United States and China to the total import amount of China and the United States) and Figure 2 (the ratio of the export amount to the United States and China to the total export amount of China and the United States), it is recognized that there could exist graphs above and below with a boundary of 15 percent. It could be another symmetry.

The symmetric graph indicates important conditions, such as expressions of economic structure and institutional mechanism. Thus, it could be understood that these expressions are not so easily revised. As long as the economic structure (which exists fundamentally) cannot be changed, and as long as the institutional mechanism cannot be modified, the situations indicated earlier are difficult to change.

In this section, we investigated the framework of Sino-American friction through information concerning international trade and concluded that such friction can be based on the economic structure and institutional mechanism and, thus, will be difficult to change.

In the next section, we conduct a general analysis of military expenditure.

3. Military Expenditure[8]

A critical aspect of the friction between the United States and China is obviously military expenditure. Based on numerical values made public, the tendency is as follows.

As shown in Table 14 and Figure 8, Chinese military expenditure has significantly increased in recent years. In particular, from the year 2011 onward, both the tendency to increase military expenditure in China and, to the contrary, the tendency to reduce military expenditure in the United

[8]The amount of the military expenditure varies from one source to another. In this chapter, we depend on statistics from the World Bank. According to the World Bank, China's military expenditure includes estimates of military spending not included in the official government budget.

States have been obvious. In fact, in the year 2011, military expenditure in the United States was 7,113 million US dollars and in China, it was 2,714 million US dollars. However, in the year 2017, military expenditure in the United States decreased to 6,097 million US dollars. In contrast, military expenditure in China increased to 4,350 million US dollars. If simply compared, the United States' military expenditure in the year 2017 decreased to 85.7 percent of its expenditure in 2011; in contrast, in China, it increased by 160 percent.

It goes without saying that because of the decrease in military expenditure by the United States and the increase in military expenditure by China, hostility between the two countries has become aggravated.

Judging from different indications, as Mearsheimer asserts, it has become clearer that China is not a "status quo power," but an "aggressive

Table 14. Military expenditure of the United States and China (2000–2017) (100 million US dollars).

Year	USA	China
2000	3,016.9	677.7
2001	3,127.4	854.1
2002	3,567.2	993.8
2003	4,152.2	1,079.8
2004	4,646.8	1,191.6
2005	5,033.5	1,344.2
2006	5,276.6	1,588.4
2007	5,569.6	1,826.9
2008	6,211.3	2,016.2
2009	6,685.7	2,438.2
2010	6,981.8	2,523.7
2011	7,113.4	2,714.3
2012	6,847.8	3,036.2
2013	6,397.0	3,335.6
2014	6,099.1	3,766.7
2015	5,961.0	3,833.9
2016	6,001.1	4,136.7
2017	6,097.6	4,350.1

Source: World Bank (Data: Global Note).

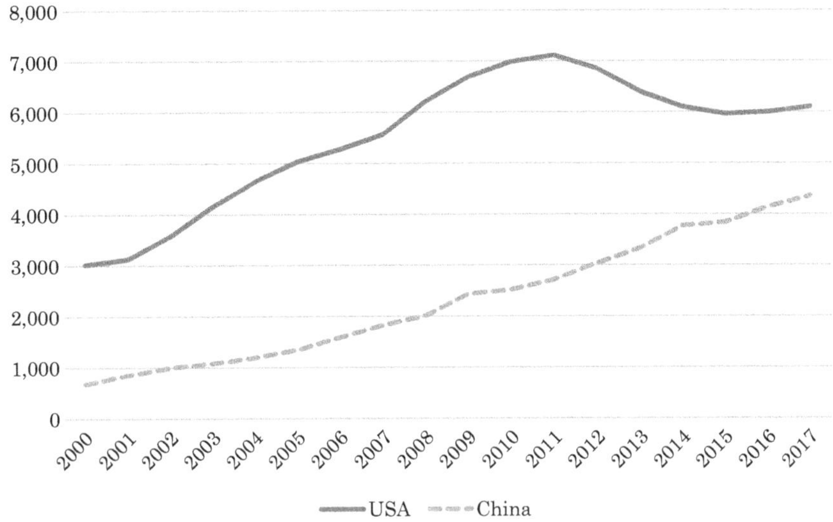

Figure 8. Military expenditure of the United States and China (2000–2017).
Source: World Bank (Data: Global Note).

state determined to achieve regional hegemony."[9] At any rate, it is difficult to insist that China would be a "status quo" country (which means that when the country develops democratically and economically, it would not engage in an arms race with the United States).

Furthermore, as far as an expansion of the People's Liberation Army is concerned, it is undoubtedly correct to say that there is an aspect of aiming for regional hegemony, but at the same time, it is undeniable that China's military spending also has the aspect of being a cost necessary for the survival of an authoritarian regime.[10] In short, in order to solidify the power base of the authoritarian regime, it is necessary to depend on the People's Liberation Army.[11] Therefore, military expenditure under the authoritarian regime could continue to expand.[12]

[9]Mearsheimer (2001, p. 402).
[10]Anami (2017, p. 210).
[11]*Ibid.*
[12]In a sense, when China develops economically and democratizes politically, it might be possible that military expenditure could be reduced. However, under the circumstances, democratization in China might be difficult and moving away from the national strategy

It is well known that China has provided finance for developing countries in order to expand its military influence. A typical example is the case of the Port of Hambantota in Sri Lanka. An article in *Nihon Keizai Shimbun* (27 June 2011) reported that Sri Lanka had proposed a strategy to improve its economic growth by utilizing the advantageously located port (in relation to marine transportation routes) to connect Europe and the Middle East to Asia. The then Cabinet Minister of International Financial Cooperation and Deputy Minister of Finance and Planning emphasized the country's "strategic location" and indicated a plan to achieve economic growth through the "hub design," serving as a transit point for logistics and tourism etc. Five harbors were indicated as the core of the "hub design," including the Port of Hambantota in the south, where large ships such as oil tankers could stop and refuel; also that, just a few kilometers offshore lies an oil transport route connecting the Middle East and Asia, which is reported to have great potential for the construction of refining facilities and other developments. In addition to these points, the article in *Nihon Keizai Shimbun* (27 June 2011) also reported support for these plans by China.[13]

Another article in *Nihon Keizai Shimbun* (10 December 2016) reported that the Sri Lankan government had stated that the rights and interests of large harbors located in the southern area could be sold to Chinese corporations. It also reported that, according to local information, the Sri Lankan government would sell 80 percent of the rights and interests of the Port of Hambantota to China Merchants Port Holdings Co., Ltd., for around 1,100 million US dollars.

About one year after the above-mentioned state of affairs, another article in *Nihon Keizai Shimbun* (21 December 2017) indicated that the Port of Hambantota in Sri Lanka was fully equipped through the assistance of China and was practically sold to a Chinese corporation because Sri Lanka could not pay China back. Moreover, it has been reported that a Chinese submarine made a call at the port. Thus, many countries are worried that China will utilize the port for military purposes.

---

of achieving regional hegemony might also be difficult. At any rate, it is difficult to judge the present China as a "status quo power," but it might be appropriate to judge the present China as an "aggressive state determined to achieve regional hegemony."

[13] It is noted that Chinese support equaled 2 billion US dollars and support by India equaled 1 billion US dollars.

In short, China provides a large amount of money to Sri Lanka, and when Sri Lanka is unable to repay China, China gets rights and interests over certain infrastructure and utilizes it for military purposes. In other words, when China develops economically and democratizes politically, China could become a status quo power.

What does this mean in terms of military technology? As far as military technology is concerned, according to Ito (2011), China has increased its production of nuclear warhead missiles every year since the middle of the 1990s. In order to realize its long-term national goal of becoming a regional hegemon in Asia and eliminating US power from the region, it is necessary for the People's Liberation Army to hold a large number of movable warheads and trajectory nuclear missiles (pp. 164–165).

Moreover, it is important to note that the Chinese government stole design technology for small, high-performance nuclear warheads for mobile multiple independently targetable reentry vehicles (MIRVs) from the United States (p. 165). Because of the theft of such a critical design technology, the nuclear technology of the People's Liberation Army can progress dramatically, and the People's Liberation Army can finally acquire the world's best nuclear weapons to compete against the nuclear forces of the United States. However, needless to say, progress in military technology should be through one's own technological progress, not through stealing. As a matter of fact, as reviewed in the next section, the Chinese government's efforts towards technological advancement are considered to be active.

Furthermore, what is also important is that, although both the US Department of Defense and the US Department of Energy were greatly startled by the theft of the nuclear technology by a Chinese secret agent in the year 1995, the Clinton Administration not only remained silent but also did not adopt any countermeasures (p. 166). In short, the Clinton Administration did nothing at all against such wrongdoing by Chinese spies. It is extremely difficult to understand why the US policy toward China was so tolerant.

In any case, the very fact that China has acquired highly advanced mobile ICBMs and SLBMs that cannot be destroyed by preemptive or retaliatory nuclear attacks by the US (p. 166) has become an extremely important security issue for both the United States and Japan.

In this section, what confirmed that China will not be a status quo power but an aggressive state determined to achieve regional hegemony, as Mearsheimer has asserted (Mearsheimer, 2001, p. 402). Also, we confirmed that the appropriate theoretical framework under which to correctly investigate China is offensive realism. We also concluded that Chinese military expenditure has been expanding, and the difference between this and the expenditure of the United States (whose military expenditure has been decreasing) has become notably smaller.

Then, what about the technological aspect? We consider it in the following section.

4. Technology

The situation regarding ZTE has already been mentioned at the beginning of this chapter. On 1 December 2018, a situation concerning Huawei Technologies Co., Ltd (hereafter Huawei) received much attention.

According to an article in *Nihon Keizai Shimbun* (7 December 2018), it was reported that the Canadian Department of Justice arrested Meng Wanzhou (Vice President and Chief Financial Officer (CFO) of Huawei), who is the daughter of Huawei's founder. It was also reported that US authorities requested a travel restriction on Meng Wanzhou on the suspicion of illegal export of manufacture from the United States to Iran; since then, the US government has imposed sanctions on Huawei. The article also reported that the US government and US Congress kept a close watch on Huawei and ZTE as they were suspected of conducting espionage on behalf of the Chinese government. The purchase of products from Huawei and ZTE by the US government was also prohibited. Furthermore, it was reported that the US Federal Communications Commission requested telecommunications companies (which received government subsidies) to not use the products of Huawei and ZTE.[14]

In fact, another article in *Nihon Keizai Shimbun* (8 December 2018) reported that Ansip Vice-Chairman of the EU shared his viewpoint at a press interview on 7 December in which he stated that such IT companies as Huawei were required to cooperate with Chinese intelligence agencies. He also said that the EU was concerned about security risks. According to yet another article in *Nihon Keizai Shimbun* (10 December 2018), the

[14]After that, the Chinese government imprisoned some Canadian people. Needless to say, it has never been clear whether or not the Canadian people's case had any relation with the arrest of Meng Wanzhou.

Japanese government formulated its guidelines regarding the procurement of information and communication equipment for central ministries and agencies and self-defense forces in order to defend against a possible leakage of confidential information on national security issues through the implantation of illegal programs. The Japanese government rejected products by Huawei, which was the largest company of communications equipment in China and was suspected of exporting products to Iran. The guidelines were applied for equipment procured after April 2019. In short, in both Europe and Japan, products of Huawei and ZTE were excluded.[15] This can be considered the beginning of the "digital cold war between the United States and China."[16]

It goes without saying that as for the relationship between military expenditure and national security, the role occupied by the technological level is assessed to be extremely important. However, because it is difficult to statistically judge the level of military technology, we consider here the number of patent applications in order to analyze the Chinese government's policy on technological progress (see Table 15 and Figure 9). Obviously, the number of Chinese patent applications has rapidly increased. As mentioned at the beginning of this chapter, it seems as if the Chinese government has decided to further a policy of "Made in China 2025" by investing big amounts in subsidies to high-tech industries and demonstrating a positive attitude toward protection of intellectual property.

To make sure of it, by using the Grubbs-Smirnov Test to see when the number of patent applications[17] significantly increased from past values and could be considered an outlier, it was found to be in 2011.[18] The result seems to agree with the values in Table 15 and Figure 9.

---

[15] For example, it was communicated that Deutsche Telekom, on 14 December, reconsidered apparatus procurement from Huawei (*Nihon Keizai Shimbun*, 15 December 2018).

[16] *Nihon Keizai Shimbun* (9 June 2018).

[17] As regards the Grubbs–Smirnov Test, see, for example, Morita (2017b).

[18] The result of the calculation indicated that it was −2.2486 (at the 5 percent significance level) in 2011 and −1.9538 in 2010. The result of the test might seem to support the assertion by Mifune (2016) that the "transposition of the direction of Chinese foreign policy" started to change direction during the second term of the Hu Jintao administration (p. 8). Moreover, the same test was implemented regarding military expenditure and nominal GDP, the result of which demonstrated that no abnormal values were measured in 2011.

Table 15. The number of patent applications in the United States and China (2000–2016).

Year	USA	China
2000	280,390	26,445
2001	293,805	31,239
2002	291,806	41,418
2003	301,737	58,757
2004	330,854	69,017
2005	383,242	97,948
2006	404,260	129,290
2007	437,353	161,308
2008	428,881	204,268
2009	397,919	241,434
2010	433,199	308,326
2011	440,632	436,170
2012	473,489	561,408
2013	501,162	734,096
2014	509,521	837,817
2015	530,662	1,010,615
2016	521,642	1,257,409

Source: WIPO (Data: Global Note).

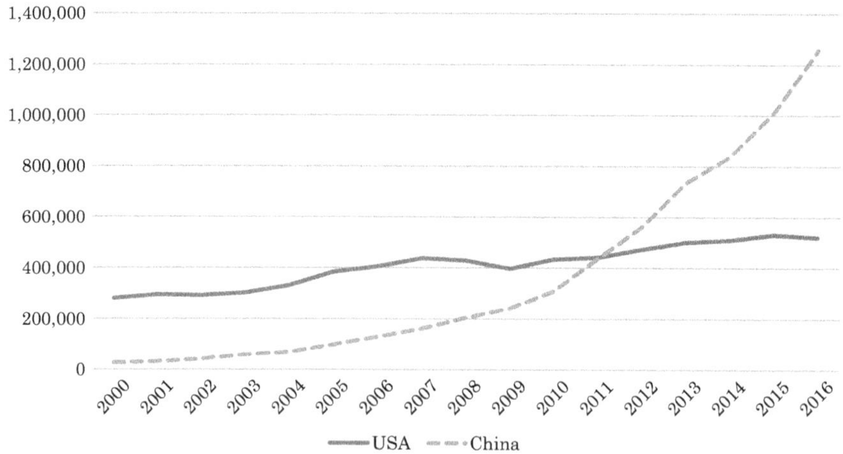

Figure 9. The number of patent applications from the United States and China (2000–2016).

Source: WIPO (Data: Global Note).

In short, China is offering a huge amount of subsidy to the high-tech industry and has shown a positive stance toward the protection of intellectual property. The rapidly increasing number of patent applications in China clearly indicates the positive stance of the Chinese government.

5. Sino-American Friction[19]

5.1. *Details*

The start of a clear confrontation between the United States and China (which is often called a "trade war") can be traced back to March 2018. That is to say, the US government introduced a draft on punitive duties against the Chinese due to infringement of intellectual property rights (on March 22).[20] On 3 April 2018, the US government made the draft public.

On 4 April 2018, China made public the items covered under retaliative duties, and the Under Secretary of Commerce of the Chinese government suggested that if an opponent attacked, the Chinese would fight to the last.

On 3 and 4 May 2018, the first conference on trade between the United States and China was held. However, on 16 May 2018, President Donald Trump stated that China ought to compromise. The second conference was held on 17 and 18 May 2018, in which high government officials of both the United States and China expressed the provisional reservation of customs duties. On 19 May 2018, Chinese Deputy Prime Minister Liu He stated that it took time to settle structural problems.

However, on 29 May 2018, the United States again expressed the initiation of duties as part of sanctions. Then, on 2 and 3 June 2018, a third conference on trade was held.

---

[19] This section is fundamentally based on the articles in *Nihon Keizai shimbun*.

[20] Furthermore, on 8 March, President Donald Trump signed a document which ordered the operation of import restrictions on steel and aluminum. The US government charged an import duty of 25 percent on steel and 10 percent on aluminum. Those import duties were applied to every country after 23 March. However, Canada and Mexico, which resumed renegotiation of NAFTA (North American Free Trade Agreement), were granted a postponement. It was further accepted that other allied countries such as Japan could be exempted from the duties after discussions.

After the third conference, the United States announced the final draft of duties for sanctions on 15 May 2018, and China also announced the imposition of retaliative duties on the same scale on 16 May.

The United States directed the consideration of additional tariffs of 200 billion US dollars on the 18th of the same month, and on the 20th, US Secretary of Commerce Wilbur Ross stated that China must be given pain, otherwise it would not stop its unfair trade practices.

On 6 July 2018, the Donald Trump administration of the United States imposed additional duties (25 percent) against Chinese products, such as industrial machinery and electronic components, which amounted to roughly 34 billion US dollars. Immediately, the Chinese government retaliated in an equivalent manner. It covered 818 items from the United States and 545 items from China, amounting to 34 billion US dollars, or 25 percent.

As indicated in an article in *Nihon Keizai Shimbun* (7 July 2018), this kind of situation reflected the domestic political affairs of the United States. According to that article, there was a confrontation between Steven T. Mnuchin (United States Secretary of the Treasury) and Robert E. Lighthizer (United States Trade Representative), which signified a confrontation between moderates (former) and hard-liners (latter). According to Mearsheimer (2001), it was a confrontation between the "engagement policy" and the "containment policy."

The same article also reported that US President Donald Trump was greatly dissatisfied by the United States trade deficit (which continued to increase). In May in 2018, the US introduced high-level talks between Mnuchin (US Secretary of the Treasury) and Liu He (Chinese Deputy Prime Minister) and pressed the Chinese side for a final concession. Initially, the moderates, including Steven T. Mnuchin, held strong influence. After the second round of talks with China in the middle of May, Mnuchin announced a joint statement that included an increase in US export to China and declared that the trade war was temporarily on hold, shelving tariffs. The hardliners quickly retaliated.

Lighthizer repeatedly explained the necessity of the imposition of duties. The media declared that China had come out on top after the talks and called Trump "weak-kneed." Trump publicly stated his discontent against the slow progress of negotiations with China.

Subsequently, on 23 August, the Trump administration inaugurated the second round of sanction duties.[21] The second round of sanctions

---

[21] The following description is based on an article in *Nihon Keizai Shimbun* (24 August 2018).

amounted to 16 billion US dollars and covered such products as semiconductors and chemicals. Due to this, China again enforced retaliative duties, whose scale was the same as that of the United States (16 billion US dollars). Both rounds of sanctions and the retaliative duties amounted to 50 billion US dollars each. An article in *Nihon Keizai Shimbun* (23 August) reported that, although both sides tried to negotiate through dialogue, President Trump never wavered from his firm stance. The trade war, which had become a burden to the economy, looked like it would continue.

Moreover, the Trump administration announced, on 24 September 2018, that a third round of sanction duties would be imposed.[22] The targets included foodstuffs and consumer electronics from China. The duties amounted to 200 billion US dollars and the additional tax rate was at first 10 percent and would increase after 2019 to 25 percent.[23] China's retaliative duties on the import of products from the United States, such as LNG and timber, amounted to 60 billion US dollars, with additional retaliative duties at the rate of 5–10 percent, which was implemented on the same day.

By the third round of the trade war, the import amount through sanctions imposed by the Trump administration against China was around 250 billion US dollars. On the contrary, the import amount through sanctions imposed by the Chinese government against the United States was around 110 billion US dollars.

What proportion do these import amounts, said to be 250 billion US dollars or 110 billion US dollars, account for?

As shown in Table 16, according to Chinese statistics, in the year 2017, the United States' import amount from China equaled 429.755 billion US dollars and the Chinese import amount from the United States equaled 153.943 billion US dollars. According to US statistics, also in the year 2017, the United States' import amount from China equaled 505.470 billion US dollars and the Chinese import amount from the United States equaled 129.894 billion US dollars.

---

[22]The following description is based on an article in *Nihon Keizai Shimbun* (25 September 2018).

[23]Thereafter, on 1 December 2018, the US government announced that the scheduled additional duties on Chinese products (which was planned to be implemented on 1 January 2019) were deferred. However, although both countries would continue to negotiate on intellectual property rights, the United States set a deadline of 90 days after which, if the negotiations were not fruitful, the US government would raise the tariff rates (see *Nihon Keizai Shimbun*, 3 December 2018).

Table 16. The GDP ratio of various countries to the world GDP (1–2003) (in percent).

	1	1000	1500	1600	1700	1820	1870	1913	1950	1973	2003
France	2.2	2.3	4.4	4.7	5.3	5.1	6.5	5.3	4.1	4.3	3.2
Germany	1.2	1.2	3.3	3.8	3.7	3.9	6.5	8.7	5.0	5.9	3.9
UK	0.3	0.7	1.1	1.8	2.9	5.2	9.0	8.2	6.5	4.2	3.1
USA	0.3	0.4	0.3	0.2	0.1	1.8	8.9	18.9	27.3	22.1	20.6
Japan	1.1	2.7	3.1	2.9	4.1	3.0	2.3	2.6	3.0	7.8	6.6
China	25.4	22.1	24.9	29.0	22.3	32.9	17.1	8.8	4.6	4.6	15.1
India	32.0	28.1	24.4	22.4	24.4	16.0	12.1	7.5	4.2	3.1	5.5

Source: Maddison (2007, p. 381).

Therefore, according to Chinese statistics, 71.5 percent of Chinese imports from the United States and 58.2 percent of US imports from China were subject to high tariffs as of 2017. According to US statistics, 84.7 percent of Chinese imports from the United States and 49.5 percent of US imports from China were subject to high tariffs as of 2017.[24]

The United States import amount from China (which become the object to the imposition of tariffs) in the year 2017 was 2.79 times greater than the Chinese import amount from the United States (according to the US statistics, it was 3.89 times greater). Because the import amounts (which become the object to the imposition of tariffs) greatly varied, if both countries competed with each other in the imposition of duties, the United States would undoubtedly be superior to China due to the larger scale of its duties.[25]

Moreover, it was reported that President Donald Trump declared that if China retaliated against the third sanction duties, the United States would impose additional duties on all the remaining imported products

[24]It was reported that the two countries were threatening each other with 50 percent and 70 percent high import duties (*Nihon Keizai Shimbun*, 25 September 2018).

[25]As indicated earlier, if China were to levy the same amount of retaliative duties (as levied by the United States as sanctions duties) on import from the United States, it would eventually run out, and then China would not be able to continue the retaliation. It goes without saying that there is a difference between the United States and China not only in terms of the import amount but also in the substitutability of imported goods by other countries (although the details on this point would not be discussed in this book).

from China.[26] As indicated earlier, China imposed retaliative duties on import products from the United States, which amounted to 60 billion US dollars with additional rates of 5–10 percent. In contrast, as President Trump stated, if the US government had invoked additional duties on all import products from China, China would never have been able to retaliate further. The situation was precarious and it took on the appearance of a war of attrition with no exit.

One could clearly recognize the tension in Sino-American relations in a speech given by US Vice President Michael Richard Pence at the Hudson Institute on 4 October 2018. Pence stated that the US foreign policy on China had changed from an "engagement policy" to a "containment policy."

5.2. *The speech by US Vice President Michael Pence*[27]

An article in *Nihon Keizai Shimbun* entitled "the speech of US Vice President Michael Pence" specifically emphasized the change in US foreign policy on China (from "engagement policy" to "containment policy") by using subtitles such as "the United States shifts from engagement to containment with China" and "the era of helping is over."

As expressed in the article, the original "engagement policy" was described, which involved economic liberalization and greater partnerships between China and the liberal and democratic world. However, China had chosen to economically attack the US and had strengthened its military power. Therefore, the United States changed the policy to a "containment policy."

As the article stated, the reason why the Trump administration changed its policy toward China was because China's presence was a threat to the hegemony of the United States in terms of both economy and national security. It undoubtedly meant that the Chinese national strategy of becoming a regional hegemon had been noticed.[28]

---

[26]*Nihon Keizai Shimbun* (25 September 2018).

[27]Readers can read the speech by Michael Pence on the Internet. The description of this section is based on an article in *Nihon Keizai Shimbun* (2 November 2018). Because the numerical values in that speech were based on statistics from the United States, they might be different from the numerical values given in this chapter.

[28]According to Rudd (2018), the United States' engagement policy with China, which covered a period of 40 years, was already finished officially and replaced by "strategic

"The speech of Michael Pence" included topics such as economy, national security, foreign policy, and the Chinese domestic situation. On the economic situation, Pence mentioned that the Chinese Communist Party made inconsistent policies on liberal and fair trade, which included tariffs, exchange operations, compulsory technology transfers, and theft of intellectual property. The speech also mentioned that the Chinese government instructed government officials and enterprises to acquire the intellectual property belonging to the United States (which formed the basis of the economic leadership of the United States) with every conceivable means, in order to lead the world economically, which resulted in China having the second highest GDP in the world. Thus, Mr. Pence expressed his opinion that successive US administrations had mostly neglected such Chinese behavior or in some cases had even assisted the Chinese. He asserted that such a period had come to an end. In short, the speech by Mr. Pence expressed the change in US policy toward China.

Speaking about national security, Mr. Pence stated that the Chinese National Security Agency had committed large-scale theft of US technology and the Chinese Communist Party had converted stolen civilian technology to military technology on a large scale. He also expressed that the US government had strengthened the role of the Committee on Foreign Investment in the United States (CFIUS) in order to protect the United States' national security from Chinese depredation. He mentioned that the US government would continue its activities against the Chinese government until China completely stopped its theft of US intellectual property. The speech by Mr. Pence therefore indicated that Chinese military advancement was mainly implemented due to the theft of US technology and not due to Chinese domestic technological development.

Another statement by Mr. Pence speech shows that Chinese vessels are regularly patrolling around the Senkaku Islands, which are under Japan's administration, also shows that, in the South China Sea, a US Navy Aegis destroyer conducting a "Freedom of Navigation Operation (FONOP)" was forced to take evasive maneuvers when a Chinese navel vessel dangerously approached within 45 yards, heightening vigilance against China's military actions in both the East China Sea and the South China Sea. Mr. Pence's speech demonstrated that the US had tightened its

---

competition." The United States' hard-line stance against China seemed to be broadly supported by US government agencies and the business community.

guard against Chinese military operations in the East China Sea and South China Sea.

Speaking about foreign policy, Pence claimed that China extended its influence using debt diplomacy. China had provided billions of dollars for infrastructure construction in Asia and Africa. Mr. Pence mentioned the Sri Lankan case, in which the Sri Lanka government incurred a vast amount of debt in order to construct a port (the commercial value of which is debatable), which was administered by a Chinese state-owned company. When the Sri Lanka government was unable to pay back the debt, the Chinese government exerted pressure to transfer the port to Chinese ownership. Mr. Pence worried about the future of the port (as a naval base of China's).

Mr. Pence also mentioned that the Chinese Communist Party had tried to persuade three countries in South and Central America to discontinue relations with Taiwan. He asserted that such Chinese actions would endanger the stability of the Taiwan Strait.

Furthermore, about Chinese relations with the United States, Mr. Pence declared that China had attempted to interfere in the domestic politics of the US and had tried to provide remuneration to US companies, movie production companies, universities, think tanks, journalists, members of state governments and federal governments, etc., for their work. He also criticized the Chinese government for mobilizing undercover agents and disguised organizations to attempt to change the American narrative on China. Mr. Pence disclosed that, due to the malicious influence and intervention by the Chinese government in the United States, the opinion about China in the United States had changed.

It goes without saying that Mr. Pence harshly criticized the human rights situation in China because China had, in the past few years, rapidly increased its control of and suppression against its own citizens by establishing unprecedented aggressive monitoring by occasionally borrowing US technology. Mr. Pence also criticized the renewed wave of persecution against Chinese Christians, Chinese Buddhists, and Chinese Muslims. He especially censured China's behavior in the Xinjiang Uyghur Autonomous Region, where one million Uygur Muslims were sent to governmental concentration camps in order to reform their thoughts.

In his speech, Pence asserted that, in the relationship with China, the United States would never compromise until the relationship became one based on fairness, reciprocity, and mutual respect for national sovereignty.

After the above-mentioned speech by Vice President Michael Pence, on the morning of October 5, the day after the speech, the Chinese Ministry of Foreign Affairs issued a spokesperson's statement saying that, as this is an unfounded accusation, we firmly oppose it. However, as the article reported,[29] the news on the speech by Mr. Pence in the Chinese media was restrained because, if the minds of the Chinese people became unsettled, the one-party rule of the Communist Party might waver, and if the anti-American sentiments of Chinese people increased, then it might be difficult to heal Sino-American relations. As the article also reported, it was in China's favor at present to have stable relations with the United States.

The purpose of addressing Vice President Pence's speech in this section is to understand it in conjunction with Mearsheimer's arguments mentioned at the beginning of this chapter. To put it briefly, Mearsheimer's concern about the engagement policy advocates' belief (if China develops democratically and economically, China would become a status quo country seeking stability and would not engage in an arms race with the United States) is clearly dismissed.[30]

Can China become a hegemon[31] in the future?

If we extrapolate from the current scale of the GDP and military expenditure, it would be possible, in the not-so-distant future, for China to catch up with and overtake the GDP and military expenditure of the United States. However, this is based on the premise that it could be estimated through extrapolation.

Just in case, we would assess the situation that can be extrapolated, in accordance with Maddison (2007). The information for making a decision is provided in Table 16 and Figure 10. Table 16 indicates the GDP ratio of various countries to the world GDP (from Maddison, 2007) and Figure 10 illustrates three countries, the United States, China, and India, from the seven countries mentioned in Table 16.

With regard to GDP, for 50 years from 1820 to 1870, the GDP ratio of the United States rapidly increased and approached that of China and

---

[29] It is the article in *Nihon Keizai Shimbun* (2 November 2018).

[30] At the same time, it should be recognized that, from the viewpoints of offensive realism, Chinese behavior (as a great power wanting to become a hegemon) might become similar to the behavior of the United States.

[31] In this book, we use the term "hegemon" based on Mearsheimer (2001).

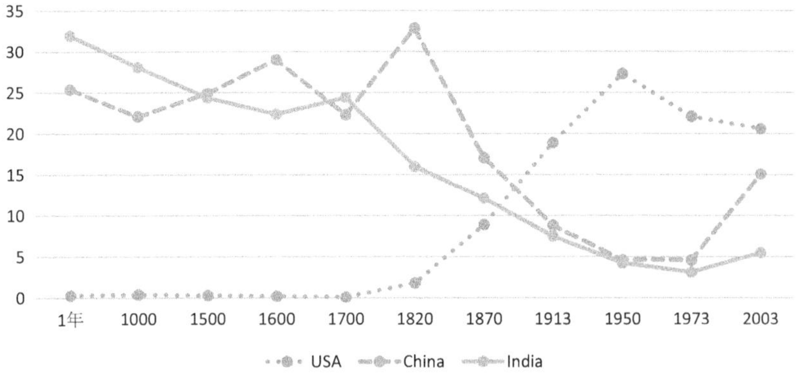

Figure 10. The GDP ratio of USA, China, and India to the world total (1–2003) (in percent).
Source: Maddison (2007, p. 381).

India. In the year 1913, the GDP ratio of the United States became much higher than that of China and India. The GDP ratio of various countries to the world GDP changed in such a drastic manner as shown in Table 16. Thus, when we extrapolate the GDP trend, it is possible for China to catch up with and overtake the scale of GDP and military expenditure of the United States.

It goes without saying that the change in the relations between the United States and China is closely connected with the change of hegemony. As shown in on Table 17, the "cycle of hegemony" occurs in accompaniment with the world-scale wars. After the Second World War, the "hegemon UK" was taken over by the "hegemon USA."

Supposing that a change from the hegemony of the USA to the hegemony of China could occur, it would become possible after a Third World War (or a similar scale serious confrontation). It is also possible that the hegemonic position of the United States is maintained after a serious confrontation between the United States and China.

As Mearsheimer (2006) asserts, China aims to become a "regional hegemon" in Asia. In order to do so, China needs to become much more powerful and will try to banish the United States from the Asian region. The United States has been a regional hegemon in the Western Hemisphere since the late 1800s. Although the United States is clearly the most powerful state on the planet today, it is not a global hegemon (p. 160). In that

Table 17. Cycle of Hegemony.

Cycle	Approximate duration	World power	Formative global conflict
I	1518–1608	Portugal	Italian wars (1499–1517)
II	1609–1713	United Provinces of the Netherlands	Spanish wars (1581–1608)
III	1714–1815	Great Britain	French wars (1618–1713)
IV	1816–1945	Great Britain	French wars (1792–1815)
V	1946–	United States of America	World wars (1914–1918, 1939–1945)

Source: Modelski and Thompson (1987, p. 86).

sense, China is trying to become a regional hegemon in the Asia. However, the United States is trying to deter China from becoming a regional hegemon. China's neighboring countries of India, Japan, Russia, Singapore, South Korea, and Vietnam are also forming a balancing coalition[32] led by the United States as they are worried about the rise of China. With regard to Taiwan, it would be difficult to suppose that the United States and Japan would approve of Chinese rule in Taiwan. Taiwan is an important player of the anti-China balancing coalition and is extremely important in a strategic sense for the security of the East Asian Sea Lane. Mearsheimer's conclusion is that international politics is an unpleasant and dangerous business, and no amount of goodwill could mitigate the intense security competition when a state seeks to become a hegemon in Eurasia. According to him, it is "tragedy of great power politics."

If China tries to become a regional hegemon in the Asian region, and if the United States (and the neighboring countries of China) does not exonerate China, a conflict might become unavoidable. As Mearsheimer asserts, it would be the logical conclusion of current international politics.[33]

[32] With respect to the balancing strategy, see Morita (2018).

[33] Moreover, Mearsheimer's assertion is that the United States has a profound interest in seeing Chinese economic growth slow down considerably in the years ahead. For much of the past decade, however, the United States has pursued a strategy intended to have the opposite effect. The US policy on China is misguided. That is because a wealthy China would not be a status quo power but an aggressive state determined to achieve regional hegemony (Japanese version, p. 517). It is rather difficult to find any evidence to doubt the Chinese aim to achieve regional hegemony.

5.3. *Peaceful rise?*

According to Rudd (2018), the US policy toward China shifted from engagement to "strategic competition," and this US hard-line stance against China is broadly supported by the US government agencies and the business community.

Moreover, considering the statement by Pan Zhongqi and Chen Zhimin (2014), it became possible for China to embark on the historical process of peaceful rise only after the initiation of the reform and opening-up policy (p. 79). The framework of China's reform and opening-up policy, China's peaceful rise, and the US engagement policy with China would become clear.

What is the "Chinese peaceful rise?"

According to Pan and Chen (2014), China's peaceful rise strategy is hard to call China's grand strategy. As previously mentioned, the process of peaceful rise actually began in 1978, and the original intention behind China's proposal of the concept of peaceful rise was not as a grand strategy for its own development, but to counter the China threat theory (p. 77).

However, the expression peaceful rise is the most suitable one to indicate the policy design for Chinese development.

And the adoption of the reform and opening-up policy immediately helped to lower the priority of military expenditures among domestic issues. Economic growth was prioritized in place of armament and China utilized the long-term stable international situation. Pan and Chen (2014), thus, described that China dispelled the negative impression that China was a country that Challenged the international system (p. 81). Pan and Chen (2014) also argued that the basic principles of Chinese foreign policy were that China should not take any conspicuous actions, should wait for opportunities, and accomplish its tasks in a favorable manner (p. 80).

In any case, according to the assertion of Pan and Chen (2014), the world for many years had a multipolar structure and China has promoted this multipolar structure since the mid-1990s (p. 82). Pan and Chen (2014) also mentioned that, from the viewpoint of controllability of a multipolar system, China firmly believes that cooperation among governments (based on sovereign states) can solve problems and create appropriate and long-term solutions (p. 84). As a matter of fact, the Chinese approach to accomplish objectives involves a combination of bilateral partnership and multilateral arrangement (p. 85). Actually, it seems to be a strategy that, while advocating a multipolar structure that could prevent the rise of hegemonism and unilateralism by a dominant superpower, actually seeks to secure influence through bilateral partnerships.

Based on the assertion of Pan and Chen (2014), is it possible that China's rise could be peaceful? If it is possible, it depends on the assessment of the concept of relationship governance. Relationship governance (which is based on the concept of interconnection that is deeply rooted in Chinese culture) could play an important role in the governance of international relations. Relationship governance is a process to deal with complicated relations within a group by political and social arrangement (p. 85). This process aspires to create mutual confidence through the establishment of a common understanding with regard to social norms and human morality by establishing order and reciprocal cooperation (p. 85).[34]

However, Pan and Chen (2014) also state that the recent escalation and intensification of maritime disputes in the East China Sea and the South China Sea are factors that could potentially derail China's path of peaceful rise and that it is widely known that China's maritime policy has become increasingly hardline, making it seem as though the strategy of peaceful rise is coming to an end (p. 95).

If straightforwardly present with reference of recent world standard views, it could be said that the maritime disputes in the East China Sea and the South China Sea are understood as evidence that China was not originally on the path of peaceful rise and that the strategy of peaceful rise, which appears to be coming to an end, never really existed. Mearsheimer, who insists that the US policy on China has been misguided for decades, agrees with this view. Actually, Mearsheimer's "offensive realism" suggests that the purpose of a nation-state is to maximize power. According to Mearsheimer, it would be difficult for a country as powerful as China to become a status quo power and thus for the Chinese rise to be peaceful.

However, as Pan and Chen (2014) argue, the reason why China insists on territorial rights over islands (including Taiwan) in the East China Sea and South China Sea has never come from an ambition to increase its power base in the international system. As Pan and Chen (2014) explain,

---

[34]It is extremely difficult to correctly recognize such abstract expressions. With regard to such expressions, Mearsheimer (2014) provides us with useful information about Confucian culture.

the relationship between China and Taiwan has seen both periods of good and bad, but China has always maintained political legitimacy over the governance of Taiwan (p. 95).

Pan and Chen (2014) state the following in their summary.

China should not deviate from its peaceful rise. An unavoidable problem for China might be how the Chinese concept (used worldwide with Chinese intrinsic characteristics and Chinese universal sense of values) develops and becomes popular and also how China's peaceful rise can be accepted by the world (p. 96).

According to Pan and Chen (2014), the world might have misunderstood China's rise as it happened at a very quick pace that was much faster than what the world expected (p. 96).

In short, the world could not accept China's rise even though it was peaceful. Therefore, when the situation becomes clear, the world could accept China. At that time, the rise of China would become evident as peaceful when viewed through the lens of globally accepted concepts that have developed and spread, alongside China's unique characteristics and values.[35]

According to Mearsheimer (2014), if China continues its striking economic growth over the next few decades, it is likely to act in accordance with the logic of offensive realism, which is to say, it will attempt to imitate the United States. China is involved in various territorial disputes, and the more powerful it is, the better able it will be to settle those disputes on terms favorable to Beijing (p. 368). Then it would be recognized that the rise of China is peaceful.

In order to become more powerful to settle territorial disputes on favorable terms, it would need to maintain overwhelming economic power, military power, and cultural influence. As Mearsheimer asserts, it is necessary for China to act in accordance with the logic of offensive realism.

Then, is it possible to refer to the tendency to act according to the logic of offensive realism as "peaceful rise"? Needless to say, "to act in accordance with the logic of offensive realism" means "not to act as a status quo power but to act as an aggressive state determined to achieve

[35]In other words, without referring to the Chinese intrinsic characteristics and the Chinese universal sense of values, can China's rise ever be recognized as peaceful?

regional hegemony." It would be impossible, under those circumstances,[36] to misrepresent such an aggressive attitude as a "peaceful rise."

On the whole, we assert in this section that it is difficult to find any basis to recognize Chinese actions as part of a "peaceful rise."

5.4. *Offensive realism*

As considered in the previous section, if we assume that China acts according to the logic of offensive realism, what could we foresee for the near future of the world?

We consider it with reference to Chapter 10 of Mearsheimer (2014).

The translator commentary and postscript (by S. Okuyama) could be used as a reference. According to a summary of it, there are two theoretical suppositions of "defensive realism" by Kenneth Waltz: (1) the international system is anarchic and (2) the aim of a nation-state is to survive. In addition to these two, the theoretical suppositions of "offensive realism" by Mearsheimer include the following: (3) a large country has an aggressive military power, (4) a large country cannot completely know what an enemy country plans, and (5) a large country will try to act rationally (Table 18 compactly presents Mearsheimer's views (2014)). Adding to those suppositions, a large country has to be aggressive enough to expand power and aspire toward world hegemony country in order to ensure national security. Based on the five suppositions, it can be estimated that China will take the same actions as the United States. As Mearsheimer asserts, China cannot rise peacefully.

Table 18. The major realist theories.

	Defensive realism	**Offensive realism**
What causes states to compete for power?	Structure of the system	Structure of the system
How much power do states want?	Not much more than what they have. States concentrate on maintaining the balance of power	All they can get. States maximize relative power, with hegemony as their ultimate goal

Source: Mearsheimer (2014, p. 22).

[36] Reason why we mention "under the circumstances" is that, it might be indefinable under the world in which China could become a single pole hegemonic country.

Although it might be obvious, there could exist such circumstances under which China could rise peacefully and the future of Sino-American relations could be viewed optimistically. According to Mearsheimer (2014), there are two types of arguments. One argument is cultural theory, which claims that China's Confucian culture will allow a rapidly growing China to avoid intense security competition with its neighbors as well as the United States. The other argument is based on a familiar liberal theory of economic interdependence. Conflict is said to be unlikely because the major countries in Asia — as well as the United States — are economically intertwined, which means that if they fight with each other, it will threaten the prosperity that is so important to all of them. On close inspection, however, neither of these theories provides a sound basis for avoiding trouble ahead in Asia (p. 403).

In regard to such an optimistic theory on China's peaceful rise, Mearsheimer offers his counterarguments.

As far as the cultural theory is concerned, there is little basis for the claim that China is an exceptional great power that eschews realist logic and instead behaves in accordance with the principles of Confucian pacifism. Almost all of the available evidence indicates that China has a rich history of trying to maximize its relative power. Furthermore, there is no good reason to think China will act differently in the future (p. 407).

Concerning the argument of economic interdependence, Mearsheimer insists as follows.

This perspective has two components. First is the claim that China's economy is inextricably bound to the economies of its potential rivals, including Japan and the United States, and a war involving them would have disastrous economic consequences for all the belligerents (p. 407). Second, prosperity is the main goal of modern states (p. 407). However, with regard to the theory of economic interdependence, because if you do not survive, you cannot prosper, political calculations often trump economic ones when they come into conflict (p. 408). Also, concerning the economic costs of war, by starting a war, a particular state might be having significant economic problems, which could put it in a position where it has little to lose economically and maybe even something to gain (p. 409). And also states sometimes start wars in the expectation that victory will bring them substantial economic and strategic benefits and that those prospective benefits will be greater than the prosperity lost from damaged interdependence (p. 409). It is said that economically interdependent countries can sometimes fight wars and still avoid incurring significant economic costs (p. 409). Thus, the above-mentioned reasons make it difficult to be confident that economic interdependence can serve as a firm foundation for peace in Asia in the decades ahead (p. 410).[37]

Therefore, Mearsheimer (2014) submits that the picture he has painted of what is likely to happen if China continues to rise is not a pretty one. Indeed, it is downright depressing (p. 410), and he asserts that there is good reason to think China will eventually pursue regional hegemony (p. 411).

In short, it is reasonable to recognize that, if China behaves in accordance with offensive realism, we can reach a conclusion that China cannot rise peacefully.

6. Conclusion

In this chapter, we focused our attention on topics such as trade, military expenditure, and technology relating to China and the United States. The "rise of China" has been tremendous, specifically in terms of the Chinese technology policy.

In Section 5, concerning the "Sino-American friction," we (1) indicated the start of the friction, (2) considered the speech by Vice President Michael Pence, (3) investigated whether or not "China's rise" could be assessed as peaceful, and (4) examined the view based on the "offensive realism."

The provisional conclusion obtained by the above-mentioned examinations will be presented as follows (because circumstances are still changing, it will be difficult to judge decidedly):

1. Economic interdependence relations between China and the United States are based on the "economic structure" and "institutional mechanism"; therefore, the relations cannot be easily revised.

---

[37]As mentioned earlier, economic interdependence between China and the United States has been strong and, thus, it is difficult to suppose that the it can be easily destroyed. In view of the present Sino-American relations, it is also difficult to find any grounds to insist that political calculations could trump economic ones. However, if behaviors of both China and the United States can be recognized in the framework of "offensive realism," it might be reasonable to think that political calculations could trump economic ones.

2. Confrontation between China and the United States seems to have intensified because of both the "American decrease" and "Chinese increase" in military expenditure.
3. We consider the occurrence of the"outlier" by the Grubbs–Smirnov Test on the Chinese number of patent applications. And the results indicate that the abnormal values occurred in the year 2011.
4. It is extremely difficult to conclude that China's rise can be peaceful.
5. Judged from the circumstances, the Chinese national strategy can be recognized as "offensive realism."
6. Chinese behavior, derived from the framework of "offensive realism," might become similar to US behavior (as a regional hegemon).
7. Assuming that China's behavior parallels that of the US, the "Sino-American friction" seems to be a confrontation not regarding a trade balance but regarding regional hegemony.
8. Therefore, we should recognize that the "Sino-American friction" can move toward an extremely serious confrontation (although it might be a long-term prospect).[38]

[38]Needless to say, it does not mean that there is no way to avoid a Sino-American war.

Part II

Chinese Foreign Relations: Case Studies

Chapter 5

An Economic Analysis of Sino-German Relations

1. Introduction

In the forthcoming time horizon of two to three decades, many believe that the status of a "hegemon" — a term referring to an overwhelmingly powerful nation in the world due to its economic power, military might, and cultural influence — would shift from the United States (US) to China.

As a matter of fact, it is apparent that US economic and military power would gradually decline, whereas those of China would (supposedly "not gradually, but rapidly") expand.

In this context, international relations surrounding Japan may serve as a representative case. In accordance with the US' withdrawal from East Asia (as a result of the decline in both its economic and military power), a military vacuum is likely to emerge. And it is expected that this vacuum could be filled by China.

As mentioned above, the probability of this occurring within the next 20–30 years is high.

From the viewpoint of the US, it could be beneficial for them to act swiftly to slow down China's march toward regional hegemony. We could recognize that various policies of the Trump administration in the US were advanced under such intentions.

From the viewpoint of China, however, it would be best to continue evading these policies and maintain a stance of patience until the emergence of a pro-China government. With the above-forecasted period, China may potentially surpass the US, given their current positions.

However, we could also recognize that the messages sent out by Xi Jinping, the current Paramount Leader of China, have never been one of evasion.

The Xi Jinping administration of China appears to have adopted various policies that were strongly criticized by the US (as well as by the United Kingdom (UK), France, and Australia[1]). The criticism was directed, among others, at policies that were branded as promoting "reeducation camps" and "forced labor" (or, in other words, "a violation of human rights") in Xinjiang Uyghur Autonomous Region; that the "one country two systems" principle in Hong Kong has been easily broken with the enactment of the "Hong Kong National Security Law"; and also that they continuously concealed the infection status of the novel coronavirus (over a period of one month or several months). Undoubtedly, it appears that these policies were implemented by taking a calculated risk of accepting criticism from international society.[2]

In summary, in recent years, Sino-American relations have differed since the period of President Obama (USA) and President Hu Jintao (China).

Then, would it be correct to assert that a large number of countries have taken a strict stance toward China? That is indeed not true. According to an article in *Nihon Keizai Shimbun* (7 August 2020), with relation to the "Hong Kong National Security Law," enacted for greater Chinese control in Hong Kong, 53 countries supported China in the United Nations Human Rights Council at the end of June 2020. The number of countries that supported the proclamation of criticism of China was only 27; nearly all were developed countries, including Japan. In other words, the "undemocratic dictatorship," which may be hard to accept for developed countries, was supported by 53 countries; in contrast, the number of countries criticizing it was limited to only about half the number. The reason why the "undemocratic dictatorship" by the Chinese Communist Party was supported could be easily recognized. According to the same article

[1] Whether or not Japan could be included in that list as of August 2020 might be a delicate matter.

[2] It would be difficult to suppose that, although they exactly predicted the infection status of the novel coronavirus, they continued concealing the situation. However, it goes without saying that what should be criticized has been the innate characteristics of the Chinese Communist Party (to keep inconvenient facts secret).

mentioned above, the countries that backed China included Cuba, Pakistan, Cambodia, and African countries, which were subsidized by China for their development fund, with exceptions being oil-producing countries in the Middle East and countries with highly influential governments. To put it rather simply, China acquired support through financing.

However, for China, in order to acquire this "support," it not only involved "financing" but also "the market." For example, with regard to automobiles, the sales figure in China in 2019 was 25,768,677, significantly larger than in the second- and third-largest markets, the US (17,480,004) and Japan (5,195,216), respectively. The Chinese market is certainly an extremely important market for auto manufacturers, as it boasts annual sales of more than 25 million automobiles. Therefore, the foreign policies of both Germany and Japan toward China must be necessarily cautious, considering that they host the industry giants Volkswagen and Toyota Motor Corp., respectively.

Particularly, the relations between Germany and China regarding Volkswagen must be handled delicately. In China's huge market, Volkswagen holds a 15–16 percent share, which exceeds that of Toyota Motor Corp. by more than double. Volkswagen's operations in China might warrant close observation. Even if the inhumane dictatorship of the Chinese Communist Party continues, it is highly uncertain whether Volkswagen would choose to exit the huge Chinese market.

In this chapter, following acknowledgment of various limitations, we investigate the Sino-German relationship, focusing primarily on its economic aspects.

The structure of this chapter is as follows: In the first section, we review the trend of international society, focusing on changes in US policy toward China as well as Germany's policy position toward China. In the second section, with regard to the characteristics of Sino-German relations, we look back at the Second Sino-Japanese War and consider the commonalities between China and Germany, assessing whether China and Germany could easily enter into an alliance. In the third section, we further consider Sino-German relations based on trade relations and foreign direct investments. In the fourth section, we investigate Volkswagen's relationship with China, which might play an important role in shaping Sino-German relations. Finally, in the last section, we present the conclusions of this chapter.

2. Where does the Problem lie?

An event that could mark the beginning of our discussion occurred in Europe in 2015, which might still be relatively fresh in readers' memory.[3] Namely, in March 2015, the UK expressed its intention to participate in the Asian Infrastructure Investment Bank (AIIB), which was led by China (UK was the first among the advanced industrialized countries).

That expression of interest from the UK presented an important opportunity for European countries to participate in the AIIB.

In September 2015, the US Environmental Protection Agency issued a notice of violation to Volkswagen (which had evaded emissions testing). Later, in October 2015, Chinese President Xi Jinping visited the UK, which subsequently led to business deals (whose total amount reached 40 billion GBP) being established between the UK and China. In light of these events, Prime Minister David Cameron expressed that Sino-UK relations have entered a new era, which President Xi Jinping described as a "golden age."

It might be easily recognized that the relations between China and Europe have grown closer, while those between China and the US have become strained.

The above-mentioned tendencies have taken on a different appearance due to various reasons, which are outlined as follows. First, in the US, the Donald Trump administration marked a shift in the conventional balance between the US and China from an "engagement policy" to a "containment policy." Second, given the criticism of Xi Jinping's administration as a "non-humanitarian dictatorship," globally, more countries and regions began reconsidering their "engagement policy" toward China. Third, needless to say, the concealment of the truth about the novel coronavirus by the Xi Jinping administration raised suspicion.

In short, there is a growing perception that the "engagement policy" toward China may be counterproductive and should be replaced by a "containment policy"; this could be a reflection of the global trend.

On 23 July 2020, US Secretary of State Mike Pompeo delivered an address deemed "historical." A summary of that address is as follows[4]: He

---

[3] The following content is based on Manabe (2016, pp. 132–134).

[4] According to an article in *Nihon Keizai Shimbun* (25 July 2020). Moreover, there could be existed some addresses called "historically." The main background of them might be the following Chinese situations described earlier in the text. Because of the problems in

stated that China has stolen valuable intellectual property and secret information related to trade, squeezed supply chains away from the US, and engaged in the use of slave labor, alleging that the main trade routes of the world have been made unsafe for international commerce. He called President Xi Jinping a real believer in bankrupt totalitarianism ideology — an ideology that could characterize China's long-standing ambition toward world hegemony under Chinese Communism. He also stated that the US cannot deal with China as a normal country, as it would any other country, and that the Chinese General Consulate in Houston, Texas, had to be closed because it was a base of espionage and intellectual property theft by China.[5] With regard to the Chinese observance of international law in the South China Sea, he observed that the US has reversed its stance of eight years, during which it (referring to the previous government) took insults lying down. Pompeo concluded that if the free world could not change communist China, China would change them.

It goes without saying that, when Mike Pompeo mentioned that the free world would try not to be changed by China, he addressed the anti-China network and sought an anti-China alliance.[6] By saying that the free world would be miserable if it allowed itself to be changed by China, many of the liberal and democratic countries might choose to join the anti-China network.[7] However, it might be probable that countries would not want to participate in this network. Germany may be expected to be one of the important non-participant countries. [8]

China such as the "Hong Kong National Security Law," "violation of human rights in Xinjiang Uyghur Autonomous Region," and "cover up of the novel coronavirus," the policies of the Chinese Communist Party led by President Xi Jinping have deviated considerably from what was considered acceptable by the international society.

[5]As a retaliatory measure, it was announced that China notified the closing of US general consulate in Chengdu City, Sichuan Province (*Nihon Keizai Shimbun*, 26 July 2020).

[6]See the article in *Nihon Keizai Shimbun* (22 July 2020). Needless to say, the assessments within the US of Pompeo's address might not be identical. Particularly, it was reported that the views on pro-Chinese media were unsparing (although we do not have any comments here on them).

[7]According to the author's subjective expression, the world in which "China would change us" seems to be practically a "world of nightmare." However, it might be correct that the number of pro-China politicians (the so-called "panda hugger politicians") in the Western world could be surprisingly large.

[8]Makabe (2016) expressed that the "possible alliance" between China and Germany could become the "strongest" and the "most atrocious." As a matter of fact, any country (not only

Table 1. Prediction of growth rate by the OECD (2020–2021) (in percent).

	(1) Re-expansion case of infection		**(2) Convergence case of infection**	
	2020	**2021**	**2020**	**2021**
World	▲7.6	2.8	▲6.0	5.2
Japan	▲7.3	▲0.5	▲6.0	2.1
USA	▲8.5	1.9	▲7.3	4.1
China	▲3.7	4.5	▲2.6	6.8
Europe	▲11.5	3.5	▲9.1	6.5

Source: OECD (Data: *Nihon Keizai Shimbun*).

On 10 June 2020, the Organization for Economic Cooperation and Development (OECD) reported the "prediction of growth rate," which consisted of the following two types of prediction: (1) "re-expansion case of infection" within the year 2020 and (2) "convergence case of infection."[9] The prediction by the OECD is shown in Table 1.

Because "a prediction is a prediction," we acknowledge its hit-and-miss nature. After having understood this limitation, when looking at the predictions, in both cases of "re-expansion case of infection" and "convergence case of infection" for countries and regions, we could observe a relatively higher rate of growth, first, for China and, second, for Europe.[10]

Moreover, on 24 June 2020, the International Monetary Fund (IMF) released the "prediction of growth rate" estimates for the years 2020 and 2021, which are shown in Table 2. According to that prediction, the country with the highest growth rate is China, followed by Europe.[11] If the

Germany) which would form an alliance with China led by the Xi Jinping administration might surely form an atrocious alliance. Also, Japan's ambiguous diplomatic stance could be quite capable of being looked upon with suspicion. However, it would not be probable that Japan would have such relations with China resembling an "alliance" in the near future because of the past history and because of national sentiment in both countries. Therefore, it could be recognized that Japan would not be considered similarly as Germany.

[9] See *Nihon Keizai Shimbun* (11 June 2020).

[10] It goes without saying that nobody has the slightest objection to insisting that one of the countries which have driven the European economy might surely be Germany.

[11] See *Nihon Keizai Shimbun* (25 June 2020). Europe here means that both the UK and the Eurozone are included.

Table 2. Prediction of growth rate by the IMF (2020–2021) (in percent).

	2020	**2021**
World	▲4.9	5.4
Japan	▲5.8	2.4
USA	▲8.0	4.5
Eurozone	▲10.2	6.0
UK	▲10.2	6.3
China	1.0	8.2
Brazil	▲9.1	3.6
Saudi Arabia	▲6.8	3.1
World trade volume	▲11.9	8.0

Source: IMF (Data: *Nihon Keizai Shimbun*).

source of the novel coronavirus is China, and if (as is commonly claimed) the Chinese government engaged in a cover-up operation resulting in the virus spreading more extensively and more seriously across the world, and if this results in an upward revision of China's relative standing in the world, then it must be said that this is a significant and tragic situation.[12]

This chapter attempts to focus our attention on Sino-German relations, which may provide useful information when investigating Sino-American relations. If we suppose that, for Germany, China is the best partner in the Asian region, and for the US, Japan is the best partner in the same region,[13] then, while considering Sino-American relations, Sino-German relations seem to be as much of critical importance as US–Japan relations.

According to an article in *Nihon Keizai Shimbun* (22 July 2020), the Tony Blair Institute for Global Change (UK) revealed the result of a public

[12] It goes without saying that it must be the unintentional result of the Chinese government. Suppose, on the contrary, if it were the intended result of the Chinese government, we could say that "the world after then" must be really miserable.

[13] It might be doubtful whether or not Japan is the best partner in the Asian region for the US (that is, the US before the Trump administration). Even if there existed a US–Japan alliance, for the US before the Trump administration, the best partner (or potentially the best partner) in the Asian region could be China. Such a way of thinking for the US seemed to be significantly changed since "the birth of the President Trump administration" and "the occurrence of the novel coronavirus."

opinion survey (held in June 2020), indicating that perceptions of the Chinese government became worse compared to levels before COVID-19, with 60 percent in the UK, 55 percent in France, 46 percent in Germany, and 54 percent in the USA responding negatively. Based on these results, the Tony Blair Institute for Global Change indicated that it became difficult for politicians in the US and Europe to not deal with Chinese situations. However, as the same article reported, the degree of "hard line" stance of German policy toward China was undoubtedly weaker than that of the policies of the UK and France. In fact, with regard to the "exclusion of Huawei" policy, Germany was withholding its participation. Also, it was reported that the then German Chancellor Angela Merkel appealed for continued talks with China. Thus, the basic principle of German policy toward China was, as yet, "change through trade."[14] It appeared to resemble the US' "engagement policy" toward China adopted by the Obama administration, which meant that the US, Europe, and Japan believed China would naturally become a liberal and democratic country with sufficient growth.[15] However, that seems to be an arbitrary prejudice held by developed countries.[16] In Communist China, such a tendency remained completely unrecognizable.[17] After the establishment of Xi Jinping's administration in China, we must acknowledge that the above-mentioned arbitrary prejudice (of developed countries) has clearly become hopelessly futile.

What exactly does an "alliance" between countries mean? The main aim of an alliance is undoubtedly national security. When we focus our

---

[14]If Germany continued to employ such an "engagement policy" toward China since the birth of the Xi Jinping administration, we have to say that it has been an extremely wrong policy.

[15]It seems for us that such an optimistic view could not be effected under the current Chinese communist administration.

[16]Could it not be arbitrary prejudice until the time of second Tiananmen Square incident?

[17]It is said that German Chancellor Angela Merkel has a "communist thought." However, because Germany is a democratic country, unless many people in Germany desire communism, Germany could not become communist. Furthermore, it was certain that, in Germany, the Hitler administration was the result of a democratic procedure. However, it was beyond doubt to insist that the enormous amount of reparation imposed by the Treaty of Versailles drove German people toward Nazism. We could not suppose that in the Germany of Merkel administration, there could exist necessary and sufficient conditions for communism.

attention on countries such as the US and China, which are either hegemonic or near-hegemonic, it would be appropriate to suppose that their actions could be recognized as "offensive realism."[18] For countries that act based on "offensive realism," although economic interests may be important, they would not be considered vital. In this sense, it is evident that China could fall within that scope, whereas contemporary Germany might not.

Supposing that there could exist relations in the above sense of an "alliance" between China and Germany, the main purpose of China would be paving a pathway toward "hegemony" (as achieved through "One Belt One Road") while that of Germany would by and large center around its "economic interest."[19]

Either way, in this chapter, we attempt to examine the economic relations between China and Germany.

3. Characteristics of Sino-German Relations

There exists an assertion stating that the Sino-Japanese War was initiated by Germany.[20] It does not matter whether or not Germany initiated the war; however, there was no place for doubt that Germany provided assistance to China (both openly and covertly). It was Germany that provided military supplies to China, enabling the latter to become a formidable adversary for the Japanese army as they worked out Chinese strategies of offense and defense which were put into practice. To the belligerent nations of China and Japan, although Germany claimed to be neutral on the surface, it was certainly a betrayal in providing facilities for

---

[18] See Mearsheimer (2001).

[19] As mentioned earlier in the footnote 14, it is hard to believe that many Germans, who democratically elect their leaders, would support an alliance with the Chinese Communist Party (especially the Xi Jinping administration), to confront the anti-China encirclement by the United States, Europe, Japan, Australia, and others. For Germany, it would be purely an "economic alliance."

[20] See Ara (2008). The Japanese title of Ara (2008) is just the same as "Sino-Japanese War was initiated by Germany." Needless to say, we might have various views concerning the country that originally initiated the Sino-Japanese War.

militaristic China. Furthermore, between Germany and Japan at that time, there existed the "German–Japanese Anti-Comintern Pact."[21]

Needless to say, Japan repeatedly protested against the concessions granted to militaristic China by Germany.[22]

It was 7 July 1937 when the "Marco Polo Bridge Incident" broke out. However, after this incident, when Kintomo Mushakoji (the ambassador of Japan to Germany) protested the arms export to China, Konstantin von Neurath (the German minister for foreign affairs) responded that Germany had aimed to suspend the arms export to China. However, Germany did not do so (and instead, it exported arms to China by transporting them through a British company in Singapore using Dutch ships).[23] As Ara (2008) described, on 16 August, the Fuhrer Adolf Hitler took counsel with Werner von Blomberg (minister for defense) and Konstantin von Neurath, in which Hitler mentioned that, although Germany would basically maintain the partnership with Japan, with regard to the dispute between Japan and China, Germany should maintain neutrality, and that, as long as China would pay with foreign exchange or raw materials and as long as it could be successfully camouflaged, Germany would continue the export to China. Moreover, Ara (2008) stated that Hitler's intention was to increase Germany's profit by continuing exports to China as before while ostensibly maintaining a posture of friendly relations with Japan, which seemed to be an unambiguous act of disloyalty.[24]

We mention various related matters, as described by Ara, in the following.[25]

The reason why Germany did not accept Japan's repeated requests was clear: its strong economic ties with China. As a matter of fact, according to the statistics of 1936, among the countries to which Germany exported arms, China held an overwhelmingly dominant position,

---

[21] It was on 25 November 1936 when the "German–Japanese Anti-Comintern Pact" ended, and as mentioned later, it was on 7 July 1937 that the "Marco Polo Bridge Incident" broke out. Therefore, we could not but doubt the effect of the international agreement (with Germany) of the "German–Japanese Anti-Comintern Pact."

[22] In Ara (2008), it was mentioned that Japan repeated ineffective protests and Germany easily dealt with them.

[23] Ara (2008, pp. 169–170).

[24] *Ibid.*, p. 171.

[25] The following depends on *ibid.*, p. 177.

accounting for 57.5 percent of the total. The second position was occupied by Bulgaria (10.5 percent) and the third by Turkey (6.1 percent). Japan occupied only 0.5 percent. The amount of arms deals between Germany and China at the time of these statistics reached 2.3 million Reichsmarks, and it increased to 8.2 million Reichsmarks in 1937 (when the Marco Polo Bridge Incident occurred).[26]

Judging from Germany's international relations, particularly considering its rearmament situation, foreign currency gained from its economic relations with China was extremely important. Thus, for Germany, the value of Japan's exports could not compare with those of China.[27] Therefore, regardless of whether this action constituted disloyalty, Germany continued its exports to China. It should be remembered that Germany prioritized economic earnings while backing up China, although it recognized disadvantages for Japan, its partner country, under the Japan–Germany Anti-Comintern Pact.

The question we seek to answer is whether the above-mentioned bilateral relations between Germany and China were a restrictive particular case of Nazi Germany with China or rather a common theme of Sino-German bilateral relations, which could be shared by the current bilateral relations between the Federal Republic of Germany and the People's Republic of China. However, generally, it seems that such an aspect could exist in international relations.[28]

If that is the case, could the Sino-German relations be easily concluded as an alliance? Needless to say, although it would be difficult to answer such a question about international relations between two countries, it seems appropriate to recognize that Sino-German relations could easily lead to an alliance.

For example, Makabe (2016) details shared characteristics between Germany and China, as shown in Table 3.[29] In fact, the author asserts that,

---

[26] Thus, the concerned battlefront in China was said to be the war between the Germany and Japanese armies (*Ibid.*, p. 172).

[27] *Ibid.*, p. 177.

[28] With regard to the cases referred to as an "intelligence war," although it would be extremely rare to be publicly announced, it might usually be daily occurrences. Concerning this matter, see, for example, Takako Cline (2018).

[29] We would not refer in this chapter whether or not there could become different opinions from Table 3. Although it is not clear what "regional hegemon in Europe" of Germany

Table 3. Shared characteristics of Germany and China.

	China	Germany
Behavioral pattern	Hegemonism in Asia	Hegemonism in Europe
Intention to economic growth	Strong	Strong
System	Communism	Feudal capitalism
Race	Multiracial	Divergence through division and unification
New industrial development	Industrial reorganization led by the government	Industry 4.0

Source: Makabe (2016, p. 14).

in the post-war world order, the paradigm shift would be occurring from an "American center" to a "China–German center." According to Makabe, both countries have many common characteristics and also have mutually complementary relations. That is to say, China wishes to obtain technological strength and creditworthiness from Germany, and Germany desires to acquire a significant share of the huge market in China.[30]

Such relations, as mentioned above, appear to be quite similar to the erstwhile mutually complementary relations between China (of Chiang Kai-shek) and Germany (of Adolf Hitler).

With regard to the relations that could easily lead to an alliance, there are several incidents that can be mentioned.

According to an article in *Newsweek* (28 July 2020), Helmut Schmidt (former chancellor) repeated his remarks defending China in relation to the Tiananmen Square protests in 1989 and became the first politician to visit China after these protests.[31] In those days, criticism against China (which

---

means, according to data from the World Bank, Germany's military expenditure in 2018 placed it in the eighth place (with Japan in the eleventh place). Neither Germany nor Japan are nuclear powers. It might be difficult to predict if Germany would become a regional hegemony in Europe in the distant future; however, it would not be easy to mention that Germany has an aim to be a hegemony or a regional hegemony.

[30] See Makabe (2016, p. 16). Concerning the wishes of China, it seems that there are a few objections. The complementary relations between Germany and China could also be realized between Japan and China. However, it would be difficult to recognize that Sino-Japanese relations could easily lead to an alliance.

[31] See *Newsweek* (Japanese version).

was denounced for the massacre of its own citizens by using tanks of the People's Liberation Army) from the international community was strong, and it faced severe sanctions. Therefore, visits such as the one made by Helmut Schmidt were expected to improve Sino-German relations.[32]

A more recent example is the stock acquisition of Deutsche Bank by HNA Group. Chinese HNA Group invested money in Deutsche Bank in February 2017, and then in March and April of the year, it advanced its stock acquisition. Then, it was reported that the Group, holding 9.92 percent of equity stock in May, became the largest shareholder.[33] However, following a deterioration in the management of HNA Group, it was said that the Chinese government might intervene, possibly leading to its nationalization. Should this situation come to pass, it is said that it would result in the Chinese government becoming the largest shareholder of Deutsche Bank.[34]

In another example, it was reported that Chinese auto manufacturer Zhejiang Geely Group Holding Co., Ltd. acquired a 9.69 percent stake in German automaker Daimler and became its largest shareholder.[35] The case in question unfolded as follows. Daimler made disclosures pursuant to the German Securities and Exchange Law. That transaction value was conceivable as a scale of one trillion yen. Because Geely is a parent company of firms such as Swedish Volvo, there was a possibility that it might exert

---

[32] With respect to the above-mentioned cases, they were not another country's affairs for Japan. After the Tiananmen Square protests, the first official visitor to China recognized as important by the Western world was Masayoshi Ito (the then chairman of the LDP General Council, Japan) and also the first country which released the freezing of international yen loans to China ahead of other countries. And first and foremost, in October 1992, the Japanese government initiated the formal visit of the Emperor to China. The Japanese government planned the restoration of international relations with China and also pushed for the return of China to international society. However, thereafter, there were no signs of improvement in Sino-Japanese relations. Although we would not investigate the reasons for that in this book, we have to say that the relations between China and Japan have never been one that could easily lead to an alliance.

[33] *Sankei News*, 24 May 2017.

[34] With regard to such situations, for example, see Watanabe (2018). Thereafter, it was announced that HNA Group sold 26.8 million stocks of Deutsche Bank with 63.4 million euros whose share decreased to be 6.3 percent (*Bloomberg*, 18 February 2019). And finally, it was reported that HNA Group came under Hainan Province government supervision (not the central government in Beijing) (*Sankei News*, 29 February 2020).

[35] See *Nihon Keizai Shimbun*, 24 February 2018.

influence on key German competitors. Also, although the aim of Geely remained uncertain, it reportedly had an interest in Daimler's battery technology.[36] With regard to this case, Watanabe (2018) reported that because the auto industry developed military technology such as engines, it is an important industry from the perspective of national security and has a substantial influence on other industries. However, regarding this situation, German Chancellor Angela Merkel reportedly indicated that there was "no violation" and showed a stance of acceptance.[37]

The state of affairs clearly indicated that Merkel demonstrated a pro-China stance during her visit to China. Makabe (2016) presented Merkel's frequent visit to China as an example to show that Germany moved toward strengthening its relations with China. After Angela Merkel took office as Chancellor, the number of times she visited Japan until October 2015 was three; in contrast, she visited China at least eight times. Judged from just the timing of visits, it is evident that Germany placed considerable emphasis on its relations with China. Moreover, Makabe (2016) reported that Merkel herself mentioned China as the most important partner in Asia.[38]

Certainly, when Germany recognized that China could be the most important partner in Asia, it had to be the kind of relations that could easily culminate into an alliance.

4. Economic Relations between China and Germany

4.1. *Trade relations between China and Germany*

In this section, we investigate the economic relations between China and Germany, comparing them with those between Germany and Japan and between Germany and the US.

First, in Section 4.1, we consider trade relations.

The first parameter is the "directional trade ratio."[39] As indicated earlier, that ratio measures the closeness of trade relations. Table 4 shows the directional trade ratio between Germany and China.

As shown in Table 4, the ratio lies within the range of 0.05–0.06, which cannot be considered a significant value. In order to compare, we

---

[36] *Ibid.*

[37] Watanabe (2018, p. 94).

[38] Makabe (2016, p. 124).

[39] Concerning the details of directional trade ratio, see Chapter 2 of this book.

Table 4. Directional trade ratio between Germany and China (2008–2018).

Year	Directional trade ratio	Year	Directional trade ratio
2008	0.048	2014	0.058
2009	0.055	2015	0.058
2010	0.061	2016	0.060
2011	0.060	2017	0.061
2012	0.057	2018	0.061
2013	0.055		

Source: JETRO *International Trade and Investment Report* (Annual Edition) and author's calculation.

Table 5. Directional trade ratio between Germany and Japan (2008–2018).

Year	Directional trade ratio	Year	Directional trade ratio
2008	0.024	2014	0.023
2009	0.025	2015	0.023
2010	0.024	2016	0.025
2011	0.024	2017	0.025
2012	0.023	2018	0.025
2013	0.023		

Source: JETRO *International Trade and Investment Report* (Annual Edition) and author's calculation.

need to know what the directional trade ratio is between Germany and Japan. Table 5 presents this value.

The ratio shown in Table 5 lies within the range of 0.023–0.026, which cannot be considered a significant value; it is also recognized as an undoubtedly smaller ratio compared to that between Germany and China.[40]

Just to be sure, we present the directional trade ratio between Germany and the US in Table 6.

The directional trade ratio between Germany and China is similar to that between Germany and the US. In contrast, the directional trade ratio between Germany and Japan indicates undoubtedly a smaller value. In order to clearly show the comparison, Figure 1 is presented. As can be seen, China has about the same ratio with the US as it does for Germany, whereas its Japanese ratio is smaller. The difference between frequencies

[40] It seems to show that, for Germany, China could be the best partner in Asia.

Table 6. Directional trade ratio between Germany and the United States (2008–2018).

Year	Directional trade ratio	Year	Directional trade ratio
2008	0.055	2014	0.057
2009	0.054	2015	0.064
2010	0.057	2016	0.061
2011	0.051	2017	0.059
2012	0.055	2018	0.059
2013	0.055		

Source: JETRO *International Trade and Investment Report* (Annual Edition) and author's calculation.

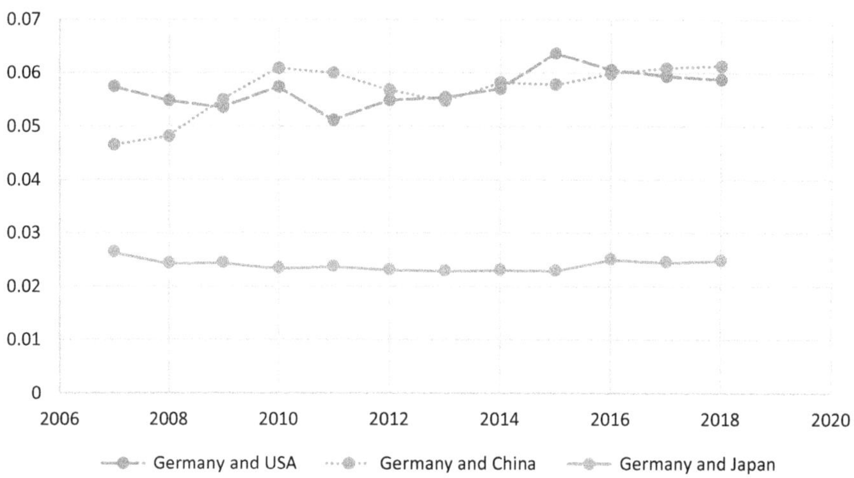

Figure 1. Directional trade ratio of Germany with each country (2007–2018).
Source: Jetro, *International Trade and Investment Report* (Annual Edition) and author's calculation.

of Merkel's visits to China and Japan might be reflected by the disparity in the ratios of 0.05–0.06 and 0.023–0.026.

The second consideration (as in the previous chapters) is about the "trade linkage index."

The "trade linkage index" focuses on whether there exists a trade distortion between the countries involved. It goes without saying that, in this section, the focus is on the distortion in trade between Germany and China — a portion explained not by comparative advantage but by characteristic factors in either country or both countries.

As explained previously, if the actual export amount from Germany to China equates to the hypothetical export amount to China, the numerical value of the index could become one. If the numerical value of the index rises above one or falls below it, this may indicate that the "distorted portion of the trade" has increased.

Table 7 shows the trade linkage index of Germany with China. For comparison, Table 8 indicates the linkage index of Germany with Japan, while Table 9 indicates its index with the US.

The trade linkage index of Germany with China and the US is approximately 0.60 and 0.65, respectively. In contrast, the trade linkage index of Germany with Japan is approximately 0.30–0.40. As previously mentioned, the potential comparative advantage value is 1.0, thus Germany's trade with China and the United States shows a value that is clearly closer to potential comparative advantage compared to its trade with Japan.

In order to vividly show the difference, Figure 2 is shown. It could easily be recognized that Figure 2 appears to be similar to Figure 1. That

Table 7. Trade linkage index of Germany with China (2008–2018).

Year	Trade linkage index	Year	Trade linkage index
2008	0.591	2014	0.617
2009	0.571	2015	0.584
2010	0.601	2016	0.629
2011	0.623	2017	0.641
2012	0.597	2018	0.641
2013	0.573		

Source: JETRO *International Trade and Investment Report* (Annual Edition) and author's calculation.

Table 8. Trade linkage index of Germany with Japan (2008–2018).

Year	Trade linkage index	Year	Trade linkage index
2008	0.281	2014	0.336
2009	0.293	2015	0.362
2010	0.296	2016	0.397
2011	0.297	2017	0.399
2012	0.314	2018	0.402
2013	0.340		

Source: JETRO *International Trade and Investment Report* (Annual Edition) and author's calculation.

Table 9. Trade linkage index of Germany with the United States (2008–2018).

Year	Trade linkage index	Year	Trade linkage index
2008	0.564	2014	0.664
2009	0.544	2015	0.698
2010	0.536	2016	0.642
2011	0.560	2017	0.652
2012	0.622	2018	0.656
2013	0.650		

Source: JETRO *International Trade and Investment Report* (Annual Edition) and author's calculation.

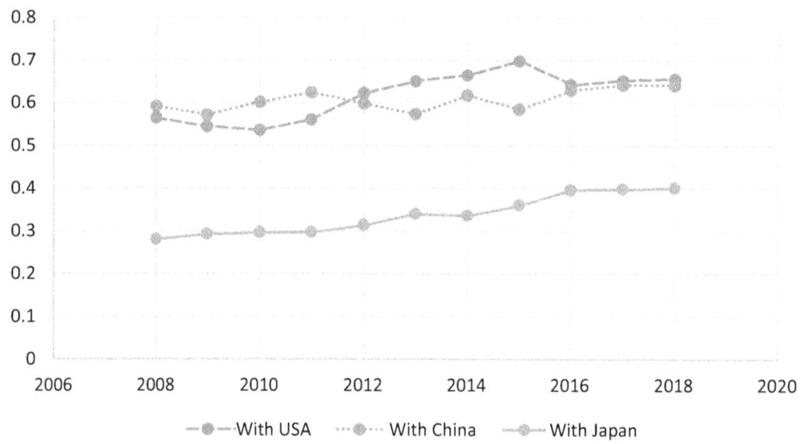

Figure 2. Trade linkage index of Germany with each country (2008–2018).

Source: JETRO *International Trade and Investment Report* (Annual Edition) and author's calculation.

is to say, as shown by the directional trade ratio, for Germany, China and the US share similarities as a trade partner country. In contrast, Japan would not be as close a partner country for German trade. As indicated previously, the difference between the frequencies of Merkel's visit to China and Japan might be reflected by the difference in the index, which lies between around 0.6 and 0.3–0.4.

Both numerical values of the directional trade ratio and the trade linkage index undoubtedly show that Japan–German relations have been less substantial than those between China and Germany. Moreover, judging from the numerical values alone, both Sino-German relations and Sino-American relations exhibit similar values.

In order to gain a better understanding of the trade relations and compare the German directional trade ratio and trade linkage index with the US, China, and Japan, we investigate here the Japanese directional trade ratio and trade linkage index with the US, China, and Germany. They are shown in Tables 10–12 and Figure 3 (directional trade ratio) and in Tables 13–15 and Figure 4 (trade linkage index).

It could be clearly seen that Figures 3 (directional trade ratio) and 4 (trade linkage index) have a similar structure to Figures 1 (directional trade ratio) and 2 (trade linkage index), respectively. That is, in all figures, only one line has a small numerical value, which is the line representing the directional trade ratio and trade linkage index between Germany and Japan. Trade relations between Germany and Japan have been undoubtedly weaker than those between Germany and the US, as well as between Germany and China.

In order to illustrate the situation more clearly (although it might be rather troublesome) regarding trade linkage index, in Figure 5, we show

Table 10. Directional trade ratio between Japan and the United States (2008–2018).

Year	Directional trade ratio	Year	Directional trade ratio
2008	0.099	2014	0.092
2009	0.096	2015	0.101
2010	0.092	2016	0.106
2011	0.086	2017	0.102
2012	0.093	2018	0.100
2013	0.092		

Source: JETRO *International Trade and Investment Report* (Annual Edition) and author's calculation.

Table 11. Directional trade ratio between Japan and China (2008–2018).

Year	Directional trade ratio	Year	Directional trade ratio
2008	0.139	2014	0.139
2009	0.154	2015	0.141
2010	0.154	2016	0.145
2011	0.150	2017	0.145
2012	0.141	2018	0.142
2013	0.138		

Source: JETRO *International Trade and Investment Report* (Annual Edition) and author's calculation.

Table 12. Directional trade ratio between Japan and Germany (2008–2018).

Year	Directional trade ratio	Year	Directional trade ratio
2008	0.024	2014	0.023
2009	0.025	2015	0.023
2010	0.024	2016	0.025
2011	0.024	2017	0.025
2012	0.023	2018	0.025
2013	0.023		

Source: JETRO *International Trade and Investment Report* (Annual Edition) and author's calculation.

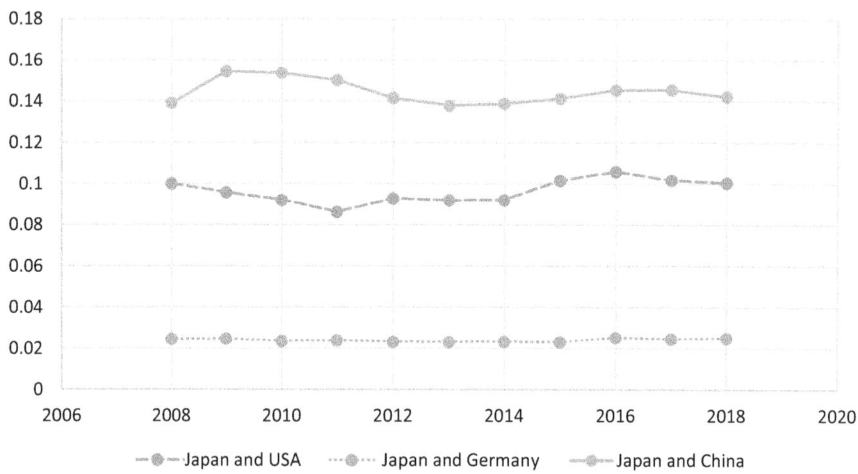

Figure 3. Directional trade ratio of Japan with each country (2008–2018).
Source: JETRO *International Trade and Investment Report* (Annual Edition) and author's calculation.

both "German index with the United States and with China" and "Japanese index with the United States and with China."

What is clearly indicated in Figure 5, in line with the earlier assertion (with the numerical value of 1.0 expressed as a potential comparative advantage level) that both the numerical values of more than 1.0 and less than 1.0 suggest a distortion, deviating from potential comparative advantage, the Japanese trade linkage index with the US and, in particular, China undoubtedly has been more than 1.0 (e.g., the Japanese trade linkage index with China in 2009 reached 2.3891). In short, there has been a clear difference in the trade linkage indexes of Germany with both the US and China,

Table 13. Trade linkage index of Japan with the United States (2008–2018).

Year	Trade linkage index	Year	Trade linkage index
2008	1.378	2014	1.461
2009	1.317	2015	1.476
2010	1.208	2016	1.461
2011	1.233	2017	1.445
2012	1.379	2018	1.447
2013	1.489		

Source: JETRO *International Trade and Investment Report* (Annual Edition) and author's calculation.

Table 14. Trade linkage index of Japan with China (2008–2018).

Year	Trade linkage index	Year	Trade linkage index
2008	2.327	2014	1.719
2009	2.389	2015	1.713
2010	2.089	2016	1.763
2011	2.007	2017	1.811
2012	1.776	2018	1.770
2013	1.688		

Source: JETRO *International Trade and Investment Report* (Annual Edition) and author's calculation.

Table 15. Trade linkage index of Japan with Germany (2008–2018).

Year	Trade linkage index	Year	Trade linkage index
2008	0.422	2014	0.417
2009	0.390	2015	0.406
2010	0.371	2016	0.409
2011	0.405	2017	0.408
2012	0.399	2018	0.426
2013	0.406		

Source: JETRO *International Trade and Investment Report* (Annual Edition) and author's calculation.

as well as Japan's with these two nations. The numerical values of the Japanese trade linkage index with the US and China have been more than 1.0 (that is, "actual export amount" becomes large); in contrast, the numerical values of the German trade linkage index with the US and China have been less than 1.0 (that is, "actual export amount" becomes small).

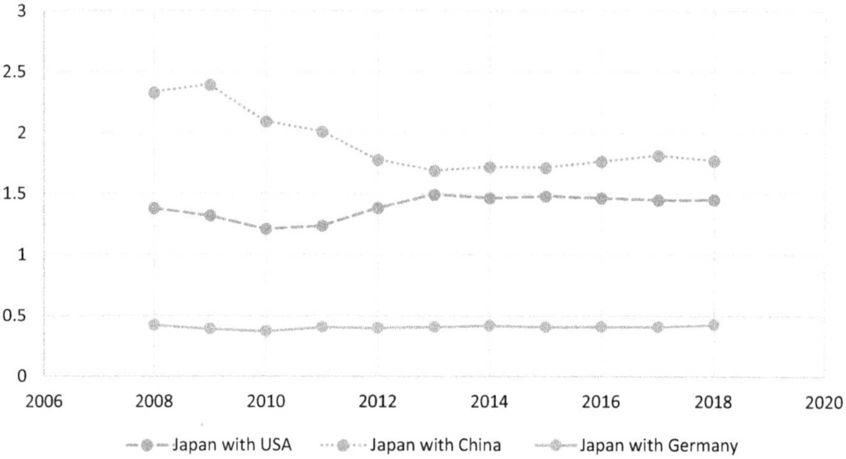

Figure 4. Trade linkage index of Japan with each country (2008–2018).

Source: JETRO *International Trade and Investment Report* (Annual Edition) and author's calculation.

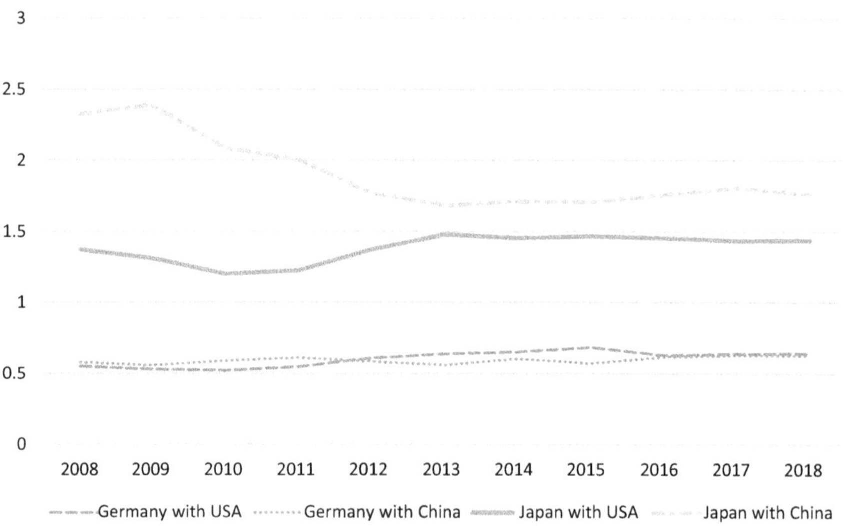

Figure 5. Trade linkage index of Japan and Germany with the United States and China (2008–2018).

Source: JETRO *International Trade and Investment Report* (Annual Edition) and author's calculation.

Similarly, although it may be rather troublesome, we can confirm here that, concerning the directional trade ratio, a similar relationship could be recognized, as shown in Figure 6. In this figure, the two lines placed at the top indicate Japan's directional trade ratio with the US and China. Because the directional trade ratio is simply the ratio of trade amount with the country concerned to the total trade amount, the ratio of Japanese trade amount with the US and China to the total Japanese trade amount is found to be undoubtedly larger than the ratio of German trade amount with the US and China to the total German trade amount.

Now, taking Japan for comparison, we consider German trade relations with China. As long as the investigation of this section is concerned, it might be appropriate to consider that the grounds upon which Germany could conclude an alliance with China may not be so strong, yet not so weak. As a matter of fact, if Germany concludes an alliance, the target country of the alliance could reasonably be either the US or China.

To reaffirm the ranking and share of German trade contributing to Chinese trade, we present Table 16 (Chinese import) and Table 17 (Chinese export).

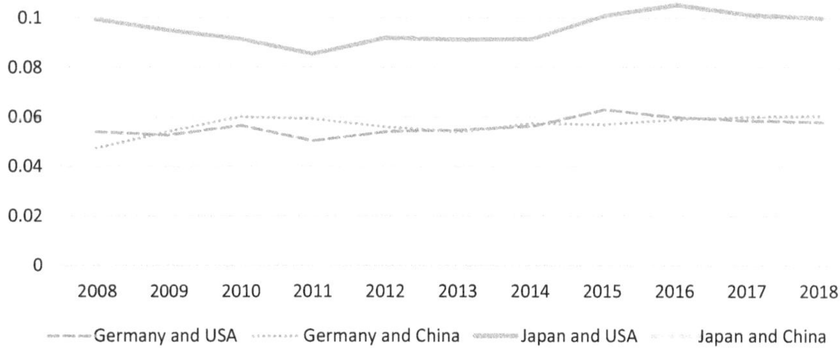

Figure 6. Directional trade ratio of Japan and Germany with the United States and China (2008–2018).

Source: JETRO *International Trade and Investment Report* (Annual Edition) and author's calculation.

Table 16. Chinese import partner countries: Ranking and ratio (2016–2019).

Year	2016		2017		2018		2019	
Ranking	Country	Ratio	Country	Ratio	Country	Ratio	Country	Ratio
1	South Korea	10.0	South Korea	9.6	South Korea	9.6	South Korea	8.4
2	Japan	9.2	Japan	9.0	Japan	8.5	Taiwan	8.3
3	Taiwan	8.8	Taiwan	8.4	Taiwan	8.3	Japan	8.3
4	USA	8.5	USA	8.4	USA	7.3	USA	5.9
5	Germany	5.4	Germany	5.3	Germany	5.0	Australia	5.8
6	Australia	4.5	Australia	5.2	Australia	4.9	Germany	5.1
7	Malaysia	3.1	Brazil	3.2	Brazil	3.6	Brazil	3.8
8	Brazil	2.9	Malaysia	2.9	Malaysia	3.0	Malaysia	3.5
9	Thailand	2.4	Thailand	2.3	Russia	2.8	Russia	2.9
10	Russia	2.0	Russia	2.2	Thailand	2.1	Saudi Arabia	2.6

Source: JETRO *International Trade and Investment Report* (Annual Edition).

Table 17. Chinese export partner countries: Ranking and ratio (2016–2019).

Year	2016		2017		2018		2019	
Ranking	Country	Ratio	Country	Ratio	Country	Ratio	Country	Ratio
1	USA	18.4	USA	19.0	USA	19.2	USA	16.8
2	Hong Kong	13.7	Hong Kong	12.3	Hong Kong	12.1	Hong Kong	11.2
3	Japan	6.2	Japan	6.1	Japan	5.9	Japan	5.7
4	South Korea	4.5	South Korea	4.5	South Korea	4.4	South Korea	4.4
5	Germany	3.1	Germany	3.1	Germany	3.1	Germany	3.2
6	India	2.8	India	3.0	India	3.1	India	3.0
7	Netherlands	2.7	Netherlands	3.0	Netherlands	2.9	Netherlands	3.0
8	UK	2.7	UK	2.5	UK	2.3	UK	2.5
9	Singapore	2.1	Singapore	2.0	Singapore	2.0	Taiwan	2.2
10	Taiwan	1.9	Taiwan	1.9	Taiwan	2.0	Singapore	2.2

Source: JETRO *International Trade and Investment Report* (Annual Edition).

Next, we confirm the ranking and share of China's contribution to German trade. They are Table 18 (German import) and Table 19 (German export).

The share of Chinese trade, as a German import partner country, constitutes about 10 percent, and China has held first place. With regard to German export partner countries, China contributes approximately

Table 18. German import partner countries: Ranking and ratio (2016–2019).

Year	2016		2017		2018		2019	
Ranking	Country	Ratio	Country	Ratio	Country	Ratio	Country	Ratio
1	China	9.8	China	9.7	China	9.8	China	10.0
2	Netherlands	8.8	Netherlands	8.8	Netherlands	9.0	Netherlands	8.9
3	France	6.9	France	6.2	France	6.0	USA	6.5
4	USA	6.1	USA	5.9	USA	5.9	France	6.0
5	Italy	5.4	Italy	5.4	Italy	5.5	Poland	5.2
6	Poland	4.9	Poland	4.9	Poland	5.1	Italy	5.2
7	Switzerland	4.6	Czech	4.5	Czech	4.4	Czech	4.3
8	Czech	4.4	Switzerland	4.4	Belgium	4.2	Switzerland	4.2
9	Austria	4.0	Austria	4.0	Austria	4.0	Belgium	3.9
10	Belgium	4.0	Belgium	3.9	UK	3.4	UK	3.5

Source: JETRO *International Trade and Investment Report* (Annual Edition).

Table 19. German export partner countries: Ranking and ratio (2016–2019).

Year	2016		2017		2018		2019	
Ranking	Country	Ratio	Country	Ratio	Country	Ratio	Country	Ratio
1	USA	8.9	USA	8.7	USA	8.6	USA	8.9
2	France	8.4	France	8.2	France	8.0	France	8.0
3	UK	7.1	China	6.7	China	7.1	China	7.2
4	Netherlands	6.6	Netherlands	6.7	Netherlands	6.9	Netherlands	6.9
5	China	6.3	UK	6.6	UK	6.2	UK	5.9
6	Italy	5.1	Italy	5.1	Italy	5.3	Italy	5.1
7	Austria	5.0	Austria	4.9	Austria	4.9	Austria	5.0
8	Poland	4.5	Poland	4.6	Poland	4.8	Poland	5.0
9	Switzerland	4.2	Switzerland	4.2	Belgium	3.4	Switzerland	4.2
10	Belgium	3.5	Belgium	3.5	Czech	3.4	Belgium	3.5

Source: JETRO *International Trade and Investment Report* (Annual Edition).

6–7 percent and has held a position between third and fifth. Then, what are the corresponding positions of the US? Among German import partner countries, its share is nearly 6 percent, holding the fourth place, and among German export partner countries, its share is approximately 9 percent, taking the first place. Therefore, we could recognize that the Chinese share and position among German import and export partner countries have been symmetrically arranged with respect to those of the US. That is, the Chinese share and position among German import partner countries have been about the same as those of the US among German export partner countries.

Then, what is the trade balance? Table 20 indicates the German trade balance with China and the ratio of that balance to the overall German trade balance with the world. Table 21 shows the German trade balance with the US and the ratio of that balance to the overall German trade balance with the world.

As shown in Tables 20 and 21, the German trade balance with China has been in deficit, while that with the US has been in surplus. However, those amounts of deficit and surplus have been different to some extent. Particularly, the situation in the latter half of the 2010s is rather clear. The amount of German surplus with the US constitutes approximately

Table 20. German trade balance with China and with whole world (2008–2018) (million EUROs, in percent).

Year	Trade balance with China (A)	Trade balance with whole world (B)	(A)/(B) (in percent)
2008	▲25,282	176,249	14.34
2009	▲18,987	134,192	14.15
2010	▲22,892	153,333	14.93
2011	▲14,546	158,087	9.20
2012	▲10,927	188,254	5.80
2013	▲6,532	197,654	3.30
2014	▲4,845	216,904	2.23
2015	▲20,273	247,684	8.19
2016	▲17,692	252,213	7.01
2017	▲14,513	244,743	5.93
2018	▲13,228	227,725	5.81

Note: (A)/(B) in this table indicates absolute values.
Source: JETRO *International Trade and Investment Report* (Annual Edition).

Table 21. German trade balance with United States and with whole world (2008–2018) (million EUROs, in percent).

Year	Trade balance with USA (A)	Trade balance with whole world (B)	(A)/(B) (in percent)
2008	25,407	176,249	14.42
2009	13,920	134,192	10.37
2010	20,507	153,333	13.37
2011	25,430	158,087	16.09
2012	36,229	188,254	19.24
2013	39,878	197,654	20.18
2014	47,477	216,904	21.89
2015	54,557	247,684	22.03
2016	49,017	252,213	19.43
2017	50,402	244,743	20.59
2018	48,785	227,725	21.42

Source: JETRO *International Trade and Investment Report* (Annual Edition).

20 ercent of the total amount of German surplus with the whole world. In contrast, the amount of German deficit with China comprises, by and large, only 5 percent (in absolute value) of the total amount of German surplus with the entire world.

Then, what is the degree of dependence on foreign trade? It is shown in Table 22 and Figure 7. Obviously, the degree of dependence on foreign trade for Germany has been much larger than that for other countries, with its average value equating to 67.18 percent. The average values for the US, Japan, and China are, respectively, 21.55 percent, 26.67 percent, and 39.17 percent.

Those tables and figures unambiguously indicate that, for Germany, foreign trade — comparatively to Japan and the US — is of greater importance to other nations involved. Moreover, because German trade with the US accounts for 20 percent of its surplus, it is quite clear that the US has been an important trading partner.

By the way, the information that could not be captured by the directional trade ratio pertains to which countries indicate a higher ratio in foreign trade with Germany and China. Table 23 and Figure 8 represent the ratio of each country's foreign trade with Germany to German trade as a whole, and Table 24 and Figure 9 show the ratio of each country's foreign trade with China to Chinese trade as a whole.

Table 22. Degree of dependence on foreign trade of each country (2008–2018) (in percent).

Year	Japan	USA	China	Germany
2008	28.69	23.30	50.56	66.88
2009	19.79	18.22	39.19	56.88
2010	23.84	21.40	44.55	64.70
2011	25.73	23.90	44.73	69.99
2012	25.89	23.72	42.47	70.28
2013	28.70	23.02	40.99	68.61
2014	30.89	22.82	38.66	67.86
2015	28.48	20.66	33.52	68.38
2016	24.64	19.48	31.19	66.61
2017	27.37	19.97	32.33	68.94
2018	29.30	20.56	32.63	69.85

Source: JETRO *International Trade and Investment Report* (Annual Edition) and author's calculation.

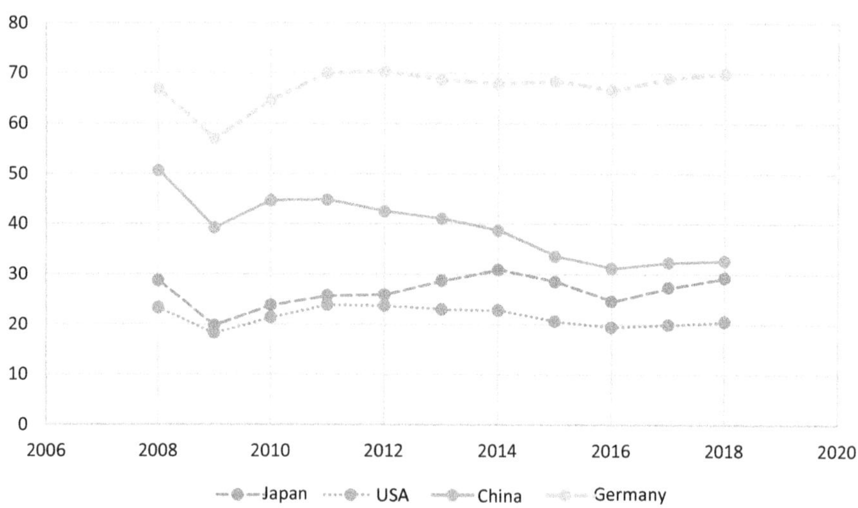

Figure 7. Degree of dependence on foreign trade of each country (2008–2018) (in percent).
Source: JETRO *International Trade and Investment Report* (Annual Edition) and author's calculation.

Table 23. The ratio of each country in foreign trade with Germany to German total trade (2008–2018) (in percent).

Year	China	USA	Japan	France	UK	Netherlands
2008	5.35	6.40	2.05	8.90	6.05	7.70
2009	6.35	6.30	2.00	9.10	5.75	7.65
2010	7.55	6.20	2.05	8.60	5.50	7.55
2011	7.45	6.20	2.00	8.50	5.60	7.80
2012	7.30	6.75	2.00	8.30	5.70	8.00
2013	7.15	6.75	1.90	8.15	5.80	8.20
2014	7.65	6.90	1.80	8.20	6.00	8.05
2015	7.85	7.90	1.75	7.85	5.75	7.95
2016	8.05	7.50	1.90	7.65	5.40	7.70
2017	8.20	7.30	1.85	7.20	5.10	7.75
2018	8.45	7.25	1.90	7.00	4.80	7.95

Source: JETRO *International Trade and Investment Report* (Annual Edition) and author's calculation.

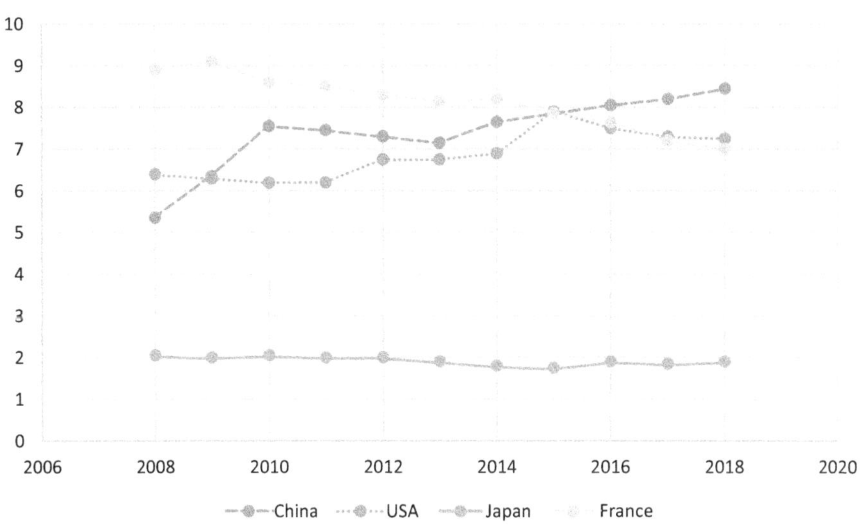

Figure 8. The ratio of each country in foreign trade with Germany to German total trade (2008–2018) (in percent).

Source: JETRO *International Trade and Investment Report* (Annual Edition) and author's calculation.

Table 24. The ratio of each country in foreign trade with China to Chinese total trade (2008–2018) (in percent).

Year	USA	Japan	Germany	Hong Kong	Taiwan	South Korea
2008	13.00	10.40	4.50	8.00	5.00	7.30
2009	13.50	10.40	4.80	7.90	4.80	7.10
2010	13.00	10.00	4.80	7.80	4.90	7.00
2011	12.30	9.40	4.60	7.80	4.40	6.70
2012	12.50	8.50	4.20	8.80	4.40	6.60
2013	12.50	7.50	3.90	9.60	4.70	6.60
2014	12.90	7.30	4.10	8.70	4.60	6.80
2015	14.10	7.00	4.00	8.70	4.80	7.00
2016	14.10	7.50	4.10	8.30	4.90	6.90
2017	14.20	7.40	4.10	7.00	4.90	6.80
2018	13.70	7.10	4.00	6.70	4.90	6.80

Source: JETRO *International Trade and Investment Report* (Annual Edition) and author's calculation.

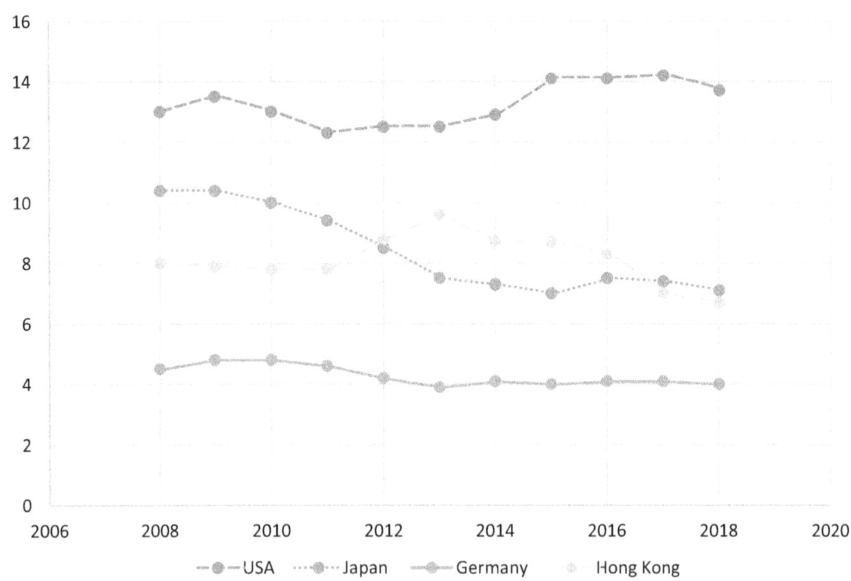

Figure 9. The ratio of each country in foreign trade with China to Chinese total trade (2008–2018) (in percent).

Source: JETRO *International Trade and Investment Report* (Annual Edition) and author's calculation.

As clearly indicated in the above tables and figures, we could recognize a significant difference between the contribution of China to German trade and that of Germany to Chinese trade. To put it briefly, although China and the US are important countries for German trade (along with France and the Netherlands), those for Chinese trade are the US and Japan (along with Hong Kong and South Korea), but not Germany. Therefore, judging from trade relations, if Germany and China were able to establish their relationship as easily conducive to forming an alliance, it appears to have originated on the German side rather than the Chinese side.[41]

4.2. *FDI relations between China and Germany: On the FDI-trade index*

In this section, we consider foreign direct investment. Particularly, we investigate it using the FDI-trade index. That is, we use here not only statistics of foreign direct investment but also, based on the data from international relations between the home country of FDI and the host country of FDI, we consider whether or not foreign direct investment between the home and host countries could actively be implemented.

Under this consideration, we utilize two types of statistics: "FDI concentration index" and "trade linkage index."

The FDI concentration index is described as follows. Considering the FDI concentration index from Germany to China, the index represents the ratio of the value obtained by dividing German outward FDI to China by China's inward FDI to the value obtained by dividing German outward FDI by the total world outward FDI. When the ratio indicates a value greater than 1.0, German FDI in China is shown to be relatively larger compared to that of other countries. Table 25 shows the FDI concentration index of Germany with China. We could recognize that there were many years with relatively higher numerical values, particularly the indices from 2009 to 2013 (in fact, the index of 2011 reached 3.6990). Therefore, for German FDI, China could be considered a relatively higher-scale host country compared to other host countries.

In order to compare the FDI concentration index of Germany with China, we would view the indices of the US (Table 26) and Japan (Table 27).

---

[41] It goes without saying that, although we would not refer them here, there might exist other circumstances on the Chinese side.

Table 25. FDI concentration index (Germany with China) (2008–2018).

Year	FDI concentration index	Year	FDI concentration index
2008	0.140	2014	0.608
2009	1.168	2015	0.475
2010	2.280	2016	1.048
2011	3.699	2017	0.322
2012	0.967	2018	0.058
2013	1.921		

Source: JETRO *International Trade and Investment Report* (Annual Edition) and author's calculation.

Table 26. FDI concentration index (the United States with China) (2008–2018).

Year	FDI concentration index	Year	FDI concentration index
2008	0.803	2014	0.192
2009	▲0.434	2015	0.263
2010	0.206	2016	0.367
2011	▲0.057	2017	0.344
2012	▲0.109	2018	▲0.632
2013	0.281		

Note: ▲ of the table indicates "excess withdrawal."
Source: JETRO *International Trade and Investment Report* (Annual Edition) and author's calculation.

Table 27. FDI concentration index (Japan with China) (2008–2018).

Year	FDI concentration index	Year	FDI concentration index
2008	0.731	2014	0.625
2009	1.622	2015	0.749
2010	0.896	2016	0.646
2011	1.512	2017	0.633
2012	1.263	2018	0.548
2013	0.764		

Source: JETRO *International Trade and Investment Report* (Annual Edition) and author's calculation.

It is evident from Tables 26 and 27 that the German FDI concentration index with China has been higher than the US and Japanese FDI concentration indices with China.

Next, as performed in a previous study,[42] we establish whether German FDI in China can be considered active or not.

FDI is an activity that is more closely related to the factors such as the culture and institutions of the target country or region than foreign trade. Although it is not easy to scientifically consider a reasonable scale of FDI between countries concerned. We examine here the strengths and weaknesses of international relations as expressed by the scale of international trade, which is shown by the trade linkage index.

The question of whether the size of German outward FDI into China is large or small should thus be judged by neither intuition nor political judgment. It should be based on the degree of closeness of the economic relations between Germany and China, and whether German outward FDI into China could be implemented with the same degree of economic relations between them.

The question mentioned above could appropriately correspond to the ratio consisting of the FDI concentration index as a numerator and the trade linkage index as a denominator, which is referred to here as the FDI-trade index. When the ratio equals 1.0, FDI relations between the two countries correspond with their international relations. When it exceeds 1.0, FDI relations between them are more active than the expected scale from international relations; whereas, when less than 1.0, they are less active than expected. Table 28 indicates the German FDI-trade index with China.

As clearly shown in Table 28, the German FDI-trade index with China has been more than 1.0 for many years (particularly in 2011, when the index reached 5.9355). Thus, we could recognize that German FDI in China has seemingly been quite large, given the international economic relations between them.

For a comparison, with regard to the FDI-trade index with China, we consider the American FDI-trade index (Table 29) and the Japanese FDI-trade index (Table 30).

As clearly indicated in Tables 29 and 30, an index value exceeding 1.0 was observed only in the American FDI-trade index in 2008, and no index

[42] With regard to the author's assertion, see, for example, Morita (2017b).

Table 28. FDI-trade index (Germany with China) (2008–2017).

Year	FDI-trade index	Year	FDI-trade index
2008	0.237	2013	3.354
2009	2.045	2014	0.986
2010	3.795	2015	0.813
2011	5.936	2016	1.665
2012	1.618	2017	0.502

Source: JETRO *International Trade and Investment Report* (Annual Edition) and author's calculation.

Table 29. FDI-trade index (the United States with China) (2008–2018).

Year	FDI-trade index	Year	FDI-trade index
2008	1.005	2014	0.269
2009	▲0.521	2015	0.331
2010	0.266	2016	0.461
2011	▲0.079	2017	0.430
2012	▲0.154	2018	▲0.966
2013	0.390		

Note: ▲ of the table indicates "excess withdrawal."
Source: JETRO *International Trade and Investment Report* (Annual Edition) and author's calculation.

Table 30. FDI-trade index (Japan with China) (2008–2018).

Year	FDI-trade index	Year	FDI-trade index
2008	0.314	2014	0.364
2009	0.679	2015	0.437
2010	0.429	2016	0.366
2011	0.753	2017	0.349
2012	0.711	2018	0.310
2013	0.452		

Source: JETRO *International Trade and Investment Report* (Annual Edition) and author's calculation.

value exceeding 1.0 was obtained in the Japanese FDI-trade index. In other words, German FDI in China has undoubtedly been larger than American and Japanese FDI in China.

Figure 10 depicts the FDI-trade index with China for Germany, the US, and Japan. It could easily be recognized that there is a clear difference, which shows an overwhelmingly larger FDI-trade index for

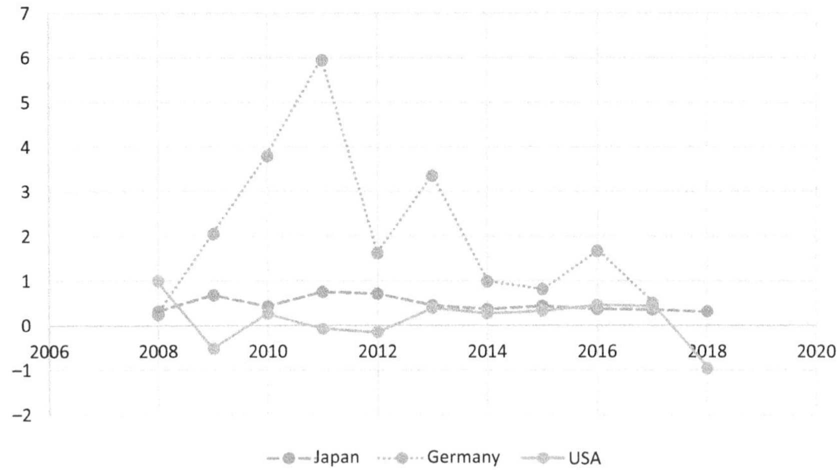

Figure 10. FDI-trade index of each country with China (2008–2018).

Source: JETRO *International Trade and Investment Report* (Annual Edition) and author's calculation.

Table 31. FDI-trade index (China with Germany) (2008–2018).

Year	FDI-trade index	Year	FDI-trade index
2008	0.063	2014	4.136
2009	0.098	2015	1.491
2010	0.626	2016	▲0.310
2011	0.208	2017	▲0.419
2012	1.158	2018	0.458
2013	0.005		

Note: ▲ of the table indicates "excess withdrawal."

Source: JETRO *International Trade and Investment Report* (Annual Edition) and author's calculation.

Germany compared to the USA and Japan. To reaffirm this, with regard to the average values, they are 1.9045 for Germany, 0.1302 for the US, and 0.4696 for Japan.

Then, what are the adverse FDI-trade indices (meaning China's FDI-trade indices with Germany, the US, and Japan)?

Table 31 shows the Chinese FDI-trade index with Germany.

As obvious from Table 30, the Chinese FDI-trade index with Germany has never been large. Although it indicates a relatively larger numerical value in 2014 and presents numerical values of more than 1.0 in 2012 and 2015, overall, they could not be considered large numerical values. That is, Chinese FDI in Germany could never be said to be large in light of international economic relations.

Then, similarly to the Chinese case, what are the American and Japanese FDI-trade indices with Germany? They are given in Tables 32 (US) and 33 (Japan). And Figure 11 shows the FDI-trade index for Germany with respect to the US, Japan, and China.

In addition, with regard to average values, they are 0.6829 for China, 1.9218 for the US, and 3.2987 for Japan. The Chinese FDI-trade index, in relation to Germany, has been predominantly smaller than that of the US and Japan. Therefore, as mentioned above, Chinese FDI in Germany could never be considered large in light of international economic relations.

Table 32. FDI-trade index (the United States with Germany) (2008–2018).

Year	FDI-trade index	Year	FDI-trade index
2008	3.564	2014	0.039
2009	1.274	2015	1.316
2010	0.523	2016	6.296
2011	1.875	2017	0.563
2012	7.091	2018	▲0.635
2013	▲0.766		

Note: ▲ of the table indicates "excess withdrawal."
Source: JETRO *International Trade and Investment Report* (Annual Edition) and author's calculation.

Table 33. FDI-trade index (Japan with Germany) (2008–2018).

Year	FDI-trade index	Year	FDI-trade index
2008	6.178	2014	1.096
2009	2.516	2015	2.387
2010	▲0.429	2016	5.967
2011	1.960	2017	2.937
2012	7.793	2018	3.339
2013	2.542		

Note: ▲ of the table indicates "excess withdrawal."
Source: JETRO *International Trade and Investment Report* (Annual Edition) and author's calculation.

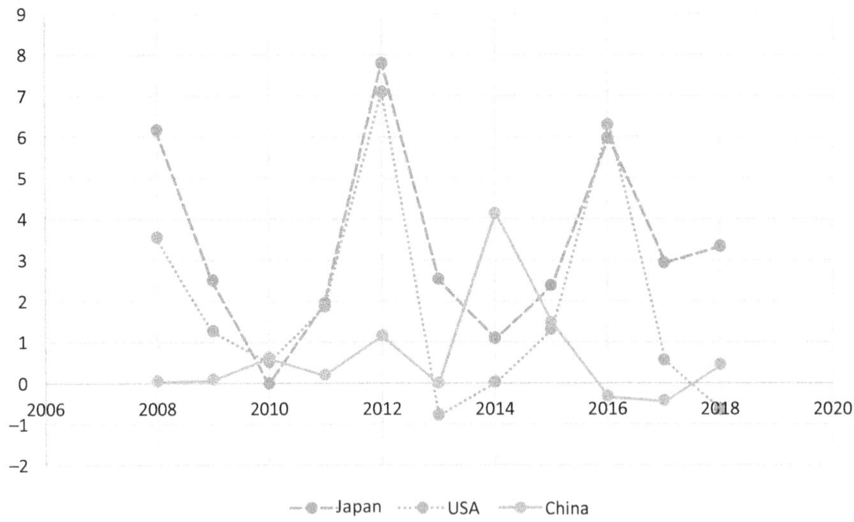

Figure 11. FDI-trade index of each country with Germany (2008–2018).

Source: JETRO *International Trade and Investment Report* (Annual Edition) and author's calculation.

As in Section 4.1, judged from trade relations, if Germany and China were able to establish relations that could easily lead to an alliance, it appears to stem more from circumstances on the German side than those on the Chinese side. Similar circumstances could be observed in FDI relations.[43]

5. On the Relations between China and Volkswagen (Germany)

On 18 September 2015, the US Environmental Protection Agency (hereafter, EPA) announced that an illegal software was detected during the emissions testing of diesel cars of Volkswagen (hereafter, VW) (which reduced the amount of exhaust gas), and VW was found to be in violation

[43] It goes without saying that they are the conclusions based on "trade relations" and "foreign direct investments." Although we would not refer them here, there might exist other circumstances on the Chinese side.

of law.[44] According to the EPA, during actually driving, the quantity of nitrogen oxides (NO_x) emitted by these cars reached 10–40 times higher than the reference value. Also, according to EPA, VW's violations dated back to its car sold since 2009.

According to the announcement by VW on 22 September 2015, the total number of cars subject to EPA regulations was 11 million all over the world, and 6.5 billion euros would be recorded in extraordinary loss for the period of July–September as costs for countermeasures.

Moreover, regarding the financing aspect, there could be a strong probability that the case might leave a trail in the future. A US media report informed us that the sanctions reached a record amount of 18 billion US dollars. Furthermore, it was reported that in other countries, plans for investigating the violation by VW's diesel cars would be expanded.

It goes without saying that, as mentioned above, in addition to the costs for countermeasure, risks such as civil penalties and litigation in the US would have a significant detrimental impact on VW's business prospects. However, according to Jürgen Bieber (an analyst at Metzler Bank), although it would take one to two years for VW to restore trust, it could still make a net profit of 13–14 billion euros. The financial structure of VW has been sound, allowing it to take the necessary countermeasures.

However, it was claimed that one of the ways by which VW would rectify this distortion was through rapid expansion. When Martin Winterkorn took office as president in 2007, the aim of "10 million in 2018" was set. In order to achieve the aim, VW expanded the production capacity in China and acquired luxury car and commercial vehicle brands one after another. In 2014, the aim of reaching 10 million was accomplished, and sales almost doubled subsequently. VW was indeed doing well.

However, despite rapid expansion by VW, its costs continued to escalate. The operating profit, as a percentage of sales (in December 2014), was 6 percent. In comparison with Toyota, whose operating profit on sales (in March 2015) was 10 percent, the business results of VW were undoubtedly inferior. According to the EPA, VW's unlawful activities involving diesel cars sold in the US began in 2009, during which the cars cleared the reference value of emissions testing using an illegal software. It was two years later when President Martin Winterkorn announced the

[44] With regard to the said case, we are dependent on the articles in *Nihon Keizai Shimbun* (during September and October 2015).

expansion on a larger scale. It could be said that the rapid expansion was accompanied by ongoing fraud.

As well known, VW's corporate governance has consisted of a special structure. Both the Porsche and Piech families (both connected to Ferdinand Porsche) hold approximately 51 percent of the voting rights. Furthermore, even now, although the Federal Government has never invested money in VW, the state of Niedersachsen holds 20 percent of the voting rights, and the prime minister of that state is a member of the supervisory board. Such shareholder composition could stabilize management. However, in emergencies such as the one exemplified here, a quick plan to deal with it might face interruptions.[45]

Nevertheless, through cooperation with the government, an aggressive attitude by the private sector has enabled China to become successful and outperform its competitors since the 1980s (in a situation where he/she is forced to switch to a defensive stance, it is said that his/her strengths may turn into weakness).

The VW scandal had an impact on China. VW sold 3.68 million cars in China, amounting to nearly 40 percent of global sales in 2014. However, the majority of the cars sold in China were gasoline cars, while the share of diesel cars was less than 0.1 percent, which were roughly 3,000 cars directly imported from Germany. The deterioration of the brand image has resulted in widespread intangible negative effects.

An article in *Nihon Keizai Shimbun* reported the following.[46]

After the disclosure of violations in diesel cars by VW in the US on "chat app" and "microblogging" platforms in China, criticism of VW from general consumers has been teeming. In China, they consider word-of-mouth communication to be important. Thus, such a fall in online reputation could lead to serious sales aggravation.

A salesperson at a VW dealership in Beijing expressed tiredly that, since German cars are recognized for their technological strength, serious issues would arise. At the time, the new car market in China had decreased for five months in a row until August 2015. Thus, the executive of a Chinese corporation in VW said with a barefaced sense of danger that, at this rate, a significant downward revision might well become necessary.

Furthermore, another article in *Nihon Keizai Shimbun* (1 October 2015) reported that, according to a German news agency, a fact was newly

[45] *Nihon Keizai Shimbun*, 26 September 2015.

[46] *Ibid.*

found out that on 28 September, when German prosecution announced the start of investigation, VW decided to use the illegal software to manipulate the amount of exhaust gas emitted by diesel cars during 2005–2006.

What exactly happened to VW in this period?

VW was troubled by poor sales in the weak US market. Furthermore, the US government announced that the environmental regulation "Tier2Bin5" in order to enforce stricter emissions control would be introduced in 2009. According to the regulation, the emissions quantity of nitrogen oxides (NO_x) over a distance of 1 kilometer must be less than 0.044 grams, which has a severity four times greater than the European standard "Euro 5." There would be no postponement period for VW.

In those days of the year 2006, VW's headquarters in Germany proceeded with the strategy called "blue motion technology," which was a project to develop diesel engines with superior environmental performance in order to improve global sales, including in markets such as China and India, rapidly growing sales quantity. It is reported that in their sights was Toyota which had been running strongly, particularly in North America.

At that time, the auto industry raced toward renewed competition. Because of expansion in emerging markets such as China and India, the condition to become a "global player" jumped up from producing "4 million cars" to producing "10 million cars." The abilities of parts procurement and raising money for research and development are deeply dependent on the scale. In the competition for major auto manufacturers to succeed and advance to the next level, it would be unacceptable for VW if it failed in becoming the best in the world and capturing the US market.

In the auto industry, there is a saying: the "wall of 10 million cars." That is, as an automaker approaches producing 10 million cars, its management becomes increasingly unsatisfactory. It is because, on the one hand, rapid growth can generate scale-related merits, but on the other hand, it may also lead to a loosening of internal controls.

As a matter of fact, General Motors went bankrupt due to loose management in 2009, and Toyota made a large-scale recall in North America in 2010. Therefore, it is easily imaginable that the pressure for goal achievement through "top down" becomes a hotbed for unlawfulness.[47]

However, it could be said that, with regard to the viciousness, the VW case might be extremely serious — a situation with no such precedent in the

---

[47] *Nihon Keizai Shimbun* (1 October 2015).

past. Regarding the amount of money, the compensation which Toyota paid for the large-scale recall in the US equaled altogether 3 billion US dollars, including out-of-court settlement payments and recall costs. In contrast, VW recorded 6.5 billion euros as a reserve fund. However, when costs such as discontinued, withholding purchase, and class action are included, it raises concerns that the total cost may reach an extraordinarily large amount.[48]

The rapid growth of VW toward 10 million cars was mostly contributed by China. However, it was lacking substance. In contrast to its success in China, VW was late to establish luxury car brands in the US compared to BMW and Mercedes-Benz. In such circumstances, the announcement by VW regarding its ambitious goal to become the world's leader in sales numbers may be viewed as significant pressure on upper-level management.[49]

In *Nihon Keizai Shimbun* (27 October 2015), a very interesting article titled "Modulating German economy (2) Dependence in China has become risk" was published. The point of the article was that a deceleration of the Chinese economy would shake the German economy. As shown earlier, one of the driving forces that enabled VW to close in on Toyota in automobile sales was undoubtedly its Chinese market penetration. One-third of VW's automobile sales were attributed to China, where its market share reached 18 percent. Also, the ratio of Chinese exports to Germany compared to global German exports rose from around 3 percent (before the financial crisis) to more than 6 percent. It was stated that Germany employed the utmost business stimulus measures in China. Therefore, it was asserted that dependency in China could become either positive or negative.[50]

Needless to say, concerning a period of 10 years up to 2014, per capita exports from Germany held the top position globally, being approximately three times higher than those of Japan. The ratio of exports to GDP in Germany was approximately 50 percent. Strong exports supported the current surplus and strong economy, leading to Germany's influential voice in the EU. However, the deceleration of the Chinese economy would shake the foundation of Germany's strong economy.

---

[48] *Ibid.*

[49] *Ibid.* The article included interviews with Mr. Takaki Nakanishi and Mr. Martin Görnich.

[50] As referred to in that article, a one percent slowdown of the Chinese economy would lead to a 0.25 percent slowdown pressure on the Euro area economy one year later. Particularly, Germany is highly dependent on China, so they would receive much stronger downgrade pressure than other countries.

Table 34. The sales ratio per country of VW in 2019 (in percent).

Country	Sales ratio
Germany	12.43
Russia	2.13
USA	5.96
Brazil	4.29
China	38.58
Japan	0.43

Source: Motor-Fan.jp(https://motor-fan.jp/article/10013300).

It might be recognized that the German situation (as described in that article) could be said to be the result of its deep dependence on China.

The global sales performance of VW in 2019 is shown in Table 34.

The quantity of car sales by VW worldwide totaled 10.9736 million, with Germany accounting for 12.43 percent, the US at 5.96 percent, and Japan at 0.43 percent. China (including Hong Kong) accounted for a much greater share of 38.58 percent (almost 40 percent), which was more than three times that of Germany.

According to an article in *Nihon Keizai Shimbun* (26 May 2020), the supreme court in Germany ordered VW to respond to the call for buyback from its German customers in light of its emissions violations. The purchase price of the car in question was 3,149,000 euros and the amount of compensation equaled 2,800,000 euros. Due to that judicial decision, similar lawsuits were initiated in Germany. It was prospectively determined that VW would compensate for its violations to at least 50,000 customers. Furthermore, for the unlawful exhaust gas emissions from diesel cars discovered in 2015, VW had to pay over 30 billion euros in penalties and compensation. In the US, in 2016, VW reached a mutual agreement with the concerned authorities regarding the buyback, leading to the automaker buying back over 350,000 vehicles and paying more than 7.4 billion US dollars. It was estimated that, due to the buyback in Germany, the costs related to its violations would range from hundreds of millions to ten hundreds of millions of euros.

According to another article in *Nihon Keizai Shimbun* (28 July 2020), the US Federal Trade Commission (FTC) announced on 27 July that, in connection with the unlawful exhaust emissions from diesel cars found out in 2015, VW paid out the out-of-court settlement payment to the purchasers in the US, which amounted to more than 9.5 billion US dollars. Thus, the compensation procedure in the US related to the emissions scandal came to a conclusion. Regarding this out-of-court settlement payment, in addition to vehicle purchase expenses, the costs of purchasing new vehicles and differences in fuel expenses were also included. Besides, there was a penalty paid to the US Department of Justice and compensation provided to customers outside the US. Therefore, ultimately, the costs paid by VW in relation to this scandal amounted to over 30 billion US dollars.

Further, in an article in *Nihon Keizai Shimbun* (26 May 2020), it was reported that, with regard to electric vehicles (EVs), VW plans to produce 11.6 million units by 2028 in China.

Although the Chinese new energy vehicle (NEV) market has been stagnant, VW has estimated its great future potential. Tesla Motors of the US has begun operations, making competition extremely intense. Under such circumstances, it was said that VW could secure a firm footing by strengthening its involvement in management.

Moreover, on 30 May 2020, a news article reported that VW deepened its "honeymoon relations" with China. The article also announced that Prime Minister Li Keqiang mediated its expansion of EVs. That is, VW announced on 29 May 2020 that they reached a basic agreement to invest money with a 50 percent stake in the parent company of Anhui Jianghuai Automobile Group Corp. Ltd. (JAC), which is a midsize state-owned automobile company, with the investment amounting to 1 billion euros. The Anhui province, where JAC established a base, is the birthplace of Prime Minister Li Keqiang. VW (which has the largest ratio of automobile sales in China) aimed to deepen its relationship with the Chinese government and strengthen its position as a leader.

Furthermore, JAC, which is wholly owned by the Anhui government, increased its capital by the end of December. VW invested money with a 50 percent stake in the form of an undertaking. Moreover, VW and JAC would increase their joint investment ratio in the EV joint venture to 75 percent. It was reported that the plan would reach a final agreement by the end of July.

However, it was also announced that the investment at the time entailed embracing a rather "dull" company. Nevertheless, there was a reason for taking the plunge, related mainly to circumstances that began approximately five years ago. Namely, in October 2015, Prime Minister Li Keqiang invited German Chancellor Angela Merkel to Hefei City, of Anhui Province.

Prime Minister Li inspected JAC in the early morning and discussed a potential collaboration between JAC and VW with Chancellor Merkel. It could be argued that the aim of the collaboration was to try to shore up JAC. Later, in 2017, both VW and JAC agreed to establish a joint venture. In those days, in China, there was a regulation deciding that the joint venture partners of foreign capital were limited to two companies. VW already had two joint venture partners: SAIC Motor Corporation Limited and FAW Group, and as such, their plan was not feasible. However, if the objective of the joint venture was EVs instead, a third partner was permitted. That change in rule was put into practice by order of Prime Minister Li.

The above-mentioned article also states that global companies like VW could not remain unaffected by international relations. The Xi Jinping administration intensified its confrontation with President Trump's administration over technological development in the high-tech field, as well as on Hong Kong and foreign trade issues. It might be estimated that, due to deepening relations with VW (which is a representative company in Germany), China aims to bring Germany closer to its camp. However, in the so-called "New Cold War" situation between China and the US, it could be probable that Germany will change its attitude toward China.

In short, the article title states that VW deepens honeymoon with China, and indeed it seems to be an aspect of a deepening honeymoon. However, at the same time, it mentions the possibility that Germany might change its stance towards China amid the Sino-American relations.

In the contemporary world, both automobile production and sales volumes in China have been overwhelmingly large. Table 35 indicates the production volumes of respective countries in order from first to tenth place, and Table 36 displays the sales volumes of respective countries in order from first to tenth place. As shown clearly from the two tables, the volumes and ratios occupied by China were predominantly large. Naturally, the huge Chinese market might be viewed as extremely attractive by VW, Toyota Motor Corp., and other automobile manufacturers. Therefore, if Sino-American relations are without significant issues, it could be less probable that Germany would change its attitude toward China.[51] Apart from the possibility of referring to the relationship between

[51]If we say in that sense, when considering the year of publication, the assertion by Makabe (2016) seems to be quite a reasonable judgment.

Table 35. Automobile production and ratio to world production of each country (2019).

Rank	Country	Production volume	The ratio (in percent)
1	China	25,720,665	28.02
2	USA	10,880,019	11.85
3	Japan	9,684,298	10.55
4	Germany	4,661,328	5.08
5	India	4,516,017	4.92
6	Mexico	3,986,794	4.34
7	South Korea	3,950,617	4.30
8	Brazil	2,944,988	3.21
9	Spain	2,822,355	3.07
10	France	2,202,460	2.40
	Whole world	91,786,861	100.0

Note: (1) Production volume of four-wheeled vehicle includes passenger cars, commercial vehicles, trucks, and buses. (2) Hong Kong is not included in China.
Source: OICA[52] (Data : Global Note).

Table 36. Automobile sales and ratio to world sales of each country (2019).

Rank	Country	Sales volume	The ratio (in percent)
1	China	25,768,677	28.21
2	USA	17,480,004	19.13
3	Japan	5,195,216	5.69
4	Germany	4,017,059	4.40
5	India	3,816,891	4.18
6	Brazil	2,787,850	3.05
7	France	2,755,696	3.02
8	UK	2,676,918	2.93
9	Italy	2,131,916	2.33
10	Canada	1,975,855	2.16
	Whole world	91,358,457	100.0

Note: (1) Production volume of four-wheeled vehicle includes passenger cars, commercial vehicles, trucks, and buses. (2) Hong Kong is not included in China.
Source: OICA (Data : Global Note).

[52]OICA stands for Organisation Internationale des Constructeurs d'Automobiles (The International Automobile Industry Association).

Table 37. Sales volume of new cars and the ratio to the total volume in China (January–May, 2020)

Company	Sales volume	Ratio to the total (in percent)
Toyota	580,100	7.3
Honda	469,644	5.9
Nissan	459,413	5.8
Mazda	76,328	1.0
Mitsubishi	29,193	0.4
VW	1,249,800	15.7
Geely Auto	420,317	5.3
Great Wall Motor	313,061	3.9
BYD Company	124,903	1.6
Total	7,957,000	100.0

Source: *Nihon Keizai Shimbun* (26 June 2020).

China and Germany as "alliance," we could easily predict that economic relations between VW and China are proceeding in close cooperation.

To reaffirm this, we refer to the sales volume of new cars in China from January to May 2020. It is shown in Table 37. As indicated in that table, Toyota occupied a 7.3 percent share, while VW held 15.7 percent, which was twice as much as Toyota's. However, due to the influence of COVID-19, when comparing these figures with those from the same period from the previous year, it was reported that Toyota experienced a decline of 7.8 percent, whereas VW saw a decrease of 20.0 percent).

In any case, in China's market — where automobile production and sales comprise over 28 percent of the global total — VW holds a share of approximately 15–16 percent. Thus, the relations between VW and China appear to be important not only for the automobile manufacturer but also for Germany's national economy. In that sense, it would be reasonable to estimate that the probability of a change in Germany's attitude toward China might be relatively small.

Looking back, an article[53] in *Reuters* (23 April 2012) reported that VW announced the construction of its new factory in Urumqi (Xinjiang Uyghur Autonomous Region) at a cost of 225 million US dollars, whose annual

[53]The URL of the concerned article (in Japan and in Japanese) is https://jp.reuters.com/article/tye83m07m-volkswagen-china-urumqi-idJPTYE83M07N20120423.

production capacity was projected to reach 50,000 from 2015 onward. It goes without saying that the Xinjiang Uyghur Autonomous Region is a poorer region in which the confrontation between the Uyghurs, who are predominantly Muslim, and the Han race continues. Due to the risks associated with confrontation, investments and production capacities have remained relatively small. Reportedly, Mr. Martin Winterkorn, the CEO of VW, mentioned that, as a pathfinder of the Chinese automobile industry, they provided important support for Chinese industrial development and for Sino-German economic relations, and he is said to have stated that, with our partners, we would expand this pioneering spirit to the western region of China. In addition to the above, Winterkorn clarified that VW (which had invested in the Chinese market ahead of other automobile manufacturers) was requested by the Chinese government to examine the potential of expanding its manufacturing base to the western region.

In short, VW quickly decided to construct a new factory in Urumqi, a poor region in western China, following the request of the Chinese government.

By the way, on 1 March 2020, the Australian Strategic Policy Institute submitted its report, which has received widespread attention around the world. The title of that report is "Uyghurs for Sale." It goes without saying that the content of that report indicated the use of Uyghur for "forced labor" (or "slave labor"). That is, the Chinese government forced Uyghurs to work at the Xinjiang Uyghur Autonomous Region in the pretext of a "reeducation camp" and also used them for "forced labor" across China at private enterprises in other areas. Naturally, "forced labor" meant reduced labor costs.[54] Thus, it was argued that the Uyghur labor force had become convenient for the supply chains of enterprises. In that sense, altogether, 82 companies (both Chinese and foreign) were named as beneficiaries of the forced labor. Of these, 11 were Japanese companies.[55] Obviously, VW was among the 82 companies.

[54]According to the report (although governmental media announced that a "good wage" could be paid), it was notified that, compared with Han Chinese, less amount of wages were paid.

[55]According to the information, the 11 Japanese companies are Hitachi, Japan Display, Mitsubishi Electric Corp., Mitsumi Electric Co., Ltd., Nintendo Co., Ltd., Panasonic, Sony, TDK, Toshiba Corp., Uniqlo, and Sharp Corp. The 82 companies featured many well-known names of automobile manufacturers, such as BMW, Jaguar, Land Rover, Mercedes-Benz, Volkswagen, and GM.

Also, with regard to the "forced labor" of Uyghurs in the Xinjiang Uyghur Autonomous Region, an article in *Politico* (25 July 2020) reported that Members of the European Parliament (MEPs) proscribed VW as an accomplice with the Chinese Communist Party in Uygur oppression. The article called VW a company with no conscience, and because it supported the "hell" of totalitarianism in the Xinjiang Uyghur Autonomous Region, it was considered an accomplice with the Chinese Communist Party.

This view, presented by the article in *Politico*, might provide useful information when considering it as part of the viewpoint on VW in the US and Europe. However, as mentioned earlier, the probability of a change in Germany's attitude toward China would remain small. Even if German companies were denounced[56] as profit oriented with no conscience and as accomplices in Uygur oppression, like VW, under such conditions, it seems reasonable to suppose that Germany would make an effort to continue its international relations with China.[57]

However, (due to the nature of the matter, it has never been touched upon here), it should be urgently added. That is, in the current situation, there exist a number of uncertain aspects. Supposing that certain actions by the Chinese Communist Party administration come to light, which even both Chancellor Merkel and VW (which have conciliatory attitudes toward China) may find it hard to accept,[58] this may lead to a potential shift in Germany's attitude toward China.

As indicated earlier, although we would not detail it here, suppose relations between Germany and China were such that could enter into an "alliance" (or "an almost alliance"), we believe that the aim of China (as mentioned based up Makabe (2016)) is to acquire German technology, know-how, and creditworthiness.[59] Furthermore, along those lines, there could exist the aim of paving a pathway toward hegemony. As far as we recognize from the current situation, therefore, it is appropriate to estimate that the likelihood of a change in Germany's attitude toward China may become relatively small.

---

[56] It would not be investigated here whether or not such denunciation is correct.

[57] Furthermore, as mentioned earlier, it could be added that (although we would not consider here) the government policy of Chancellor Merkel based on her "communist thought" shared politically with the Chinese Communist Party administration.

[58] Unfortunately, because the situations at this moment seem to be extremely uncertain, we have to say that it is hard to specify and assume what would happen in the near future.

[59] Makabe (2016, p. 16).

6. Conclusion

The assertions presented in this chapter are as follows:

(1) There could exist an insistence that the Sino-Japanese War was devised by Germany.
Without questioning the truth of the matter, the fact that while Japan signed the Anti-Comintern Pact with Germany on one hand, it provided weapons and various conveniences to China, with which it was at war, was clearly an act of betrayal. From this situation, we can gain a clear understanding of the characteristics of German relations with China.
(2) The role of China in German trade and that of Germany in Chinese trade have been quite different. To put it briefly, important countries for German trade have been China and the US (along with France and the Netherlands); in contrast, important countries for Chinese trade have been the US and Japan (along with Hong Kong and South Korea), but not Germany. Thus, from the viewpoint of trade relations, if both Germany and China make establishing an alliance easy, it seems to originate more from the German side than the Chinese side.
(3) It could be said that German FDI in China has seemed to be rather large in light of international economic relations between the two countries. In contrast, however, Chinese FDI in Germany has never seemed to be large in light of international economic relations between them. Therefore, similar circumstances in trade relations, as mentioned above, could also be recognized in FDI relations. Therefore, from the perspective of FDI relations, if both Germany and China make it easy to form an alliance, again it appears to be originating primarily from circumstances on the German side rather than those on the Chinese side.
(4) VW's relations with China seem to be quite interesting when we consider Sino-German relations. One of the forces that drove VW to close in on Toyota's leading position in automobile sales was, of course, the penetration into the Chinese market. To be sure, the rapid growth of VW toward manufacturing 10 million cars was mainly attributed to its expansion in China. However, it lacks substance. Unlike its success in China, VW trailed its competitors BMW and Mercedes-Benz in establishing luxury car brands in the US. In such circumstances, VW's used illegal software during emissions testing

of its diesel cars with the aim of reaching the top spot in global vehicle sales numbers.

(5) In addition to the illegal software case, VW was denounced as an accomplice of the Chinese Communist Party in Uygur oppression because of the construction of its factory in Urumqi (Xinjiang Uyghur Autonomous Region), and it benefited from low-cost supply chains established with the "forced labor" of Uyghurs.

(6) Considering these situations, it seems reasonable to suggest that the probability of a shift in Germany's attitude toward China may become small. Even if VW were denounced as profit oriented with no conscience and as an accomplice in Uygur oppression with the Chinese Communist Party, it can be expected that Germany would make an effort to continue its international relations with China.

(7) However, (due to the nature of the matter, it has never been touched upon here), it should be urgently added. In the current situation, there exist a number of uncertain aspects. Supposing that certain actions by the Chinese Communist Party administration come to light, which even both Chancellor Merkel and VW (which have conciliatory attitudes toward China) may find it hard to accept, this may lead to a potential shift in Germany's attitude toward China.

Chapter 6

An Economic Analysis of Sino-Australian Relations

1. Introduction

Australia is sometimes called the "canary in the coal mine" in terms of intervention by the Chinese Communist Party.[1] The "canary in the coal mine" refers to times in the past when canaries were used to detect poisonous gases that arose in coal mines. If the canary stopped making a noise, people would realize that a poisonous gas had been emitted and could protect human life. By extension, taking finance as an example, the volatility index is usually called the "canary in the coal mine" as it can provide information on the abnormality of the market price (or unfavorable development).

In short, in a field, a canary is a tool by which probable risk (or unfavorable development) can be quickly observed.

Therefore, in this chapter, the canary is a tool to judge whether or not there is a risk for a nation of interference by the Chinese Communist Party.

In this chapter, Australia is called the "canary in the coal mine" and we investigate the economic relations between Australia and China during a period when relations between the two countries have been getting worse.

In *Nihon Keizai Shimbun* (7 May 2021), an article entitled "China 'indefinitely halts' economic dialogue with Australia — retaliation amid deteriorating relations?" was published. According to the article, the National Development and Reform Commission (NDRC) of China

[1] See Garnaut (2018).

announced on 7 May 2021 that all talks on strategic economic activities with Australia would stop indefinitely. This announcement by the NDRC was in retaliation against the Morrison administration's reassessment of a lease agreement of a commercial harbor between a Chinese company and a local-level government in Australia. The National Development and Reform Commission of China criticized some Australian government personnel as having prejudiced thoughts against China and also having a Cold War mentality, which led to this "indefinite stop." In response to this matter, Mr. Dan Tehan (the Australian Ministry of Trade, Sightseeing, and Investment) stated on 6 May that because strategic economic talks were an important place to talk about problems, the "indefinite stop" was quite unfortunate.

Furthermore, *Nikkei Ryutsu Shimbun* (28 May 2021) published an article that indicated that the customs movement of edible grapes from Australia was delayed in China, which was reported by the producer's group in Australia. According to Jeff Scot, chief executive officer (CEO) of ATGA, the customs procedures were delayed for around 6 weeks. Every year from April to May, 300 containers of such grapes were exported to China every week. However, around the time when the article was written, only 120–150 containers per week had been exported to China. In short, this was considered retaliation by the Chinese authority (by delaying customs procedures). Therefore, the article concluded that, triggered by the request by Australian Prime Minister Morrison to independently investigate the origin of the COVID-19 virus, Sino-Australian relations had worsened.

However, clear deterioration of the relationship between China and Australia started in 2017. It was reported then that Prime Minister Malcolm Turnbull was considered a pro-China politician. But Mr. Turnbull changed his attitude in the latter half of 2017. It was revealed that a parliament member had received financial assistance from a Chinese national and had spoken in favor of China regarding the South China Sea issue. This led to strong opposition and public opinion in Australia on "Chinese interference in Australian domestic affairs" (*Nihon Keizai Shimbun*, 22 May 2018). However, as reported by that article, the Australian attitude toward China has been a smoldering issue for many years. In 2016, it was found out that a former cabinet minister took the position of an adviser for the Chinese company "Landbridge Group" which had hired Darwin Port (a northern point of strategic importance in

Australia) for a long period. It was also recognized that the inflow of investment money from China was one of the reasons for a recent increase in housing prices. These incidents hardened the opinions of the Australian public. However, in 2014, when President Xi Jinping had visited Australia for the G20 and made a speech at the Australian Parliament, the opinion toward China had been positive. But when news got out of a contract made by a state government of Australia to lend Darwin Port for 99 years to a Chinese company in October 2015, the atmosphere in Australia started to change (Okano, 2021).

In this chapter, we consider the economic aspect of Sino-Australian relations in view of the deterioration of relations between the countries.

The structure of this chapter is as follows: In the second section, we review the Chinese tendency toward hegemony. In the third section, we consider international trade relations between Australia and China and compare the same with trade relations between Japan and China and between Germany and China. In the fourth section, we investigate the foreign direct investment relations between Australia and China and compare the same with the foreign direct investment relations between Japan and China and between Germany and China. In the last section, we submit an overview of this chapter.

2. On the Hegemony of China

2.1. *Beijing Consensus*

After the end of the Cold War between the United States and the USSR, the American system based on "liberalism, democracy, and market economy" was accepted as the model for systemic transition by former socialist countries on advice and encouragement from the International Monetary Fund (IMF). We call such a system the "Washington Consensus."

At that time, the focus was not on the transition itself, but on a "strategy" to implement the transition, which was either "shock therapy" (to implement a transition rapidly and at one stroke) or "gradualism" (to implement a transition gradually).

The "strategy" of China was taken into consideration as China's transition was successful. Stanley Fischer (2002) evaluated the Chinese transition and stated that economic growth in China was led by political stability which did not exist in other transition countries. However, at the same time, Fischer mentioned that, in the future, China would shoulder a large fiscal burden due to the accumulation of bad debt by state-owned banks[2].

The "Chinese model" was an important subject of debate. However, it was a subject within the framework of a transition strategy. The main aim of transition was the framework of "liberalism, democracy, and market economy." In other words, it was assumed that if the Chinese economy grew large enough, a massive middle class could be established which could lead Chinese people to request liberalism, democracy, and a market economy. The extremely conciliatory pro-Chinese foreign policy of the US Clinton administration of those days gave credence to such a way of thinking.

However, such a thought process was mistaken. China's aim was not liberalism, democracy, and market economy but the attainment of hegemony under the leadership of the Chinese Communist Party.[3]

In 1992, Jeffrey Sachs published his analysis on the success of "shock therapy" based on the success of Poland. In 1994, the Sachs and Woo model was investigated by comparing ex-USSR countries with China.[4]

China was isolated in international society because of sanctions after the second Tiananmen Square incident on 4 June 1989. In order to support China's reintegration into the international community, Japan was the first to lift the freeze on yen loans to China and made the Emperor's visit to China a reality.

The Chinese ambition to become a hegemon was not apparent. However, it is clear that in Western developed countries there was a significant lack of vigilance towards China.

In October 1992, based on a speech by Deng Xiaoping, accelerated economic reform was implemented in China. At this time, Western developed countries (particularly in the United States) were not wary of China.[5]

---

[2]Hayashi (2002, p. 158).

[3]While China can be called a "socialist market economy," it is neither liberal nor democratic. Also, it could never be a market economy in the normal sense.

[4]See Sachs (1993) and Sachs and Woo (1994).

[5]Numerous politicians in Western developed countries did not regard China with enough cautiousness. What could be the plausible reasons for this lack of wariness?

John Mearsheimer (2001, 2006, 2014), a political scientist, was the one who sounded the warning against America's engagement policy toward China. In his book (2001), he said that China did not have enough latent power to become a regional hegemon. However, he claimed that it was too late for the United States to reverse course and slow down the rise of China.[6] The US government did not reverse course until the Trump administration.

The author of this book indicated in an article (2017a) that the GNP levels cited by Mearsheimer (2001) showed China's GNP at 1,180 billion US dollars and Japan's GNP at 4,090 million US dollars. However, in 2014, China's GDP equaled 10,000 billion US dollars and Japan's was 4,600 US dollars. The big difference in GDP between China and Japan was due to the US engagement policy with China. Thus, Japan's national security situation in 2021 has worsened. However, the situation related with China in which Japan is sitting on its hands and observing has not changed.[7]

With regard to China, the views that could be regarded as focusing on Chinese specific strategies are those of Ramo (2004) and Halper (2010).[8]

According to the cover of the Japanese version of Halper (2010), it states that in regions such as Africa, the Middle East, and Latin America, countries under dictatorial and oppressive regimes are abandoning the "Washington Consensus," which mandates democratization, information transparency, and the emphasis on human rights, and are instead focusing on the "Beijing Consensus," an economic growth model led by state-driven authoritarianism. In the Chapter 3 of Halper (2010), citing James Mann, it was stated that all the dictatorships in existence in the world have received support from China.

In short, the "Washington Consensus" aimed to reach a system of "liberalism, democracy, and market economy." In order to reach that system, there were two alternatives available: "shock therapy" (to implement a transition rapidly and at one stroke) and "gradualism" (to implement a transition gradually). Therefore, considering China is a successful example of gradualism, it was wrongly assumed that China's aim was to achieve "liberalism, democracy, and market economy."

---

[6] Mearsheimer (2001, p. 518) (Japanese version).

[7] With regard to Sino-Japanese relations, see Chapter 8 of this book.

[8] Both are titled *The Beijing Consensus*.

Contrary to the Washington Consensus, the "Beijing Consensus" is a regime of authoritarianism led by a nation-state. James Mann asserted that all dictatorships in the world have received support from China. According to an article in *Yomiuri Shimbun* (1 July 2021), Canada (which is a member of the G7) voiced concern about the human rights situations in the Xinjiang Uyghur Autonomous Region, Hong Kong, and Tibet at the United Nations Human Rights Council (UNHRC) held in Geneva, Switzerland. There were 44 countries that endorsed Canada's views, including the United States, Japan, European countries, and Australia. In contrast, Belarus, which has been criticized by the United States and European countries for its oppression of domestic opposition parties, defended China and claimed the support of 64 countries in its assertions that the circumstances in Hong Kong, Xinjiang, and Tibet are China's domestic administrative matters. Although Belarus did not name the 64 countries, it was a matter of concern that there were 44 against China but 64 supporting China. Many countries seem to have adopted an authoritarian regime led by a nation-state.

2.2. *Interference and manipulation by the Chinese Communist Party*

Okano (2021) stated the following about Sino-Australian relations.

Sino-Australian relations have deteriorated since 2016. As mentioned earlier, Australia and China were closest in 2014. In that year, President Xi Jinping visited Australia in accordance with the G20 and made a speech at the Australian parliament. Both countries agreed to upgrade their relationship and strategic partnership and agreed to sign the FTA. However, when a northern state government in Australia made a contract to lend Darwin Port for 99 years to a Chinese company in October 2015, the atmosphere in Australia started to change (Okano, 2021). Darwin Port is near the stationing facilities of the United States Marines. Thus, the United States expressed dissatisfaction with Australia. Within Australia, the Australian people voiced wariness against China on increased investments by Chinese companies particularly in infrastructure-related industries. The Australian government then blocked Chinese companies from buying its electric power grid and large-scale farms in Australia due to public outcry in 2016. Australia also started to heed the warning of a

Chinese invasion of Pacific Island countries, which can be considered the "backyard" of Australia.[9]

According to an Australian diplomatic white paper published in November 2017, the change in Australia's views on China is notable. The diplomatic white paper reexamined the international situation from a long-term viewpoint and specified that China was challenging the American hegemonic position. It also demonstrated Australia's strong sense of caution against China.[10]

Table 1 shows the principal events after 2014, a year in which relations between China and Australia were the closest.

In 2015, the Northern Territory state government of Australia made a contract with a Chinese company to lend Darwin Port for 99 years.

Because Darwin Port is near the stationing facilities of United States Marines, the United States expressed dissatisfaction with Australia. The Australian people also grew wary toward China regarding issues of national security.

In 2016, Australia rejected the sale of large-scale farms to Chinese companies, requested China to accept the South China Sea decision (which denied the territorial right of China), and also rejected the sale of its power grid to Chinese state-owned companies. Due to these activities of the Australian government, Sino-Australian relations worsened.

However, in Fukushima (2020), it is claimed Sino-Australian relations conclusively worsened due to an event that occurred in June 2017. At that time, the Australian national broadcaster ABC and independent media Fairfax broadcast a documentary program that provided detailed information on the influence of the Chinese Communist Party in Australian society due to which Australian national opinion shifted against the Chinese Communist Party (p. 274).

Regardless of the direct trigger, Sino-Australian relations conclusively worsened in 2017.

The common assumption of Chinese foreign relations with Australia can be understood based on the title of Hamilton's work (2018), *Silent Invasion*.

In Chapter 6 of Hamilton's work (2018), the situation of the Port of Hambantota (Sri Lanka) was described. When the Sri Lankan government

[9] Okano (2021, p. 2).

[10] *Ibid.*

Table 1. Principal events of Sino-Australian relations after 2014.

Year	Month	Events
2014	11	President Xi Jinping visited Australia and made a speech in the parliament. Both countries agreed to upgrade their relationship and strategic partnership and agreed to sign the FTA.
2015	10	The Northern Territory of Australia signed a contract to lend Darwin Port for 99 years to a Chinese company.
		Effectuation of FTA between Australia and China.
	12	Inauguration of AIIB (Australia participated in AIIB as the original member country).
2016	2	Australia published a Defense White Paper.
	4	Australia rejected the large-scale sale of farms to Chinese companies.
	7	Australia requested that China accept the South China Sea decision (which denied the territorial rights of China).
	8	Australia rejected the sale of its power network to Chinese state-owned companies.
2017	After the middle of 2017	The Australian public's anxiety against the influence of the Chinese Communist Party in Australian society increased.
	11	Australia published a Diplomatic White Paper.
	12	Australia submitted a bill to block interference in domestic affairs by foreign governments and foreigners.
2018	2	The cancellation of interchange projects between Australia and China came to light.
	8	The Australian government decided to remove Huawei from its 5G system.
2019	1	Delay in customs clearance of coal from Australia at multiple ports in China.
	9	Prime Minister Scott Morrison commented that China was not a "developing country" (which can receive preferential treatment from the WTO) but a new "developed country."
	11	Prime Minister Scott Morrison and Prime Minister Li Keqiang had a conference in Bangkok.
2020	4	After the statement by Australia demanding an independent investigation into the origin of the coronavirus, Sino-Australian relations deteriorated greatly.

Source: Okano (2012, p. 3).

announced that it would sell the Port of Hambantota to the China Merchants shipping company (which owns the Port of Newcastle), the community rioted. A huge new industrial park in Sri Lanka promised as part of the Silk Road development would have dispossessed local farmers. Local politicians did not want to become a "Chinese colony." At the inauguration of the industrial zone, the Chinese ambassador promised 5 billion dollars and 100,000 jobs. However, the ambassador did not mention that Hambantota Port is strategically important to China's projection of naval power in the Indian Ocean. In July 2017, Sri Lanka found it necessary to sell a seventy percent stake in the port to China in a bid to repay a Chinese loan obtained to build the facility. The creation of crippling indebtedness is a powerful Chinese tool under OBOR ("One Belt One Road") (pp. 174–175).

As Hamilton (2018) indicated, the "debt trap" is a powerful Chinese tool. Nowadays, this situation is common in the international community.

Although it is difficult to imagine that developed countries such as Australia and Japan could fall into a debt trap, there are several ways of trapping countries including "retaliation" (in other words, "interference" and "manipulation").

Hamilton (2018) mentions such cases.[11] In 2010, when the dissident writer Liu Xiaobo was awarded the Nobel Peace Prize, the Chinese Communist Party was embarrassed and angry. Although the Norwegian government played no role in the decision, Beijing retaliated by sharply cutting Norway's exports of salmon to China.[12] Free trade talks were abandoned and diplomatic relations went into deep freeze (p. 194). Oslo was chastened. When the Dalai Lama visited Norway four years later, the

[11]This chapter relies on Hamilton (2018) for specific cases and does not claim a shared perception of an invasion by China. For the purposes of this chapter, it is sufficient to have an outline of certain aspects of Sino-Australian relations, namely an overview of the "interference" by the Chinese Communist Party.

[12]As Hamilton indicated, the Norwegian government played no role in the decision on the Nobel Peace Prize. However, the selection of Nobel Peace Prize winners is implemented by the Nobel Committee and the nomination of 5 members of the Committee is enforced by the Norwegian parliament. In that sense, the Norwegian parliament plays a role. However, the Norwegian government is not involved. In China, because there is no "separation of the three powers" (administration, legislation, and judicature), there is no differentiation between legislative power and administrative power.

prime minister refused to meet him. According to "a study," a country's exports to China are liable to fall by eight percent[13] if its president or prime minister meets the Dalai Lama.[14] In short, although it there is no economic rationality for it, meeting with the Dalai Lama could reduce a country's exports to China by eight percent.

It goes without saying that the reverse case could also exist.

Chapter seven of Hamilton (2018) starts with the following sentence:

"In August 2002 the media jubilantly reported that an Australia-based consortium had just won, against fierce competition, a contract to supply natural gas to Guangdong province." The then Prime Minister John Howard declared that winning the bid for 25 billion dollars was "a gold medal performance" and the fruit of close engagement with China.[15]

It was reported that it was a close-run competition, with Australia's chances of beating Qatar, Malaysia, Russia, and Indonesia looking poor only two weeks before the bid was won.

---

[13]According to Blackwell and Harris (2016), export levels to China drop by an average of 8.1 percent after meetings between a prime minister or monarch and the exiled Tibetan leader, a decrease that takes roughly two years to rebound (pp. 129–130). Additionally, "A study" refers to Fuchs and Klann (2010), with the subtitle "Dalai Lama Effect on International Trade."

[14]Blackwell and Harris (2016, p. 130). As a matter of fact, although the Norwegian government played no role in the decision on the Nobel Peace Prize, the Chinese Communist Party retaliated against the Norwegian government. Thus, if there were meetings between a prime minister and the Dalai Lama, the Norwegian government would naturally worry about retaliation from the Chinese Communist Party.

[15]On 9 August 2002, *Nihon Keizai Shimbun* reported that Australian Prime Minister John Howard announced on the 8th that a contract had been signed with China for the export of liquefied natural gas (LNG) worth a total of 25 billion Australian dollars. The LNG would be received at China's first LNG terminal, which is being built in Guangdong Province by China National Offshore Oil Corporation (CNOOC) and others. It would be supplied for power generation and city gas in the Pearl River Delta region, including Shenzhen and Guangzhou. Given that China would become a major customer for the Northwest continental shelf gas field, CNOOC is also considering participating in the gas field's capital investment. In addition, resource companies operating in Australia are strengthening ties with China, which has future potential, as export to Japan have stalled. Prime Minister Howard, who met with Chinese President Jiang Zemin during his visit to China in May 2002, worked to promote Australian LNG. On the 8th, the Prime Minister welcomed the contract, saying it symbolizes a new bilateral partnership in the resource sector.

Chen Yonglin, who was a political officer in the Chinese consulate in Sydney at the time and had been following the events closely, later revealed that the Guangdong government was about to award the contract to Indonesia, which tendered the lowest price, until the CCP's Central Committee in Beijing ordered it be given to Australia. "They thought that Australia was really important," said Chen, "and that at the time Australia had totally turned towards America, so they thought we should use economic means to bring Australia back."[16]

Aware of how quickly Australia responded when an economic string was pulled, from then onward, Beijing decided to "use economic measures to guide Australia." After all, Prime Minister Howard had refused to meet the Dalai Lama while Beijing dangled the carrot of the 25-billion-dollar deal.

Rory Medcalf stated that essentially Beijing wanted from its commercial partners the same thing it wanted from its own people — economic benefits in return for submission on politics and security.[17] In short, the only reason why China engages in exports and imports is because of compliance on politics and security and not because of economic rationality.

3. International Trade Relations between Australia and China

3.1. *Australian economy: An overview*

In this section, we provide an overview of the Australian economy along with an outline of the real GDP growth rate, unemployment rate, and military expenditure.

In the following sections of this chapter, similarly, we would look at similar data regarding Australia. For comparison purposes, we would also like to examine the same data for Japan, Germany, and China which is a counterpart in the Sino-Australian relations.

[16]The result of that fierce competition should be recognized as unconnected to economic rationality.

[17]Such claims by Medcalf are a citation from Hamilton (2018).

First, the real GDP growth rates, as shown in Table 2 and Figure 1, of Australia, Japan, Germany, and China are discussed.

The real GDP growth rate of Australia was negative in 2020. The real GDP growth rates of Japan and Germany in 2020 were also negative. Although the real GDP growth rate of China was positive (the real GDP growth rate in 2018 and 2019 was 6.73 percent and 5.82 percent, respectively), the growth rate in 2020 was significantly lower at 2.27 percent.

Table 2. Real GDP growth rate of Australia (2008–2020) (in percent).

Year	Real GDP growth rate	Year	Real GDP growth rate
2008	2.67	2015	2.32
2009	1.88	2016	2.73
2010	2.36	2017	2.41
2011	2.85	2018	2.84
2012	3.80	2019	1.95
2013	2.13	2020	▲2.44
2014	2.57		

Source: IMF (Note: Global Note).

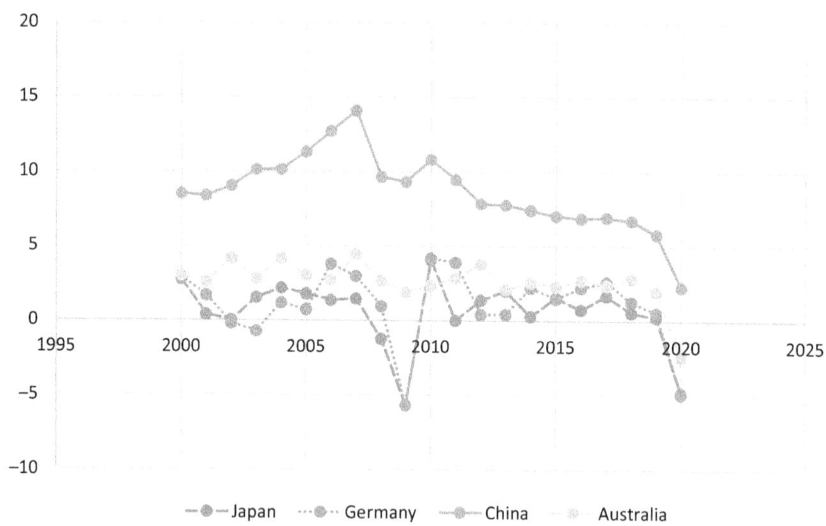

Figure 1. Real GDP growth rate of each country (2000–2020) (in percent).

Source: IMF (Data: Global Note).

The poor GDP growth rates of Australia in 2020 were influenced by the COVID-19 pandemic; so, although the tendency was global, the deterioration of Sino-Australian relations could have also been a factor.

Second, the statistics of unemployment, as indicated in Table 3 and Figure 2, for Australia Japan, Germany, and China are provided.

Table 3. Unemployment rate of Australia (2008–2020) (in percent).

Year	Unemployment rate	Year	Unemployment rate
2008	4.25	2015	6.05
2009	5.58	2016	5.70
2010	5.21	2017	5.58
2011	5.08	2018	5.29
2012	5.23	2019	5.15
2013	5.66	2020	6.51
2014	6.06		

Source: IMF (Data: Global Note).

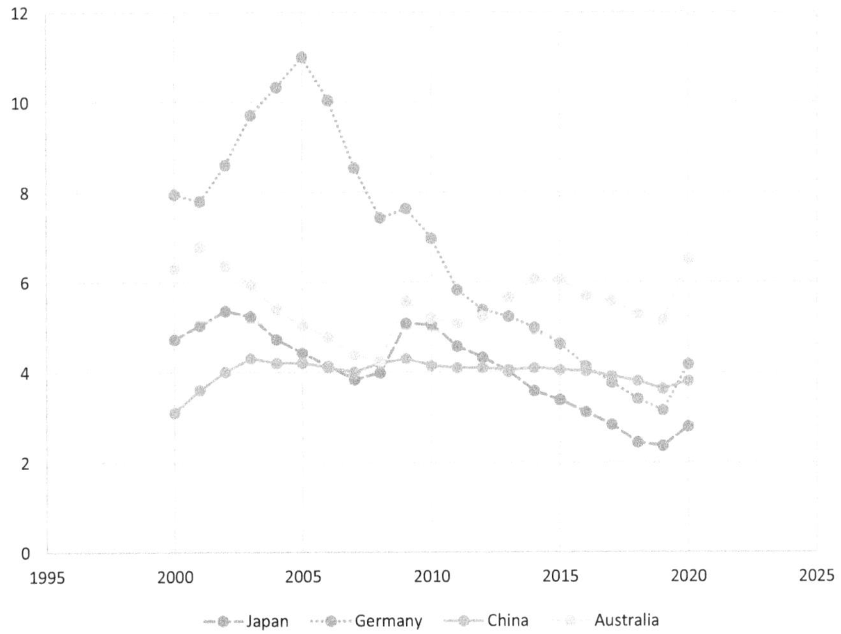

Figure 2. Unemployment rate of each country (2000–2020) (in percent).

Source: IMF (Data: Global Note).

In all four countries, the unemployment rate undoubtedly deteriorated from 2019 to 2020. That is to say, the ratio of unemployment grew from 5.15 percent to 6.51 percent for Australia, from 2.36 percent to 2.79 percent for Japan, from 3.15 percent to 4.18 percent for Germany, and from 3.62 percent to 3.80 percent for China.

Thus, the worsened unemployment rate in Australia was influenced by the COVID-19 pandemic; so, although the tendency was global, the deterioration of Sino-Australian relations could have also been a factor.

In 2020, both the real GDP growth rate and unemployment rate, not only in Australia but also in the whole world, were significantly worse than previous years mainly due to the COVID-19 pandemic.

Third, as indicated in Table 4 and Figure 3, the military expenditure of Australia Japan, Germany, and China is provided.

The increase of China's military expenditure has been remarkable. The huge difference in military expenditure between Australia and China can be easily understood. Of the four countries, only China is a nuclear state. If a war between Australia and China breaks out, the result is obvious. Australia (which is a non-nuclear-weapon state and does not have a large military expenditure) cannot independently start a war with China. With regard to military expenditure in 2019, Australia spent 25.912 billion US dollars, Japan 47.690 billion US dollars, and Germany 49.277 billion US dollars. In contrast, China's military expenditure in 2019 was 261.082 billion US dollars. China's military expenditure in 2019 was ten times more than Australian military expenditure in 2019.

Australia's military expenditure in 2018 was less than its expenditure in 2017 and its expenditure in 2019 was less than the amount in 2018. In light of the deterioration in Sino-Australian relations, if the Australian

Table 4. Military expenditure of Australia (2008–2019) (million US dollars).

Year	Military expenditure	Year	Military expenditure
2008	18,633	2014	25,784
2009	18,960	2015	24,046
2010	23,218	2016	26,383
2011	26,597	2017	27,691
2012	26,217	2018	26,840
2013	24,825	2019	25,912

Source: World Bank (Data: Global Note).

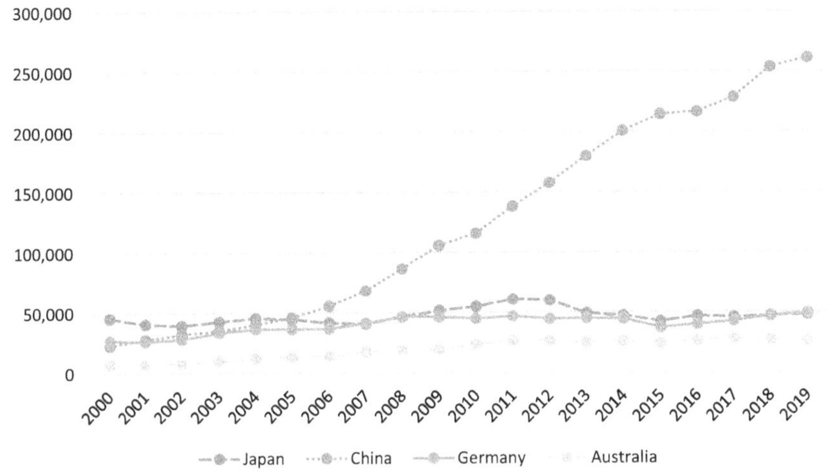

Figure 3. Military expenditure of each country (with China) (2000–2019).
Source: World Bank (Data: Global Note).

government was seriously worried about national security, it would have increased its military expenditure to some extent.

In the next section, therefore, we consider Sino-Australian relations in 2018 and 2019.

3.2. *Australia's foreign trade relations with China: An overview*

In this section, we review the import partner countries and export partner countries of China and Australia in international trade. They are shown as Table 16 (import of China) and Table 17 (export of China) in Chapter 5.

Australia's ratio among China's import partner countries was 4.5−5.2 percent, ranking it at the fifth or sixth position. Australia's ratio among Chinese export partner countries was less than 2 percent, which ranks it at the twelfth or fourteenth position. Thus, needless to say, Australia's ratio and rank are neither large nor high. The country that occupied a larger ratio and a higher rank in both Chinese imports and exports was the United States. The US ratio among Chinese import partner countries was around 8 percent, ranking it at the fourth position. The US ratio among Chinese export partner countries was almost 20 percent, ranking it first.

Then, what was China's position (ratio and rank) as Australia's import and export partner country? Tables 5 and 6 show the import and export partner countries, respectively, of Australia.

China's ratio among Australian import partner countries was 22–25 percent, giving it the first rank (in 2019, China's ratio was 2.13 times greater than the ratio of the USA, which was ranked second). China's ratio among Australian export partner countries was generally 32–38 percent, ranking it in first place in 2019, Japan occupied the second rank with a ratio of 14.9 percent; however, China's ratio was 2.58 times higher).

In 2018, China's ratio among Australia's import partner countries and export partner countries was larger than its ratio in 2017, and China's ratio in 2019 was larger than that in 2018. This makes it difficult to recognize the signs of the decisive deterioration of Sino-Australian relations, which started in 2017.

Table 7 and Figure 4 indicate the trade balance of Australia with China and the trade balance of Australia with the whole world. Table 8 and Figure 5 show the trade balance of China with the whole world.

As clearly shown in Figure 4, from 2012 to 2017, Australia's trade balance with China greatly exceeded its trade balance with the whole world.

However, in 2019, Australia's trade balance with the whole world slightly exceeded its trade balance with China.

Table 5. Australian import partner countries: Ranking and ratio (2016–2019).

	2016		2017		2018		2019	
Ranking	**Country**	**Ratio**	**Country**	**Ratio**	**Country**	**Ratio**	**Country**	**Ratio**
1	China	23.3	China	22.2	China	24.5	China	25.8
2	USA	11.3	USA	10.3	USA	10.3	USA	12.1
3	Japan	7.7	Japan	7.3	Japan	7.4	Japan	7.0
4	Thailand	5.7	South Korea	7.2	Germany	4.9	Thailand	4.8
5	Germany	5.3	Thailand	5.0	Thailand	4.9	Germany	4.8
6	South Korea	4.3	Germany	4.7	South Korea	4.3	South Korea	4.0
7	Malaysia	3.7	Malaysia	3.8	Malaysia	4.3	Malaysia	3.6
8	New Zealand	3.0	Singapore	2.8	Singapore	3.8	Singapore	3.4
9	UK	2.8	New Zealand	2.7	New Zealand	2.6	New Zealand	2.5
10	Singapore	2.7	UK	2.4	UK	2.4	UK	2.3

Source: JETRO International Trade and Investment Report (Annual Edition).

Table 6. Australian export partner countries: Ranking and ratio (2016–2019).

	2016		2017		2018		2019	
Ranking	**Country**	**Ratio**	**Country**	**Ratio**	**Country**	**Ratio**	**Country**	**Ratio**
1	China	31.6	China	33.0	China	34.2	China	38.4
2	Japan	13.8	Japan	14.6	Japan	16.1	Japan	14.9
3	South Korea	6.7	South Korea	6.7	South Korea	6.9	South Korea	6.7
4	USA	4.7	India	5.2	India	4.8	UK	3.9
5	India	4.3	Hong Kong	4.0	USA	3.8	USA	3.9
6	UK	3.9	USA	3.9	Taiwan	3.1	India	3.7
7	Hong Kong	3.9	New Zealand	3.0	Hong Kong	3.0	Taiwan	3.3
8	New Zealand	3.4	Taiwan	2.9	Singapore	2.9	Singapore	3.1
9	Taiwan	2.8	Indonesia	2.2	New Zealand	2.8	New Zealand	2.6
10	Singapore	2.1	Singapore	2.2	Malaysia	2.1	Malaysia	2.3

Source: JETRO International Trade and Investment Report (Annual Edition).

Table 7. Trade balance of Australia with China and with the whole world (2008–2019) (million Australian dollars).

Year	Trade balance with China	Trade balance with the whole world
2008	▲2,835	▲3,447
2009	6,635	▲4,119
2010	19,146	20,993
2011	29,318	34,728
2012	28,688	5,978
2013	47,100	20,846
2014	37,459	13,666
2015	19,269	▲17,228
2016	21,848	2,927
2017	35,575	12,978
2018	43,211	40,282
2019	70,292	82,204

Source: JETRO International Trade and Investment Report (Annual Edition) and the author's calculation.

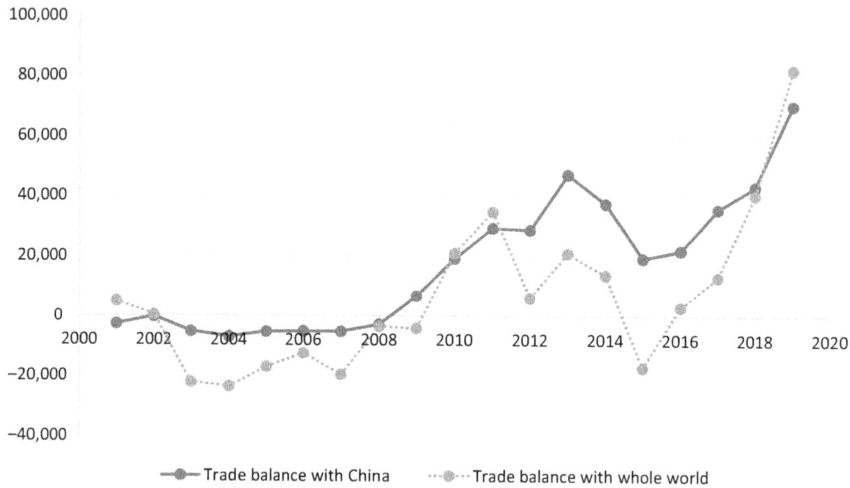

Figure 4. Trade balance of Australia with China and with the whole world (2001–2019).

Source: JETRO International Trade and Investment Report (Annual Edition) and the author's calculation.

Table 8. Trade balance of China with the whole world (2008–2019) (million US dollars).

Year	Trade balance	Year	Trade balance
2008	298,126	2014	383,060
2009	195,689	2015	593,902
2010	181,507	2016	509,707
2011	154,897	2017	419,554
2012	230,309	2018	350,947
2013	259,015	2019	421,071

Source: UNCTAD (Note: Global Note).

In 2018, Australia's trade surplus with China and with the whole world was greater than its trade surplus in both cases in 2017, and likewise, these values in 2019 were greater than those in 2018.

Australia's degree of dependence on foreign trade is indicated in Table 9 and Figure 6.

Germany's degree of dependence on foreign trade was much larger than that of other countries. The mean value of Germany from the year 2008 to 2019 was 67.90 percent. Similarly, the mean value of Australia

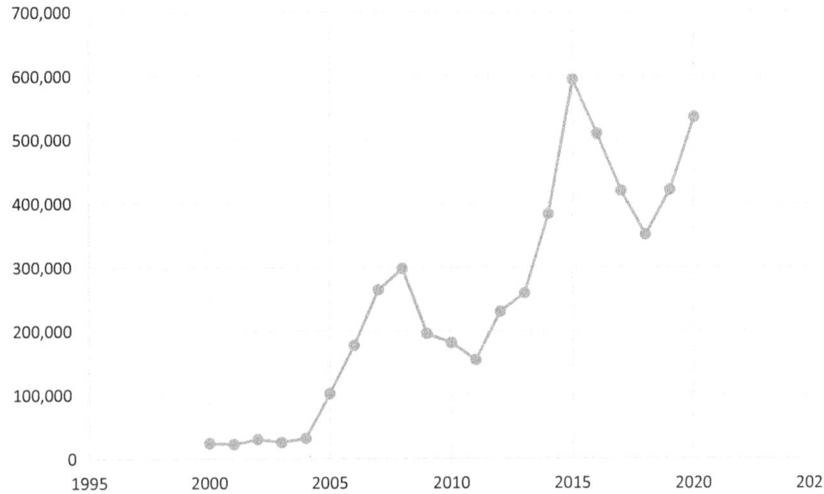

Figure 5. Trade balance of China with the whole world (2000–2020).
Source: UNCTAD (Data: Global Note).

Table 9. Degree of dependence on foreign trade of each country (2008–2019) (in percent).

Year	Japan	Australia	China	Germany
2008	28.69	36.08	50.6	67.55
2009	19.79	30.89	39.26	57.45
2010	23.84	31.93	44.65	65.16
2011	25.73	33.65	44.85	70.33
2012	25.89	33.01	42.61	70.61
2013	28.7	32.47	41.15	68.99
2014	30.89	32.69	38.82	68.21
2015	28.51	31.66	33.67	68.83
2016	24.75	29.81	31.34	67.24
2017	27.44	31.94	32.58	69.65
2018	29.38	34.05	32.63	70.56
2019	27.31	35.37	30.73	70.18

Source: UNCTAD (Note: Global Note) and the author's calculation.

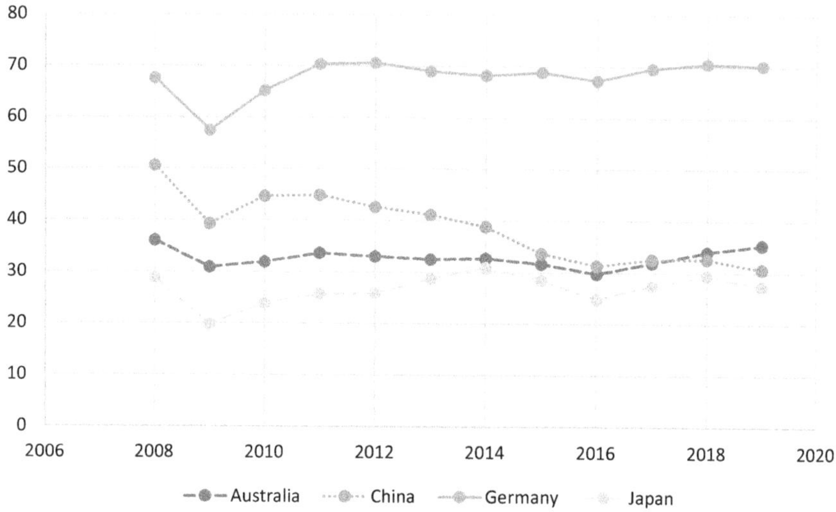

Figure 6. Degree of dependence on foreign trade of each country (2008–2019) (in percent).

Source: UNCTAD (Note: Global Note) and the author's calculation.

was 32.80 percent, Japan 26.74 percent, and China 38.57 percent. Thus, the degree of dependence of Germany was 2.07 times higher than that of Australia.

Australia's degree of dependence on foreign trade in 2019 was larger than that in 2018, which was larger than that in 2017.

In the following section, we compare Sino-Australian economic relations to Sino-German and Sino-Japanese economic relations.

3.3. *International trade relations between Australia and China: Directional trade ratio*

Our first consideration is the "directional trade ratio." This ratio measures the closeness of trade relations between the countries concerned.

Table 10 shows the directional trade ratio between Australia and China.

The directional trade ratio between Australia and China was consistently more than 0.1 from the year 2009 and was more than 0.15 from the year 2013.

Table 10. Directional trade ratio between Australia and China (2008–2019).

Year	Directional trade ratio	Year	Directional trade ratio
2008	0.087	2014	0.152
2009	0.112	2015	0.153
2010	0.126	2016	0.152
2011	0.133	2017	0.155
2012	0.136	2018	0.165
2013	0.157	2019	0.183

Source: JETRO International Trade and Investment Report (Annual Edition) and the author's calculation.

Table 11. Directional trade ratio between Germany and China (2008–2019).

Year	Directional trade ratio	Year	Directional trade ratio
2008	0.048	2014	0.058
2009	0.055	2015	0.059
2010	0.061	2016	0.060
2011	0.060	2017	0.061
2012	0.057	2018	0.061
2013	0.055	2019	0.063

Source: JETRO International Trade and Investment Report (Annual Edition) and the author's calculation.

Furthermore, the directional trade ratio between Australia and China in 2019 was larger than the ratio in 2018, which was larger than the ratio in 2017.

For comparison, we can see the directional trade ratio (1) between Germany and China in Table 11 and (2) between Japan and China in Table 12.

The directional trade ratio between Germany and China was 0.05–0.06, which was not a large numerical value. Comparatively, the directional trade ratio between Australia and China represented a larger value.

Table 12 shows the directional trade ratio between Japan and China, which was 0.14–0.15, a value that is similar to the ratio between Australia and China and is rather different from the ratio between Germany and China.

Table 12. Directional trade ratio between Japan and China (2008–2019).

Year	Directional trade ratio	Year	Directional trade ratio
2008	0.139	2014	0.139
2009	0.154	2015	0.141
2010	0.154	2016	0.145
2011	0.150	2017	0.145
2012	0.144	2018	0.142
2013	0.138	2019	0.141

Source: JETRO International Trade and Investment Report (Annual Edition) and the author's calculation.

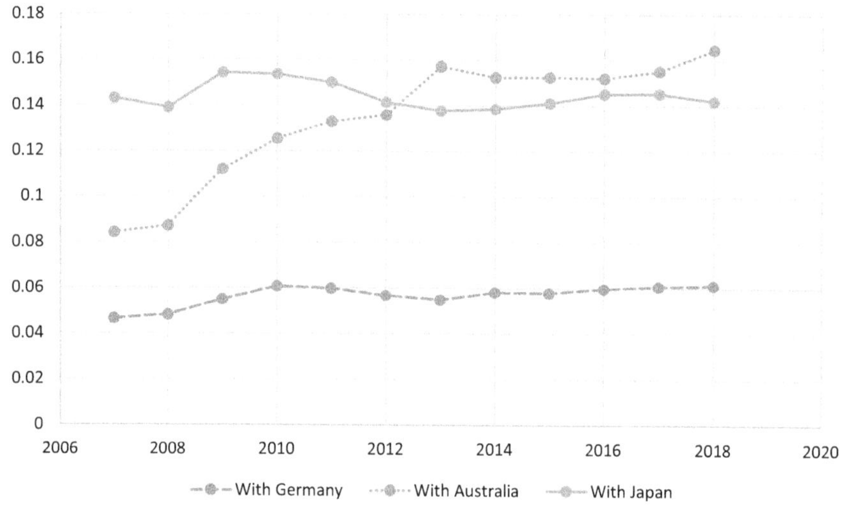

Figure 7. Directional trade ratio of China with each country (2007–2018).
Source: JETRO International Trade and Investment Report (Annual Edition) and the author's calculation.

Figure 7 illustrates the directional trade ratio of China with Australia, Germany, and Japan, from which it is easy to recognize the difference.

The directional trade ratios of China with Australia and Japan have shown similar numerical values in recent years. The directional trade ratio between China and Australia in 2008 was lower than 0.1, which was smaller than the ratio between China and Japan (0.14). However, since then, the directional trade ratio between China and Australia increased rapidly. Thus, since the year 2013, the directional trade ratio between China and Australia has consistently been greater than the ratio between China and Japan.

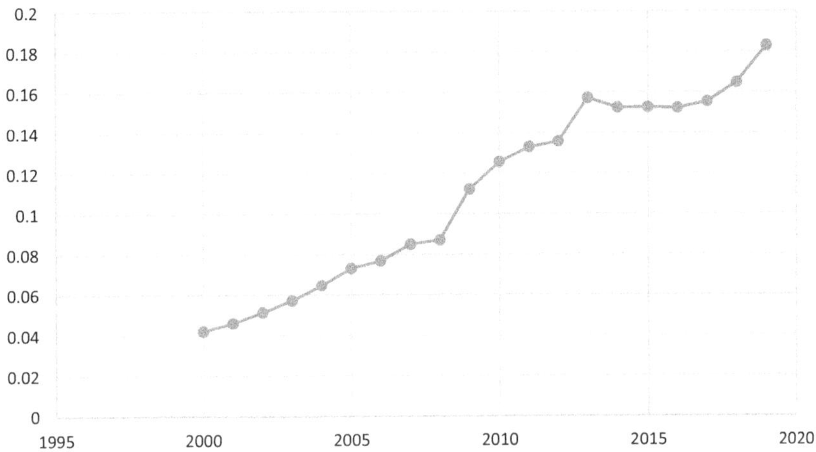

Figure 8. Directional trade ratio between China and Australia (2000–2019).
Source: JETRO Global Trade and Investment Report (Annual Edition) and the author's calculation.

For reference, Figure 8 indicates the directional trade ratio between China and Australia since the year 2000.

Since 2000, the directional trade ratio between China and Australia has consistently increased. A big jump in value occurred from 2008 (0.0871) to 2009 (0.1121) and from 2012 (0.1358) to 2013 (0.1571).

Therefore, it should be noted that, as previously mentioned, the directional trade ratio increased in both 2018 and 2019. According to Table 10, the value was significant 0.1647 in 2018 and 0.1829 in 2019.

As previously mentioned, when examining through the directional trade ratio, it is evident that, as the same as in earlier, with keeping in mind that the decisive deterioration of Sino-Australian relations started in 2017, there is no evidence that the values of the directional trade ratio between Australia and China decreased in 2018 and 2019.

3.4. *International trade relations between Australia and China: Trade linkage index*

In this section, we investigate the trade linkage index focusing on Sino-Australian relations. As explained before, the trade linkage index focuses on whether there are trade distortions between the two countries engaged in trade (in this chapter, Australia and China). The trade linkage index is used as a measure of distortion of trade. In this section, we analyze a distortion in the trade between Australia and other countries (the existence of a portion that is considered to be explained not by comparative advantage, but by factors unique to either Australia or its trading partner countries).

If Australia's actual export amount to China equals the hypothetical export amount to China, the numerical value of the index will be one. If the numerical value of the index is higher (or lower) than one, the "distorted portion of the trade" becomes bigger.

Table 13 shows the trade linkage index of Australia with China. Table 14 shows the trade linkage index of China with Australia. Figure 9 provides an illustration of these indexes.

If the numerical value of the index is higher (or lower) than one, the "distorted portion of the trade" is bigger. Therefore, Australia's foreign trade with China and China's foreign trade with Australia will be judged

Table 13. Trade linkage index of Australia with China (2008–2019).

Year	Trade linkage index	Year	Trade linkage index
2008	2.123	2014	3.157
2009	2.732	2015	3.177
2010	2.717	2016	3.152
2011	2.784	2017	3.146
2012	2.901	2018	3.101
2013	3.367	2019	3.456

Source: JETRO International Trade and Investment Report (Annual Edition) and the author's calculation.

Table 14. Trade linkage index of China with Australia (2008–2019).

Year	Trade linkage index	Year	Trade linkage index
2008	1.267	2014	1.353
2009	1.462	2015	1.467
2010	1.395	2016	1.495
2011	1.414	2017	1.447
2012	1.320	2018	1.624
2013	1.337	2019	1.687

Source: JETRO International Trade and Investment Report (Annual Edition) and the author's calculation.

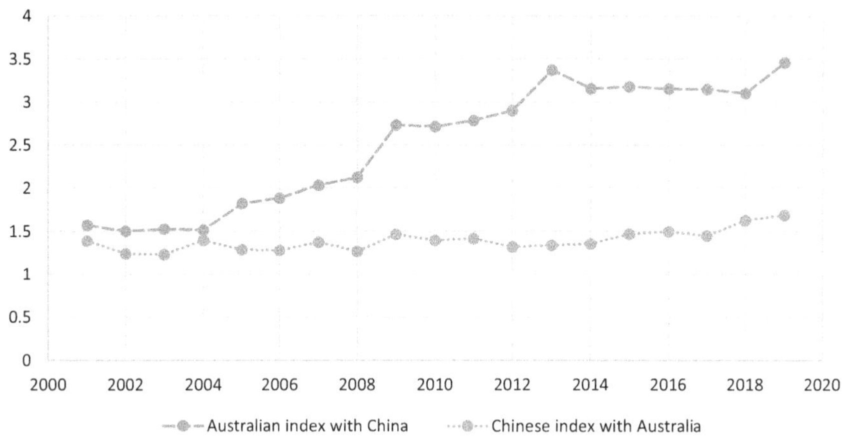

Figure 9. Trade linkage index of Australia with China and China with Australia (2001–2019).

Source: JETRO International Trade and Investment Report (Annual Edition) and the author's calculation.

based on whether the "distortion" is bigger. Furthermore, as clearly shown in Figure 9, the distortion in Australia's foreign trade with China expanded from 2004. In contrast, the distortion in China's foreign trade with Australia has not significantly changed. Thus, there could exist some kind of factors that are distorting Australia's foreign trade with China.

Additionally, it should be noted that (as mentioned earlier, with keeping in mind that the decisive deterioration of Sino-Australian relations started in 2017) when looking at Australian trade linkage index with China, it could be seen that in 2018, it was slightly smaller than in 2017, and in 2019, it was significantly larger than in 2018. Furthermore, regarding China's trade linkage index with Australia, it was larger in 2018 compared to 2017 and even larger in 2019 compared to 2018.

For reference, we consider the Japanese and German trade linkage indexes with China, which are represented in Tables 15 and 16, respectively.

As clearly indicated in Table 15, the trade linkage index of Japan with China was 2.0, based on which one can judge that the actual export amount was large. However, as shown in Table 16, the trade linkage index of Germany with China was less than 1.0, based on which one can judge that the actual export amount was never large.

Table 15. Trade linkage index of Japan with China (2008–2019).

Year	Trade linkage index	Year	Trade linkage index
2008	2.327	2014	1.719
2009	2.389	2015	1.713
2010	2.089	2016	1.763
2011	2.007	2017	1.811
2012	1.776	2018	1.770
2013	1.688	2019	1.707

Source: JETRO International Trade and Investment Report (Annual Edition) and the author's calculation.

Table 16. Trade linkage index of Germany with China (2008–2019).

Year	Trade linkage index	Year	Trade linkage index
2008	0.591	2014	0.617
2009	0.571	2015	0.5841
2010	0.601	2016	0.629
2011	0.623	2017	0.641
2012	0.597	2018	0.641
2013	0.573	2019	0.648

Source: JETRO International Trade and Investment Report (Annual Edition) and the author's calculation.

Figure 10 illustrates the trade linkage indexes of Australia, Japan, and Germany with China. The trade linkage index of Germany with China was small. In contrast, those of both Australia and Japan with China were large. Since 2009, the numerical value of the Australian index increased but the numerical value of the Japanese index decreased. In particular, the numerical value of the Japanese index has been less than 2.0 since 2012. In contrast, the numerical value of the Australian index has been more than 3.0 since 2013.

In any case, the trade linkage index of Australia with China has recorded a much larger numerical value than the trade linkage indexes of Japan and Germany with China.

What about the trade linkage index of China with Australia? As shown in Table 14, the index recorded a range between 1.2 and 1.6, indicating that the numerical values were neither small nor large.

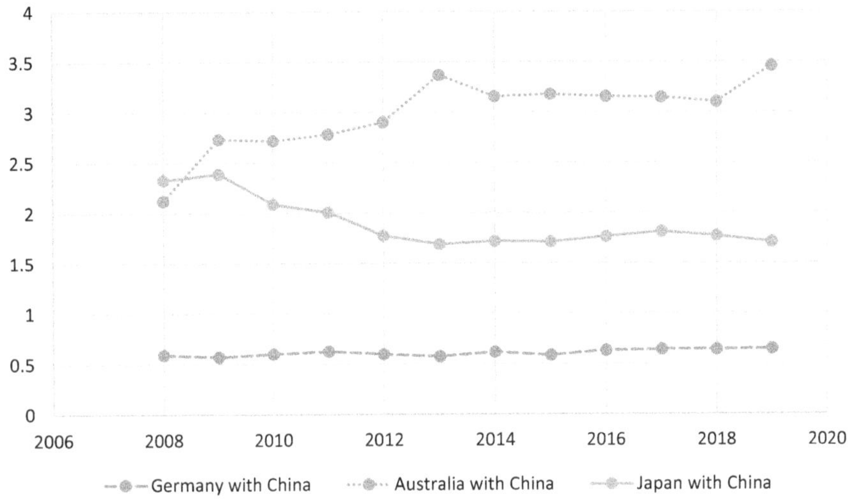

Figure 10. Trade linkage indexes of Australia, Japan, and Germany with China (2008–2019).

Source: JETRO Global Trade and Investment Report (Annual Edition) and the author's calculation.

Particularly when compared to the trade linkage index of Australia with China (which is approximately around 3.0), it could not be said to be a high value. To illustrate this, Figure 9 shows both the trade linkage index of China with Australia and that of Australia with China.

The main assertion of this section is, therefore, that it might be difficult to recognize the significant negative influences on Australian foreign trade relations with China in 2018 and 2019.

For reference, we would consider similar investigations with regard to Sino-Japanese relations and Sino-German relations.

Table 17 indicates the trade linkage index of China with Japan. Figure 11 shows altogether the trade linkage index of Japan with China and China with Japan. The figure undoubtedly different from Figure 9, which presents the trade linkage index of Australia with China and China with Australia. Although the trade linkage index of Japan with China is slightly larger than the trade linkage index of China with Japan, both values are similar.

Table 18 indicates the trade linkage index of China with Germany. Figure 12 shows the trade linkage index of Germany with China and China with Germany. As clearly shown in the figure, although the trade

Table 17. The trade linkage index of China with Japan (2008–2019).

Year	Trade linkage index	Year	Trade linkage index
2008	1.773	2014	1.437
2009	1.878	2015	1.516
2010	1.664	2016	1.608
2011	1.628	2017	1.585
2012	1.489	2018	1.531
2013	1.478	2019	1.479

Source: JETRO International Trade and Investment Report (Annual Edition) and the author's calculation.

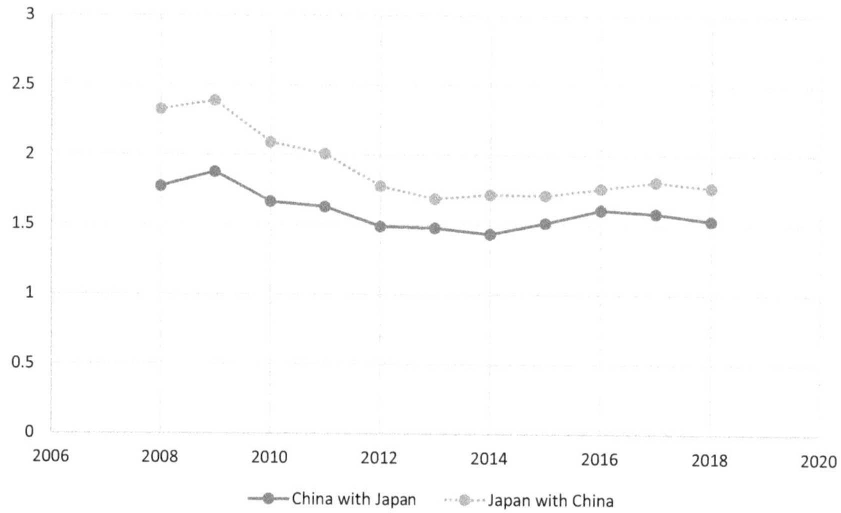

Figure 11. The trade linkage index of China with Japan and Japan with China (2008–2018).

Source: JETRO International Trade and Investment Report (Annual Edition) and the author's calculation.

linkage index of Germany with China could be slightly larger than the trade linkage index of China with Germany, both figures remain by and large at the same level (the trade linkage index of China with Germany indicated a downward trend; however, since 2013, the index remains generally at the same level).

Table 18. The trade linkage index of China with Germany (2008–2019).

Year	Trade linkage index	Year	Trade linkage index
2008	0.570	2014	0.467
2009	0.565	2015	0.476
2010	0.606	2016	0.464
2011	0.571	2017	0.473
2012	0.517	2018	0.469
2013	0.467	2019	0.479

Source: JETRO International Trade and Investment Report (Annual Edition) and the author's calculation.

3.5. *International trade relations between Australia and China: Degree of dependence on the export of a country to a specific country*

In this section, we focus on the trade linkage index of Australia with China and China with Australia, the trade linkage index of Japan with China and the China with Japan, and the trade linkage index of Germany with China and China with Germany. We particularly analyze the differences among these indexes. The focal point of this analysis is the concept of the degree of dependence on the export of a country (Australia) to a specific country (China) and the tendency of that degree of dependence.

The degree of dependence on export is usually defined as the proportion of a country's economy that relies on exports, expressed as the ratio of export value to GDP and other indicators. The purpose is to recognize the degree of dependence on the export of Australia to China and observe the tendency of that degree of dependence.

Therefore, in this section, first, we investigate the usual degree of dependence on the export of Australia; second, we confirm the trade linkage index of Australia with China; and third, we consider the degree of dependence on the export of Australia to a specific country (that is to say, China).

Figure 13 indicates the degree of dependence on the exports (in general) of Australia and China.

As explained earlier, the trade linkage index is focused on whether or not there exists a trade distortion between the countries concerned.

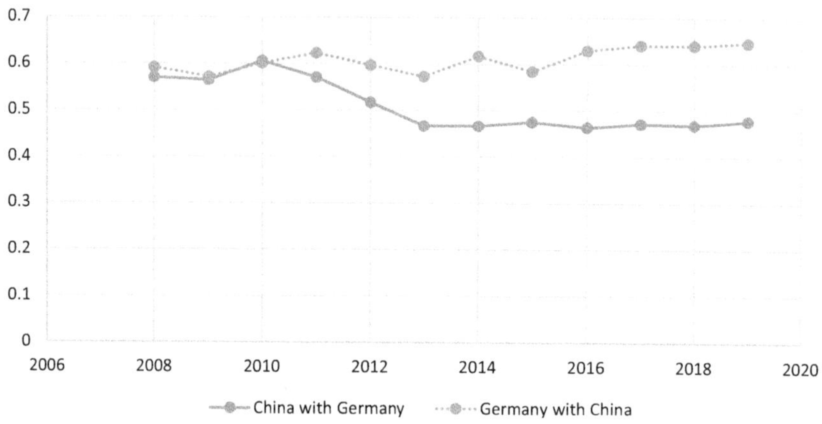

Figure 12. The trade linkage index of China with Germany and Germany with China (2008–2019).

Source: JETRO International Trade and Investment Report (Annual Edition) and the author's calculation.

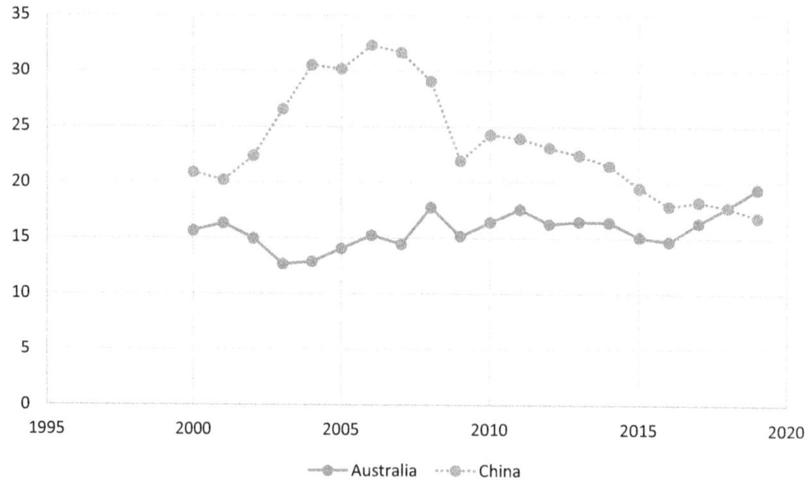

Figure 13. Degree of dependence on the exports of Australia and China (2000–2019) (in percent).

Source: JETRO International Trade and Investment Report (Annual Edition) and the author's calculation.

Actually, it is used as a measure of distortion of trade. The distortion of Australian exports to China has been bigger than the distortion of Chinese exports to Australia. The difference between the two is shown as a ratio, which is recognized as the degree of dependence on the export of Australia to China. As indicated earlier, if the above-mentioned ratio equals 1.0, it means the mutual distortion of the respective countries has the same numerical value, which indicates that the distortions on both sides have the same value, and the magnitude of the portion explained by factors other than comparative advantage is the same. However, if it exceeds 1.0, it means that the portion of exports from Australia to China that could be explained by factors other than comparative advantage is greater than the portion of exports from China to Australia that could be explained by factors other than comparative advantage. In other words, it indicates whether the degree of deviation from comparative advantage of export from Australia to China exceeds that of exports from China to Australia (whether it is above 1.0) and by how much (what value it takes).

In this chapter, we refer to such numerical values the degree of dependence on export (of a country concerned) to a specific country.[18]

Table 19 shows numerical values of "the degree of dependence on the export of Australia to China." Undoubtedly, these values largely exceed the numerical value of 1.0. In order to compare, we present "the degree of dependence on the export of Japan to China" (Table 20) and "the degree of dependence on the export of Germany to China" (Table 21). Figure 14 shows the degree of dependence on the export of the three countries to China.

As clearly shown in Figure 14, the degree of dependence on the export of Australia to China was much larger than the Japanese degree and German degree. The degree of dependence on the export of Japan to China had large numerical values from 2008 to 2011, but then the values fell and were similar to the German degree.

In other words, it could be seen that Australian exports to China had significantly deviated from their comparative advantage (with a deviation far greater than that of China's exports to Australia from their comparative advantage).

---

[18] In Chapter 7 of this book, we designate the same definition as "the degree of dependence on export III."

Table 19. Degree of dependence on the export of Australia to China (2008–2019) (in percent).

Year	The degree of dependence on export	Year	The degree of dependence on export
2008	1.676	2014	2.333
2009	1.869	2015	2.166
2010	1.948	2016	2.108
2011	1.969	2017	2.174
2012	2.198	2018	1.909
2013	2.519	2019	2.048

Source: JETRO International Trade and Investment Report (Annual Edition) and the author's calculation.

Table 20. Degree of dependence on the export of Japan to China (2008–2019) (in percent).

Year	The degree of dependence on export	Year	The degree of dependence on export
2008	1.312	2014	1.196
2009	1.272	2015	1.130
2010	1.256	2016	1.097
2011	1.232	2017	1.143
2012	1.193	2018	1.156
2013	1.142	2019	1.155

Source: JETRO International Trade and Investment Report (Annual Edition) and the author's calculation.

The degree of dependence on the export of Australia to China is shown in Table 22 and Figure 15.

As shown in Table 22 and Figure 15, the numerical value of the degree of dependence on the export of Australia to China increased from 2005 and reached a peak in 2013. After that, the degree started a downward trend and showed smaller numerical values such as 1.9092 in 2018 and 2.0484 in 2019.

As mentioned previously, according to the definition of the degree of dependence on export to a specific country in this book, if the deviation from comparative advantage of exports from Australia to China is equal

Table 21. Degree of dependence on the export of Germany to China (2008–2019) (in percent).

Year	The degree of dependence on export	Year	The degree of dependence on export
2008	1.038	2014	1.320
2009	1.012	2015	1.228
2010	0.993	2016	1.355
2011	1.092	2017	1.357
2012	1.155	2018	1.365
2013	1.227	2019	1.351

Source: JETRO International Trade and Investment Report (Annual Edition) and the author's calculation.

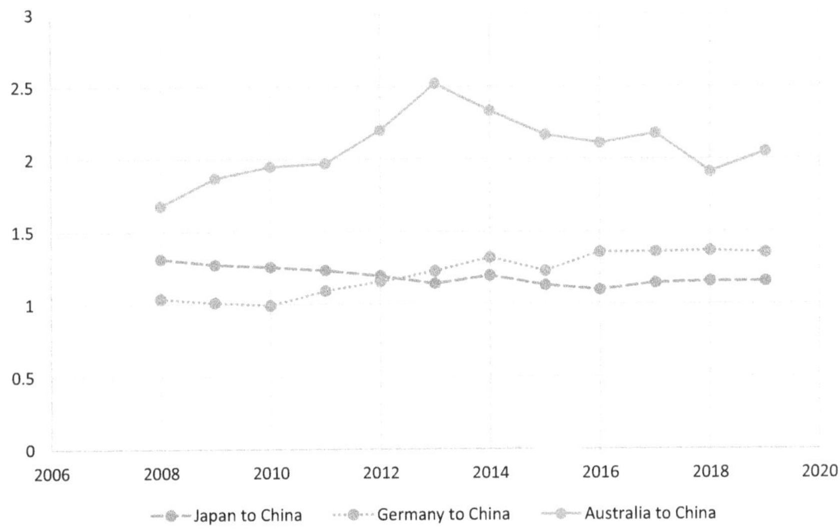

Figure 14. Degree of dependence on the export of each country to China (2008–2019) (in percent).

Source: JETRO International Trade and Investment Report (Annual Edition) and the author's calculation.

to the deviation from comparative advantage of exports from China to Australia, it takes a value of 1.0, and if the difference in the deviation exceeds, it means that the value is greater than 1.0. Needless to say, the larger the value above 1.0, the greater the difference in the deviation.

Table 22. Degree of dependence on the export of Australia to China (2001–2019) (in percent).

Year	The degree of dependence on export	Year	The degree of dependence on export
2001	1.131	2011	1.969
2002	1.220	2012	2.198
2003	1.237	2013	2.519
2004	1.088	2014	2.333
2005	1.416	2015	2.166
2006	1.473	2016	2.108
2007	1.479	2017	2.174
2008	1.676	2018	1.909
2009	1.869	2019	2.048
2010	1.948		

Source: JETRO International Trade and Investment Report (Annual Edition) and the author's calculation.

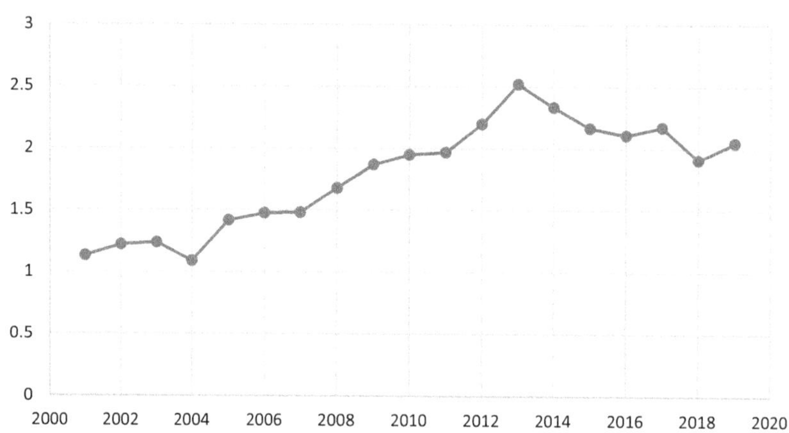

Figure 15. Degree of dependence on the export of Australia to China (2001–2019) (in percent).

Source: JETRO International Trade and Investment Report (Annual Edition) and the author's calculation.

Therefore, the fact that the degree of dependence on export of Australia to China peaked at a value of 2.5193 in 2013 and then entered a downward trend means that "the degree of deviation from comparative advantage of Australian exports to China" has approached "the degree of deviation from comparative advantage of Chinese export to Australia." Thus, since 2014, the difference in the degree of deviation from comparative advantage between the Australian export to China and the Chinese export to Australia has become smaller.[19]

3.6. *International trade relations between Australia and China: Outline in 2018 and 2019*

Before the end of this section, based on *Global Trade and Investment Report* (JETRO), we take a look at the international trade of Australia in 2018 and 2019.

In 2018, the real GDP growth rate of Australia was 2.8 percent, which achieved a 26-consecutive-year economic expansion. Of the real GDP growth rate, the growth rate of exports was 5.0 percent and the growth rate of imports was 3.9 percent.

When we observe exports by item in 2018, minerals and fuel occupied more than 60 percent of the total exports, out of which coal ranked first (accounting for 19.4 percent of the total exports). Coal increased from 17.0 percent the previous year and surpassed iron ore. In contrast, iron ore (ranked second) increased by 0.3 percent compared to the previous year. However, depending on the economic expansion in China (which occupied the first ranking in exports to Australia), more iron ore exports were expected. Natural gas (ranked third) increased to 69.0 percent compared to the previous year, with a value of 43.297 billion Australian dollars in 2018.

With regard to exports by country and region, China (which exceeded Japan and ranked first in exports in Australia in 2009) maintained the first ranking consistently. After that, the Chinese ratio continued to expand and was 34.2 percent of the total exports in Australia.

[19]As Australia and China were at their best in terms of cooperation in 2014, the result of this analysis might be interesting. Since 2014, the degree of dependence on the export of Australia to China has become smaller. More detailed analyses on the result of the degree of dependence on exports are necessary.

When we observe imports by item, manufactured goods occupied 64.3 percent of the total imports. The ratio of computers, communication equipment, and passenger cars is high as usual. Also, chemicals and petroleum products occupied a large ratio. Regarding the expansion rate, the values of both civil engineering heavy equipment (44.0 percent compared to the previous year) and freight cars (21.2 percent compared to the previous year) largely increased.

With regard to imports by country and region, China occupied 24.5 percent of the total imports and ranked first. Observed by item, communications equipment (8.527 billion Australian dollars) and computers (6.481 billion Australian dollars) occupied 20 percent of the total imports from China. The principal imports from the United States (ranked second) were passenger cars (2.041 billion Australian dollars) and aviation instruments and space appliances (1.253 billion Australian dollars).

In 2019 (because of increased uncertainty in the global economy, droughts, and large-scale forest fires), the real GDP growth rate was 1.8 percent, which was significantly less compared to the previous year. Of the real GDP growth rate, the growth rate of exports was 3.20 percent and the growth rate of imports was negative 1.29 percent.

When we observe exports by item, iron ore (ranked first) occupied 24.7 percent of the total exports and increased to 51.8 percent compared to the previous year. The main reason for that increase was the supply shortage due to a dam-break accident in an iron ore mine in Brazil in January 2019, which caused iron ore prices to soar. More than 80 percent of the iron ore in Australia was exported to China. On the other hand, the total exports of coal (ranked second) decreased to 4.3 percent due to the tendency of coal prices to fall. Natural gas (ranked third) was favorable with a value of 12.4 percent compared to the previous year, and the main export countries were Japan, China, and South Korea.

With regard to exports by country and region, since 2009, exports to China have been valued at 38.4 percent of the total exports. The percent of resource exports such as iron ore, coal, and natural gas increased to 26.2 percent compared to the previous year. Next to China, Japan, South Korea, the UK, and the USA occupied the top positions.

When we observe imports by item, petroleum products occupied the largest ratio, which had decreased by 0.1 percent compared to the previous year. The main import countries were Singapore, South Korea, and Japan. The next ranked import item was a passenger car. However, just as domestic automobile sales had decreased over 21 consecutive months until December 2019, the import of automobiles was 4.5 percent lower than the previous year.

With regard to imports by country and region, imports from China occupied roughly 25 percent of the whole imports, with a robust growth of 6.2 percent over the previous year, ranking first. The main import items were communications equipment, computers, and petroleum products. Because of the increase in import of air navigation and space appliance parts, medicines, and crude oil, imports from the United States recorded a 11.9 percent growth over the previous year, ranking second.

As can be seen from this overview, there was no impact of the deterioration of the relationship between China and Australia.

However, according to *Global Trade and Investment Report* (2020 version by JETRO), with China being its largest foreign trade partner country, tensions in Australia have run high. The Chinese government announced in May 2020 that China would levy a duty on the import of barley from Australia, which was a combined total of 80.5 percent, including an anti-dumping duties of 73.6 percent and compensation duties of 6.9 percent. Moreover, in the same month, because of a technical issue, China suspended the import of beef from the 4 main meat-processing plants in Australia. In August 2020, the Chinese Department of Commerce announced that it had initiated anti-dumping and anti-subsidy investigations into Australian wine. This highlights the rising tensions in trade between Australia and China.

Furthermore, an article in *Nihon Keizai Shimbun* (26 August 2021) reported that Australia increased pressure against China regarding human rights issues. The Australian government announced in August that they would implement a law amendment to impose sanctions against foreign government officials who have participated in the violation of human rights. Australia also decided to participate in joint military training with the United States, Japan, and India. Because China greatly depends on Australian iron ore, Australia realized that even if it coerced China, China would not be able to carry out strong retaliatory economic sanctions against Australia. The Australian Department of Defense announced (23 August 2021) that the Australian navy would participate in the "Malabar" joint military training implemented by the United States, Japan, and India. Australia had participated in the "Malabar" training in 2007. However, because China expressed discomfort against Australian participation, Australia stopped participating until 2020. According to *Nihon Keizai*

Shimbun, Australia's participation 2 years in a row in the joint operations proves that it highly values the "Quad" (cooperation among the United States, Japan, Australia, and India) over China. Furthermore, Prime Minister Morrison's strong posture against China could have been because China depends on Australia for more than 60 percent of its iron ore. According to the Chinese customs office, China's import quantity from Australia in 2020 (when Sino-Australian relations deteriorated because of an Australian request for an independent investigation into the COVID-19 pandemic) was 7 percent more than the previous year. Moreover, according to Australian Department of Foreign Affairs and Trade, Australia's export of goods to China in 2020 amounted to 147.8 billion Australian dollars, which was one percent less than the previous year. However, because Australia's total export amount decreased, the ratio occupied by China increased from 38.3 percent (in 2019) to 40.7 percent (in 2020). Nonetheless, unless Australia increased the pressure on China, there was a possibility that China could implement economic sanctions irrespective of the economic damages to itself. Thus, the Morrison Administration acted in concert with the United States regarding its foreign policy toward China; on the other hand, the Morrison administration also showed consideration toward China.

In short, China weighed the advantages of economic sanctions against Australia against the disadvantages of economic damage to itself and decided that it could not implement economic sanctions against Australia.

As stated earlier, the influence of the deterioration of Sino-Australian relations in the international trade of Australia in 2018 and 2019 is not perceptible.

4. FDI Relationship between Australia and China: On the FDI Trade Index

In this section, we consider the FDI relationship between Australia and China. We do not investigate the numerical values of FDI but considered whether or not the FDI between Australia and China has been enforced positively, based on international relations between the home country and the host country.

We use the FDI concentration index and the trade linkage index.

FDI concentration index is presented as follows. When considering the FDI concentration index from Australia to China, this index represents the ratio of the value obtained by dividing "Australian outward FDI in China" by "China's inward FDI" as the numerator, and "Australian outward FDI" by "the total outward FDI worldwide" as the denominator. When the ratio is more than 1.0, Australian FDI to China is bigger than that of other countries.

Table 23 indicates the FDI concentration index of Australia with China.

As Table 23 shows, the fundamental numerical values might be small. When the absolute value is large, it is negative. In contrast, when the index is not more than 1.0, it is positive. Therefore, Australian FDI in China is comparatively smaller than that of other countries.

For comparison, we review the FDI concentration indexes of Germany and Japan with China in Tables 24 and 25, respectively.

Table 23. FDI concentration index (Australia with China) (2008–2019).

Year	FDI concentration index	Year	FDI concentration index
2008	0.363	2014	▲12.776
2009	▲0.870	2015	▲0.302
2010	0.039	2016	▲0.519
2011	0.137	2017	▲3.209
2012	0.418	2018	0.938
2013	0.788	2019	0.349

Note: ▲ indicates excess withdrawal.

Source: JETRO International Trade and Investment Report (Annual Edition) and the author's calculation.

Table 24. FDI concentration index (Germany with China) (2008–2019).

Year	FDI concentration index	Year	FDI concentration index
2008	0.140	2014	0.608
2009	1.168	2015	0.475
2010	2.280	2016	1.048
2011	3.699	2017	0.322
2012	0.967	2018	0.058
2013	1.921	2019	0.437

Source: JETRO International Trade and Investment Report (Annual Edition) and the author's calculation.

Table 25. FDI concentration index (Japan with China) (2008–2019).

Year	FDI concentration index	Year	FDI concentration index
2008	0.732	2014	0.625
2009	1.622	2015	0.749
2010	0.896	2016	0.646
2011	1.512	2017	0.633
2012	1.263	2018	0.548
2013	0.764	2019	0.590

Source: JETRO International Trade and Investment Report (Annual Edition) and the author's calculation.

As shown in Tables 24 and 27, the FDI concentration index of Germany with China was undoubtedly larger than the index of Japan with China.

In this section, we would pose the question, as the author has in previous arguments, "is Australian FDI in China considered active or not?"[20]

Instead of asking if the FDI is large or small, one can judge by asking if the FDI can be implemented with the same degree of economic relations as the other countries being considered. Therefore, the FDI trade index consists of the FDI concentration index as a numerator and the trade linkage index as a denominator.

Therefore, when the FDI trade index is equal to 1.0, FDI relations between the two countries are considered to correspond with their international relations. When the index is more than 1.0, FDI relations between them are more active than expected based on their international relations. When the index is less than 1.0, FDI relations between them are less active than expected. Table 26 indicates the FDI trade index of Australia with China.

As clearly indicated in Table 26, in the FDI trade index of Australia with China, there were many years of "excess withdrawal" and no year with a large numerical value (in the positive sense). Therefore, it could be said that Australian FDI in China has never been active in the context of international economic relations.

From 2014 to 2017, the FDI trade index of Australia with China was negative. In contrast, in 2018 and 2019, the index was positive. Thus, the

[20]Regarding the author's assertions, see, for example, Morita (2017b).

Table 26. FDI trade index (Australia with China) (2008–2019).

Year	FDI trade index	Year	FDI trade index
2008	0.171	2014	▲4.180
2009	▲0.319	2015	▲0.095
2010	0.014	2016	▲0.165
2011	0.049	2017	▲1.020
2012	0.144	2018	0.303
2013	0.234	2019	0.101

Note: ▲ indicates excess withdrawal.
Source: JETRO International Trade and Investment Report (Annual Edition) and the author's calculation.

Table 27. FDI trade index (Germany with China) (2008–2019).

Year	FDI trade index	Year	FDI trade index
2008	0.237	2014	0.986
2009	2.045	2015	0.813
2010	3.795	2016	1.665
2011	5.936	2017	0.502
2012	1.618	2018	0.340
2013	3.354	2019	0.677

Source: JETRO International Trade and Investment Report (Annual Edition) and the author's calculation.

FDI trade index of Australia with China was undoubtedly smaller in 2018 and 2019 compared to years before 2017.

The FDI trade index of Germany with China and Japan with China are shown in Tables 27 and 28, respectively.

As indicated in Tables 27 and 28, the FDI trade index of Germany with China was more than 1.0 for many years (particularly in 2011, the index reached 5.9355; however, after 2014, except for 2016, the index was less than 1.0 every year). Therefore, in light of international economic relations, the German FDI trade index with China became active (at least until 2013). In contrast, the FDI trade index of Japan with China was not more than 1.0 for any year. That is to say, both Australian and Japanese FDIs with China were less active than the German FDI with China.

Table 28. FDI trade index (Japan with China) (2008–2019).

Year	FDI trade index	Year	FDI trade index
2008	0.314	2014	0.364
2009	0.679	2015	0.437
2010	0.429	2016	0.366
2011	0.753	2017	0.349
2012	0.711	2018	0.313
2013	0.452	2019	0.322

Source: JETRO International Trade and Investment Report (Annual Edition) and the author's calculation.

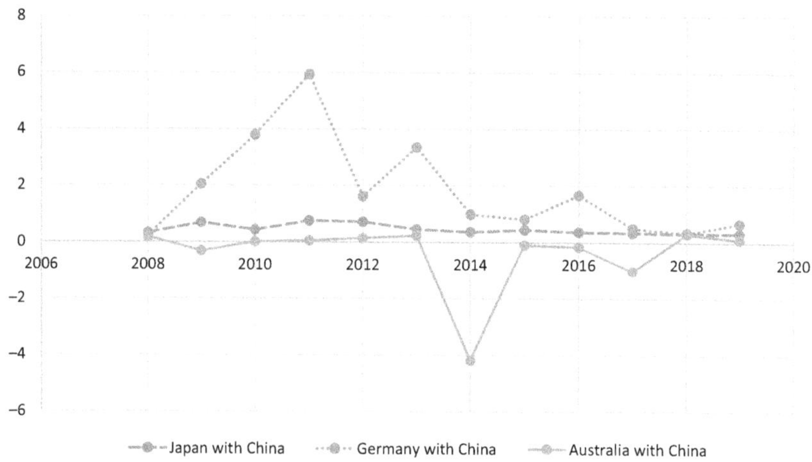

Figure 16. FDI trade index of each country with China (2008–2019).

Source: JETRO Global Trade and Investment Report (Annual Edition) and the author's calculation.

Figure 16 shows the FDI trade indexes of Australia, Germany, and Japan with China. Until the year 2013, the FDI trade index of Germany with China was larger than the index of Australia and Japan. Moreover, the FDI trade index of Australia with China was smaller than that of Japan. The average values are as follows: Germany 1.8305, Japan 0.4575, and Australia negative 0.3969.

Now, the FDI trade indexes of China with Australia, Germany, and Japan are shown in Tables 29, 30, and 31, respectively. Figure 17 represents them altogether.

Table 29. FDI trade index (China with Australia) (2008–2019).

Year	FDI trade index	Year	FDI trade index
2008	1.279	2014	0.809
2009	1.628	2015	1.303
2010	0.724	2016	0.441
2011	0.771	2017	0.624
2012	0.455	2018	0.128
2013	0.578	2019	0.330

Source: JETRO International Trade and Investment Report (Annual Edition) and the author's calculation.

Table 30. FDI trade index (China with Germany) (2008–2019).

Year	FDI trade index	Year	FDI trade index
2008	0.063	2014	4.136
2009	0.098	2015	1.491
2010	0.626	2016	▲0.310
2011	0.208	2017	▲0.419
2012	1.158	2018	0.308
2013	0.005	2019	0.827

Note: ▲ indicates excess withdrawal.
Source: JETRO International Trade and Investment Report (Annual Edition) and the author's calculation.

Table 31. FDI trade index (China with Japan) (2008–2019)

Year	FDI trade index	Year	FDI trade index
2008	0.035	2014	2.318
2009	▲0.193	2015	▲1.877
2010	▲3.022	2016	▲0.055
2011	▲0.991	2017	0.671
2012	0.461	2018	0.094
2013	0.574	2019	0.122

Note: ▲ indicates excess withdrawal.
Source: JETRO International Trade and Investment Report (Annual Edition) and the author's calculation.

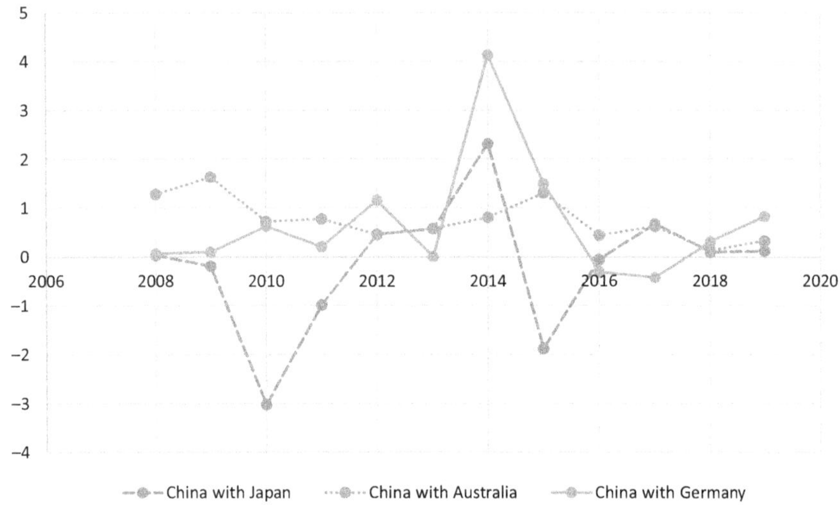

Figure 17. FDI trade index of China with each country (2008–2019).

Source: JETRO International Trade and Investment Report (Annual Edition) and the author's calculation.

We first review the FDI trade index of China with Australia. There were many years when the index was less than 1.0; such a tendency became evident particularly after 2010. Therefore, the Chinese FDI with Australia could not be large due to economic relations between the two countries.

The FDI trade index of China with Germany is not large due to economic relations between the two countries. Although in 2014 the value was rather large (4.1360), in 2012 and 2015, the values were more than 1.0 but not large numerical values. In short, the Chinese FDI with Germany could not be large due to economic relations between the two countries. With regard to the FDI trade index of China with Japan, the tendency of the index was remarkable. It was more than 1.0 in only one year. In other years, the numerical values of the index were either less than 1.0 or negative.

As investigated in this section, the FDI trade index of Australia with China was undoubtedly negative from 2016 to 2017 but became positive from 2018 to 2019. Thus, it is difficult to note any negative influences due to a deterioration of Sino-Australian relations.[21]

[21] Interestingly, the FDI trade index of China with Australia shows a downward tendency from the peak year of 2015 (1.3029), including in 2018 and 2019.

5. Conclusion

In this chapter, we consider Sino-Australian relations, in particular the economic aspect. We also compare Sino-Australian relations with Sino-Japanese relations and Sino-German relations. Our focus is on Sino-Australian relations in 2018 and 2019 and gauging the possible impact in a deterioration of relations in 2017.

Based on our investigations in this chapter, it is difficult to verify if the decisive deterioration in Sino-Australian relations in 2017 has had a significant economic impact.

Our conclusions are as follows:

(1) In 2019, the military expenditure of Australia was 25.912 billion US dollars, while that of Japan was 47.690 billion US dollars and Germany was 49.277 billion US dollars. In contrast, the military expenditure of China was 261.082 billion US dollars, incomparably larger than that of Australia, Germany, and Japan. In fact, the Chinese military expenditure in 2019 was 10 times more than the Australian military expenditure. The military expenditure of Australia in 2019 was smaller than the amount in 2018, which was smaller than the amount in 2017.

(2) Next, regarding the ranking and ratio of Australian import and export countries, the ratio of China in Australian imports and exports (ranked first in both) was larger in 2018 that in 2017, and even larger in 2019 than in 2018. The Australian trade surplus (both with China and the whole world) in 2019 was larger than that in 2018, which was larger than that in 2017.

(3) The degree of dependence on foreign trade in Australia, Japan, China, and Germany in 2018/ 2019 was as follows: Germany 67.90 percent, Australia 32.80 percent, Japan 26.74 percent, and China 38.57 percent. Compared with Germany, the average value of Australia was substantially smaller. Also, the degree of dependence on foreign trade in Australia was larger in 2019 was larger than that in 2018, which was larger than that in 2017.

(4) With regard to the directional trade ratio with China, the numerical value of the ratio of Germany was small. The numerical value of the ratio of both Australia and Japan was undoubtedly larger than that of Germany. Concerning the directional trade ratios of Japan and Australia with China, after 2013, the ratios of Australia were larger

than those of Japan. Also, the directional trade ratio of Australia with China in 2019 was larger than the ratio in 2018, which was larger than the ratio in 2017.

(5) The trade linkage index of Germany with China was small; in contrast, the trade linkage indices of Australia and Japan with China were rather large. After 2009, the numerical values of the trade linkage index of Australia had an upward tendency but those of Japan had a downward tendency. The trade linkage index of Australia with China in 2018 was slightly smaller than the index in 2017, but the index in 2019 was substantially larger than the index in 2018.

(6) The degree of export dependence of Australia on China was undoubtedly larger than the degree export dependence of Germany and Japan on China. The degree of export dependence of Australia on China peaked in 2013 and after that experienced a downward trend, due to which the degrees in 2018 and 2019 were slightly smaller than before. Therefore, it is considered that the "degree of deviation from comparative advantage" (as defined in this book) in Australian exports to China has been decreasing overall since 2014.[22]

(7) With respect to the FDI trade index with China, the FDI trade index of Germany was larger than those of Japan and Australia. In particular, the Australian FDI trade index with China was smaller than that of Japan. The FDI trade index of Australia with China from 2014 to 2017 was negative but positive in 2018 and 2019. Thus, it could not be said that the FDI trade index of Australia with China in 2018 and 2019 was significantly smaller compared to the period before 2017.

Therefore, although there was a decisive deterioration in Sino-Australian relations in terms of international politics and national security, there was no influence of this on economic relations between the two countries.[23]

[22] The author of this book considers that a more detailed analysis of these results is necessary. As stated in the previous footnote 20, this is a subject for future consideration.

[23] It goes without saying that the question of why such results were obtained remains. The author of this book would like to take the opportunity to review this matter future.

Chapter 7

A Political Economy of Cross-Strait Relations

1. Introduction

An article in *Nihon Keizai Shimbun* (16 December 2021) reported a conclusion reached by the Japan Economic Research Center that China's GDP would exceed the United States' GDP in the year 2033. The reversal period would be later than the estimate from last December (2020), which suggested it could be as early as 2028. Furthermore, it is forecasted that in the year 2050, the US's GDP will exceed China's GDP once again. This is because of (1) the tightening of regulations for private enterprises by the Chinese government, (2) a decrease in the growth of productivity, and (3) a labor shortage due to population decline in the long run.[1]

A "reversal" and a "second reversal" of nominal GDP between China and the United States will have a significant impact on the economy, politics, national security, etc., of countries in the Asia Oceania region (including Japan, Taiwan, Australia, and South Korea).

In Chapter 6 of this book, we analyzed the economic relations between Australia and China from the point of view of Australia, which is a "canary in the coal mine" in terms of intervention by the Chinese

[1] In that article, it is also reported that the per capita nominal GDP of Japan (which indicates personal wealth) would be less than that of South Korea in 2027 and Taiwan in 2028. This is because of the delayed digital transformation in the field of administration, the poor increase in labor productivity, etc.

Communist Party. It might be dangerous, in terms of an uncertain future, for countries and regions to have any relations with China (Chinese Communist Party). Taiwan has always experienced this danger and it is accepted nowadays that there might be an emergency situation involving Taiwan in the near future.

With regard to Sino-Australian relations, as mentioned in Chapter 6, although there has been a "decisive deterioration in Sino-Australian relations" in terms of international politics and national security, at this time, it has not affected the economic relationship between the two countries.[2]

In this chapter, we focus our attention on contemporary Taiwan and analyze the political economy of Cross-Strait Relations with reference to Sino-Australian relations.

The fundamental strategy of Taiwan has been to maintain the status quo and neither "independence" from China nor "unification" with China. Taiwan has never wanted to trigger a Chinese invasion and has thus has never demanded an independent state of Taiwan. To put it simply, Taiwan's policy is to perform a "sensitive balance." The Tsai Ing-wen administration of Taiwan, advocated a new policy of facing south, which indicates that Taiwan will seek to associate with countries to its south. However, the Taiwanese policy of rejecting China has to be implemented based on a "sensitive balance."

In this chapter, we analyze Cross-Strait relations with a particular focus on the political economy of Taiwan and its "sensitive balance" policy.

The structure of this chapter is as follows: After the introduction, in the second section, we consider the "Taiwan emergency situation." In the third section, we review the general situation of the Taiwanese economy. In the fourth section, we analyze the international trade in Taiwan and also consider the countries with which Taiwan is conducting trade. In the fifth section, we analyze the international trade relations of Taiwan and China. In the sixth section, we investigate the three degrees of dependence on export. In the seventh and eighth sections, we consider the outward FDI of Taiwan. And finally, in the ninth section, we provide an overview of the chapter.

---

[2]Also in that footnote, it states that, it goes without saying, the question of why such results were obtained remains.

2. Rise of China and the Status quo of Taiwan

Ever since China has been progressing and has occupied an important position in international society, the international issues involving China have increased. Therefore, international society needs an appropriate framework to understand China's behavior.

Even if China asserts itself in a different way, its behavior would still fall under the "realism" framework. The framework of "realism" has two sub-types: "offensive realism" and "defensive realism."

Waltz's (1979) assertion that "realism is the best without any adjectives to qualify"[3] is undoubtedly correct. The type of realism — whether offensive or defensive — depends on the situation and the best way to secure national security.[4]

However, the Chinese Communist Party's present behavior can be categorized as offensive realism. There is no room for doubt that "China's rise" has been unpeaceful.[5]

As the policy of the Xi Jinping administration is offensive realism, the possibility of an emergency situation in Taiwan is very real and could occur in the next 5–10 years with a rather high probability.[6]

2.1. *Taiwan's emergency situation (1) — What is the peaceful rise of China?*

What does the "peaceful rise of China" mean? As mentioned in Chapter 4, Pan and Chen (2014) asserted that China has given a false impression to

---

[3] Waltz (1979, p. ix) (Japanese version), preface to Japanese version.

[4] *Ibid.*

[5] See Mearsheimer (2006).

[6] Scott Harold and Satoru Mori described in an article in *Newsweek* (Japanese version, 21 September 2021) that the commanding officer of the US Indo-Pacific Command (Philip Davidson) asserted at a public hearing of the Senate Armed Services Committee that the threat of a Chinese invasion of Taiwan was imminent (within 6 years after his statement). Two weeks later, his successor, John C. Aquilino, also warned that this threat could be realized sooner than usual (p. 34). If it occurs "within 6 years after this" or "much nearer" the year 2021, both the United States and Japan will be forced to deal with such a threat. If a Chinese invasion of Taiwan were to occur, both the United States and Japan will be caught in the conflict (p. 34).

the whole world on its supposed "peaceful rise." In the new era of Chinese further peaceful rise, the inevitable challenge is how to develop and disseminate concepts that combine Chinese unique characteristics with universal values and are accepted globally, and how to deepen and promote Chinese peaceful rise in the world (p. 96). According to Pan and Chen (2014), China's rise was too speedy and smooth, which created a false impression for the whole world (p. 96).

In short, although China's rise seems peaceful, it was too quick for the whole world to accept as peaceful. Therefore, it is when the world embraces China that the situation would become clear, and at that time, it would be evident that Chinese rise (characterized by its unique features and values) is peaceful in light of the globally accepted concept.

In Chapter 4, we also provided the analysis conducted by Mearsheimer (2014). According to him, if China continues its striking economic growth over the next few decades, it is likely to act in accordance with the logic of offensive realism and it will imitate the United States. China is involved in various territorial disputes and the more powerful it gets, the better able it will be to settle those disputes on terms favorable to Beijing (p. 368).

If this were to happen, as Pan and Chen (2014) stated, we will recognize that the rise of China has been peaceful.

It goes without saying, in order to be "more powerful" to settle the disputes on terms favorable to Beijing, it is necessary to maintain its overwhelming economic power, military power, and cultural influence. Based on Mearsheimer's expression, it is indispensable for China to act in accordance with the logic of offensive realism.

Then, is it possible for its actions to be construed as a "peaceful rise?" Needless to say, to act in accordance with the logic of offensive realism means to act as an invasive country and seek the position of regional hegemony. Under the existing conditions, these actions cannot be accepted as constituting a "peaceful rise."[7]

In short, it is difficult to find any grounds to recognize China's actions as constituting a "peaceful rise."

---

[7]In a world in which China is the hegemon (i.e., not the existing conditions), its actions might be accepted as constituting a "peaceful rise."

2.2. *Taiwan's emergency situation (2) — The world of "offensive realism"*

As mentioned in Section 2.1, if we suppose that China acts in accordance with the logic of offensive realism, what does that mean for "Taiwan's emergency situation?"

We answer this question based on Chapter 10 of Mearsheimer's work (2014).[8]

According to the translator's explanation and postscript by Masashi Okuyama, the theoretical assumptions of "defensive realism" by K. N. Waltz are as follows: (1) The international system is anarchic and (2) survival is the primary goal of a nation. In addition to these two, Mearsheimer asserted the additional three assumptions: (3) Great powers inherently possess some offensive military capability, (4) states can never be certain about other states' intentions, and (5) great powers are rational actors (pp. 30–31). If such assumptions are accepted, great powers are compelled to become aggressive and aspire to the position of global hegemony in order to ensure their own national security. Therefore, based on these five assumptions, we recognize that China will behave as the United States has done. Also, Mearsheimer advocated that China cannot rise peacefully.

However, there are opposing views that China could rise peacefully and the future of Sino-American relations is peaceful. According to Mearsheimer (2014), there are two reasons for such assertions: (1) The first reason is based on a cultural theory that China's Confucian culture will ensure that it avoids intense security competition with its neighbors as well as with the United States. (2) The other reason is based on the familiar liberal theory of economic interdependence, that is to say, conflict is unlikely because the major countries in Asia — as well as the United States — are economically intertwined, which means that if they fight with each other, it will threaten the prosperity that is so important to all of them (p. 403).

Mearsheimer's rejection of the opposing views is based on the following. With regard to the cultural theory, there is little basis for the claim that China is an exceptional great power that eschews realist logic and instead behaves in accordance with the principles of Confucian pacifism. Almost all the available evidence indicates that China has a rich

---

[8] Chapter 10 is entitled "Can China Rise Peacefully?"

history of trying to maximize its relative power. Furthermore, there is no good reason to think China will act differently in the future (p. 407). Concerning the theory of economic interdependence, this perspective has two components: (1) the claim that China's economy is inextricably bound to the economies of its potential rivals, including Japan and the United States, and a war involving them would have disastrous economic consequences for all the belligerents; (2) the claim that prosperity is the main goal of modern states. However, the basic tenet of the theory of economic interdependence is that "if you do not survive, you cannot prosper." So, at the most basic level, political calculations often trump economic ones when it comes to conflict. This is certainly true regarding matters of national security (p. 408). With respect to the "economic costs" of a war, a country has little to lose economically and maybe even something to gain by starting a war (p. 409). Also, states sometimes start wars with the expectation that victory will bring them substantial economic and strategic benefits and that those prospective benefits will be greater than the prosperity lost from damaged interdependence (p. 409). Economically interdependent countries can sometimes fight wars and still avoid incurring significant economic costs (p. 409). Thus, it is hard to be confident that economic interdependence can serve as a firm foundation for peace in Asia in the decades ahead (p. 410).

Mearsheimer stated that if China continued to rise, the future will be tricky for other countries and downright depressing (p. 410). According to him, there is good reason to think China will eventually pursue regional hegemony (p. 411). Based on the five assumptions mentioned earlier, this depressing conclusion rings true.

In support of Mearsheimer's assertion, history is littered with civil wars wherein there was substantial economic interdependence between the combatants before the fighting broke out (p. 408). In short, although there could exist substantial economic interdependence, fighting could break out among the countries concerned.

If we consider China's behavior within the framework of "offensive realism," we reach a conclusion that China's rise can never be peaceful.

Therefore, as seen within the framework of "offensive realism," a Taiwanese emergency situation will break out sooner or later.[9]

---

[9]As former Prime Minister Shinzo Abe asserted (*Nihon Keizai Shimbun*, 2 December 2021), an emergency in Taiwan constitutes an emergency in Japan, which will occur sooner or later.

2.3. *Status quo of Taiwan*

What do we think about the situation in Taiwan?

Regarding Taiwan, there is no room for discussion. As is well known, the fundamental strategy of Taiwan has been to maintain the "status quo."[10]

Tsai Ing-wen (former president of Taiwan) mentioned that the policy of cross-strait relations should transcend the arguments of political parties and the government should refer to different opinions. When a leader creates a policy, he or she should ensure that it is accepted by society. The accepted position within Taiwan is to maintain the "status quo."[11]

Actually, it is difficult to imagine that Taiwan, while keeping a close eye on China, would believe that if the Chinese economy continues to develop, it will eventually transform into a liberal and democratic country or that if it transforms into a liberal and democratic country, it will no longer attack militarily other countries or regions. Thus, we recognize that the fundamental strategy of Taiwan is neither "liberal" nor "idealistic."

In other words, the fundamental strategy of Taiwan is self-preservation, meaning that only if its national security is threatened will Taiwan participate in a conflict.[12]

Nihon Keizai Shimbun (20 November 2021) published an article entitled "Hong Kong, the pro-China group has acquired almost exclusively possession." The article claimed that in the Hong Kong parliamentary elections of 19 December 2021, a pro-China party would acquire an almost exclusive majority. The Credentials Committee of Hong Kong (which examines the candidates in the elections) released its examination results and finalized the composition of the election: There were 90 seats to be won; only 4 candidates introduced themselves as "pro-democracy." The 2021 parliamentary election in Hong Kong was the first one to be implemented after the Xi Jinping administration drastically revised the electoral system with the slogan "the reign of patriots." There were 154 candidates running for the 90 seats, out of which 153 were accepted to run for Parliament. There were 9 candidates who claimed to be neutral, none of whom was well known. Thus, there

---

[10] The "status quo" policy of Taiwan has various features which are not discussed in this book. With regard to the "status quo" policy, see, for example, Matsuda and Shimizu (2018).

[11] Tsai Ing-wen (2015, p. 211).

[12] Such a strategy might be called "defensive."

Table 1. The identities of Taiwanese people (1992–2021 (June)) (in percent).

Year	Taiwanese	Chinese
1992	17.6	25.5
2000	36.9	12.5
2008	48.4	4.0
2012	54.3	3.6
2016	58.2	3.4
2018	54.5	3.6
2021 (June)	63.3	2.7

Source: Election Study Center National Chengchi University.

is a possibility that some of them were encouraged to stand as candidates by the Chinese authority.[13]

In short, the above-mentioned situation undoubtedly demonstrated that liberalism and democracy in Hong Kong have been suppressed by the Chinese authority's leadership. Such a situation in Hong Kong must have troubled the Tsai Ing-wen administration in Taiwan, which viewed "liberalism and democracy" as important.

In the Taiwan presidential election (11 January 2020), Tsai Ing-wen won an overwhelming victory. Two of the main factors for this victory were the "Fugitive Offenders Ordinance Amendment Bill 2019" passed in Hong Kong and the suppression of the large-scale demonstrations against the "Amendment Bill" in Hong Kong, both of which were led by the Chinese Communist Party.

According to a 1992 questionnaire asking the Taiwanese people if they identified as Taiwanese or Chinese, only 25.5 percent identified as Chinese; however, in June 2021, the ratio drastically decreased to 2.7 percent. In contrast, in 1992, only 17.6 percent of the people identified as Taiwanese, which drastically increased to 63.3 percent in June 2021. The data are shown in Table 1.

[13] The article in *Nihon Keizai Shimbun* (21 December 2021) announced that, in the parliamentary election in Hong Kong, the pro-China group acquired 89 seats out of 90, which was 99 percent of the total. It also reported that the voting rate equaled 30.2 percent, which was less than the previous voting rate of the 2016 parliamentary election (58 percent).

According to another article in *Nihon Keizai Shimbun* (23 October 2021), Mr. Biden (the then president of the United States) was asked at a campaign rally held in Maryland if the United States would defend Taiwan if Taiwan was attacked by China; he asserted that the United States was responsible for Taiwan's defense. The article also reported that, immediately after this exchange, the press secretary of the White House amended the President's statement and stated that the US foreign policy had not been modified. Jen Psaki (the White House press secretary) emphasized at the press conference (held on 22 October) that the defense relations between the United States and Taiwan were based on the "Taiwan Relations Act" established in 1979. It was reported that although the United States supported Taiwan in improving its self-defense capacity and in settling its disputes with China peacefully, the United States is not obligated to defend Taiwan.

In short, as far as the "Taiwan Relations Act" is concerned, the United States has never been obligated to defend Taiwan.[14]

Furthermore, another article in *Nihon Keizai Shimbun* (9 November 2021) reported on the 6th Plenum of the 19th Central Committee of the Chinese Communist Party. The Xi Jinping administration has been especially perplexed by the "political status of Taiwan." The greater the pressure that China applies on Taiwan, the stronger the intention of independence in Taiwan becomes, and the harder the criticism against China from across the world. The United States has become much clearer in its involvement in the Taiwan issue, and recently members of the European Parliament from the European Union (EU) have visited Taiwan, indicating that the EU is also moving closer to Taiwan. In relations with the United States, an online meeting is scheduled with President Biden. However, there are no signs of a "détente" because there is a major gap due to the "human rights problems" and the "political status of Taiwan." Concerning Sino-Australian relations (which used to be good), because Australia asserted the need to investigate the origin of the COVID-19 pandemic, China retaliated by successively imposing sanctions against Australia on foreign trade, which led to a decisive deterioration of Sino-Australian relations. "AUKUS," which is a national security framework established by the UK, US, and Australia (in September 2021), has enabled

[14] It is not known whether or not the United States will defend Taiwan if Taiwan is attacked militarily by China.

Australia to obtain the technology to build nuclear submarines. This is a "nightmare" for China.

Chinese media personnel reported that the economy is slowing down and foreign policy is not going well. Governance will become increasingly difficult next year.

In particular, the trend of the UK, the US, and Australia of building nuclear submarines has led to Australia possessing 8 nuclear submarines, thereby drastically changing the power balance in Asia in geopolitical and military aspects.[15]

The actions of Australia and Taiwan against the Chinese Communist Party administration, as well as the movements of Western developed countries, centered on the United States and the United Kingdom, towards Australia and Taiwan have forced us to inevitably recognize the situations of "Taiwan's emergency situation."

As mentioned earlier, the Taiwanese people never wished Taiwan was a "sovereign state." As shown in Table 1, the ratio of those identifying themselves as Taiwanese (not as Chinese) has overwhelmingly increased. However, this is not the same as wishing Taiwan was a "sovereign state." Similar to Table 1, Table 2 shows data taken from the home page of the Election Study Center (National Chengchi University).

That is to say, a "unification" with China has no more than 2–4 percent approval and "independence" from China has 5–7 percent approval. The ratio of people wanting to maintain status quo has remained 70–80 percent since 2008. Furthermore, with regard to the details of the "status quo," the ratio of "Taiwanese" people wanting "independence in the future" increased to reach 25.8 percent in June 2020. At present, there is no change in maintaining the "status quo." In short, many Taiwanese people wish to maintain the "status quo".

At the same time, it seems like the United States, Japan, and European countries have found positive benefits in the "status quo" of Taiwan.

Only one country might try to disturb the Taiwanese "status quo" in order to unify and that is China. Therefore, "Taiwan's emergency situation" — whether or not it occurs and, if it does occur, when and how — fully depends on the Chinese Communist Party.[16]

---

[15] See the article (by James G. Stavridis) in *Nihon Keizai Shimbun* (23 October 2021).

[16] Therefore, if the "Taiwan's emergency situation" does not occur, it would likely be due to a situation that requires some changes within the Chinese Communist Party leadership.

Table 2. The outlook of the Taiwanese people (1994–2020 (June)) (in percent).

Year	Unification	Independence	Status quo (for the time being)	Status quo (forever)	Status quo (independence in the future)
1994	4.4	3.1	38.5	9.8	8.0
2000	2.0	3.1	29.5	19.2	11.6
2008	1.5	7.1	35.8	21.5	16.0
2012	1.7	4.8	33.9	27.7	15.1
2016	1.7	4.6	33.3	26.1	18.3
2018	3.1	5.0	33.4	24.0	15.1
2020 (June)	1.5	5.9	28.2	27.5	25.8

Source: Election Study Center, National Chengchi University.

The situation is extremely dangerous, in which China (under the framework of "offensive realism") has rapidly increased its military power and economic power, exists close to Taiwan, and also aspires to unify.

Thus, it might not be easy for Taiwan to survive.[17]

One of the fundamental policies of the Tsai Ing-wen administration in Taiwan was the "New Southbound Policy" (in other words, to stop depending on China).

China's most important dispute is over Taiwan, which Beijing is deeply committed to making an integral part of China once again. The present government in Taiwan, however, believes it is a sovereign country and has no interest in being reintegrated into China. However, Taiwanese leaders do not advertise their independence for fear it will provoke China to invade Taiwan (p. 375).

The following assertion by Mearsheimer (2014) could be helpful:

"Given the importance of these territorial disputes to China, coupled with the apparent difficulty of resolving them through the give-and-take

[17]It goes without saying, as previously mentioned, a "Taiwan's emergency situation" is highly likely to become a "Japan's emergency situation." For Japan, it cannot be considered someone else's problem.

> of diplomacy, the best way for China to settle them on favorable terms is probably via coercion. Specifically, a China that is much more powerful than any of its neighbors will be in a good position to use military threats to force the other side to accept a deal largely on China's terms. And if that does not work, China can always unsheathe the sword and go to war to get its way" (p. 376).

That is to say, it seems likely that coercion or the actual use of force is the only plausible way China is going to regain Taiwan. Therefore, becoming a regional hegemon is the best pathway for China to resolve its various territorial disputes on favorable terms (p. 376).[18]

If we assume that the Chinese way includes "coercion or the actual use of force," then when China becomes a regional hegemon, Taiwan's emergency situation will definitely come to pass.

When the United States' military power and economic power decline (at least, significantly decline compared with China's military power and economic power), the United States will withdraw from the East Asian region. At that time, a conflict between Taiwan (and Japan) and China is likely to occur.[19]

As Mearsheimer (2014) asserted, Taiwanese leaders do not advertise their independence for fear it will provoke China to invade Taiwan. Moreover, other countries, including the United States, Japan, and European countries, have found positive benefits in the "status quo" of Taiwan. In short, the only country which has the incentive to start a conflict with Taiwan is China, not Taiwan itself, Australia, the United States, Japan, or European countries.

3. General Situation of the Taiwanese Economy

In this section, we take a look at the general situation of the Taiwanese economy, which includes the GDP growth rate, unemployment rate, trade balance, and military expenditure.

---

[18] It seems like China has hastened its preparations in the hopes of moving toward the "best pathway."

[19] In this book, we do not consider a situation of Taiwan and Japan implementing "nuclear armament" and possibly defending both countries in cases of emergency situations.

Table 3. The present state of affairs of Taiwan and Australia.

	Taiwan	Australia
Population (ten thousand)	2,360	2,569
Nominal GDP (hundred million US dollars)	6,050	13,593
Per capita nominal GDP (US dollars)	26,528	52,825
Real GDP growth rate in percent	2.71	1.4
Military expenditure (hundred million US dollars)	107.6	325.4[a]
Major industries	Manufacturing industry (electronics/electrical), Chemicals, Steel, Machinery	Mining, Finance/insurance, Wholesale/retailing, Construction
Unemployment rate (in percent)	3.73	4.90

Note: [a]According to the home page of the Ministry of Foreign Affairs (Japan), 1 Australian dollar equals 0.7297 US dollars.
Source: Ministry of Foreign Affairs (Japan).

We provide a comparison of Taiwan and Australia in Table 3.[20]

With regard to the population, Taiwan has 23.60 million people and Australia 25.69 million, which is not a big difference. However, concerning the economic scale, there are considerably big differences. As for nominal GDP, Taiwan's GPD is 605.0 billion US dollars and Australia's is 1,359.3 billion US dollars. Therefore, the per capita nominal GDP of Taiwan is 26.528 thousand US dollars and Australia's per capita nominal GDP is 52.825 thousand US dollars. In 2019, Taiwan's real GDP growth rate was 2.71 percent. In contrast, Australia's real GDP growth rate was 1.40 percent in the 2020/2021 fiscal year. Taiwan's military expenditure amounted to 10.76 billion US dollars,[21] while Australia spent 32.54 billion

[20]Table 3 is based on information from the home page of the Ministry of Foreign Affairs (Japan).

[21]The website of the Ministry of Foreign Affairs (Japan) states, according to The *Military Balance* 2018 etc.

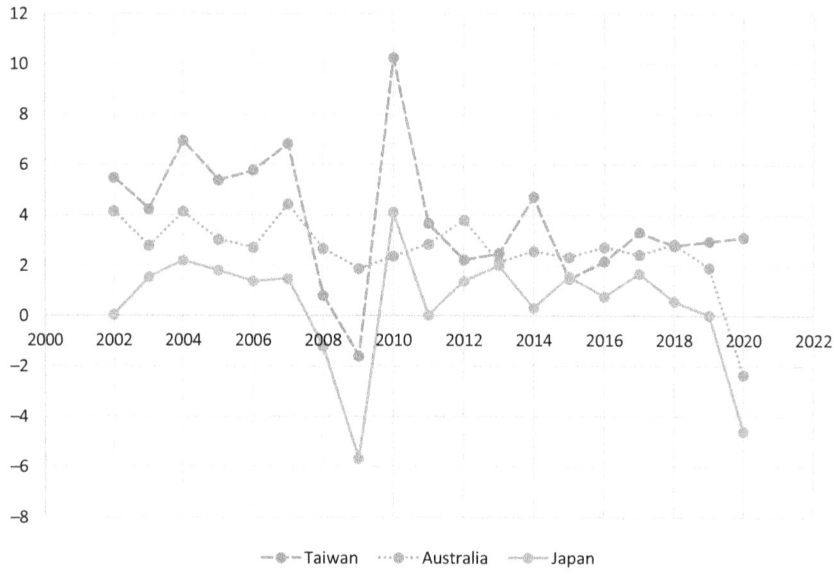

Figure 1. Real GDP growth rate of each country (2002–2020) (in percent).
Source: IMF (Data: Global Note).

US dollars in the 2021/2022 fiscal year, which was a big difference. Taiwan's unemployment rate was 3.73 percent (the average in 2019) and Australia's was 4.90 percent (in the 2020/2021 fiscal year). Taiwan's major industry is manufacturing. In contrast, Australia's major industries are mining, finance, and insurance, which is considerably different from that of Taiwan.

We provide more details regarding various items in the following.

First, the real GDP growth rate is indicated in Figure 1. In 2020, Taiwan recorded a positive real GDP growth rate (3.12 percent). The negative influence on economic activities due to the COVID-19 pandemic was slight, there were new business opportunities due to the application of new technology and remote working, and there was an expansion in the export of electronic components and information and communication equipment due to external demand, all of which contributed to Taiwan's positive economic growth rate.[22] Many business opportunities were created by the coronavirus crisis. Taiwan protected itself against the COVID-19 pandemic by closing entry and exit points from China. Furthermore,

[22] See *Global Trade and Investment Report* (JETRO, 2021).

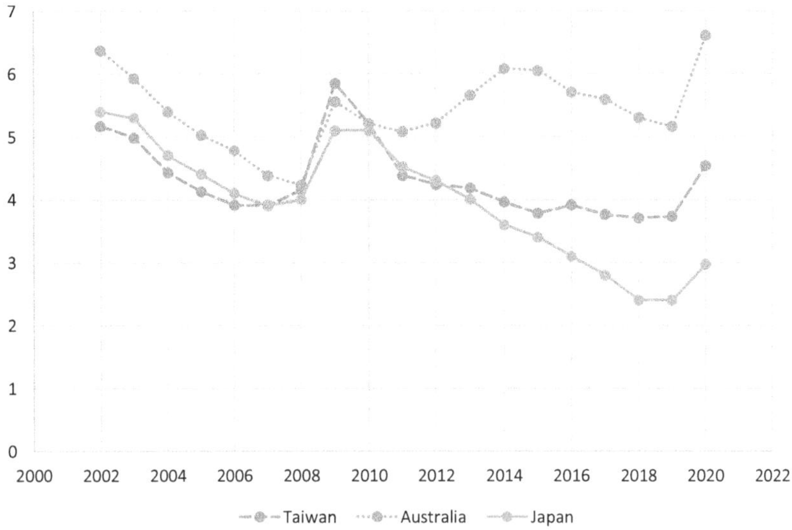

Figure 2. Unemployment rate of each country (2002–2020) (in percent).
Source: ILO (Data: Global Note).

there was a significant deterioration of economic growth rate in 2009 in all countries due to the "financial crisis."

Second, the unemployment rate is shown in Figure 2. In any country, the unemployment rate in 2020 was worse than it had been previously due to the COVID-19 pandemic. Taiwan's unemployment in 2020 was 1.22 times the 2019 rate, Australia's 1.28 times, Japan's 1.24 times, Hong Kong's 1.96 times, and South Korea's 1.09 times. The decline in the unemployment rate in South Korea was lower. The numerical value of the unemployment rate for both Australia (6.61 percent) and Hong Kong (5.80 percent) was large, but it was small for Japan (2.97 percent). The numerical value of the unemployment rate of Taiwan was 4.54 percent and of South Korea was 4.07 percent.

Third, the trade balance is indicated in Figure 3, showing the trade balance since 2002. For Taiwan, the amount indicated a constant surplus and upward trend. For Japan, the amount fluctuated strongly. For Australia, there were several years of a trade deficit but less intense than for Japan. The trade balance in Taiwan has shown a firm tendency toward a trade surplus.

Fourth, military expenditure is shown in Figure 4 (both China and Israel are included for reference). China's military expenditure has been overwhelmingly larger than that of other countries. The expenditure of

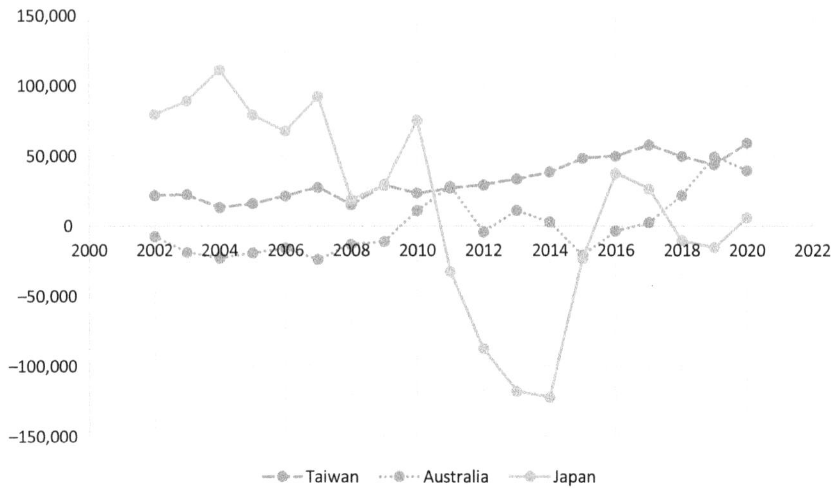

Figure 3. Trade balance of each country (2002–2020).

Source: UNCTAD (Data: Global Note).

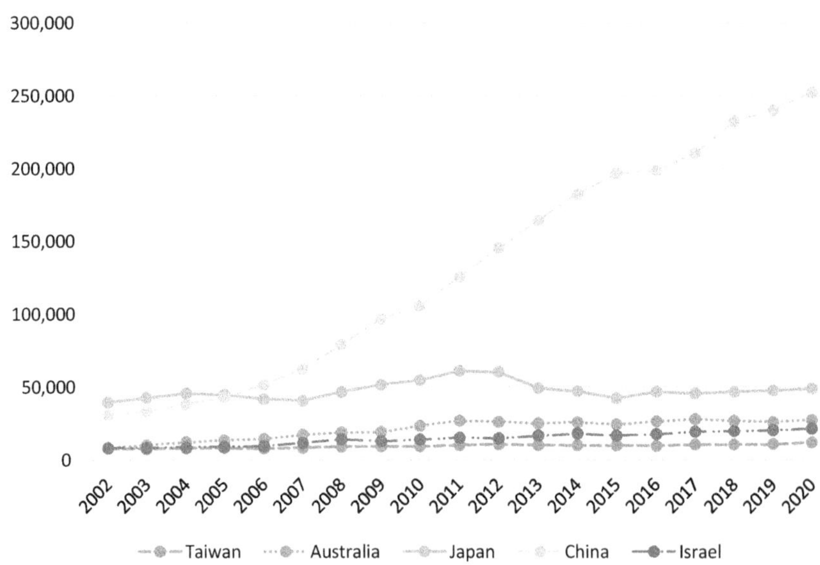

Figure 4. Military expenditure of each country (with China) (2002–2020).

Source: World Bank (Data: Global Note).

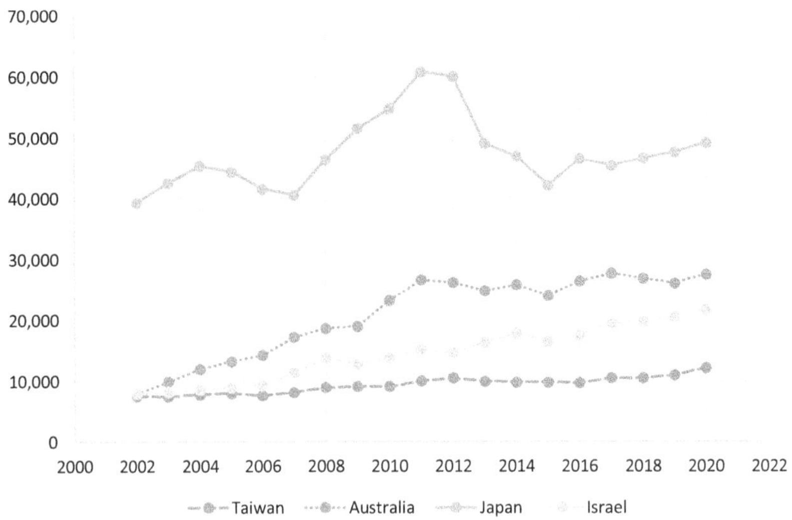

Figure 5. Military expenditure of each country (without China) (2002–2020).
Source: World Bank (Data: Global Note).

both Taiwan and Israel (particularly Taiwan) has been extremely small. For reference, the military expenditure of some countries (except for China) is indicated in Figure 5.

As shown in Figure 5, the military expenditure of Japan has been larger and that of both Taiwan and Israel has been smaller.

What about the ratio of military expenditure to GDP (as indicated in Figure 6)?

As shown in Figure 6, the military expenditure to GDP ratio of Israel is larger than that of other countries (it reached 5–6 percent). Both Taiwan and Australia have never had a large ratio: Taiwan's ratio has never been more than 2 percent and Australia's ratio was 2.08 percent, 2.00 percent, and 2.06 percent, respectively, in 2016, 2017, and 2020. Japan's ratio has been smaller compared to that of other countries (by and large the ratio has been less than 1.00 percent and it reach 1.00 percent in 2020).

Figure 7 shows that the military expenditure of China is equal to the combined military expenditure of other countries. It goes without saying that China's military expenditure ratio compared to Taiwan (which has the smallest military expenditure) has been the largest.

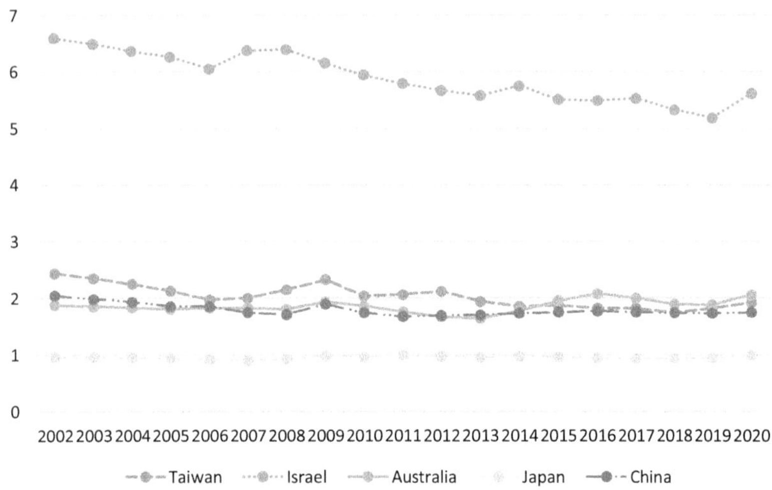

Figure 6. The ratio of military expenditure to GDP of each country (2002–2020) (in percent).

Source: World Bank (Data: Global Note) and the author's calculation.

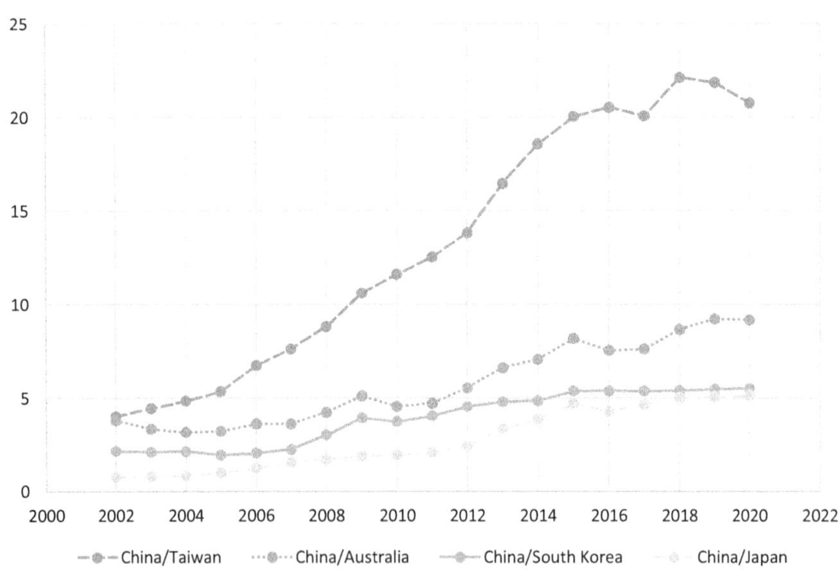

Figure 7. The ratio of Chinese military expenditure to that of each country (2002–2020).

Source: World Bank (Data: Global Note) and the author's calculation.

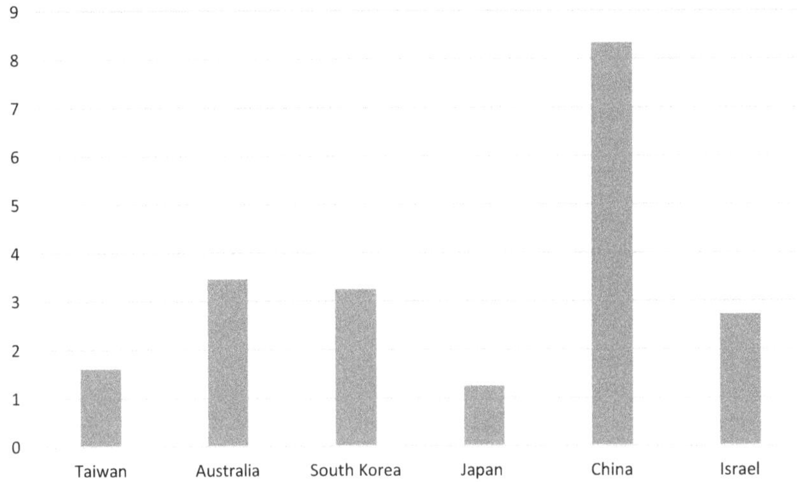

Figure 8. The increase of military expenditure of each country.

Source: World Bank (Data: Global Note).

The increase in military expenditure is illustrated in Figure 8, which shows how many times the military expenditure in 2020 is compared to that in 2002. Needless to say, China's military expenditure grew at the highest rate among the countries concerned. In contrast, the expansion in military expenditure of Taiwan and Japan was the smallest, which was interesting considering both countries have been exposed to the menace of Chinese military attacks.[23]

4. International trade of Taiwan

4.1. *The overview of Taiwanese international trade: Outline of the years 2019 and 2020*

We take a short look at Taiwanese international trade based on JETRO (2020, 2021).[24]

[23] Could we recognize that such situations reflect their policies of relying on the United States for their national securities?

[24] See JETRO *Global Trade and Investment Report* (2020, 2021). Section 3.1 has citations from JETRO (2020, 2021).

According to the Taiwanese Ministry of Finance, Taiwan's trade amount in 2019 was 329.1940 billion US dollars in exports (indicating a 1.4 percent decrease compared to the previous year) and 285.6938 billion US dollars in imports (showing a 0.3 percent increase compared to the previous year). Both exports and imports reached their respective second largest ever values. The trade balance in 2019 was a surplus of 43.533 US dollars. According to the analysis of the Ministry of Finance, although the trend of world trade slowed down due to the Sino-American trade friction, the restructuring of the global supply chains, which caused an expansion of the production capabilities in Taiwan, offset the negative factors related to international trade.

With regard to exports by country and region in 2019, except for some countries and regions, the trend was weak. Although China (which occupied the first ranking in export ratio) recorded a 4.9 percent decrease compared to the previous year, its ratio combined with Hong Kong has exceeded 40 percent for four consecutive years. Exports to China of such items as chemical products, plastic, rubber, and machinery decreased stably; however, export of electronic components remained strong.[25] Exports to ASEAN (occupying the second ranking) recorded a 7.2 percent decrease compared to the previous year (which decreased by 0.7 percent compared to the previous year) because of the Sino-American trade friction. Exports to the United States (occupying the third ranking) were at an all-time high at 17.1 percent compared to the previous year. Similarly, exports to Japan were the highest on record with an increase of 2.1 percent compared to the previous year.

When we observe exports by item, machinery and electrical equipment (which occupied 57.7 percent of the total exports) reached a 3.8 percent increase compared to the previous year. Electronic components increased 1.6 percent compared to the previous year. However, the electronic components sector has become polarized. Integrated circuits (ICs), which account for 30 percent of exports, increased by 4.6 percent more than previous year, but diodes (including LEDs) and solar battery

[25] Australian exports to China accounted for 38.4 percent of the total, with resource exports such as iron ore, natural gas, and coal performing particularly well, increasing by 26.2 percent (JETRO, *Global Trade and Investment Report*, 2020). On the other hand, Taiwan's exports to China in the same year accounted for 27.9 percent of the total, and as mentioned in the text, electronic components have been performing steadily.

decreased by 16.8 percent and 67.1 percent respectively compared with previous year.

With regard to imports by country and region in 2019, imports from China (ranked first) were the highest on record at 57.385 billion US dollars, which showed an increase of 6.7 percent compared to the previous year. Imports from China have seen a significant increase in electronic components, information and communication equipment, and also the integrated circuits (largest amount of import and increasing by 20.6 percent more than previous year). The rate of imports from Japan (which occupied the second rank) was 0.3 percent less than the previous year. The rate of imports from ASEAN and the United States was 1.3 percent more and 5.2 percent more, respectively, than the previous year.

When we observe imports by item, because the prices of raw materials in international trade decreased, the import of the items concerned decreased greatly. The imports of crude oil and mineral products, chemicals, and base metals/base metal products decreased 11.4 percent, 8.5 percent, and 11.0 percent, respectively, compared to the previous year. On the other hand, imports of machinery and electrical equipment (which were 42.6 percent of the total imports) increased by 11.8 percent compared to the previous year.

According to the Ministry of Finance of Taiwan, the trade amount of Taiwan in 2020 amounted to 345.2107 billion US dollars in exports (indicating a 4.9 percent increase compared to the previous year and reaching the highest amount on record) and 285.8172 billion US dollars in imports (showing a 0.1 percent increase compared to the previous year). Thus, the trade balance in 2020 amounted to a 59.3935 billion US dollar surplus. In 2020, due to the Sino-American trade friction and the COVID-29 pandemic, the trends of trade protectionism, diversification of global supply chains, and expanding production models through localization and digitalization.

With regard to exports by country and region in 2020, exports to China, the United States, Hong Kong, and Japan were the highest on record. China (which ranks first in export ratio) experienced an 11.6 percent increase compared to the previous year, and when including Hong Kong, the export ratio has surpassed 40 percent for five consecutive years. In terms of exports to China, electronic components (products using 5th Generation (5G) Mobile Communication Systems and artificial intelligence (AI)) were the main items and their export increased compared to the previous year. In terms of exports to ASEAN (which occupied the second ranking in the exports ratio), there was a 1.3 percent decrease consecutively over three years. Although exports to the Philippines and Indonesia decreased, exports to Singapore and Malaysia increased. Exports to the United States (which occupied the third ranking in the exports ratio) increased by 9.3 percent compared to the previous year and were the highest on record.

When we observe exports by item, machinery and electrical equipment (which occupied 60.0 percent of the total exports) reached a 14.8 percent increase compared to the previous year, in which electronic components increased by 20.5 percent compared to previous year because of the active demand for products that utilized the new techniques of 5G and AI. The export of information and communication equipment saw a 15.3 percent increase compared to the previous year due to several factors, including the regional reshoring of Taiwanese companies and order transfer progress, the expansion of 5G infrastructure, and the increased demand associated with the rise of online business during the COVID-19 pandemic.

With regard to imports by country and region in 2020, imports from China (ranked first) were the highest on record at 63.576 billion US dollars, which was an increase of 10.8 percent compared to the previous year. With the reorganization of the supply chain, Taiwanese companies have increased their regional production, and imports of electronic components from China have risen. The import of integrated circuits recorded an 11.9 percent increase compared to the previous year. Imports from Japan (which occupied the second rank) were 4.2 percent more than the previous year. Imports from Europe recorded an all-time high, with 0.6 percent more than the previous year. Imports from ASEAN were the highest on record with 2.6 percent more than the previous year, in which both Singapore and Vietnam recorded the highest ever values. In contrast, imports from the United States recorded a 6.8 percent decrease compared to the previous year because of delays in the purchase of manufacturing equipment for semiconductors (due to the COVID-19 pandemic).

When we observe imports by item, imports of machinery and electrical equipment (which occupied 47.5 percent of the total imports) increased by 11.6 percent compared to the previous year because of an increase in the import of electrical equipment and components. The import of crude oil and mineral products, chemicals, and base metals/ base metal products decreased by 30.7 percent, 1.6 percent, and 2.1 percent, respectively, compared to the previous year because of the decrease in the prices of raw materials in international trade due to the COVID-19 pandemic.

4.2. *International trade partners of Taiwan*

In this section, we consider China as the international trade partner of Taiwan in comparison with Australia.

The position of China (ranking and ratio) in terms of international trade with Taiwan is shown in Tables 4 (import to Taiwan) and 5 (export from Taiwan). Also, the position of Taiwan (ranking and ratio) in terms of international trade with China is indicated in Tables 16 (import to China) and 17 (export from China).

In the previous chapter, we examined the case of Australia. For more information on Australia's foreign trade relations with China, please refer to Section 3.2 of Chapter 6.

In this chapter, we conduct an investigation about Taiwan's foreign trade relations with China.

China's share among Taiwan's import partner countries was 19–20 percent, giving it the first rank (in 2019, compared to the second-rank country Japan, China's share was 1.31 times greater than that of Japan). Also, China's share among Taiwan's export partner countries was generally 27–29 percent, which once again gave it the first rank (in 2019, the United States occupied the second rank, and compared to the United States, China's share was 1.99 times greater). Taiwan's share among

Table 4. Taiwanese import partner countries: Ranking and ratio (2016–2019).

	2016		2017		2018		2019	
Ranking	**Country**	**Ratio**	**Country**	**Ratio**	**Country**	**Ratio**	**Country**	**Ratio**
1	China	19.1	China	19.3	China	18.8	China	20.1
2	Japan	17.6	Japan	16.2	Japan	15.4	Japan	15.4
3	USA	12.4	USA	11.7	USA	12.1	USA	12.2
4	South Korea	6.4	South Korea	6.5	South Korea	6.8	South Korea	6.2
5	Singapore	5.6	Singapore	3.4	Australia	3.3	Malaysia	3.6
6	Malaysia	2.7	Australia	3.2	Malaysia	3.2	Australia	3.5
7	Indonesia	1.9	Malaysia	2.8	Singapore	2.9	Singapore	2.8
8	Thailand	1.7	Indonesia	1.9	Indonesia	1.9	Vietnam	1.8
9	Vietnam	1.2	Thailand	1.7	Thailand	1.6	Indonesia	1.6
10	Philippines	1.0	Vietnam	1.2	Vietnam	1.3	Thailand	1.5

Source: JETRO International Trade and Investment Report (Annual Edition).

Table 5. Taiwanese export partner countries: Ranking and ratio (2016–2019).

	2016		2017		2018		2019	
Ranking	**Country**	**Ratio**	**Country**	**Ratio**	**Country**	**Ratio**	**Country**	**Ratio**
1	China	26.4	China	28.0	China	28.8	China	27.9
2	Hong Kong	13.7	Hong Kong	13.0	Hong Kong	12.4	USA	14.0
3	USA	12.0	USA	11.6	USA	11.8	Hong Kong	12.3
4	Japan	7.0	Japan	6.6	Japan	6.9	Japan	7.1
5	Singapore	5.8	Singapore	5.6	Singapore	5.2	Singapore	5.5
6	South Korea	4.6	South Korea	4.6	South Korea	4.8	South Korea	5.1
7	Vietnam	3.4	Vietnam	3.3	Vietnam	3.2	Vietnam	3.3
8	Philippines	3.1	Malaysia	3.3	Malaysia	3.2	Malaysia	2.9
9	Malaysia	2.8	Philippines	3.0	Philippines	2.7	Philippines	1.9
10	Thailand	2.0	Thailand	2.0	Thailand	1.8	Thailand	1.7

Source: JETRO International Trade and Investment Report (Annual Edition).

China's import partner countries was 8–9 percent, giving Taiwan the second or third rank. And, Taiwan's share among China's export partner countries was generally 2 percent, ranking it ninth or tenth. Thus, Taiwan's ratio and rank were not high in terms of trade with China. The country that occupied a larger ratio and higher rank in both Chinese imports and exports was the United States.

This is the summary of international trade for China and Taiwan. China's ratio among Taiwan's export partner countries was 27–29 percent and China's ratio among Australia's export partner countries was 32–38 percent. Moreover, China's ratio among Taiwan's import partner countries was 19–20 percent and China's ratio among Australia's import partner countries was 22–25 percent. China ranked first in all the cases mentioned. Obviously, China's ratios in Australian exports and imports were larger than its ratios in Taiwanese exports and imports. In conclusion, for both Taiwan and Australia, their exports and imports are greatly dependent on China.

Keeping in mind the "New Southbound Policy" of the Tsai Ing-wen administration in Taiwan, the ratios of China and ASEAN in Taiwanese exports and imports are shown in Figures 9 (exports) and 10 (imports).

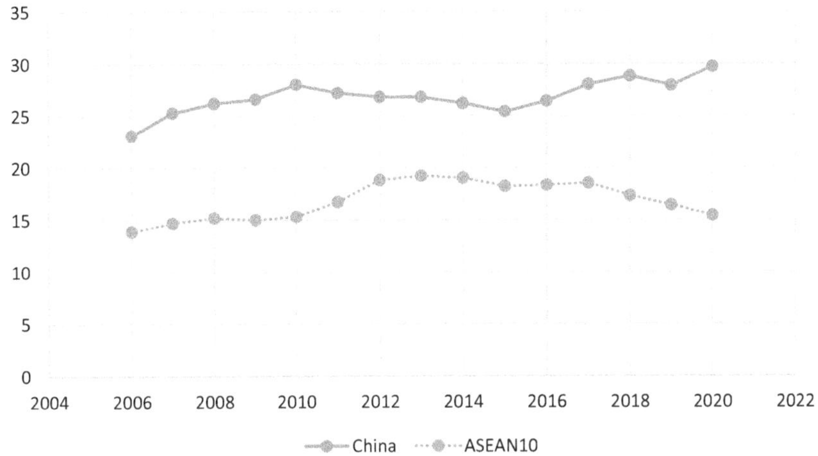

Figure 9. The ratios of China and ASEAN in Taiwanese exports (2006–2020) (in percent).

Source: JETRO Global Trade and Investment Report (Annual Edition) and the author's calculation.

As indicated in both figures, China's export ratios are increasing (particularly since 2015) and import ratios are also increasing (approximately constant); in contrast, the export ratios of ASEAN were decreasing (particularly since 2014) and import ratios remained unchanged.

In short, in spite of the aim of the "New Southbound Policy" of the Tsai Ing-wen administration in Taiwan, Taiwan's dependence on China has not reduced.

5. Taiwan's International Trade Relations with China: Directional Trade Ratio

In this section, we consider the directional trade ratio of Taiwan's international trade with China.

As mentioned earlier in this book (Chapter 2), the directional trade ratio measures the closeness of trade relations between the countries concerned. Figure 11 shows the directional trade ratio between China and Taiwan, China and Australia, and China and Japan. According to Figure 11, since 2013, the directional trade ratio between China and Australia has been larger, and the ratio between China and Taiwan and between China and Japan has been smaller.

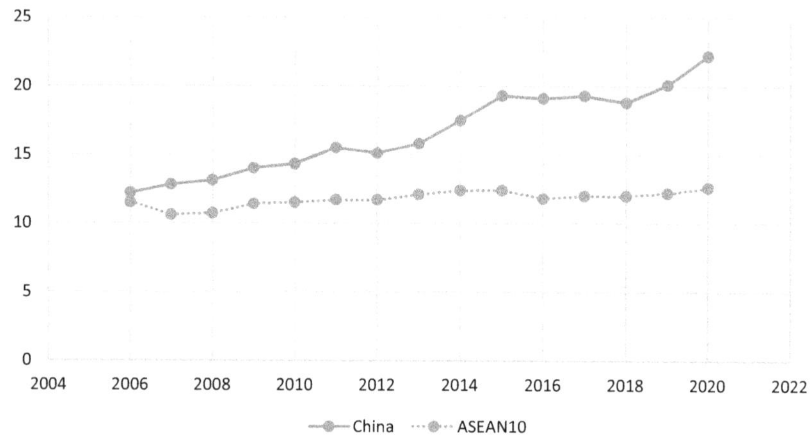

Figure 10. The ratios of China and ASEAN in Taiwanese imports (2006–2020) (in percent).

Source: JETRO Global Trade and Investment Report (Annual Edition) and the author's calculation.

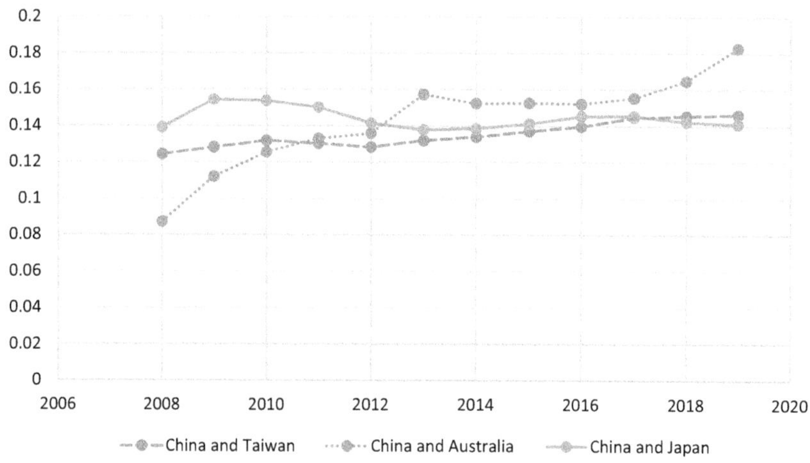

Figure 11. Directional trade ratio between China and each country (2008–2019).

Source: JETRO Global Trade and Investment Report (Annual Edition) and the author's calculation.

With regard to the directional trade ratio between China and Taiwan, it shows a slow but steady increase (the ratio was 0.1397 in 2016 and 0.1462 in 2019).

6. Three Degrees of Dependence on Export

In this section, we consider three degrees of dependence on export. The first is the degree of dependence on export in the usual sense, which is the numerical value obtained from the total export amount of the country concerned divided by the nominal GDP amount of that country. The second is the numerical value in which the total export amount of the country concerned is exchanged for the export amount to China of that country. The third is the degree of dependence on export to a specific country, which was utilized in Chapter 6.

As explained in Chapter 6 regarding the degree of dependence on export to a specific country, the trade linkage index focuses on whether or not there exists a trade distortion between the countries concerned. Actually, the trade linkage index is used as a measure of distorting trade. It is clear that the distortion of Taiwanese exports to China has been bigger than the distortion of Chinese exports to Taiwan. In this chapter, the difference between the distortion of Taiwanese exports to China and the distortion of Chinese exports to Taiwan is shown as a ratio, which is recognized as the degree of dependence on exports of Taiwan to China. If the ratio is 1.0, both countries have equal mutual distortion, meaning the portion not explained by comparative advantage is the same. If the ratio is more than 1.0, the portion not explained by comparative advantage in Taiwanese exports to China is larger than in Chinese exports to Taiwan. In other words, it demonstrates that "the degree of deviation from comparative advantage" in Taiwanese exports to China exceeds "the degree of deviation from comparative advantage" in Chinese exports to Taiwan (more than 1.0); the numerical value also indicates the level of difference between Taiwanese exports to China and Chinese exports to Taiwan.

As given in Chapter 6, we call such numerical values the degree of dependence on exports (of a country) to a specific country.

In this chapter, for convenience, we label the three degrees of dependence on export as follows: (1) the degree of dependence on export I, (2) the degree of dependence on export II, and (3) the degree of dependence on export III.

Figure 12 indicates the degree I of Taiwan, Australia, Japan, and South Korea from 2006 to 2020.

The degree of dependence on export I of Taiwan was predominantly the largest followed by that of South Korea. The values of both Australia and Japan were never large.

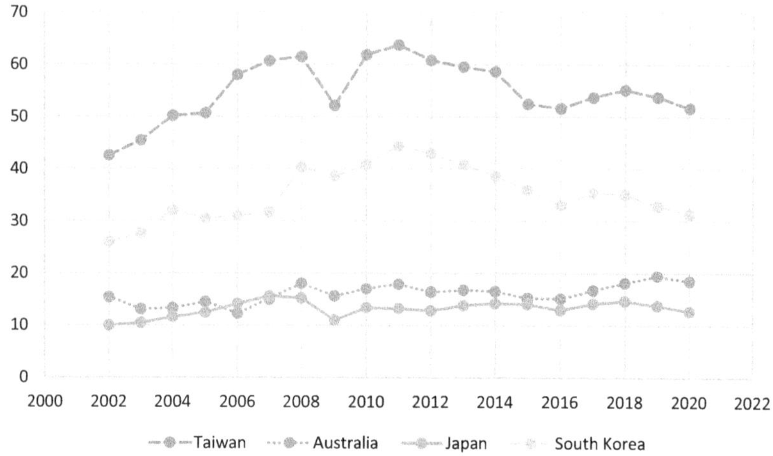

Figure 12. Degree of dependence on export I of each country (2002–2020).
Source: JETRO Global Trade and Investment Report (Annual Edition) and the author's calculation.

Figure 13 shows the degree II of Taiwan, Australia, Japan, and South Korea from 2006 to 2020. The degree of dependence on export II of Taiwan was overwhelmingly the largest followed by South Korea was larger and then Australia. In contrast, the degree of dependence on export II of Japan was never large.

Based on the degree of dependence on export II of Taiwan, we can assume that the "New Southbound Policy" of the Tsai Ing-wen administration was not successful as there was no reduction of dependence on China since 2016. Rather, the dependence on China was the lowest in 2015 (13.32 percent), but then rose again (15.33 percent in 2020).

Figure 14 shows the degree of dependence on export III. What is notable in Figure 14 is that, while Taiwan had overwhelmingly largest values in the degree of dependence on export I and II, in the case of degree of dependence on export III, its value intersects with Australia's in 2012. Since then, Australia's value has generally exceeded Taiwan's.[26]

South Korea (after 2008) and Japan's degrees of dependence on export III were undoubtedly smaller than those of Taiwan and Australia.

Thus, in connection with President Tsai Ing-wen's "New Southbound Policy," it is worth mentioning that the degree of dependence on export III

[26]With regard to the degree of dependence on export III, it seems that the influence of Chinese imports on resources from Australia was significant.

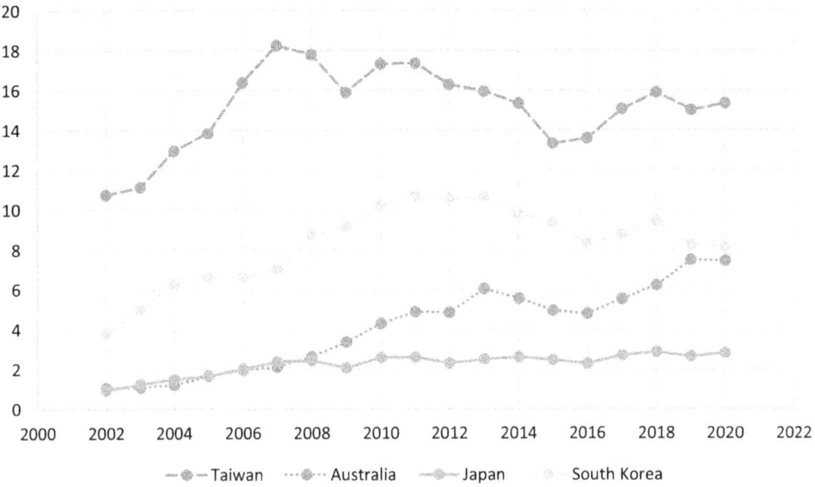

Figure 13. Degree of dependence on export II of each country (2002–2020).
Source: JETRO Global Trade and Investment Report (Annual Edition) and the author's calculation.

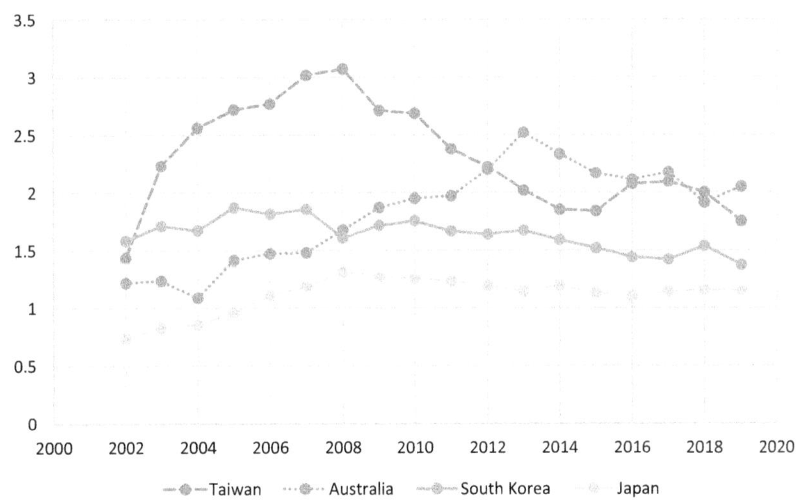

Figure 14. Degree of dependence on export III of each country (2002–2019).
Source: JETRO Global Trade and Investment Report (Annual Edition) and the author's calculation.

(towards China) increased in 2016 and 2017, and has been gradually decreasing since then. However, it does not seem to exhibit a clear downward trend.[27]

7. Foreign Direct Investment

In this section, we consider foreign direct investment in Taiwan. We would examine the amount of foreign direct investment (based on approvals) and the ratio of each country in Taiwanese total FDI amount. These are illustrated in Figures 15 and 16. In their figures, Taiwan's FDI to China, Vietnam, and Singapore is indicated.

According to Figure 15, please note the following observations: (1) Particularly after 2016, the Taiwanese FDI to China rapidly decreased and (2) although the Taiwanese FDI to Vietnam and Singapore was never

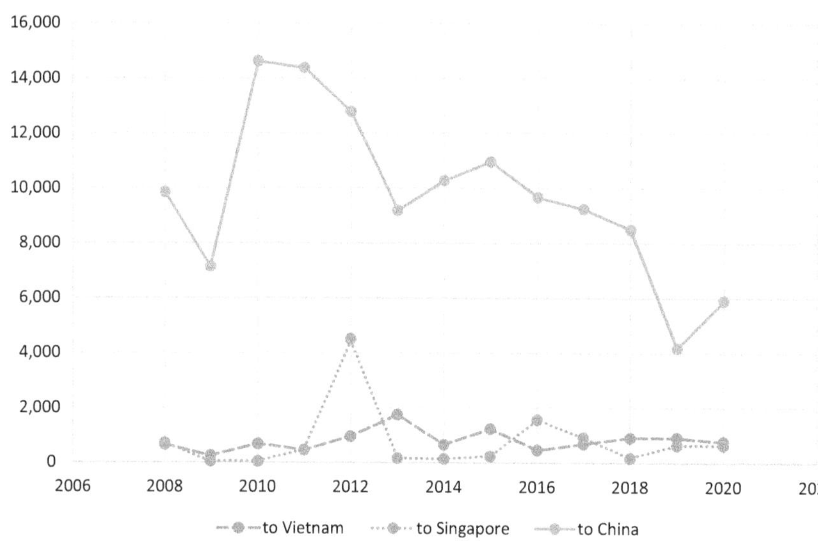

Figure 15. Taiwan's FDI amount to each country (2008–2020).
Source: JETRO Global Trade and Investment Report (Annual Edition).

[27]A more detailed analysis is required.

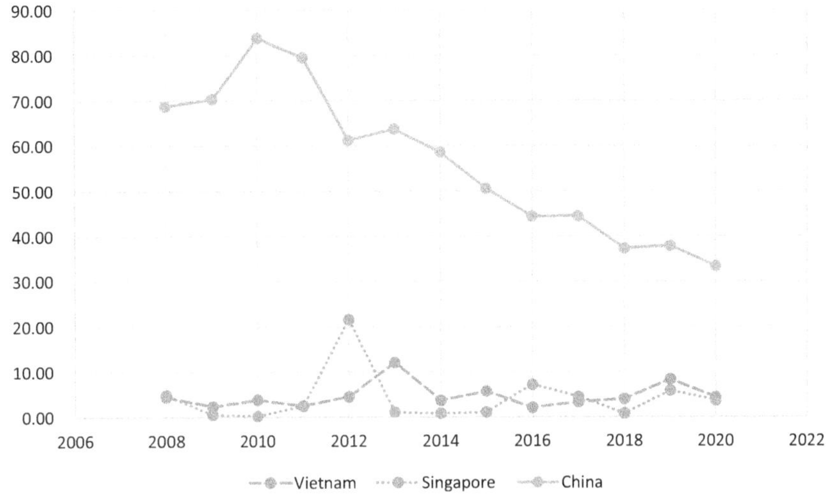

Figure 16. The ratio of Taiwan's FDI amount to each country (2008–2020).
Source: JETRO Global Trade and Investment Report (Annual Edition) and the author's calculation.

large compared to the FDI to China, it was generally steady (in particular, the Taiwanese FDI to Vietnam, which was even or increased moderately).[28]

The declining trend in Taiwanese FDI to China becomes even more evident when examining the ratio of each country in Taiwanese total FDI. This is illustrated in Figure 16. Similar to Figure 15, Figure 16 indicates the ratio of Taiwanese FDI to China, Vietnam, and Singapore. After the peak year (2010), the ratio of Taiwanese FDI to China rapidly decreased (it was 33.35 percent in 2020 compared to 83.80 percent in 2010).

Therefore, as previously observed, while the degree of export dependency II of Taiwan has never shown a clear trend of reducing dependence on China since 2016, the situation with FDI suggests a move towards reducing dependence on China (since 2010).

Next, we consider the "FDI concentration index" which provides the following data. The FDI concentration index is defined as follows. When considering the Taiwanese FDI in China, the index is represented by the value obtained by dividing Taiwan's outward FDI in China by China's

[28] With regard to that tendency, see Sako (2020, p. 1).

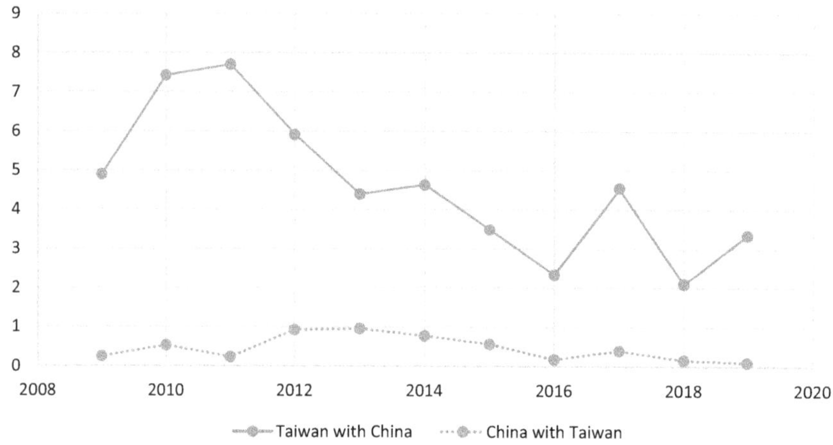

Figure 17. FDI concentration index (China and Taiwan) (2009–2019).

Source: JETRO Global Trade and Investment Report (Annual Edition) and the author's calculation.

total inward FDI as the numerator, and Taiwan's total outward FDI by the world's total outward FDI as the denominator. When the ratio is more than 1.0, the Taiwanese FDI in China is relatively bigger than that in other countries. Figure 17 shows the Taiwanese FDI concentration index in China (called "Taiwan with China") and the Chinese FDI concentration index in Taiwan (called "China with Taiwan").

Evidently, the Taiwanese FDI concentration index in China has been more than 1.0; however, in contrast, the Chinese FDI concentration index in Taiwan has been less than 1.0. The Taiwanese FDI concentration index in China has been fluctuating greatly since 2016; so, it might be difficult to recognize its general tendency. However, the numerical values of the index are between 2.0 and 4.5, which seem to be rather large.

With respect to the "FDI concentration index," as clearly shown in Figure 17, there has been no declining trend Taiwanese FDI concentration index in China since 2016.

8. Foreign Direct Investment: FDI Trade Index

In this section, we consider the Taiwanese outward FDI in China through the FDI trade index. We gauge whether the size of the FDI between the home country and host country is large or not based not on the amount of

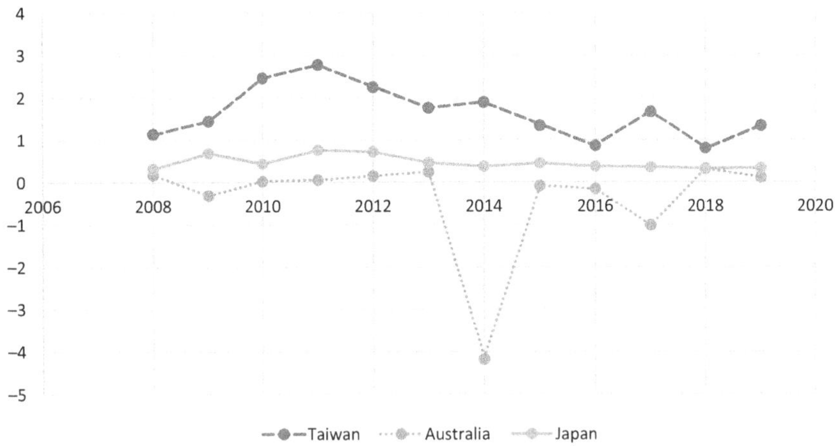

Figure 18. FDI trade index of China with each country (2008–2019).

Source: JETRO Global Trade and Investment Report (Annual Edition) and the author's calculation.

FDI but on the foreign relations between the home country and host country.

In order to determine whether FDI is active, that is, whether the scale of FDI is large or small, it is necessary to consider it in the context of the strength of international economic relations. Therefore, the FDI trade index consists of the FDI concentration index as a numerator and the trade linkage index as a denominator. Therefore, the FDI trade index of 1.0 indicates that the level of FDI relations is perfectly aligned with the international economic relations between the respective countries as represented by international relations. When the FDI trade index is more than 1.0, FDI relations between the two countries are more active than expected based on their international relations, and when the index is less than 1.0, FDI relations between them are less active than expected. Figure 18 shows the FDI trade index of China with Taiwan, Australia, and Japan.

As indicated in Figure 18, only Taiwan has an index of more than 1.0; in contrast, the index of both Japan and Australia did not reach 1.0.

Figure 19 indicates the FDI trade index of China with Taiwan and the FDI trade index of Taiwan with China. It indicates that the Chinese FDI trade index with Taiwan did not reach 1.0. This means that, in light of international economic relations, the Taiwanese FDI trade index with China is large, but, in contrast, the Chinese FDI trade index with Taiwan is small.

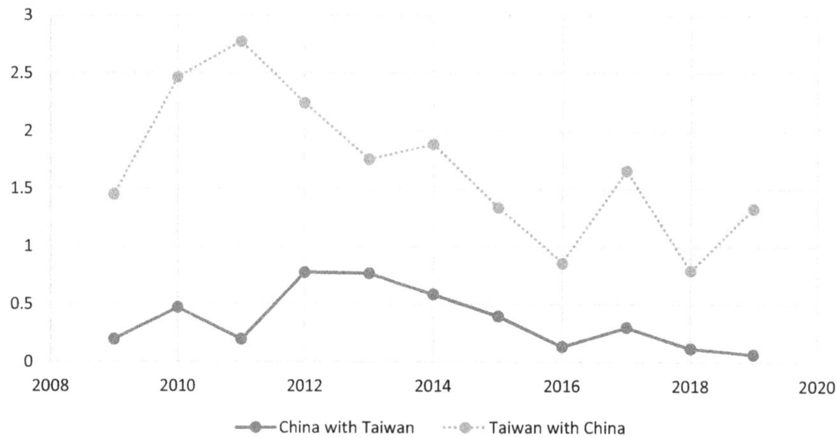

Figure 19. FDI trade index (China and Taiwan) (2009–2020).

Source: JETRO Global Trade and Investment Report (Annual Edition) and the author's calculation.

With respect to the Taiwanese FDI trade index with China, since 2016, it has fluctuated heavily and might be difficult to judge correctly.

9. Conclusion

The following is a brief summary of the investigation in this chapter:

1. If we consider China's behavior under the framework of "offensive realism," the rational conclusion is that China's rise can never be peaceful. Thus, under the framework of "offensive realism," we can conclude that a conflict involving Taiwan will break out sooner or later.
2. If the term "Taiwan's emergency situations" refers to a situation where military threats are used or war is initiated, then when China becomes a regional hegemon, "Taiwan's emergency situations" will inevitably occur. The only country which has the incentive to get into a confrontation with Taiwan is China, not Taiwan itself, Australia, the United States, Japan, or European countries.
3. Taiwan recorded a positive growth rate (3.12 percent) in 2020 due to the following: (1) the negative influence on economic activities due to the COVID-19 pandemic was slight; (2) new business opportunities

were created due to the application of new technologies and remote working; and (3) the export of electronic components and information and communication equipment expanded due to external demand.

4. The trade balance of Taiwan recorded showed a robust surplus trend, which was different from that of Australia and Japan, which fluctuated repeatedly.
5. We examined the ratio of military expenditure in 2020 to that in 2002. China's expansion of military expenditure was predominantly the largest. In contrast, the expansion of military expenditure of Taiwan and Japan was smaller, which is interesting as both countries have faced the threat of attack from China.
6. The Chinese ratio of Taiwanese exports was 27–29 percent and the Chinese ratio of Australian exports was 32–38 percent. The Chinese ratio of Taiwanese imports was 19–20 percent and the Chinese ratio of Australian imports was 22–25 percent. Obviously, the Chinese ratios in Australian exports and imports were larger than those in Taiwanese exports and imports. However, China topped the rankings for all iterations.
7. The ratios of Taiwanese exports and imports relating to China increased and those relating to ASEAN either decreased (export) or remained unchanged (import). If the "New Southbound Policy" of the Tsai Ing-wen administration in Taiwan aimed to reduce Taiwan's dependence on China, it did not materialize.
8. Since 2013, the directional trade ratio between China and Australia has been larger, and the ratios between China and Taiwan and China and Japan have been smaller than the ratio between China and Australia. The directional trade ratio between China and Taiwan has shown a gradual upward trend since 2016.
9. When we observe the degree of export dependency II of Taiwan, there has been no reduction of dependence on China since 2016. Rather, the dependence was at its lowest in 2015 and then continued to rise. The "New Southbound Policy" of the Tsai Ing-wen administration was not successful. The numerical values of the degree of export dependency III of Taiwan increased in 2016 and 2017 and after that gradually decreased. However, the tendency to decrease is not obvious.
10. The Taiwanese FDI to China has rapidly decreased. Although the Taiwanese FDI to Vietnam and Singapore was never large compared to the FDI to China, it was generally steady; in particular, the

Taiwanese FDI to Vietnam was level or had increased moderately. Therefore, based on the Taiwanese FDI to China, we note that there was no reduction in dependence on China. The situation of "reducing dependence on China" in terms of FDI can also be observed from the ratio of other countries to the total Taiwanese FDI.

11. However, there has been no discernible declining trend since 2016 in the Taiwanese FDI concentration index in China.
12. With respect to the Taiwanese FDI trade index with China, it has heavily fluctuated since 2016 and might be difficult to judge correctly.

Chapter 8

A Political Economy of Sino-Japanese Relations

1. Introduction

In the second part of this book, we have investigated some cases of international relations of different countries with China. In this chapter, we examine the current circumstances of Sino-Japanese relations.

First, in this chapter, we discuss a very interesting chapter from a book written by Koo (1996).[1] Koo (1996) mentioned that, in 1996, when the Japanese considered the future of Japan, the most important matter was what they would do if China continued to highly develop and became much stronger both militarily and economically. Would Japan allow itself to be ordered by China? Would Japan hurriedly attempt rearmament? Or would Japan plan its future based on its relationship with the US? Such discussions are also necessary for contemporary Japan. Koo (1996) also asserted that Japan should start planning its action steps against China before it is too late. With regard to the Koo's assertions (which were asserted in 1996), we could not recognize that, in Japan, there has been sufficient discussion on how Japan should respond to China, which has gained significant military and economic power. Naturally, we could not also recognize that there has been enough debate on rearmament in Japan.

Akita published his opinion on Sino-Japanese relations in an article in *Nihon Keizai Shimbun* (6 September 2022) titled "Age of Cold Peace." According to Akita (2022), the future of Sino-Japanese relations could be

[1] Please see Chapter 1 of this book where we have cited Koo's assertions.

viewed as "cold peace." In order to successfully maintain Sino-Japanese relations without armed conflict under this "cold peace," the following three conditions must be fulfilled: First, a multilayered channel for dialogue among government leaders, cadremen, and authorities should be constructed. Second, economic cooperation for mutual benefit should be promoted. Third, a stable military balance could be maintained between China on the one hand and the USA and Japan on the other. Moreover, Akita (2022) mentioned that, as history shows, when military balance collapses, a dispute occurs easily.

Akita (2022) continued to assert that, because of China's rapid military expansion, its military would dominate the combined might of the Japanese Self-Defense Forces and the US Indo-Pacific Command (as claimed by a former official of the US Department of Defense). Therefore, an important condition for sustainable peace would be for both Japan and the United States to expand their investments in defense in the region in order to restore military balance with China.

Akita (2022) also mentioned that, since 2010 when the GDP of China and Japan reversed (more China and less Japan), the balance of power began to change, and China no longer regarded Japan as an equal partner and instead pursued a superpower to confront with the United States.

In short, because the military power between Japan and China is unbalanced, the relationship between Japan and China will never be equal. Therefore, Akita (2022) asserted that as things stand, there is a high chance of a dispute between China and Japan.

Based on the current Sino-Japanese relations, serious issues have arisen in China.

According to an article in *Nihon Keizai Shimbun* (23 October 2022), President Xi Jinping had extended his leadership into an exceptional third term, but both Prime Minister Li Keqiang and Chairman of Chinese People's Political Consultative Conference Wang Yang (whose relations with Xi Jinping were said to be poor) would retire from their leadership positions. This meant more concentration of power in the hands of Xi Jinping. In the same article, it was communicated that Deputy Prime Minister Hu Chunhua (from the Communist Youth League) would be promoted. Aside from Hu Chunhua, most members of the standing committee had close relationships with Xi Jinping, so it was expected that the standing committee would be a pro-Xi Jinping faction.

However, another article in *Nihon Keizai Shimbun* (26 October 2022) made different claims about the circumstances of the standing committee. On 23 October, after the party congress, Xi's third-term leadership was inaugurated. (Prime Minister) Li Keqiang and (Chairman of the National Committee of the Chinese People's Political Consultative Conference) Wang Yang, who come from the Communist Youth League were removed from the top leadership. (Deputy Prime Minister) Hu Chunhua, also from the Communist Youth League and considered a candidate for Prime Minister, was demoted from the Politburo.

In short, because both Li Keqiang and Wang Yang (who were 67 years old) retired from their posts, and Hu Chunhua (who was 59 years old) was demoted, even more power was concentration in the hands of Xi Jinping. Such circumstances did not augur well for Sino-Japanese relations as China had never regarded Japan as an equal partner and seemed intent on confronting the United States.

In facing such times, to borrow the expression we just saw from Koo, Japanese people should seriously consider whether Japan would readily comply with China's demands.

Sino-Japanese relations have a long history and have accumulated numerous problems to be resolved. Sino-Japanese relations after 2009 have been poor, with the possibility of disputes arising easily. The start of the third Xi Jinping administration accelerated the situation. As a matter of fact, Mori (2017) also considers this period as "the fourth period" of Sino-Japanese relations, lamenting that we have entered an era of confrontation over the sea and territories and that the possibility of easing tensions is slim (p. 3). Mori (2017) asserted that the reason for the unstable relations between China and Japan included the conflict of interests regarding territories in the East China Sea, and the violent power relationship between China and Japan in recent years, and the structural vulnerability of Sino-Japanese relations since the start of their normalization process (p. 86).

Thus, in this chapter, we discuss neither the historical territorial issues nor the issues relating to past wars, but focus on the period that Mori cited as "the fourth period." We investigate the Sino-Japanese political economy. In Koo's words once again, it could be rephrased as the question of whether Japan would readily comply with China's demands.

In this chapter, we make note of the following two critical matters. First, according to Akita (2022), as history shows, when military balance collapses, a dispute occurs easily. Second, according to Mearsheimer (2014), in almost every case of civil war, there was substantial economic interdependence between the combatants before the fighting broke out.[2] In fact, the current Sino-Japanese relations (according to Mori's terminology, the "fourth period") could be described as one where the military balance is significantly disrupted, yet there is a state of economic interdependence. In this chapter, we focus our attention on Japan, which has faced much upheaval due to its relationships with China and the US.

Therefore, we analyze contemporary Sino-Japanese relations and make comparisons to Sino-Australian relations and Cross-Strait relations. Thus, the structure of this chapter is as follows: In the second section, we review the statistics of the countries concerned. In the third section, we investigate international trade relations with China. In the fourth section, we consider foreign direct investment relations with China. In the fifth section, we study the political economy of Sino-Japanese relations. In the last section, we conclude the chapter.

2. Several Statistics of Countries Concerned

In this section, we review the economic and military statistics of Japan, China, Australia, and Taiwan.[3] We have provided tables and figures on

[2] See Mearsheimer (2014, p. 408). Needless to say, Mearsheimer's remark is utilized to support the assertion that political calculations often trump economic ones.

This is certainly true regarding matters of national security. However, at the same time, this is not to deny that it might serve as a brake on war in certain circumstances (p. 410). We consider that point a bit more. Hamada (2007) mentioned that, because there is almost no research on the connection between currency and peace, He himself, using a rough estimate, suggests that by using the estimate that trade volume would triple with a common currency — applying Oneal and Russett (1997) — the likelihood of war could be said to decrease by approximately 15 percent (p. 99). In short, there could be conflicting claims regarding "economic interdependence" and "the likelihood of war." However, as Mearsheimer (2014) argued, in almost every case, there was substantial economic interdependence between the combatants before fighting broke out (p. 408). Particularly when considering the relationships between China and Japan, Australia, and Taiwan (keeping in mind China's dictatorial political system), it is impossible to completely rule out the possibility of war, and it seems that the probability is (perhaps rapidly) increasing.

[3] In this chapter, in order to avoid complications, we avoid focusing on the United States.

Table 1. Real GDP growth rate of each country (2008–2020) (in percent).

Year	Australia	Taiwan	China	Japan
2008	2.56	0.80	9.59	▲1.22
2009	1.91	▲1.61	9.45	▲5.69
2010	2.44	10.25	10.61	4.10
2011	2.83	3.67	9.55	0.02
2012	3.78	2.22	7.85	1.38
2013	2.21	2.48	7.77	2.01
2014	2.55	4.72	7.39	0.30
2015	2.31	1.47	7.02	1.56
2016	2.70	2.17	6.85	0.75
2017	2.38	3.31	6.95	1.68
2018	2.78	2.79	6.75	0.64
2019	1.98	3.06	5.95	▲0.36
2020	▲2.14	3.36	2.24	▲4.62

Source: IMF (Data: Global Note).

the real GDP growth rate, military expenditure, the ratio of GDP to military expenditure, the unemployment rate, trade balance, the degree of dependence on foreign trade, the degree of dependence on export, and the Japanese, Australian, and Taiwanese degrees of dependence on export to China.

As the real GDP growth rate shows in Table 1 and Figure 1, China's growth rate has been generally higher than that of other countries. However, in 2020, the growth rate of Taiwan became higher than that of China. Moreover, the real GDP growth rate of China has been lower than 8 percent from 2012 onward, with no indication of increasing.[4] Japan has the lowest rate of real GDP growth.

Table 2 and Figure 2 indicate the military expenditure of the four countries.

China's military expenditure has been conspicuously larger than that of other countries. In addition to the greater military expenditure, the rate of increase has also been rapid. The military expenditure of Australia,

[4] As shown in Table 2 and Figure 2, China's military expenditure has increased significantly.

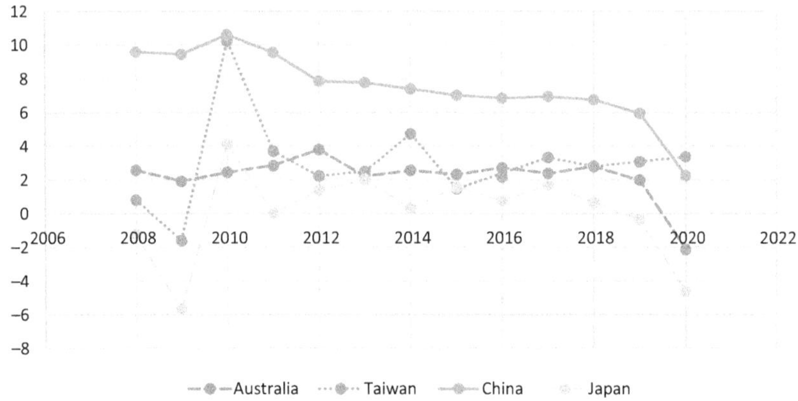

Figure 1. Real GDP growth rate of each country (2008–2020) (in percent).
Source: IMF (Data: Global Note).

Table 2. Military expenditure of each country (2008–2020) (million US dollars).

Year	Australia	Taiwan	China	Japan
2008	18,633	8,960	78,841	46,361
2009	18,960	9,123	96,602	51,465
2010	23,218	9,092	105,523	54,655
2011	26,597	9,998	125,286	60,762
2012	26,217	10,497	145,128	60,012
2013	24,825	9,964	164,071	49,024
2014	25,784	9,802	182,109	46,903
2015	24,046	9,803	196,539	42,106
2016	26,383	9,664	198,538	46,471
2017	27,691	10,480	210,443	45,387
2018	26,840	10,505	232,531	46,618
2019	26,079	10,993	240,333	47,609
2020	27,536	12,155	252,304	49,149

Source: World Bank (Data: Global Note).

Taiwan, and Japan is by and large slight; however, the expenditure of China shows a considerable increase.

Table 3 and Figure 3 show the ratio of GDP to military expenditure of the four countries. China's ratio has never been larger than that of other

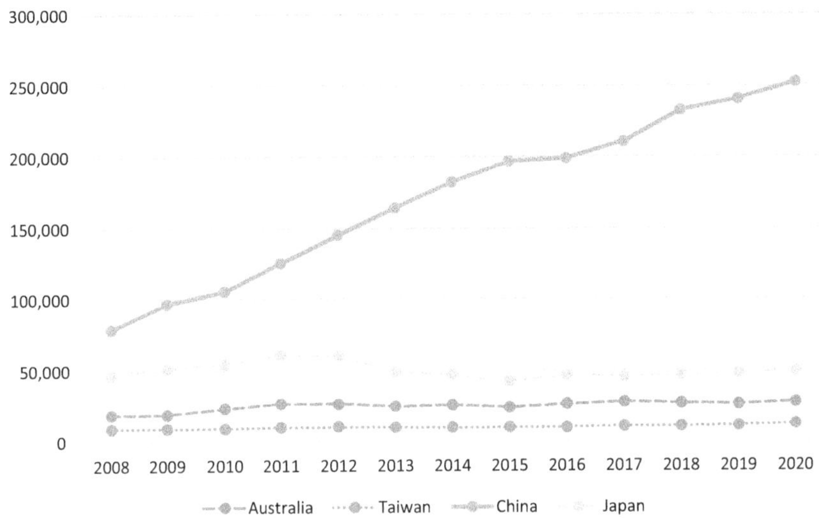

Figure 2. Military expenditure of each country (2008–2020).

Source: World Bank (Data: Global Note).

Table 3. The ratio of military expenditure to GDP of each country (2008–2020) (in percent).

Year	Australia	Taiwan	China	Japan
2008	1.80	2.15	1.71	0.92
2009	1.93	2.33	1.89	0.98
2010	1.86	2.04	1.74	0.96
2011	1.76	2.06	1.67	0.99
2012	1.67	2.12	1.69	0.97
2013	1.64	1.94	1.70	0.95
2014	1.77	1.85	1.73	0.97
2015	1.95	1.87	1.75	0.96
2016	2.08	1.82	1.77	0.95
2017	2.00	1.82	1.75	0.93
2018	1.89	1.74	1.74	0.94
2019	1.88	1.82	1.73	0.94
2020	2.06	1.92	1.75	0.99

Source: World Bank (Data: Global Note) and the author's calculation.

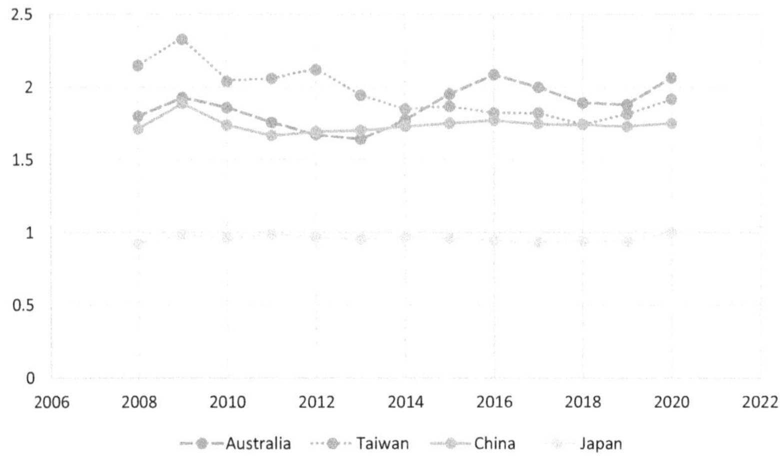

Figure 3. The ratio of military expenditure to GDP of each country (2008–2020) (in percent).

Source: World Bank (Data: Global Note) and the author's calculation.

countries. Until 2014, Taiwan had the largest GDP to military expenditure ratio and, after 2015, Australia had the largest ratio. Japan always had the lowest ratio. The ratios of China, Australia, and Taiwan have been around 2 percent; however, Japan's ratio has only been 1 percent.[5]

In any case, as Japan is a non-nuclear-weapon state, its ratio of GDP to military expenditure is around 1 percent. Thus, Japan's national security is extremely precarious because its neighbor China has nuclear weapons and spends an enormous amount on its military.

Table 4 and Figure 4 show the unemployment rate of each country. In 2020, because of the COVID-19 crisis, the unemployment rate of each country increased. However, the actual state of each country was not the

[5]An article in *Nihon Keizai Shimbun* (29 November 2022, internet version) reported that Prime Minister Kishida directed cabinet ministers to increase the ratio of GDP to military expenditure to 2 percent. In this case, the new military expenditure would have been around 11 trillion yen. However, in the initial budget on military expenditure in 2022, the amount was 5.4005 trillion yen and the ratio of GDP to military expenditure was 0.96 percent. Needless to say, although this was a directive by the prime minister, it will take time to realize it. According to the statistics of the World Bank, Japan's ratio of GDP to military expenditure was 1.02 percent in 2021 and 1.08 percent in 2022, which are less than 2 percent.

Table 4. The unemployment rate of each country (2008–2020) (in percent).

Year	Australia	Taiwan	China	Japan
2008	4.2	4.2	4.6	4.0
2009	5.6	5.9	4.7	5.1
2010	5.2	5.2	4.5	5.1
2011	5.1	4.4	4.6	4.6
2012	5.2	4.2	4.6	4.4
2013	5.7	4.2	4.6	4.0
2014	6.1	4.0	4.6	3.6
2015	6.1	3.8	4.6	3.4
2016	5.7	3.9	4.5	3.1
2017	5.6	3.8	4.4	2.8
2018	5.3	3.7	4.3	2.4
2019	5.2	3.7	4.5	2.4
2020	6.5	3.8	5.0	2.8

Source: ILO (Data: Global Note).

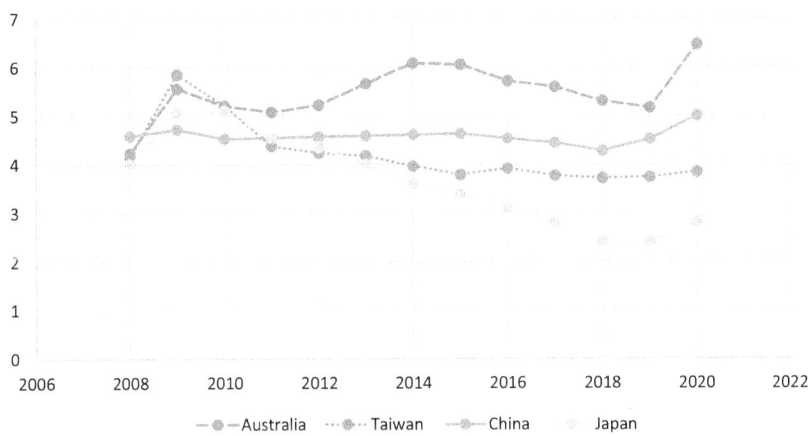

Figure 4. The unemployment rate of each country (2008–2020) (in percent).
Source: ILO (Data: Global Note).

same. In Australia, the real GDP growth rate decreased to a negative and the unemployment rate increased to more than 6 percent. On the contrary, in Taiwan, the real GDP growth rate remained positive in 2020 and the unemployment rate was less than 4 percent. In Japan, the GDP growth rate was the lowest among the four countries and the unemployment rate was also the lowest.

Table 5 and Figure 5 show the trade balance of the four countries. China's record of trade balance has been overwhelmingly large. In China,

Table 5. Trade balance of each country (2008–2021) (million US dollars).

Year	Australia	Taiwan	China	Japan
2008	▲13,016	15,181	298,126	18,878
2009	▲11,140	29,304	195,689	28,738
2010	10,995	23,364	181,507	75,715
2011	28,032	26,820	154,897	▲32,197
2012	▲4,265	29,085	230,309	▲87,276
2013	10,841	33,418	259,015	▲117,730
2014	2,623	38,242	383,060	▲122,005
2015	▲20,817	48,124	593,902	▲23,196
2016	▲3,765	49,753	509,707	37,324
2017	2,351	57,983	419,554	26,233
2018	21,712	49,576	350,947	▲10,344
2019	49,441	43,458	421,071	▲15,392
2020	38,999	59,139	523,988	5,859
2021	83,664	65,592	675,202	▲12,944

Source: UNCTAD (Data: Global Note).

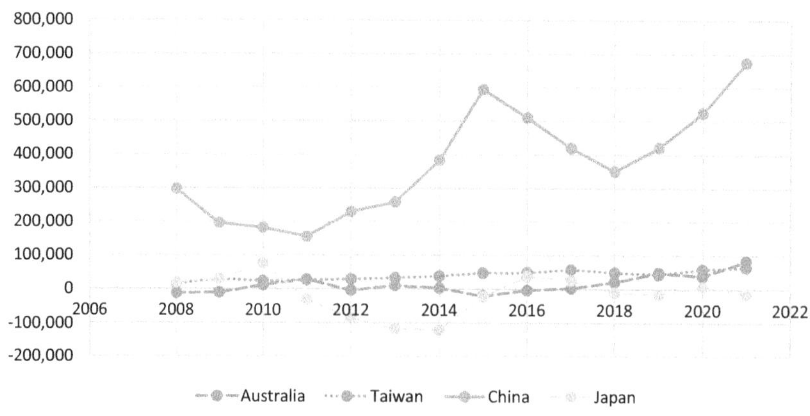

Figure 5. Trade balance of each country (2008–2021).

Source: UNCTAD (Data: Global Note).

after bottoming out in 2011, it decreased again from 2015 to 2018. However, from 2019 to 2021, the trade balance greatly increased. Both Taiwan and Australia experienced a leveling of the trade balance. Although Japan's trade balance fluctuated, in comparison with China both the deficit and surplus of Japan were not large.

Table 6 and Figure 6 show the degree of dependence on foreign trade of each country. Taiwan's degree of dependence was much higher than that of other countries. Therefore, it might be easily recognizable that, if any trade barriers were imposed, the impact on Taiwan would also be significant.

Table 7 and Figure 7 represent the degree of dependence on the export of each country, calculated by replacing the numerator of the degree of dependence on foreign trade with the total export amount. Taiwan's degree of dependence on export is of a large value. Thus, to reiterate, if such export barriers were imposed, the impact on Taiwan would also be significant.

Table 8 and Figure 8 show the degree of dependence on the export of each country to China, which means that the degree of dependence on

Table 6. Degree of dependence on foreign trade of each country (2008–2021) (in percent).

Year	Australia	Taiwan	China	Japan
2008	36.08	122.51	50.60	28.30
2009	30.89	99.95	39.26	19.57
2010	31.93	121.67	44.65	23.60
2011	33.65	126.12	44.85	25.41
2012	33.01	147.53	42.61	25.61
2013	32.47	139.36	41.15	28.39
2014	32.70	131.56	38.69	30.60
2015	31.69	113.47	33.53	28.16
2016	29.85	100.83	31.07	24.37
2017	31.92	102.27	32.14	27.04
2018	33.95	102.42	32.06	29.00
2019	35.87	98.64	30.67	26.97
2020	32.35	92.00	30.63	24.40
2021	35.16	105.63	33.93	29.96

Source: UNCTAD (Data: Global Note) and the author's calculation.

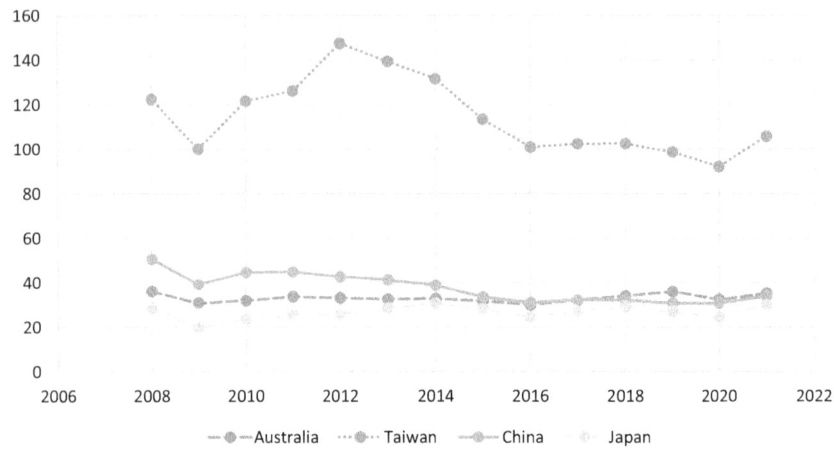

Figure 6. Degree of dependence on foreign trade of each country (2008–2021) (in percent).

Source: UNCTAD (Data: Global Note) and the author's calculation.

Table 7. Degree of dependence on the export of each country (2008–2021) (in percent).

Year	Australia	Taiwan	China	Japan
2008	17.73	64.76	29.05	14.70
2009	15.16	55.01	21.94	10.33
2010	16.41	64.99	24.28	12.74
2011	17.56	67.16	23.94	12.67
2012	16.25	78.74	23.13	12.38
2013	16.47	75.00	22.45	13.33
2014	16.42	71.41	21.42	14.29
2015	15.07	63.58	19.37	14.00
2016	14.70	56.95	17.71	12.69
2017	16.33	58.01	18.00	13.97
2018	17.70	56.71	17.40	14.60
2019	19.68	54.03	16.71	13.50
2020	17.62	51.59	17.05	12.46
2021	20.14	58.57	18.59	15.13

Source: UNCTAD (Data: Global Note) and the author's calculation.

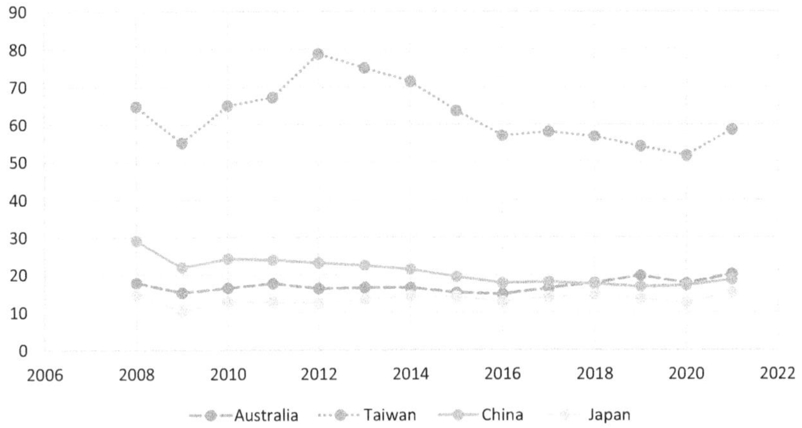

Figure 7. Degree of dependence on the export of each country (2008–2021) (in percent).
Source: UNCTAD (Data: Global Note) and the author's calculation.

Table 8. Degree of dependence on the export to China of each country (2008–2020) (in percent).

Year	Australia	Taiwan	Japan
2008	2.75	17.79	2.43
2009	3.16	15.89	2.07
2010	4.11	17.32	2.59
2011	4.67	17.35	2.59
2012	4.81	16.29	2.31
2013	5.97	15.94	2.49
2014	5.53	15.34	2.60
2015	4.90	13.32	2.46
2016	4.76	13.60	2.28
2017	5.54	15.06	2.69
2018	6.20	15.88	2.86
2019	7.50	15.00	2.63
2020	7.43	15.33	2.80

Source: JETRO International Trade and Investment Report (Annual Edition) and the author's calculation.

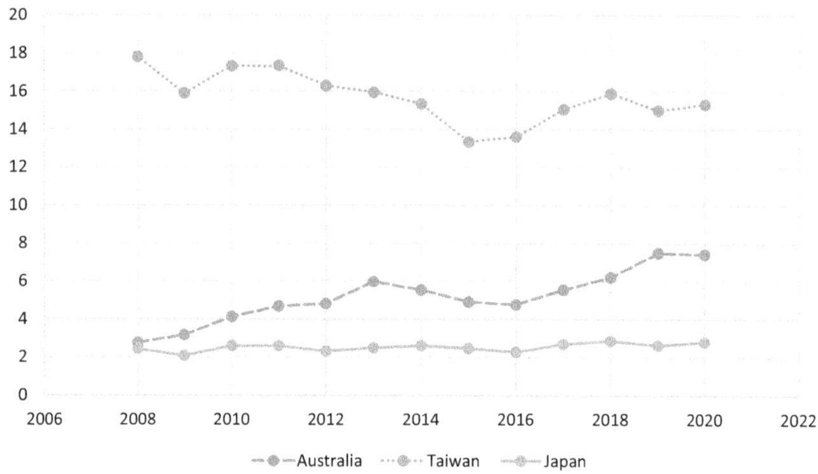

Figure 8. Degree of dependence on the export to China of each country (2008–2020) (in percent).

Source: JETRO Global Trade and Investment Report (Annual Edition) and the author's calculation.

foreign trade and on export are calculated by replacing the numerator with the total export amount to China. Taiwan's degree of dependence on exports to China is high, growing from 14 percent to 18 percent. Australia's degree of dependence on exports to China grew from 2 percent to 8 percent. Japan degree of dependence on exports to China is little more than 2 percent and shows no fluctuation.

As shown by values on the degree of dependence on foreign trade, the degree of dependence on exports, and the degree of dependence on exports to China, Taiwan has the highest values. Therefore, we could easily recognize that, if barriers were imposed on foreign trade, exports, and exports to China of Taiwan, the impact would also be significant.

3. Foreign Trade with China

3.1. *Import partner countries and export partner countries*

In this section, we review the import partner countries and export partner countries of Japan, China, Australia, and Taiwan. The values are shown in Tables 9 to 16.

Table 9. China's import partner countries: Ranking and ratio (2017–2020).

Year	2017		2018		2019		2020	
Ranking	**Country**	**Ratio**	**Country**	**Ratio**	**Country**	**Ratio**	**Country**	**Ratio**
1	South Korea	9.6	South Korea	9.6	South Korea	8.4	Taiwan	9.8
2	Japan	9.0	Japan	8.5	Taiwan	8.3	Japan	8.5
3	Taiwan	8.4	Taiwan	8.3	Japan	8.3	South Korea	8.4
4	USA	8.4	USA	7.3	USA	5.9	USA	6.6
5	Germany	5.3	Germany	5.0	Australia	5.8	Australia	5.6
6	Australia	5.2	Australia	4.9	Germany	5.1	Germany	5.3
7	Brazil	3.2	Brazil	3.6	Brazil	3.8	Brazil	4.1
8	Malaysia	2.9	Malaysia	3.0	Malaysia	3.5	Vietnam	3.8
9	Thailand	2.3	Russia	2.8	Russia	2.9	Malaysia	3.6
10	Russia	2.2	Thailand	2.1	Saudi Arabia	2.6	Thailand	2.3

Source: JETRO International Trade and Investment Report (Annual Edition).

Table 10. China's export partner countries: Ranking and ratio (2017–2020).

Year	2017		2018		2019		2020	
Ranking	**Country**	**Ratio**	**Country**	**Ratio**	**Country**	**Ratio**	**Country**	**Ratio**
1	USA	19.0	USA	19.2	USA	16.8	USA	17.4
2	Hong Kong	12.3	Hong Kong	12.1	Hong Kong	11.2	Hong Kong	10.5
3	Japan	6.1	Japan	5.9	Japan	5.7	Japan	5.5
4	South Korea	4.5	South Korea	4.4	South Korea	4.4	Germany	5.2
5	Germany	3.1	Germany	3.1	Germany	3.2	Vietnam	4.4
6	India	3.0	India	3.1	India	3.0	South Korea	4.3
7	Netherlands	3.0	Netherlands	2.9	Netherlands	3.0	UK	2.8
8	UK	2.5	UK	2.3	UK	2.5	India	2.6
9	Singapore	2.0	Singapore	2.0	Taiwan	2.2	Taiwan	2.3
10	Taiwan	1.9	Taiwan	2.0	Singapore	2.2	Malaysia	2.2

Source: JETRO International Trade and Investment Report (Annual Edition).

Table 11. Japan's import partner countries: Ranking and ratio (2017–2020).

	2017		2018		2019		2020	
Ranking	**Country**	**Ratio**	**Country**	**Ratio**	**Country**	**Ratio**	**Country**	**Ratio**
1	China	24.5	China	23.2	China	23.5	China	25.8
2	USA	10.7	USA	10.9	USA	11.0	USA	11.0
3	Australia	5.8	Australia	6.1	Australia	6.3	Australia	5.6
4	South Korea	4.2	Saudi Arabia	4.5	South Korea	4.1	Taiwan	4.2
5	Saudi Arabia	4.1	South Korea	4.3	Saudi Arabia	3.8	South Korea	4.2
6	Taiwan	3.8	UAE	3.7	Taiwan	3.7	Thailand	3.7
7	Germany	3.5	Taiwan	3.6	UAE	3.6	Vietnam	3.5
8	Thailand	3.4	Germany	3.5	Thailand	3.5	Germany	3.3
9	UAE	3.1	Thailand	3.4	Germany	3.5	Saudi Arabia	2.9
10	Indonesia	3.0	Indonesia	2.9	Vietnam	3.1	UAE	2.6

Source: JETRO International Trade and Investment Report (Annual Edition).

Table 12. Japan's export partner countries: Ranking and ratio (2017–2020).

	2017		2018		2019		2020	
Ranking	**Country**	**Ratio**	**Country**	**Ratio**	**Country**	**Ratio**	**Country**	**Ratio**
1	USA	19.3	China	19.5	USA	19.8	China	22.1
2	China	19.0	USA	19.0	China	19.1	USA	18.4
3	South Korea	7.6	South Korea	7.1	South Korea	6.6	South Korea	7.0
4	Taiwan	5.8	Taiwan	5.7	Taiwan	6.1	Taiwan	6.9
5	Hong Kong	5.1	Hong Kong	4.7	Hong Kong	4.8	Hong Kong	5.0
6	Thailand	4.2	Thailand	4.4	Thailand	4.3	Thailand	4.0
7	Singapore	3.2	Singapore	3.2	Germany	2.9	Singapore	2.8
8	Germany	2.7	Germany	2.8	Singapore	2.9	Germany	2.7
9	Australia	2.3	Australia	2.3	Vietnam	2.3	Vietnam	2.7
10	Vietnam	2.2	Vietnam	2.2	Australia	2.1	Malaysia	2.0

Source: JETRO International Trade and Investment Report (Annual Edition).

Table 13. Australia's import partner countries: Ranking and ratio (2017–2020).

	2017		2018		2019		2020	
Ranking	**Country**	**Ratio**	**Country**	**Ratio**	**Country**	**Ratio**	**Country**	**Ratio**
1	China	22.2	China	24.5	China	25.8	China	28.8
2	USA	10.3	USA	10.3	USA	12.1	USA	11.9
3	Japan	7.3	Japan	7.4	Japan	7.0	Japan	6.1
4	South Korea	7.2	Germany	4.9	Thailand	4.8	Thailand	4.9
5	Thailand	5.0	Thailand	4.9	Germany	4.8	Germany	4.6
6	Germany	4.7	South Korea	4.3	South Korea	4.0	Malaysia	3.3
7	Malaysia	3.8	Malaysia	4.3	Malaysia	3.6	South Korea	3.1
8	Singapore	2.8	Singapore	3.8	Singapore	3.4	Singapore	2.5
9	New Zealand	2.7	New Zealand	2.6	New Zealand	2.5	New Zealand	2.4
10	UK	2.4	UK	2.4	UK	2.3	UK	2.4

Source: JETRO International Trade and Investment Report (Annual Edition).

Table 14. Australia's export partner countries: Ranking and ratio (2017–2020).

	2017		2018		2019		2020	
Ranking	**Country**	**Ratio**	**Country**	**Ratio**	**Country**	**Ratio**	**Country**	**Ratio**
1	China	33.0	China	34.2	China	38.4	China	40.3
2	Japan	14.6	Japan	16.1	Japan	14.9	Japan	12.4
3	South Korea	6.7	South Korea	6.9	South Korea	6.7	South Korea	6.6
4	India	5.2	India	4.8	UK	3.9	USA	5.4
5	Hong Kong	4.0	USA	3.8	USA	3.9	UK	4.1
6	USA	3.9	Taiwan	3.1	India	3.7	Singapore	3.5
7	New Zealand	3.0	Hong Kong	3.0	Taiwan	3.3	New Zealand	2.8
8	Taiwan	2.9	Singapore	2.9	Singapore	3.1	India	2.8
9	Indonesia	2.2	New Zealand	2.8	New Zealand	2.6	Taiwan	2.8
10	Singapore	2.2	Malaysia	2.1	Malaysia	2.3	Hong Kong	2.0

Source: JETRO International Trade and Investment Report (Annual Edition).

Table 15. Taiwan's import partner countries: Ranking and ratio (2017–2020).

	2017		2018		2019		2020	
Ranking	**Country**	**Ratio**	**Country**	**Ratio**	**Country**	**Ratio**	**Country**	**Ratio**
1	China	19.3	China	18.8	China	20.1	China	22.2
2	Japan	16.2	Japan	15.4	Japan	15.4	Japan	16.1
3	USA	11.7	USA	12.1	USA	12.2	USA	11.4
4	South Korea	6.5	South Korea	6.8	South Korea	6.2	South Korea	7.2
5	Singapore	3.4	Australia	3.3	Malaysia	3.6	Malaysia	3.5
6	Australia	3.2	Malaysia	3.2	Australia	3.5	Singapore	3.1
7	Malaysia	2.8	Singapore	2.9	Singapore	2.8	Australia	2.8
8	Indonesia	1.9	Indonesia	1.9	Vietnam	1.8	Vietnam	1.9
9	Thailand	1.7	Thailand	1.6	Indonesia	1.6	Thailand	1.6
10	Vietnam	1.2	Vietnam	1.3	Thailand	1.5	Indonesia	1.6

Source: JETRO International Trade and Investment Report (Annual Edition).

Table 16. Taiwan's export partner countries: Ranking and ratio (2017–2020).

	2017		2018		2019		2020	
Ranking	**Country**	**Ratio**	**Country**	**Ratio**	**Country**	**Ratio**	**Country**	**Ratio**
1	China	28.0	China	28.8	China	27.9	China	29.7
2	Hong Kong	13.0	Hong Kong	12.4	USA	14.0	USA	14.6
3	USA	11.6	USA	11.8	Hong Kong	12.3	Hong Kong	14.2
4	Japan	6.6	Japan	6.9	Japan	7.1	Japan	6.8
5	Singapore	5.6	Singapore	5.2	Singapore	5.5	Singapore	5.5
6	South Korea	4.6	South Korea	4.8	South Korea	5.1	South Korea	4.4
7	Vietnam	3.3	Vietnam	3.2	Vietnam	3.3	Vietnam	3.0
8	Malaysia	3.3	Malaysia	3.2	Malaysia	2.9	Malaysia	2.7
9	Philippines	3.0	Philippines	2.7	Philippines	1.9	Philippines	1.6
10	Thailand	2.0	Thailand	1.8	Thailand	1.7	Thailand	1.5

Source: JETRO International Trade and Investment Report (Annual Edition).

Tables 9 and 10 show China's import and export partner countries, respectively. With regard to import partner countries, South Korea, Japan, and Taiwan occupy larger ratios than other countries, each accounting for 8 percent to 10 percent. The United States occupies a ratio of 6 percent to 8 percent (Australia, 5 percent to 6 percent). In short, as import partner countries of China, countries with larger ratios are South Korea, Japan, and Taiwan, followed by the United States and Australia. Concerning export partner countries, the United States has an overwhelmingly large ratio of 17 percent to 20 percent. After the United States, Hong Kong occupies a 10 percent to 12 percent ratio. Japan, South Korea, and Germany follow with the next larger ratio of 3 percent to 6 percent.

Regarding Japan, its ratio as an import partner country of China is 8 percent to 9 percent and ratio as an export partner country is roughly 6 percent. Japan occupies the second or third place as an import partner country and as the third place as an export partner country.

Tables 11 and 12 show Japan's import and export partner countries, respectively. Concerning import partner countries, China occupies a predominantly large ratio of roughly 25 percent (quarter). The second place is occupied by the United States with a ratio of 10 percent to 11 percent. Australia (in the third place) accounts for 5 percent to 6 percent. Regarding export partner countries, the United States and China occupy the first and second places, respectively, with ratios of roughly 20 percent. In short, China has a 25-percent ratio as the import partner country and a 20-percent ratio as the export partner country of Japan. It is difficult to imagine the foreign trade of Japan without China as China's impact on Japan as both an import partner and an export partner is immense. Therefore, if there is a conflict between China and Japan, the economic impact on both countries will be serious.

Tables 13 and 14 show the import partner countries and export partner countries, respectively, of Australia. both import and export partner country, China's ratio as both an import and an export partner country has been predominantly large. China's ratio as an import partner country is 25 percent to 30 percent and as an export partner country is 35 percent and 40 percent. Moreover, as an import partner country, the United States occupies the second place with a 10 percent to 12 percent ratio. As an export partner country, the second place is occupied by Japan, with a ratio of 12 percent to 16 percent. Although the United States and Japan occupy the second place, there is a big difference between them and the country in first place

(China). As an export partner country, Taiwan has a ratio of 2 percent to 3 percent. However, as an import partner country, Taiwan is placed lower than the tenth-place country (the UK). It is difficult to imagine the foreign trade of Australia without China. Therefore, the impact on Australian of any conflict with China will be serious. However, as an import partner country of China, Australia has a ratio of 5 percent to 6 percent, ranking fifth or sixth. As an export partner country, the ratio of Australia is lower than tenth-place countries (Taiwan, Singapore, and Malaysia).

Tables 15 and 16 represent the import and export partner countries, respectively, of Taiwan. China's ratio as both an import and an export partner country has been overwhelmingly large. As an export partner country, China occupies a ratio of 30 percent. As an import partner country, China's ratio is roughly 20 percent. As an import partner country, Japan occupies a ratio of 15 percent and as an export partner country, the United States occupies a ratio of nearly 15 percent. Although Japan and the United States occupy the rank as the second positions in import and export, respectively, there is a big difference between them and China.

Australia occupies around a 3 percent of ratio as an import partner country; however, as an export partner country, Australia is positioned lower than the tenth rank country (Thailand). Therefore, based on China's ratios, in case of conflict between Taiwan and China, the impact on Taiwan could be very serious. Taiwan occupies the ratio of 8 percent to 10 percent, ranking first to third, as an import partner country of China. As an export partner country, Taiwan has held a ratio of 1 percent to 2 percent, with a ranking of ninth to tenth. Thus, in case of conflict between Taiwan and China (except for Chinese exports to Taiwan), the impact on both Taiwan and China could be very significant.

3.2. *Directional trade ratio*

In this section, we consider the directional trade ratio[6] of the countries concerned.

As mentioned in Chapter 2, directional trade ratio measures the closeness of trade relations between the countries concerned. Table 17 and Figure 9 show the directional trade ratio between China and three countries.

---

[6]With regard to the details of the directional trade ratio, see Smoker (1965) and Chapter 2 of this book. Also see, for example, Morita (2021).

Table 17. Directional trade ratio between China and each country (2008–2020).

Year	Japan	Australia	Taiwan
2008	0.139	0.087	0.124
2009	0.154	0.112	0.128
2010	0.154	0.126	0.132
2011	0.150	0.133	0.130
2012	0.141	0.136	0.128
2013	0.138	0.157	0.132
2014	0.139	0.152	0.134
2015	0.141	0.153	0.137
2016	0.145	0.152	0.140
2017	0.145	0.155	0.145
2018	0.142	0.165	0.145
2019	0.141	0.183	0.146
2020	0.154	0.194	0.160

Source: JETRO International Trade and Investment Report (Annual Edition) and the author's calculation.

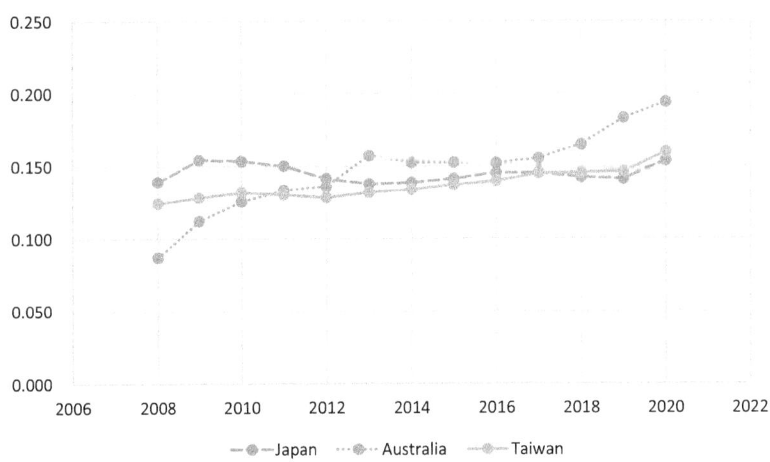

Figure 9. Directional trade ratio between China and each country (2008–2020).

Source: JETRO International Trade and Investment Report (Annual Edition) and the author's calculation.

Based on the directional trade ratio, each of the three countries has a rather large value. Australia takes larger values than Japan and Taiwan, particularly since 2013. Further, from 2012 onward (since the formation of the Xi Jinping administration in China), no country has seen a clear decrease in directional trade ratio with China. Th ratios of both Japan and Taiwan remain level, while that of Australia has experienced an increase.

3.3. *Trade linkage index*

In this section, we investigate the trade linkage index.[7] As mentioned earlier, this index analyzes whether or not there exists a trade distortion between the countries concerned. Actually, the trade linkage index is used as a measure of distortion of trade. In this section, we focus on the distortion in the trade between China and the three countries concerned (a portion that is explained not by the comparative advantage but by characteristic factors in China or both countries engaged in trade).

We explain the trade linkage index as follows using the example of the trade linkage index of Japan with the trade partner country China —.

The index is equal to the ratio of the value obtained by dividing Japan's exports to China by China's total imports, to the value obtained by dividing Japan's total exports by the world total exports. If Japan's actual export amount to China equals Japan's hypothetical export amount to China, the numerical value of the trade linkage index between Japan and China would equal 1.0. If the numerical value of the trade linkage index becomes larger than 1.0 (or smaller than 1.0), then the trade distortion between Japan and China would be larger. If the trade linkage index becomes larger than 1.0, then the trade distortion would be bigger and the actual export amount would be bigger. On the contrary, if the trade linkage index becomes smaller than 1.0, then the trade distortion becomes bigger and the actual export amount would be smaller.

Table 18 and Figure 10 show the trade linkage index between each of three countries (Japan, Australia, and Taiwan) and China.

Each country has an index of more than 1.0, which shows that foreign trade with China has been relatively larger compared to trade with other

[7]With regard to the details of the trade linkage index, see Chapter 2 of this book.

countries. In particular, Australia has had an index of more than 3.0 since 2013, which clearly indicates that Australian trade with China has been very active.

Table 19 and Figure 11 show the trade linkage index between China and each of three countries (Japan, Australia and Taiwan).

With regard to China's trade linkage index with each country, every numerical value is more than 1.0, which shows that China's trade with each country has been relatively larger compared to that of other countries. Also, those numerical values show that, until 2017, China's trade linkage index with Japan was larger than its trade index with Australia and Taiwan. However, since 2018, China's trade linkage index with Australia is larger than its index with Japan and Taiwan.

Therefore, it is evident that trade, both in terms of each country's trade with China and China's trade with each country, is relatively larger compared to trade with other countries in the world. In particular, Australia's trade with China has been very active. Until 2017, China's

Table 18. Japan, Australia, and Taiwan's trade linkage index with China (2008–2020).

Year	Japan	Australia	Taiwan
2008	2.33	2.12	3.81
2009	2.39	2.73	3.38
2010	2.09	2.72	3.01
2011	2.01	2.78	2.78
2012	1.78	2.90	2.64
2013	1.69	3.37	2.50
2014	1.72	3.16	2.45
2015	1.71	3.18	2.61
2016	1.76	3.15	2.74
2017	1.81	3.15	2.75
2018	1.77	3.10	2.65
2019	1.72	3.42	2.52
2020	1.86	3.37	2.67

Source: JETRO International Trade and Investment Report (Annual Edition) and the author's calculation.

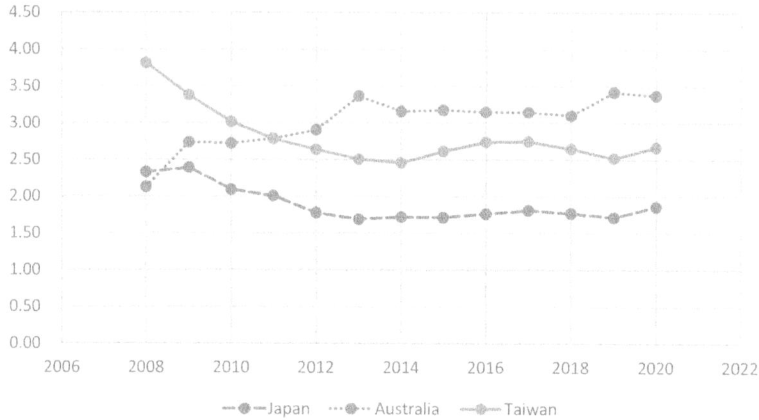

Figure 10. Japan, Australia, and Taiwan's trade linkage index with China (2008–2020).
Source: JETRO International Trade and Investment Report (Annual Edition) and the author's calculation.

Table 19. China's trade linkage index with each country (2008–2020).

Year	Japan	Australia	Taiwan
2008	1.77	1.27	1.25
2009	1.88	1.46	1.25
2010	1.66	1.40	1.12
2011	1.63	1.41	1.17
2012	1.49	1.32	1.19
2013	1.48	1.34	1.24
2014	1.44	1.35	1.33
2015	1.52	1.47	1.42
2016	1.61	1.50	1.32
2017	1.59	1.45	1.31
2018	1.53	1.62	1.32
2019	1.49	1.69	1.44
2020	1.51	1.75	1.04

Source: JETRO International Trade and Investment Report (Annual Edition) and the author's calculation.

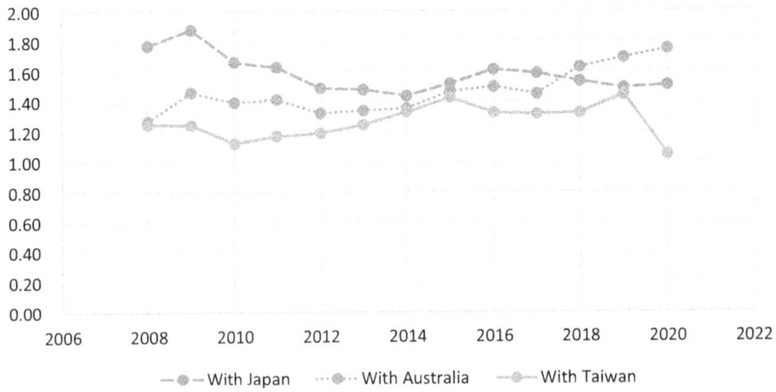

Figure 11. China's trade linkage index with each country (2008–2020).

Source: JETRO International Trade and Investment Report (Annual Edition) and the author's calculation.

trade with Japan was considerably active, and since 2018, China's trade with Australia has been very active.

3.4. *On the foreign direct investment*

In this section, we investigate foreign direct investment for which we employ two kinds of statistics: the FDI concentration index and the FDI trade index.

The FDI concentration index is indicated as follows. We suppose here the FDI concentration index of Japan with China, the index represents the ratio of the value obtained by dividing Japan's outward FDI in China by China's total inward FDI, to the value obtained by dividing Japan's total outward FDI by world total outward FDI. When the ratio is more than 1.0, Japanese FDI into China is bigger than that of other countries. Table 20 and Figure 12 show the FDI concentration index of China with Taiwan[8] and Taiwan with China.[9]

In the same way, Table 21 and Figure 13 show the FDI concentration index of China with Australia and Australia with China. Table 22 and

[8] Here, we label this "China with Taiwan."

[9] In the same way, we label this "Taiwan with China." Similar terminology is used hereinafter.

Table 20. FDI concentration index (China and Taiwan) (2009–2018).

Year	China with Taiwan	Taiwan with China
2009	0.242	4.886
2010	0.525	7.421
2011	0.228	7.696
2012	0.920	5.908
2013	0.953	4.388
2014	0.772	4.620
2015	0.560	3.486
2016	0.174	2.340
2017	0.392	4.545
2018	0.155	2.097
2019	0.096	3.346
2020	0.048	2.051

Source: JETRO International Trade and Investment Report (Annual Edition) and the author's calculation.

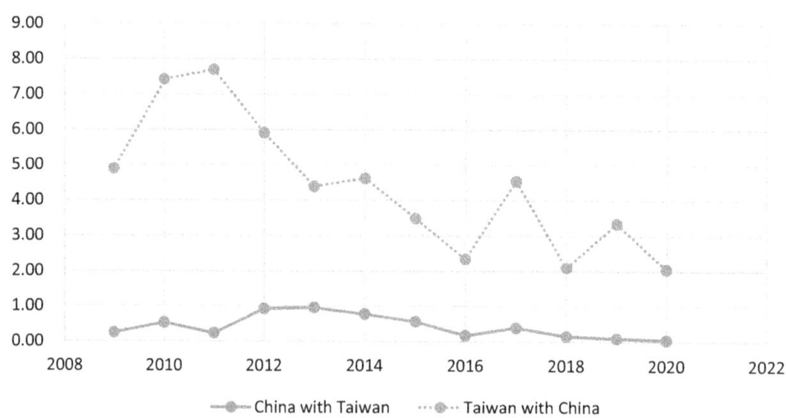

Figure 12. FDI concentration index (China and Taiwan) (2009–2020).

Source: JETRO International Trade and Investment Report (Annual Edition) and the author's calculation.

Figure 14 show the FDI concentration index of China with Japan and Japan with China.

As mentioned earlier, when the numerical value of the FDI concentration index is more than 1.0, Japan's FDI into China is relatively

Table 21. FDI concentration index (China and Australia) (2008–2020).

Year	China with Australia	Australia with China
2008	1.620	0.363
2009	2.380	▲0.870
2010	1.010	0.039
2011	1.090	0.137
2012	0.600	0.418
2013	0.772	0.788
2014	1.095	▲13.194
2015	1.911	▲0.303
2016	0.659	▲0.519
2017	0.903	▲3.209
2018	0.208	0.938
2019	0.557	0.346
2020	0.308	▲0.311

Note: ▲ indicates excess withdrawal.
Source: JETRO International Trade and Investment Report (Annual Edition) and the author's calculation.

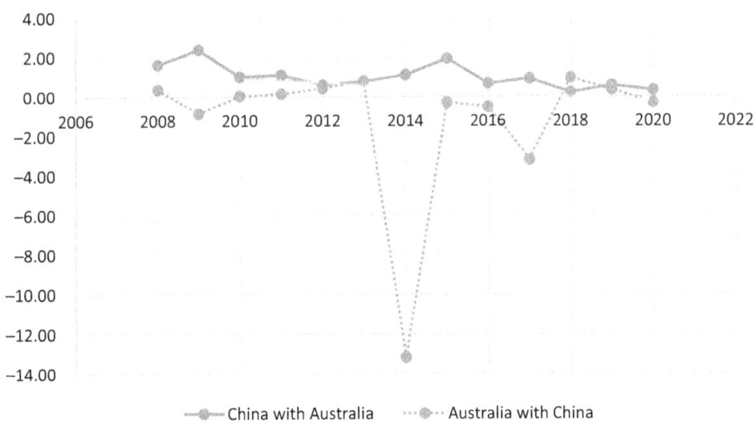

Figure 13. FDI concentration index (China and Australia) (2008–2020).

Source: JETRO International Trade and Investment Report (Annual Edition) and the author's calculation.

Table 22. FDI concentration index (China and Japan) (2008–2020).

Year	China with Japan	Japan with China
2008	0.061	0.732
2009	▲0.362	1.622
2010	▲5.029	0.896
2011	▲1.613	1.512
2012	0.687	1.263
2013	0.849	0.764
2014	3.330	0.625
2015	▲2.845	0.749
2016	▲0.088	0.646
2017	1.063	0.633
2018	0.144	0.548
2019	0.181	0.550
2020	0.235	0.483

Note: ▲ indicates excess withdrawal.
Source: JETRO International Trade and Investment Report (Annual Edition) and the author's calculation.

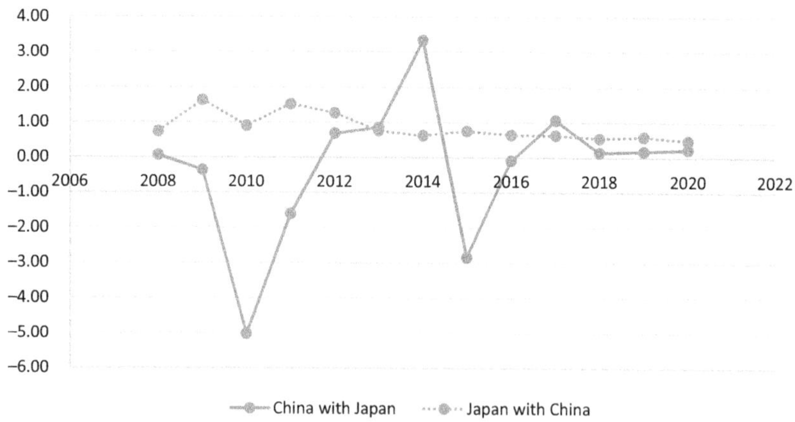

Figure 14. FDI concentration index (China and Japan) (2008–2020).
Source: JETRO International Trade and Investment Report (Annual Edition) and the author's calculation.

bigger than its FDI into other countries. On the contrary, when the numerical value of the FDI concentration index is less than 1.0, Japan's FDI into China is relatively smaller than its FDI into other countries.

The FDI concentration index of Taiwan with China is more than 1.0. The FDI concentration index of China with Australia was undoubtedly more than 1.0 over a span of 6 years, although since 2016, that index has been less than 1.0. The FDI concentration index of Japan with China was more than 1.0 for 3 years and the FDI concentration index of China with Japan was more than 1.0 over a period of 2 years.

In short, only the FDI concentration index of Taiwan with China has constantly been more than 1.0.

Next, we consider the FDI trade index.

The FDI trade index could be used as follows. The FDI trade index is a measure used to assess whether FDI is active, meaning whether the scale of FDI is large or small, by comparing it against the strength of international economic relations. Therefore, the FDI trade index consists of the FDI concentration index as the numerator and the trade linkage index as the denominator. Thus, when the FDI trade index equals 1.0, FDI relations between the two countries correspond with their international relations. When it is more than 1.0, FDI relations between them are more active than expected from international relations. When it is less than 1.0, FDI relations between them are less active than expected.

Table 23 and Figure 15 show the FDI trade index of China with Taiwan and Taiwan with China. In the same way, Table 24 and Figure 16 show the FDI trade index of China with Australia and Australia with China. Table 25 and Figure 17 show the FDI trade index of China with Japan and Japan with China.

As indicated before, we can judge whether the numerical value of the FDI trade index is more than 1.0 or less than 1.0.

The FDI trade index of Taiwan with China has been more than 1.0 for many years; however, the FDI trade index of China with Taiwan is constantly less than 1.0.

The FDI trade index of China with Australia was more than 1.0 for three years, but in other years, that index was less than 1.0.

The FDI trade index of China with Japan had a large numerical value only in 2014; in all other years, it was less than 1.0. The FDI trade index of Japan with China was consistently less than 1.0.

Table 23. FDI trade index (China and Taiwan) (2009–2020).

Year	China with Taiwan	Taiwan with China
2009	0.195	1.447
2010	0.468	2.462
2011	0.195	2.770
2012	0.775	2.241
2013	0.767	1.752
2014	0.581	1.883
2015	0.393	1.334
2016	0.132	0.854
2017	0.299	1.655
2018	0.117	0.793
2019	0.067	1.328
2020	0.046	0.769

Source: JETRO International Trade and Investment Report (Annual Edition) and the author's calculation.

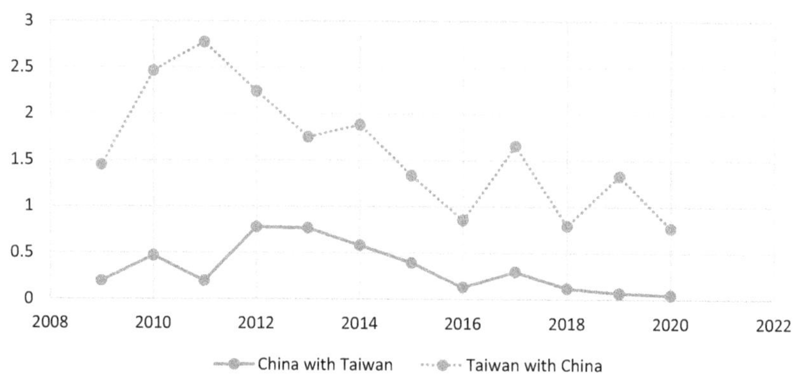

Figure 15. FDI trade index (China and Taiwan) (2009–2020).

Source: JETRO International Trade and Investment Report (Annual Edition) and the author's calculation.

When viewed through FDI trade ratio, it is evident that Taiwan's FDI in China is active (in terms of international economic relations). However, for other countries, it is difficult to recognize such active FDI (in terms of international economic relations, and thus in the context of this chapter).

Table 24. FDI trade index (China and Australia) (2008–2020).

Year	China with Australia	Australia with China
2008	1.279	0.171
2009	1.628	▲0.319
2010	0.724	0.014
2011	0.771	0.049
2012	0.455	0.144
2013	0.578	0.234
2014	0.809	▲4.180
2015	1.303	▲0.095
2016	0.441	▲0.165
2017	0.624	▲1.020
2018	0.128	0.303
2019	0.330	0.101
2020	0.177	▲0.092

Note: ▲ indicates excess withdrawal.
Source: JETRO International Trade and Investment Report (Annual Edition) and the author's calculation.

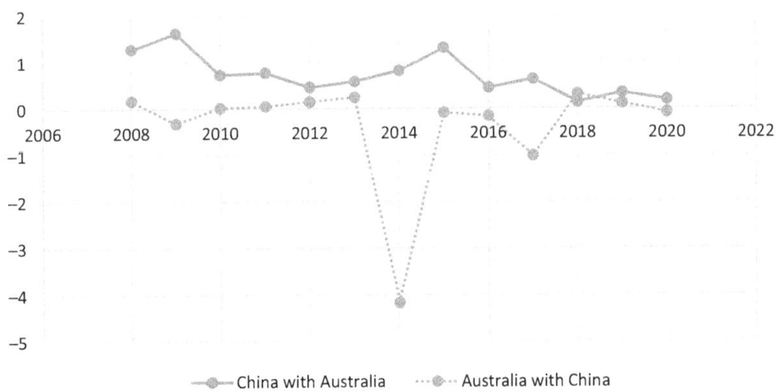

Figure 16. FDI trade index (China and Australia) (2008–2020).

Source: JETRO International Trade and Investment Report (Annual Edition) and the author's calculation.

Table 25. FDI trade index (China and Japan) (2008–2020).

Year	China with Japan	Japan with China
2008	0.035	0.314
2009	▲0.193	0.679
2010	▲3.022	0.429
2011	▲0.991	0.753
2012	0.461	0.711
2013	0.574	0.452
2014	2.318	0.364
2015	▲1.877	0.437
2016	▲0.055	0.366
2017	0.671	0.349
2018	0.094	0.313
2019	0.122	0.322
2020	0.156	0.260

Note: ▲ indicates excess withdrawal.
Source: JETRO International Trade and Investment Report (Annual Edition) and the author's calculation.

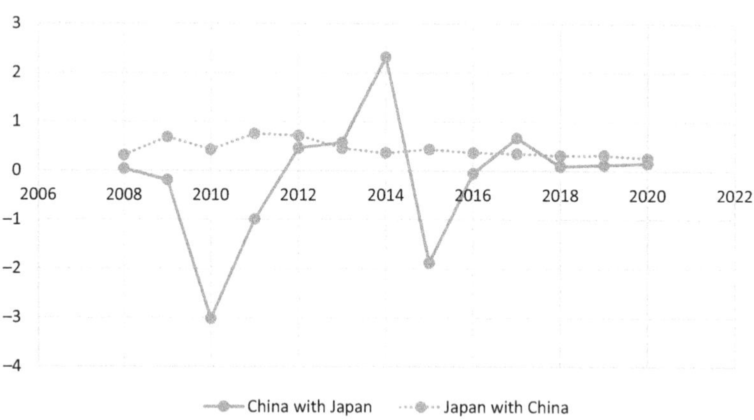

Figure 17. FDI trade index (China and Japan) (2008–2020).

Source: JETRO International Trade and Investment Report (Annual Edition) and the author's calculation.

In short, only Taiwanese FDI into China can be called active.

Considering that only Taiwan's FDI concentration index in China consistently exceeds 1.0, it could be concluded that the active FDI is only Taiwan's outward FDI in China.

In this chapter, we have viewed the general situation of Japan, Australia, Taiwan, and China, and also have viewed the economic relations between the three countries and China.

It is quite clear that Japan's economic relations with China are close as those of Australia and Taiwan with China. As stated earlier, In case of conflict between China and Japan, the impact on both countries would be significant.

However, as stated at the beginning of this chapter, according to Mearsheimer (2014), in almost every case of civil war, there was substantial economic interdependence between the combatants before the fighting broke out[10] and, as indicated by Akita (2022), as history shows, when the military balance between two countries collapses, a dispute occurs.

On one hand, there is a strong economic relations with China, as seen from the perspective of economic relations. However, on the other hand, as confirmed by the overview of each country, there is the significant fact that the "military balance" with China is greatly shifting due to China's overwhelmingly large military expenditure (as well as its nuclear capabilities) compared to other countries.

When focusing on Sino-Japanese relations, "military balance," which is the third condition according to Akita (2022), refers to a military balance between China on the one hand and the USA and Japan on the other. So, the military balance does not refer to "China" and "Japan" but rather "China" and "the USA and Japan."

In fact, when referring to the military balance between"China" and "USA and Japan," it suggests that the balance is maintained even in terms of nuclear weapons. This implies that Japan is effectively protected by the "nuclear umbrella of the USA."

However, could the"nuclear umbrella of the USA" truly function effectively?

Therefore, the crucial term to examine is the "nuclear umbrella of the USA."

---

[10] See Mearsheimer (2014, p. 408).

Japan recognizes that if it cannot be defended under the "nuclear umbrella of the USA" in case of war, it would be completely destroyed.[11]

However, it remains unclear if Japan will be defended by the USA in such a case.

It has been the result of the Japanese government's stance. As Kanehara directly mentioned in Ohta *et al.* (2022), in Japan–United States summits, the nuclear issue has never been a topic of serious discussion and the Japanese side has never asked if Japan would be protected by the USA in the case of any eventuality (p. 194).

4. The Political Economy of Sino-Japanese Relations

4.1. *China: The ultimate goal is hegemony*

According to the closing remarks in Mori (2017), She is convinced that the Sino-Japanese relations ultimately boils down to problems within Japan and that she has always thought that 80 percent of the Sino-Japanese relations is Japan's problem. In that context, one of the unresolved feelings about 1972 is that the problem of how to settle the responsibility for the war remains ambiguous for the Japanese. Also she believes that this casts a shadow over today's Sino-Japanese relations, making them tense and somewhat dampened (pp. 246–247).

Mori (2017) added that it was hopelessly difficult for such issues of past wars to be settled, providing a pessimistic prognosis for Sino-Japanese relations (p. 251).

In any case, China's strong diplomatic stance from the year 2009 to 2010, in particular after the emergence of the Xi Jinping administration, has changed the structure of Sino-Japanese relations.[12]

Mori (2017) mentioned that, among the experts on China, there exists an argument that Chinese diplomacy has changed to a stronger stance from

[11]Destruction in this context means that Japan would become dependent on China.

[12]For example, Eto (2018) mentioned that Sino-Japanese relations in the 2020s had become very strained ("summary" of (2018)). Such an assessment has been common among experts on China like Mori (2017) and Eto (2018). Moreover, Morita (2017b) mentions that the view of the "G2" gradually changed around 2009 to 2010, and points out Hosoya's (2012) assertion that Chinese diplomacy shifted its course around this time, showing a more assertive stance regarding its "core interests" (p. 324). In terms of the shift to a more assertive stance in Chinese diplomacy, it seems to be a similar trend.

the year 2009 or 2010, as represented by Hu Jintao's speeches given at the Envoy Conference in July 2009 (p. 207). According to Yoshikazu Shimizu, Jin Canrong (an international political scientist at Renmin University, China) provided the following explanation on China's stronger stance at an event held in Tokyo in October 2010. First, many realist scholars criticized the appeasement policy of diplomacy, which they claim has not furthered Chinese national interests. Second, as China's interests overseas have increased, protection of those interests has become necessary. Third, because those demanding a stronger stance are vocal within China, diplomatic compromise has never been acceptable to them (p. 208).

It seems therefore that it is necessary to formulate an effective plan to deal with the new Chinese stance.

In the field of international politics, what is it that states are believed to be trying to maximize?

What states try to maximize is the assurance of their security. However, of course, the existence of a state is not always continuously secured by security. Ito (2012) mentioned that, according to the analysis of a scholar of international politics, over the past two centuries, there have been 51 countries that were merged into or conquered by other countries through attacks or invasions. The average death rate of a nation due to such attacks was 24 percent (p. 152).

Needless to say, this death rate is variable based on different circumstances confronted by the country concerned, but it averages to 24 percent.

Japan is surrounded by nuclear power states such as the United States, China, North Korea, and Russia. Moreover, the Xi Jinping administration seems to be seriously considering an annexation of Taiwan, which will definitely have an impact on Japan.

Due to its history, Japan has been a potential enemy country in the "Enemy Clauses" of the "Charter of the United Nations." Thus, even if Japan were to protest against China, if China were to accuse Japan of an act of aggression (for example, regarding the defense of Taiwan), China could attack Japan without needing the approval of the United Nations Security Council. Thus, Japan has been placed in a disadvantageous situation.[13]

[13] The "Enemy Clauses" are indicated in Articles 53, 77, and 107 of the "Charter of the United Nations." The aim of the clauses is as follows. When an "old enemy country" of the Allied Forces of World War II (Japan, Germany, Italy, Bulgaria, Hungary, Rumania,

For contemporary Japan, a possible death rate of 24 percent has a serious meaning.

Moreover, China's aim is not to maintain the balance of power but to maximize relative power (to become a hegemony).[14] Table 18 in Chapter 4 is a table concisely presented by Mearsheimer (2014), illustrating the characteristics of "offensive realism" and "defensive realism."

Japan is located opposite China across the short distance of the East China Sea. Although China is a nuclear state, Japan has never been one. In 2020, China's ratio of GDP to military expenditure was 1.75 percent. In contrast, that of Japan was only 0.99 percent. In 2020, China's total military expenditure was 252.3 billion US dollars and Japan's was 49.1 billion US dollars, which was less than 20 percent the expenditure of China. Thus, it is doubtful whether or not a "balance of power" could exist between China and Japan. However, US military bases exist in various places in Japan. Therefore, the US has been trying to establish a "balance of power" between China on the one hand and the USA and Japan on the

---

and Finland) performs an act of invasion, the act of preventing the invasion is permitted without requiring the approval of the United Nations Security Council. Therefore, supposing that China identifies any Japanese action as an invasion, China could perform sanctions against Japan. The author of this book gives an example: If China tries to invade Taiwan and Japan tries to prevent the Chinese invasion, China could conduct a military operation against its "old enemy country" Japan without requiring the approval of the United Nations Security Council. In short, if China simply states that any Japanese action is an invasion, whether true or not, China could attack Japan. Japan cannot disobey the "Enemy Clauses." Furthermore, because the "Enemy Clauses" are "outdated," at the 50th United Nations General Assembly in 1995, based on counsel by the United Nations Special Committee on the Charter of the United Nations (UNSCCUN), a revision and deletion of the "Enemy Clauses" was adopted with 155 agreements, 0 opposition, and 3 abstentions. However, the effectuation of the revision of the Charter has to be ratified by more than two-thirds of member countries, including the 5 permanent members of the United Nations Security Council (USA, UK, France, Russia, and China). It is expected that it might take more time to revise the "Enemy Clauses." Thus, for Japan, the prospect of changing the unfavorable situation of the "Enemy Clauses" remains elusive.

[14] With regard to such an assertion, there are very few different opinions. As for Japan, this chapter does not attempt to define whether it is "realist" or "idealist," among other things (for such points, see, for example, Kamiya (2012)). However, it is certain that post-World War II Japan is not "offensive realist." From the perspective of maintaining the existing balance of power, it might be considered "defensive realist" in the sense of Mearsheimer (2014). Nevertheless, this chapter does not attempt to define such terms.

other.[15] It is thus reasonable to suppose that, in order to confront China, Japan will depend on the nuclear umbrella of the United States.

As mentioned earlier, according to Akita (2022), in order to successfully maintain Sino-Japanese relations without armed conflict under a cold peace, three conditions must be satisfied. The third condition is that a stable military balance should be secured between China on the one hand and the USA and Japan on the other.

However, as mentioned in Akita's article, based on the present circumstances, because of China's rapid military expansion, even the combined might of the Japanese Self-Defense Forces and the US Indo-Pacific Command is unlikely to defeat the Chinese military. Therefore, in the interests of sustainable peace, both Japan and the United States should expand their investments in defense in order to restore a military balance with China.[16] However, Akita's article did not refer to nuclear arms. So, the existence of a "nuclear umbrella" remains unspoken.

In any case, based on the framework of "offensive realism," China's ultimate goal is to become a hegemon. As Xi Jinping's regime begins its third term, it seems natural that neither Li Keqiang, Wang Yang, nor Hu Chunhua are included in the "China Seven." As Morita (2021) asserted, it is reasonable to reach the conclusion that any upheaval in China would not be peaceful; therefore, it is also reasonable to think that the "liberation of Taiwan" might occur sooner or later (p. 6).

4.2. *Japan: Making little, ambiguous progress*

As the late former Prime Minister Shinzo Abe asserted, "Taiwan's emergency is Japan's emergency." If Taiwan wis under the control of China, it will be extremely difficult for Japan to practice jurisdiction over the Senkaku Islands. Moreover, the safety of the sea lane of Japan might be threatened. Thus, the oil transportation route from the Middle East to Japan could be seriously affected.

Based on China's framework of "offensive realism," the "liberation of Taiwan" might occur sooner or later.

---

[15]According to the home page of the Tokyo Metropolitan Government Bureau of Urban Development, as of 31 March 2021, there are 131 US military bases across Japan.

[16]It might be necessary to expand the investment in defense in order to restore military balance with China. That is to say, at present, a military balance cannot be established.

However, in contrast, Japan's behavior has led to little progress that is ambiguous.

These behaviors by Japan are not a recent development. Progress has been slow and ambiguous in terms of the Constitution, nuclear issues, and the US–Japan security arrangement.[17]

In this chapter, we would examine these realities by reflecting on the views of Schaller (1997), Murata (2009), and Ito (2011, 2012).[18]

4.2.1. *Description of Michael Schaller*

According to Schaller (1997) (in the words of Seymour Hersh),[19] US Secretary of State Henry Kissinger visited both Japan and China in November 1973 and became deeply suspicion of both countries. He predicted that Japan, prodded by the oil crisis, would "go nuclear at some time" (p. 251). That is to say, securing oil is a matter of such importance that as long as China is a nuclear power, in order to maintain the "balance of power," Japan would be compelled to go nuclear at some point. So, if China acts based on the logic of "offensive realism," Japan has to go nuclear at some time, or else the security of Japan will remain precarious.

According to Schaller (1997), when Secretary of Defense Melvin Laird visited Tokyo in July 1971, he and his aides hinted that Washington favored a nuclear-armed Japan (p. 230). Richard Sneider, a state department Japan specialist and former NSC staff member then serving as deputy chief of the mission in Tokyo, recalled that Nixon offered to remove American nuclear weapons from Okinawa and told Sato that the United States would "understand" if Japan decided to "go nuclear" (p. 213). Nixon's views echoed remarks made by Kissinger to his staff the previous year. Moreover, Nixon argued that Japan should play a military and economic role in Asia, suggesting, yet again, that it reconsider its attitude toward nuclear weapons (p. 243). In contrast, Sato refused to yield on the issue of nuclear weapons. The overwhelming majority of the Japanese parliament and citizens

[17]Japan has not taken any action to revise the Constitution of Japan and the Treaty of Mutual Cooperation and Security between Japan and the United States of America.

[18]It goes without saying that conservative tendencies could be inferred from such a name list. This is because, as previously mentioned, the aim of this section is to address how to deal with the collapse of military balance.

[19]Seymour Hersh is an investigative journalist from the United States.

oppose nuclear weapons, while Sato had all he could handle refuting Chinese accusations of resurgent militarism (p. 243).[20]

In short, at the beginning of the 1970s, both President Nixon and Secretary of State Kissinger recommended that Japan go nuclear. In contrast, Prime Minister Sato did not agree with their request because of the overwhelming opposition by the Diet and the Japanese public and expedient refutation against Chinese accusations of resurgent militarism.[21]

However, at a conference with Zhou Enlai in 22 October 1971, Kissinger asserted that the United States would oppose the nuclear armament of Japan.[22] Although we do not investigate when and how Kissinger's stance changed in this book, there is no doubt that the changing relations of the US with China had an influence on Kissinger's views.

However, at any rate, from the viewpoint of Kissinger, Japan could be compelled to go nuclear. This is an inevitable conclusion from the point of view of the "balance of power" in international politics.[23]

4.2.2. *Reminiscence of Ryohei Murata*

The discussion on Japan's nuclear armament could also be seen in Murata (2009).[24] As is well known, Murata worked for the Ministry of Foreign

---

[20] Schaller is a specialist in American history, not a specialist in Japanese issues. According to Ito, this constitutes the positive aspect of that book. Specifically, because Schaller is neither a Japan expert nor a Japan specialist for any institution, he could speak freely (i.e., tell the truth). Ito's perspective could be seen on the online program (see Kan Ito, *Earnest Chat*, the fourth).

[21] According to Ito (Kan Ito, *Earnest Chat*, the fourth), there are 3 the United States presidents who encouraged Japan to go nuclear — Eisenhower, Nixon, and Trump. However, the United States as a whole is generally opposed to the nuclear armament of Japan. According to Ito, it has been the United States' position that, even if China, North Korea, and Russia have nuclear weapons, the United States would never allow Japan to have nuclear weapons. Therefore, as long as both the United States and China remain in their positions, Japan would need to have extraordinary political power to be able to have an "independent nuclear deterrent force." It is difficult to judge at present whether or not such a politician with extraordinary political power will arise in Japan.

[22] Mori and Masuda (2014, p. 198).

[23] If Japan does not opt for nuclear armament, it would directly affect the "balance of power" and might continue to exist as a dependency of a foreign country (China).

[24] Although the citation from Murata (2009) is not quoted to avoid complication, all citations are from the second volume (Chapter 13).

Affairs in Japan as Vice-Minister for Foreign Affairs and as Ambassador to the United States, which means that he held extremely important posts successively.

Murata emphasized the following crucial matters: (1) Japan should develop its own limited "nuclear deterrence" with submarine capability, similar to the UK and France, in order to safeguard national security. (2) Japan must not place much confidence in the "nuclear umbrella" of the United States (p. 320). These matters were specified in his book (2009).[25,26]

We investigate Murata's assertions with a wider perspective because it could be beneficial in terms of Japan's foreign policy.

Murata declared in his book (Chapter 13) that, when working for the Ministry of Foreign Affairs for around 42 years, he spent his days thinking of three kinds of conflict, which were all realized and remain extant.

According to Murata, the first conflict was particularly an inner rebellion and resistance concerning the constitution and the government's official view on it. He stated that he has always inwardly resented the origin of this constitution and continued to hate certain provisions (such as the Preamble and Chapter 2, Article 9, Paragraph 2) as the imposition by the victorious country on the defeated country (p. 279).

The second conflict came from the structure of the "Japan–US Alliance" and the "Treaty of Mutual Cooperation and Security between Japan and the United States" which formed the base of the Japan–US Alliance (p. 285).

The third conflict came from the dependency of Japan on the United States due to which Japanese diplomacy was conducted in accordance with the intentions of the United States. Murata felt uneasy due to the mentality of his colleagues at the Ministry of Foreign Affairs because of their excessive dependency on the United States (p. 298).

---

[25]Those assertions might have already been specified in the first edition in 2008.

[26]The author of this book is unaware of any stories indicating that Murata's candid reflections, having served in extremely important positions within the Ministry of Foreign Affairs, had a noticeable impact on the foreign policy of that time (in a way that was clear to everyone). It is also worth mentioning that the late Shoichi Nakagawa, former Minister of Finance, was engaged in nuclear-related discussions during this period. His so-called "drunken press conference" occurred in February 2009 following the G7 Finance Ministers and Central Bank Governors' Meeting. He lost his seat in the 45th general election of the House of Representatives in August 2009 and passed away in October 2009.

We analyze the three conflicts from the viewpoints of this chapter.

With regard to the Constitution of Japan, his conflict was particularly based on the Preamble and Chapter 2 (Article 9, Paragraph 2).

According to the preamble of the Constitution of Japan, Japan is determined to preserve its security and existence, trusting in the justice and faith of the peace-loving peoples of the world. In other words, the peoples of the world, including (of course, in today's terms) China, North Korea, and Russia, are peace-loving, and Japan has decided to trust in their justice and faith to secure our safety and survival. Therefore, as stated in Article 9, Paragraph 2, if Japanese people do not maintain land, sea, and air forces, as well as other war potential and do not recognize the right of belligerency of the state, the international community could continue to be peaceful.

The "Constitution of Japan" can be considered as "made in the USA" as it was drafted by 16 American professional soldiers and 8 American private citizens for (only) over seven days from February 4 to February 10, 1946[27] (p. 284).

Murata (2009) therefore advocated that the current constitution should cease to have effect and a new constitution should be established (p. 285).

Over the years, US–Japan security arrangements have been based on the "Treaty of Mutual Cooperation and Security between Japan and the United States," and the "Japan–US Alliance" has been executed, whose core is US–Japan security arrangements. Murata asserted that, although the international situation has changed substantially, the "Treaty of Mutual Cooperation and Security between Japan and the United States" has never been revised even once and 48 years have already passed since its institution. Why should this treaty be maintained (p. 287)?

For example, regarding Japan's burden of US military expenses, it is pointed out that since the United States is allowed to use Japanese territory and, in a sense, helps with Japan's defense as a side job, there is fundamentally no obligation for Japan to bear the world's highest US military expenses (pp. 290–291). In 2002, the ratio of host nation spending for US forces stationed in Japan reached 75 percent, which was by far the

[27]Murata asserted in his book (2009) that the Preamble is a curious article that is unworthy of being read because it was obviously written by Americans from a lowly culture that it is full of falsehood (p. 281). Still, of the 24 American professional soldiers and American private citizens, only 4 had any experience in law. Thus, Murata said that the Constitution of Japan was made in the USA. However, the "Constitution of Japan" has never been revised.

highest of any country (Germany's ratio was 33 percent and South Korea's 40 percent) with US forces.

Furthermore, concerning the validity of the "nuclear umbrella" of the United States, Murata's view is that the effectiveness of the US "nuclear umbrella" is considered by more intellectually inclined Japanese to have only limited effectiveness and will eventually disappear. This is the correct judgment (p. 291). According to Murata, confidence in the "nuclear umbrella" of the United States had already fallen (p. 320) and it was believed that Japan would not be covered by the "nuclear umbrella" of the United States.

Murata (2009) stated that, in US–Japan security relations, there is one major issue in the US–Japan security arrangement that no one touches upon (page 293), and that is, in the event that Taiwan is subjected to military action by China in the future, the United States intentionally does not mention how the US would act (pp. 293–294). Murata (2009) asserted that, as long as it could not be completely ruled out that the United States could use military force in order to defend Taiwan from China, military confrontation between Japan and China is something no one desires, but it is a possibility (p. 294).

It exists the other matter related with Murata (2009) in this chapter that, when Murata was appointed as the Ambassador to the United States, Henry C. Stackpole (a rear admiral and a "Commander of US Forces in Okinawa" in those days) stated that 'the US–Japan Security Treaty is a "cap on the bottle" to prevent Japan from once again becoming a "military superpower." In short, this is the "cap on the bottle" theory. However, Murata describes that, considering the realities of the 21st century, Japan will never become a military superpower again, and thus Murata feels that "Stackpole, don't be so stupid" (pp. 292–293).

In short, Murata recognized that Japanese dependency on the United States could allow the US to do things its own way. The author of this book shares the sentiment based on experiences during the US–Japan trade friction, when America interfered in the Japanese economy.

Nonetheless, Murata (2009) mentioned that the mutual interest of the United States and Japan is in ensuring the accord is followed, and major differences might not occur between the two sides in the foreseeable future (p. 299).[28]

---

[28]This point might be different from the analysis of Ito, which is considered in the next section. As shown in the next section, Ito (2011) claimed that the true intention of the

Of the three problems enumerated by Murata, the third one is that while American interactions with Japan and China have obviously been different, he could not understand why American dealings with China have been much more conciliatory than those with Japan. According to Murata, in the 1980s, when he was the ambassador to the United States, the Japanese trade surplus to the United States amounted to around 50 billion US dollars for which the United States pressed Japan to provide concessions under the threat of retaliation. However, with regard to China, the Chinese trade surplus to the United States is several times more than the amount of Japan's surplus in the 1980s; moreover, some Chinese articles for export to the United States have threatened some US industries. Furthermore, China's promiscuous protection for intellectual property rights is a target of global criticism. However, the American approach to China has been much more conciliatory than its approach to Japan in the 1980s (p. 303). Furthermore, Murata claimed that the US Congress had double standards because it regarded Japan as a dependency even in the economic field, but has regarded China as an equal country (p. 304).

These issues explain Murata's feelings on the relations between the United States, China, and Japan.

4.2.3. *Analysis of Kan Ito*[29]

We have cited Koo (1996) in Chapter 1 and earlier in this chapter. As described earlier, although Koo's analysis was conducted in the mid-1990s, it is relevant even now. Actually, the three alternatives presented at the beginning of this chapter could be applied to present Japan. They are (1) to strengthen the "Japan–US Alliance," (2) to liaise with China, and (3) to pursue independent defense.

However, what is not necessarily clear in this context is what the United States' intentions are within the US–Japan alliance, and how China would treat Japan if Japan became a vassal state of China.[30] With regard

---

United States has never been to protect Japan, but to Japan hinder from defending itself independently.

[29]Concerning this section, see also Morita (2017b).

[30]The author of this book believes that one of the things Japan should be preparing for right now — this is no joke — is to simulate how China would treat the Japanese people if Japan were to become a vassal state of China. Perhaps, the closer such a simulation is to reality,

to the "Japan–US Alliance," it really depends on the real intentions of the United States and whether it offers protection to Japan.

Regarding the three alternatives, interesting analyses have been offered by Ito (2011, 2012) and Kusaka and Ito (2011). Because we rarely have the opportunity to know what the United States' true intentions regarding the "Japan–US Alliance" are. From this perspective, the points raised by Ito (2011), (2012), and Kusaka and Ito (2011) seem quite "unexpected" for the general Japanese public. According to them, the real intention of the United States has never been to protect Japan but has to demilitarized Japan because the United States has regarded Japan as a "potential enemy country." If it is correct, it narrows Japan's options in one fell swoop. When we suppose the premise that the majority of Japanese people would not want to depend on China, the alternative left for Japan becomes even more limited. The only one alternative left for Japan is independent defense.

What is independent defense? Usually, it means that a country can be defended by its own military force, indicating a system wherein a country's national security could never depend on other countries' military forces. The "independent defense" asserted by Ito (2011, 2012) and Kusaka and Ito (2011) undoubtedly means an "independent nuclear deterrent force." However, because an "independent nuclear deterrent force" — in other words, independent "nuclear armament" — might not be supported by the majority of Japanese people,[31] Japan would be unable

---

the more Japanese people would think that an independent nuclear deterrent (rather than dependence on the United States) is necessary.

[31]On 28 February 2022, *Nihon Keizai Shimbun* reported under the headline "Mr. Abe Mentions Nuclear Sharing Policy" that Former Prime Minister Shinzo Abe (Liberal Democratic Party) discussed the policy of "nuclear sharing," where some European countries manage US nuclear weapons on the Fuji TV program on 27 February 2022. Mr. Abe also argued that Japan should also discuss this issue, pointing out that countries like Belgium and Germany, which are NATO members, jointly operate US nuclear weapons. Mr. Abe particularly emphasized the need to consider various options in Japan.

Regarding this matter, Hashimoto (2022), a third-generation atomic bomb victim, mentioned the results of a viewer survey conducted during the Fuji TV program on 6 March 2022. The survey showed that 76 percent of the 91,628 valid respondents supported the "nuclear sharing," indicating a clear public demand for it (pp. 28–29).

However, as mentioned in the article entitled "Why the Suddenly Emerged Nuclear Sharing Theory Missed the Mark" in the *Toyo Keizai Online* dated 12 July 2022, the current situation is that it has missed the mark." The relevant article from *Toyo Keizai Online*

to build an "independent nuclear deterrent force." If the allied country, the United States, does not take responsibility for the security of its ally, Japan (if the "nuclear umbrella" does not function), the outcome is clear. As China might equal the United States in economic power and military power in the near future, it is a reasonable goal for Japan to become a dependency of China.

Therefore, Ito argues that Japan would eventually have no choice but to pursue "nuclear armament" in the sense of an "independent nuclear deterrent." This is also the theoretical conclusion of scholars such as Huntington, Mearsheimer, and Waltz, as listed by Ito. Actually, according to Ito's logic, (A) Japan should not depend on the United States for its their national security, (B) the majority of Japanese people would not want to depend on China, and (C) as Japan is surrounded by nuclear powers (the United States, China, North Korea, and Russia), it is indispensable for a Japanese independent defense to have a nuclear deterrence capability. Therefore, Japan has to develop its independent nuclear deterrent force.

According to Ito's argument, which is based on the premise and claims of the realist group that he cites as the mainstream in the world, it is the concept of the "balance of power." As long as Japan's neighboring countries have nuclear weapons, it has no option but to "go nuclear."

---

is as follows. Among politicians and experts, it is widely understood that under the US–Japan alliance and the US nuclear umbrella, the US deterrence is already in effect. Therefore, placing nuclear weapons in Japan would make it an easy target for attacks and is not considered a wise move. Additionally, the US is unlikely to agree to nuclear sharing with Japan as it would complicate the operation of nuclear weapons and lead to nuclear proliferation.

That said, the fact that 76 percent support nuclear sharing is something unimaginable a few years ago. In light of the idea that "we should not taboo the discussion," it could be considered a significant step forward. However, it should be noted that the "shared nuclear weapons," although deployed in Japan, could not be used without the agreement of both the US and Japan. In other words, the agreement of the US is necessary.

As stated in the above article from *Toyo Keizai Online*, it is realistic to assume that the US is unlikely to agree to nuclear sharing with Japan. For reference, the "nuclear armament" advocated by Ito (2011), (2012) and Kusaka and Ito (2011) refers to independent nuclear deterrence. It is not the "nuclear umbrella" relying on US nuclear weapons (nor "nuclear sharing"), but rather Japan's "independent nuclear deterrence" without relying on US nuclear weapons. It remains doubtful whether many Japanese people would support this.

If Japan cannot depend on the nuclear weapons of an allied country, the remaining alternative is (1) to capitulate to an enemy country or (2) develop its own independent nuclear deterrent force.

In short, what Ito asserts is that based on the mainstream theory in the field of political science, the only alternative for Japan at present is to become a nuclear power.[32]

4.2.4. *On the possession of nuclear submarines*

An article in *Nihon Keizai Shimbun* (20 June 2022) reported that Prime Minister Fumio Kishida (President of the Liberal Democratic Party) expressed a cautious stance on the possession of nuclear submarines during the Fuji TV program on 19 June 2022. He pointed out that it would require enormous costs and a large number of personnel for development. There are many things that Japan had to do before getting a nuclear submarine.[33]

An article in *Sankei Shimbun* (20 June 2022, internet version) reported that Prime Minister Fumio Kishida (LDP President) discussed his careful stance on the possession of a nuclear submarine. The Constitutional Democratic Party and the Komeito Party also expressed negative views, while the Japanese Communist Party, Reiwa Shinsengumi, and the Social Democratic Party opposed it. In contrast, the Japan Innovation Party and

---

[32] Ito claimed that the United States has regarded Japan as a potential enemy country. Thus, the natural consequence of it is that the nuclear umbrella of the United States would not work effectively for Japan.

[33] Regarding Prime Minister Kishida's stance on nuclear issues, citing Hashimoto (2022), (Prime Minister Kishida) emphasized in a press conference when asked by a reporter, "Can you protect the lives of the people while adhering to the Three Non-Nuclear Principles amid the increasing risk of a Russian nuclear attack?" that he "believes it can be done." However, there was no concrete basis for this, and it was as if he was speaking in terms of spirit alone, much like the Imperial Headquarters' announcements to the public that they would surely win the war (p. 21). It goes without saying that merely "believing it can be done" is not enough to protect the lives of the people. Furthermore, according to the article of *Sankei Shimbun* (2 March 2022, internet version), Prime Minister Fumio Kishida stated clearly in the Budget Committee of the upper house of the Diet in the morning of March 2 that the government does not intend to discuss "nuclear sharing," which involves deploying and jointly operating US nuclear weapons on Japanese territory. In short, Prime Minister Kishida is likely maintaining the Three Non-Nuclear Principles while still relying on the effective function of the US nuclear umbrella.

The Party to Protect the People from NHK encouraged the idea of a nuclear submarine. The Democratic Party For The People agreed to consider it.

According to the above-mentioned article, the representative of the Japan Innovation Party (Ichiro Matsui) declared that, in order to strengthen deterrence, Japan should have higher performance forces. The leader of the Party to Protect the People from NHK (Takashi Tachibana) emphasized that, unless Japan has a substantive defense capability, it would be unable to protect its citizens from China. The representative of the Democratic Party For The People (Yuichiro Tamaki) asserted that surveillance and reconnaissance capabilities are important, and a nuclear submarine could stay submerged for 3 to 4 months. It was accepted that not only a nuclear submarine but also new technologies should be considered.

An article in *Nihon Keizai Shimbun* (15 November 2022) announced that, under AUKUS (which is a framework for national security established by the United States, the UK, and Australia in September 2021), both the United States and the UK have been providing know-how for the construction of nuclear submarines to Australia under high secrecy.

At first, the plan was to construct a nuclear submarine in a shipbuilding yard in Australia. However, in that case, the deployment of nuclear submarines is expected to occur in the 2040s. In that time, the existing "conventional diesel-electric submarine" in Australia would reach its term of expiration. The Australian government plans to extend the service life of existing conventional submarines, but concerns have arisen about a potential gap period nonetheless. Therefore, the Australian side is inquiring about building the first one or two submarines at shipyards in the United States or UK. Thus, the First Sea Lord and Chief of the Naval Staff (the top of uniformed members of the armed forces) of the UK describes that many options are considering to determine the best route for Australia to possess and operate nuclear submarines. Details would become clearer once the US President and the Prime Ministers of the UK and Australia reach an agreement. In short, in order to reach a military balance with China, both the United States and the UK intent to cooperate with Australia to offer it submarine capability.

As investigated in this chapter, the Australian economy depends greatly on China. Thus, if Australia proceeds to economically decouple with China, the economic cost for Australia will be high.

Then, unless Australia changes its economic dependence on China, in order to secure its national security, it does not have many options.

Australia's plan involves the possession of a nuclear submarine. Needless to say, it can be considered a nuclear deterrent force.

The Japanese economy is also deeply dependent on China. Thus, similar to Australia, unless Japan proceeds to the decouple from China and changes its economic dependence on China, it does not have many alternatives to ensure its national security. An important plan is the possession of a nuclear submarine, thereby forming an independent nuclear deterrent force.[34]

The TV program on 19 June 2022, asked the nine party leaders about the possession of nuclear submarines as the effective countermeasure. As mentioned earlier, Prime Minister Fumio Kishida (LDP President) shared his thoughts.

5. Conclusion

In this chapter, we mentioned the three conditions for the future of Sino-Japanese relations involving "cold peace." The three conditions are as follows: First, a multilayered channel for communication between government leaders, cadremen, and government authorities should be constructed. Second, economic cooperation for mutual benefit should be promoted. Third, a stable military balance should be secured between China on the one hand and the USA and Japan on the other.

As investigated in this chapter, similar to Australia and Taiwan, because Japan's economy depends greatly on China, if Japan proceeds to economically decouple from China, the economic cost for Japan will be very high. With regard to the "military balance," Japan's national security completely depends on the "nuclear umbrella" of the United States. However, to secure a military balance with China, which has expended a huge amount of money on developing its military sectors including nuclear power, it would be indispensable for Japan to have an independent

[34]Murata (2009) assertion, as referred in the Section 4.2.2 in this chapter, is as follows. Japan should have its own limited nuclear deterrence capability within a nuclear submarine, similar to those owned by the UK and France. This option has the least objections. When nuclear weapons are deployed on submarines, the bases where they are stored would not be targeted and attacked, and they are inherently difficult to detect. Therefore, whether it is the United States, Europe, or Russia, it becomes possible to approach very close and carry out a nuclear attack.

nuclear deterrent force. This is particularly important because if the military balance collapses, a dispute could occur.

Based on the present situation of US–Japan security arrangements, it might not be easy for Japan to develop its independent nuclear deterrent force. However, in order to maintain Sino-Japanese relations without decoupling the strong economic ties that have been established and without leading to conflict under a "cold peace," it is first necessary to verify through dialogue with the United States whether the "nuclear umbrella" is functioning effectively.[35] This is just the first thing that Japan would need to do. The next thing for Japan to do is to develop its independent nuclear deterrent force.

---

[35] It is certainly possible that being in an ambiguous state itself serves as a deterrent. However, it seems necessary to refer to Australia on this point. In Ohta *et al.* (2022), Takamizawa speaks about US–Australian relations as follows. Australia allows the use of its territory and assets, but the premise is the sharing of all information. If questions are raised about how operations are conducted, the United States is obligated to answer, regardless of the content. He understands that decisions are made based on this information, or the decisions made are accepted and that there might be a difference between US–Japan and US–Australia in this regard. When negotiating with the US, such kind of topics are sharply rejected. He feels that efforts are needed to somehow overcome this (pp. 222–223).

Concluding Remarks

As mentioned in the preface, this book is a sequel to the previous book written by the author (Morita, 2017b). This book consists of two parts and eight chapters.

With regard to the chapters, the author has presented the different outcomes of different periods. Thus, each chapter presents proper nouns corresponding to each period.

In the four chapters of Part I, the analyses focus on the "Sino-American relationship," with emphasis on understanding "China's behavior."

The aim of Part II of this book is, simply, to appropriately identify the occurrence of "non-economic situations" based on the scientific framework of economics, and to develop such methods.

The analysis in Part II concerns "Taiwan's emergency situation." In other words, the occurrence of a "non-economic situation" refers to the "annexation of Taiwan by China." Therefore, it could be said that it is about discovering and developing methods to appropriately analyze "Taiwan's emergency situations" based on the scientific framework of economics.

In the four chapters of Part I, we analyzed the "codependency relationship between the United States and China" and "Sino-American friction." We focused our attention on Sino-American relations because of the relative deterioration of the United States' economic and military power and the relative (and absolute) advancement of China's economic and military power.

Faced with such serious facts, we have to accurately analyze the behaviors of the United States and China. In this book, based on the analyses of Mearsheimer, their behaviors could be appropriately analyzed within the framework in international politics called "offensive realism." The framework of "offensive realism" tells us that both the United States and China take actions to ensure their national security. In other words, the most important aim for them is not the "peace and stability of international society" but becoming a "hegemon" (or "regional hegemon"). In other words, their behaviors are not based on the framework of "idealism."

Suppose both the United States and China act according to the framework of "offensive realism," an extremely serious conflict between the "present hegemon" and "future hegemon" would be unavoidable. Therefore, it is necessary to understand "when" and "how" this extremely serious conflict would occur. It is essential for us to consider how to offer appropriate recommendations that could effectively tackle these critically significant questions.

When we analyze Sino-American relations, it is necessary to focus on economic aspects. The United States faces a situation of "exorbitant privilege" while China faces a situation of the "undervaluation of the renminbi." Therefore, in the United States, the phenomenon of "excess consumption" occurs and in China, the phenomenon of "underconsumption" occurs. As a result, a phenomenon of "codependency relationship between the United States and China" has developed.

In this book, unfortunately, we cannot analyze the future of the "codependency relationship between the United States and China." We have to think about how to provide some appropriate advice that could effectively address such important future views.

In the four chapters of Part II, we investigate Chinese foreign policies and Chinese foreign relations with some countries through case studies. The target countries are Germany (Chapter 5), Australia (Chapter 6), Taiwan (Chapter 7), and Japan (Chapter 8).

To be more specific, the subject of analysis is Taiwan's emergency situation. In order to analyze the subject, the case studies mentioned in the chapters can serve as a reference.

We investigate the foreign trade relations and foreign direct investment relations of those countries with China. However, at the moment, there is no precedent to the Taiwan situation. Australia, Taiwan, and Japan have had extremely strong economic ties with China. Therefore, it might be very difficult to find a precedent to the annexation of Taiwan by China.

Then, are there any effective measures to prevent a conflict relating to Taiwan while also avoiding a decoupling of economic relations with

China? We investigate the most effective measure to prevent the occurrence of a Taiwanese conflict in Chapter 8 through an analysis targeting Japan. According to former Prime Minister Shinzo Abe, "Taiwan's emergency is Japan's emergency." In that sense, the role that Japan plays in this issue is very important. What could be the effective measure to prevent a "Japanese emergency?"

Japan still adheres to the "Three Non-Nuclear Principles." The three principles include (1) not possessing nuclear weapons, (2) not producing nuclear weapons, and (3) not allowing the introduction of nuclear weapons. It might be difficult to ensure national security while adhering to the "three non-nuclear principles." After all, a large number of nuclear weapons are possessed by China, North Korea, and Russia.

The perception of the Japanese people has been gradually changing. Particularly since the Xi Jinping administration in China was established, the pace of change in Japan has accelerated.

The policy which former Prime Minister Shinzo Abe advocated is "nuclear sharing." However, the policy to promote nuclear sharing has ended in failure. The main reason for this is based on the assumption that the United States would not be willing to share nuclear weapons with Japan. It has also never been clear whether or not the "nuclear umbrella" of the United States covers Japan. Therefore, the problem comes down to what the true intentions of the United States were in establishing the US–Japan Security Treaty system.

According to Ito (2014), the true intention of US foreign policy was not to secure itself against attack by other countries but to regard the protectorate (Japan) as a potential enemy. Thus, the United States has opposed Japan's independent defense.

If we understand that "Taiwan's emergency is Japan's emergency," the true intention of the United States' foreign policy becomes clear. The national security of Japan, which does not include nuclear weapons, is extremely precarious. And if the national security of Japan is extremely precarious, the national security of Taiwan is also extremely precarious.

Then, can Japan reach a position of "independent defense?" In order to do so, it is necessary for Japan to have "overwhelming political power." In other words, it depends on whether or not a great statesperson with overwhelming political power will appear in Japan. In order for Japan to confront both the United States and China and promote an independent defense system, overwhelming political power is indispensable in Japan. As a matter of fact, even if all Japanese people wish for Japan to have its own independent defense, if both the United States and China are against this, it will unfortunately be very difficult for a great statesperson to appear who can realize such a security policy for Japan.

When we think so, in the end, it becomes clear that in part I the "exorbitant privilege" of the United States can become an important keyword, and in part II, what the "true intention" of the United States regarding the establishment of the US–Japan Security Treaty system is can become the important term that we should elucidate. In short, after investigating China's foreign policies, it has become clear that the United States could play an important role. Therefore, the author would like to attempt an analysis focusing primarily on the United States's foreign policies on another occasion.

At the close of this book, the author would like to express his gratitude for splendid editorial work by World Scientific, particularly (in no particular order) Ms.Venkatesh Sandhya and Mr. Aanand Jayaraman, whose patience and wisdom are greatly appreciated.

Finally, most important, I thank my beloved wife who passed away in 2019, to whom I owe so much. This book is dedicated to my beloved late wife.

Bibliography

Akita, H. (2022). Sino-Japanese "Cold Peace" days (in Japanese), *Nihon Keizai Shimbun* (6 September 2022).

Allison, G. (2017). *Destined for War*, Boston, Massachusetts: Houghton Mifflin Harcourt.

Anami, Y. (2017). *Why China Continue Military Expansion* (in Japanese), Tokyo: Shinchosensho.

Ara, K. (2008). *Sino-Japanese War Was Designed by Germany* (in Japanese), Tokyo: Shougakukan.

Armitage, R.L., Nye, J.S., and Sunohara, T. (2010). *US-Japan Alliance vs. China and North Korea* (in Japanese), Tokyo: Bungeishunju.

Bergsten, F. (2008). "A partnership of equals: How Washington should respond to China's economic challenge", *Foreign Affairs*, 87(4).

Bergsten, F. and Cline, W.R. (1985). *The United States-Japan Economic Problem*, Washington, DC: Institute for International Economics.

Blackwell, R.D. and Harris, J.M. (2017). *War by Other Means*, Cambridge, MA: Harvard University Press.

Станковский, С. (1988). "Внешнеэкономическая политика ЯПОНИИ", *Внешняя Торговпя*, Декаьерь.

Chen, Y. and Morita, K. (2010). *Political Economy of Systemic Transition and Development in China* (in Japanese), Tokyo: Taga Shuppan.

Chen, Y. and Morita, K. (2011). "A political economy of integration and security" (in Japanese), *Hiroshima Economic Review*, 35(1).

Chen, Y. and Morita, K. (2013). "Toward an East Asian economic community", in Rosefields, S.S., Kuboniwa, M., and Mizobata, S. (eds), *Prevention and Crisis Management*, Singapore: World Scientific Publishing.

Chen, Y. and Morita, K. (2015). *Chinese Model and Development in China* (in Japanese), Tokyo: Taga Shuppan.

Chen, Y. (2009). *Transition and Development in China: Towards Shared Growth*, Farnham: Ashgate Publishing.

Chen, Z. (1995). *Income Distribution in the Stage of Economic Growth* (in Chinese), Shanghai: Shanghai People's Publishing.

Chijiwa, Y. (2022). *National Security of Postwar Japan* (in Japanese), Tokyo: Chukoushinsho.

Cline, T. (2018). *Whole Aspect of Espionage on Which Japanese People Do Not Know*, Tokyo: Kairyusha.

Dietz, R. (1986). "Soviet foregone gains in trade with the CMEA six: A reappraisal", *Comparative Economic Studies*, 28(2) (Summer).

Economy, E.C. and Segal, A. (2009). "Why the United States and China are not ready to upgrade ties", *Foreign Affairs*, 88(3).

Eichengreen, B. (2011). *Exorbitant Privilege: The Rise and Fall of the Dollar and the Future of the International Monetary System*, Oxford: Oxford University Press.

Ершов, М. и Станковский, С. (1988). "Провлемы развития Советско-Американского экономческого сотрудничества", *Внешняя Торговля*, Февраль.

Eto, N. (2019). "Sino-Japanese relations reconsidered" (in Japanese), *Financial Review*, 138.

Ferguson, N. (2007). *The War of the World: Twentieth-Century Conflict and the Descent of the West*, London: Penguin Press

Ferguson, N. and Schularick, M. (2007). "'Chimerica' and the global asset market boom", *International Finance*, 10(3).

Ferguson, N. and Schularick, M. (2009). "The end of Chimerica", *Harvard Business School Working Paper* 10-037.

Ferguson, N. and Schularick, M. (2011). "The end of Chimerica", *International Finance*, 14(1).

Fischer, S. (2002). "Ten years of transition: Looking back and looking forward", *IMF Staff Papers*, 48(Special Issue).

Fuchs, A. and Klann, N.H. (2010). "Paying a visit: The Dalai Lama effect on international trade", Paper presented at Silvaplana, July.

Fukuoka, M. (1986). *Introduction to Economics* (in Japanese), Tokyo: Nihon Keizai Shimbunsha.

Fukushima, T. (2020). "'Canary of the coal mine': Australian relations with China" (in Japanese), *Chinese Foreign Policies and Foreign Countries' Relations with China*, March, The Japan Institute of International Affairs (JIIA).

Garnaut, J. (2018). "How China interferes in Australia: And how democracies can push back", *Foreign Affairs* (9), March.

Gilpin, R. (1975). *US Power and Multinational Corporation*, New York: Basic Books.

Gingrich, N. (2019). *Trump vs. China*, New York: Hanchette Book Group.

Golden, D. (2017). *Spy Schools*, Vancouver: Raincoat Books.

Halper, S. (2010). *The Beijing Consensus*, New York: Basic Books.

Hamada, K. (1982). *Political Economy of International Finance* (in Japanese), Tokyo: Soubunsha.

Hamada, K. (2007). "Economic integration and national security in Asia" (in Japanese), in Yabushita, S. and Shimizu, K. (eds.), *Political Economy of Regional Integration* (in Japanese), Tokyo: Toyo Keizai Shinpousha.

Hamilton, C. (2018). *Silent Invasion: China's Influence in Australia*, Richmond: Hardie Grant Books.

Hamilton, C. and Ohlberg, M. (2020). *Hidden Hand: Exposing How the Chinese Communist Party Is Reshaping the World*, Richmond: Hardie Grant Books.

Hanai, H. (1988). *The Structure of US-Japan Conflict* (in Japanese), Tokyo: Koudansha.

Harold, S. and Mori, S. (2021). How US and Japan make provision for Chinese military attack, *Newsweek* (Japanese version), 21 September.

Hashimoto, K. (2022). *I Want to Assert Because I Am a Grandchild of Atomic Bomb Victims: Japan Must Have Nuclear Armament* (in Japanese), Tokyo: Wac.

Hayashi, T. (2002). "Lessons from ten years of transition towards market economy: IMF staff paper" (in Japanese), *Journal of JBIC Institute*, 12.

Holzman, F.D. (1974). *Foreign Trade under Central Planning*, Cambridge: Harvard University Press.

Holzman, F.D. (1976). *International Trade under Communism*, New York: Basic Books.

Hosoya, Y. (2012). *International Order* (in Japanese), Tokyo: Chuoukouron Shinsha.

Huntington, E. (1915). *Civilization and Climate*, New Haven: Yale University Press.

Huntington, S.P. (1968). *The Political Order in Changing Society*, New Haven: Yale University Press.

Huntington, S.P. (1996). *The Clash of Civilizations and the Remaking of World Order*, New York: Simon & Schuster.

Huntington, S.P. (1998). *Japan's Choice in the 21st Century* (lecture).

Inoguchi, K. (1987). *Post Hegemony System and Japanese Selection* (in Japanese), Tokyo: Chikumashobou.

Ito, K. (1993). *Taiwan* (in Japanese), Tokyo: Chukoushinsho.

Ito, K. (2011). *Chinese Nuclear Strategy Would Make Japan Grovel* (in Japanese), Tokyo: Shougakukan.

Ito, K. (2012). *Self-Destruction of US Empire* (in Japanese), Tokyo: Bungeishunju.

Jingu, T. (2015). "A change of balance of payments in China" (in Japanese), *Chinese Financial Market*, May.

Jones, H. (2010). *Chinamerica: Why the Future of America Is China*, New York: McGraw-Hill.

Kaldor, N. (1955–1956). "Alternative theories of distribution", *The Review of Economic Studies*, 23(2).

Kamiya, M. (2012). "Outlook on power of realist in Japan" (in Japanese), *International Security* (in Japanese), 39(4).

Kase, E. and Stokes, H.S. (2012). *Why US Began the War to Japan* (in Japanese), Tokyo: Shodenshashinsho.

Kawakami, M. (2015). "Chapter 1: Political economy of cross-strait relations: Focusing on a mechanism of Chinese influence" (in Japanese), in Kawakami, M. (ed.), *Analysis of Economic Sociology on Taiwan under Ma Ying-jeou Administration* (in Japanese).

Kawakami, M. and Wu, J.M. (eds.) (2021). *A Political Sociology of China Factor: Penetration of Influence into Taiwan* (in Japanese), Tokyo: Hakusuisha.

Kawamura, T. (2003). *Contemporary American Economy* (in Japanese), Tokyo: Yuhikaku Aruma.

Kawasoe, K. (2020). *The True Character of Coronavirus Xi Jinping Has Suppressed* (in Japanese), Tokyo: WAC.

Keohane, R.O. (1984). *After Hegemony*, Princeton: Princeton University Press.

Kimura, H. (1987). "Basic determinants of Soviet-Japanese relations: Backgrounds, framework, perceptions, and issues", *Acta Slavica Iaponica*, 5.

Kissinger, H.A. (2011, 2012). *On China*, London: Penguin Books.

Komiya, R. (1983). Tasks for adjustment of US-Japan economic relations (in Japanese), *Japan Institute of International Affairs*.

Komiya, R. (1994). *Economics of Trade Surplus and Deficit* (in Japanese), Tokyo: Toyo Keizai Shinpousha.

Komiya, R. (2008). "Personal history of mine" (in Japanese), *Nihon Keizai Shimbun,* September 2008.

Komiya, R. and Amano, A. (1972). *International Economics* (in Japanese), Tokyo: Iwanami.

Komiya, R., Okuno, M. and Suzumura, K. (eds.) (1984). *Industrial Policy of Japan* (in Japanese), Tokyo: Tokyo University Press.

Kondo, D. (2021). *Taiwan vs China: History of 100 Years of Machinations* (in Japanese), Tokyo: Businesssha.

Koo, R. (1994). *Good Appreciation of Yen and Bad Appreciation of Yen* (in Japanese), Tokyo: Toyo Keizai.

Koo, R. (1996). *Depreciation of Yen by Speculation and Appreciation of Yen by Actual Demand* (in Japanese), Tokyo: Toyo Keizai.

Kusaka, K. and Ito, K. (2011). *Get a Move on Independent Defense* (in Japanese), Tokyo: Rihakusha.

Lin Yi-fu. (1992). *Institution, Technology and Agricultural Development in China* (in Chinese), Shanghai: Shanghai Joint Publishing Company.
Maddison, A. (2007). *Contours of the World Economy, 1-2030AD: Essays in Macro-Economic History*, Oxford: Oxford University Press.
Makabe, A. (2016). *VW Unfairness and Sino-German Economic Alliance* (in Japanese), Tokyo: Shougakukan.
Mann, J. (2007). *The China Fantasy: How Our Leaders Explain Away Chinese Repression*, New York: Viking Books.
Marrese, M. and Vanous, J. (1983). *Soviet Subsidization of Trade with Eastern Europe: A Soviet Perspective*, Berkeley: Institute of International Studies, University of California.
Marumo, A. (2002). *US Economy: Limits of the Principle of Market Supremacy* (in Japanese), Tokyo: Chuoukeizaisha.
Matsuda, Y. and Shimizu, R. (eds.) (2018). *Political Relations of Contemporary Taiwan and Cross-Strait Relations* (in Japanese), Kyoto: Kouyou Shobou.
Matsuo, F. (2017). *USA and China* (in Japanese), Tokyo: Iwanami.
Mearsheimer, J.J. (2001). *The Tragedy of Great Power Politics*, New York: W. W. Norton & Company.
Mearsheimer, J.J. (2006). "China's unpeaceful rise", *Current History*, April.
Mearsheimer, J.J. (2014). *The Tragedy of Great Power Politics* (updated edition), New York: W. W. Norton & Company.
Medcalf, R. (2017). "China's economic leverage: Perception and reality", National Security College, Australian National University, *Policy Options Paper*, No. 2.
Mendershausen, H. (1959). "Terms of Trade between the Soviet Union and smaller communist countries, 1955–1957", *The Review of Economics and Statistics*, 41(2).
Mendershausen, H. (1960). "Terms of Soviet-satellite trade: A broadened analysis", *The Review of Economics and Statistics*, 42(2).
Mifune, E. (2016). *Diplomatic Strategy of China* (in Japanese), Tokyo: Koudansha Sensho.
Miyazaki, M. (2019). *Chinazi* (in Japanese), Tokyo: Tokuma Shoten.
Miyazaki, M. and Kawaguchi, M.E. (2014). *Why Chinese Get along Well with German?* (in Japanese), Tokyo: WAC.
Modelski, G. and Thompson, W.R. (1987). "Testing Cobweb models of the long cycle", in Modelski, G. (ed.), *Exploring Long Cycle*, Boulder: Lynne Rienner Publishers.
Mori, K. (2017). *Drifting of Sino-Japanese Relations* (in Japanese), Tokyo: Iwanami Shinsho.

Mori, K. and Masuda, H. (supervising a translation) (2004). *Memorandum of Conversation between Zhou en-lai and Kissinger* (in Japanese), Tokyo: Iwanami.

Mori, K. and Mori, K. (translation) (2001). *Memorandum of Conversation, February 21, 1972: Nixon's Trip to China* (in Japanese), Nagoya: Nagoya University Press.

Morita, K. (1978). "Economic analysis of international commodity agreements" (in Japanese), *Developing Economies* (in Japanese), 19(9).

Morita, K. (1986). "Second economy in Poland" (in Japanese), *Developing Economies* (in Japanese), 27(2).

Morita, K. (1988a). "Economic relations of Poland with the third world" (in Japanese), *The Economic Review*, 38(3–4).

Morita, K. (1988b). "Economic analysis of foreign policy in Japan" (in Japanese), in Iwata, K. and Ishikawa, T. (eds.), *Studies on Japanese Economy* (in Japanese), Tokyo: Tokyo University Press.

Morita, K. (1988c). "Economic analysis of East-West relations" (in Japanese), Annual Report, Japan Academy for International Trade and Business.

Morita, K. (1997). "Systemic transition toward market economy in Poland: On the Balcerowicz program", *Journal of International Development and Cooperation* (in Japanese), 3(1).

Morita, K. (2002). *Economic Reforms and Commodity Futures Market in Central Europe* (in Japanese), Tokyo: Taga Shuppan.

Morita, K. (2004). *Economic Reforms and Capital Markets in Central Europe*, Farnham: Ashgate Publishing.

Morita, K. (2016a). "A political economy of systemic transition and bubble phenomena: A comparison of China with Hungary", *Zeszyty Naukowe Uczelni Vistula*, 48(3).

Morita, K. (2016b), "Economic analysis of East-South relations" (in Japanese), *Hiroshima Economic Review* (in Japanese), 40(1–2).

Morita, K. (2017a). "An economic analysis of the codependency relations between USA and China: United States excess consumption and Chinese under consumption" (in Japanese), *Hiroshima Economic Review* (in Japanese), 41(1–2).

Morita, K. (2017b). *Emerging Capital Markets and Transition in Contemporary China*, Singapore: World Scientific Publishing.

Morita, K. (2018). "A political economy of the codependency relations between USA and China: Current situations and prospect" (in Japanese), *Hiroshima Economic Review* (in Japanese), 41(3).

Morita, K. (2019). "A political economy of Sino-American conflict" (in Japanese), *Hiroshima Economic Review* (in Japanese), 42(3).

Morita, K. (2020). "An economic analysis of Sino-German relations" (in Japanese), *Hiroshima Economic Review* (in Japanese), 44(1–2).

Morita, K. (2021). “An economic analysis of Sino-Australian relations” (in Japanese), *Hiroshima Economic Review* (in Japanese), 45(1–2).
Morita, K. (2022). “A political economy of cross-strait relations” (in Japanese), *Hiroshima Economic Review* (in Japanese), 45(3).
Morita, K. (2023). “A political economy of Sino-Japanese relations” (in Japanese), *Hiroshima Economic Review* (in Japanese), 46(3).
Morita, K. and Chen, Y. (2008a). “A sociological study of transition: China and Central Europe”, *Economic Papers* (Warsaw School of Economics, Institute for International Studies), 43.
Morita, K. and Chen, Y. (2008b). “Regional integration and path dependence: Asian integration” (in Japanese), *Hiroshima Economic Review* (in Japanese), 32(1).
Morita, K. and Chen, Y. (2009a). “Japanese FDI in Central Europe and China: Consequences and trends”, in Pickles, J. (ed.), *Globalization and Regionalization in Post-Socialist Economies*, New York: Palgrave Macmillan.
Morita, K. and Chen, Y. (2009b). “A political economy of friction with the United States: Current situation and prospects of the Sino-American relations” (in Japanese), *Hiroshima Economic Review* (in Japanese), 33(3).
Morita, K. and Chen, Y. (2009c). *Chinese Economic Reforms and Capital Markets* (in Japanese), Tokyo: Taga Shuppan.
Morita, K. and Chen, Y. (2010a). “Regional integration and path dependence: EU and East Asia”, *Economic Papers* (Warsaw School of Economics, Institute for International Studies), 44.
Morita, K. and Chen, Y. (2010b). *Transition, Regional Development and Globalization: China and Central Europe*, Singapore: World Scientific Publishing.
Morita, K. and Chen, Y. (2013). “A political economy of ‘the rise of China’: Outward foreign direct investment, mercantilism and international system” (in Japanese), *Hiroshima Economic Review* (in Japanese), 36(3).
Murata, R. (2009). *Reminiscences Vol. 1 and Vol. 2* (in Japanese), Kyoto: Minerva Shobou.
Nakanishi, T. (2013). *Toyota vs. VW* (in Japanese), Tokyo: Nihon Keizai Shimbunsha.
Navarro, P. (2015). *Crouching Tiger*, Amherst, New York: Prometheus Books.
Needham, N.J.T.M. (1991). *Science and Civilization in China*, Cambridge: Cambridge University Press.
Negishi, T. and Watanabe, F. (eds.), *International Trade of Japan* (in Japanese), Tokyo: Iwanami.
Nossel, S. (2004). “Smart power”, *Foreign Affairs*, April.
Nye, J.S. (2004). *Soft Power: The Means to Success in World Politics*, Cambridge: Perseus Books Group.

Nye, J.S. (2012). "China's soft power deficit", *Wall Street Journal,* 8 May.
Okano, Y. (2021). "Conflict of Sino-Australian relations is deepened" (in Japanese), *Mitsui & CO., LTD. Strategy Research Institute*, March, 2021.
Okazaki, H. (1983). *What Is the Strategic Thought* (in Japanese), Tokyo: Chukoushinsho.
Okazaki, H. (1984a). *Note on Information and Strategy* (in Japanese), Tokyo: PHP Research Institute.
Okazaki, H. (1984b). *Nation State and Intelligence* (in Japanese), Tokyo: Bungeishunju.
Olson, M. (1982). *The Rise and Decline of Nations*, New Haven: Yale University Press.
Olson, M. and Zeckhauser, R. (1966). "An economic theory of alliances", *The Review of Economics and Statistics*, 48(3).
Oneal, J.R. and Russett, B.M. (1997). "The classical liberals were right: Democracy, interdependence, and conflict, 1950–1985", *International Studies Quarterly,* 41(2).
Oneal, J.R., Russet, B.M., and Berbaum, M.L. (2003). "Causes of peace: Democracy, interdependence, and international organizations, 1885-1992", *International Studies Quarterly*, 47(3).
Ota, M., Kanehara, N., Takamizawa, N., and Banshou, K. (2022). *Our Real Intention on Nuclear Arms* (in Japanese), Tokyo: Shinchoshinsho.
Pan, Z. and Chen, Z. (2014). "Peaceful rise, multipolar system and Chinese foreign policies" (in Japanese), Inoguchi, T. (supervision), in Inoguchi, T. and Ikenberry, G.J. (eds.), *Japan, USA and China* (in Japanese), Tokyo: Hara Shobou.
Paszynski, M. (1982). "Stosunki gospodarcze Polski z 'trzecim swiatem'", *Sprawy Miedzynarodowe*, Styczen-Luty.
Pickles, J. (ed.) (2008). *Globalization and Regionalization in Post-Socialist Economies*, New York: Palgrave Macmillan.
Polanyi, K. (1957). *The Great Transformation*, Boston: Beacon Press.
Polanyi, K., Arensberg, C.M., and Pearson, H.W. (eds.) (1957). *Trade and Market in the Early Empires*, The Free Press; The Falcons Wing Press.
Ramo, J.C. (2004). *The Beijing Consensus*, London: The Foreign Policy Centre.
Rickards, J. (2012). *Currency Wars: The Making of the Next Global Crisis*, New York: Penguin Random House.
Rickards, J. (2014). *The Death of Money: The Coming Collapse of the International Monetary System*, New York: Penguin Random House.
Roach, S. (2014). *Unbalanced: The Codependency of America and China*, New Haven: Yale University Press.
Rosecrance, R. (1986). *The Rise of the Trading State*, New York: Basic Books.
Rudd, K. (2018). "How to avoid the Sino-American war", *Foreign Affairs Report* (Japanese version), 12.

Ruggie, J.G. (1975). "International responses to technology: Concepts and trends", *International Organization*, 29(3).

Sachs, J.D. (1993). *Poland's Jump to the Market Economy*, Cambridge, MA: The MIT Press.

Sachs, J.D. and Woo, W.T. (1994). "Reforms in China and Russia", *Economic Policy*, 9(18).

Sahashi, R. (2021). *Sino-American Conflict* (in Japanese), Tokyo: Chukoushinsho.

Sakamoto, M. (1986). *International System in Pax Americana* (in Japanese), Tokyo: Yuhikaku.

Sako, K. (2020). "Future of the New Southbound policy of Taiwan" (in Japanese), *Mizuho Insight* (Mizuho Research Institute), 18 May.

Schaller, M. (1997). *Altered States: The United States and Japan since the Occupation*, New York: Oxford University Press.

Shibata, S. and Hasegawa, T. (2012). *Economic Policies of Chinese Communist Party* (in Japanese), Tokyo: Koudansha.

Shimizu, K. (2021). *Taiwan's Emergency: A Risk of Sino-American Conflict* (in Japanese), Tokyo: Heibonshashinsho.

Shirai, S. (2004). *Renminbi and Chinese Economy* (in Japanese), Tokyo: Nihon Keizai Shimbunsha.

Snidal, D. (1985). "The limits of hegemonic stability theory", *International Organization*, 39(4).

Spero, J.E. (1981). *The Politics of International Economic Relations* (2nd edn.), New York: St. Martin's Press.

Spero, J.E. (1985). *The Politics of International Economic Relations* (3rd edn.), London: George Allen & Unwin.

Stein, A.A. (1983). "Coordination and collaboration: Regimes in an anarchic world", in Krasner, S.D. (ed.), *International Regimes*, Ithaca: Cornell University Press.

Tachibanaki, T. (1998). *Economic Disparity in Japan* (in Japanese), Tokyo: Iwanami Shinsho.

Tsai Ing-wen (2015) (Maehara, S. (supervision), Abe, Y., Shinohara, S., and A. Tsumura (translation) (2016)). *New Era Taiwan* (in Japanese), Tokyo: Hakusuisha.

Tsugami, T. (2011). *China Stands at a Crossroads* (in Japanese), Tokyo: Nihon Keizai Shimbunsha.

Tsugami, T. (2013). *Demise of Rise of China* (in Japanese), Tokyo: Nihon Keizai Shimbunsha.

Tsugami, T. (2017). *Analysis on the Reality of Sino-American Economic War* (in Japanese), Tokyo: PHP Shinsho.

Waltz, K.N. (1979). *Theory of International Politics*, New York: McGraw-Hill.

Watanabe, S. (2016). *Analysis on US Policy toward Japan* (in Japanese), Tokyo: Soushisha.

Watanabe, T. (2018). *Sino-American Trade War* (in Japanese), Tokyo: Tokuma Shoten.

Wu, J. (2004). *Economic Reforms of Contemporary China* (in Chinese), Shanghai: Shanghai Yuandong Publishing.

Yamazawa, I. (1971). "Analysis of international trade linkage index of the world" (in Japanese), in Negishi T. and Watanabe, F. (eds.), *International Trade of Japan* (in Japanese), Tokyo: Iwanami.

Zielinski, T. (1983). "Kraje Socjalistyczne-Trzeci Swiat: Stosunki gospodarcze w latach 1970-81", *Rynki Zagraniczne*, Czerwiec.

Index

www.ingramcontent.com/pod-product-compliance
Ingram Content Group UK Ltd.
Pitfield, Milton Keynes, MK11 3LW, UK
UKHW020402150926
8624IPUK00004B/299